D0481961

Quest

Also by Charles Pasternak

The Molecules Within Us: Our Body in Health and Disease (1998)
Introduction to Human Biochemistry (1979)
The Biochemistry of Differentiation (1970)

CHARLES PASTERNAK

The Essence
of Humanity

Quest

WILEY

Published in 2003 by John Wiley & Sons Ltd, The Atrium, Southern Gate, Chichester, West Sussex PO19 8SQ, England

Telephone (+44) 1243 779777

Email (for orders and customer service enquiries): cs-books@wiley.co.uk
Visit our Home Page on www.wileyeurope.com or www.wiley.com

Other Wiley Editorial Offices

John Wiley & Sons Inc., 111 River Street, Hoboken, NJ 07030, USA

Jossey-Bass, 989 Market Street, San Francisco, CA 94103-1741, USA

Wiley-VCH Verlag GmbH, Boschstr. 12, D-69469 Weinheim, Germany

John Wiley & Sons Australia Ltd, 33 Park Road, Milton, Queensland 4064, Australia

John Wiley & Sons (Asia) Pte Ltd, 2 Clementi Loop #02-01, Jin Xing Distripark, Singapore 129809

John Wiley & Sons Canada Ltd, 22 Worcester Road, Etobicoke, Ontario, Canada M9W 1L1

Wiley also publishes its books in a variety of electronic formats. Some content that appears in print may not be available in electronic books.

British Library Cataloguing in Publication Data

A catalogue record for this book is available from the British Library

ISBN 0-470-85144-9

Typeset in 10/13pt Photina by Mathematical Composition Setters Ltd, Salisbury, Wiltshire
Printed and bound in Great Britain by Biddles Ltd, Guildford and King's Lynn
This book is printed on acid-free paper responsibly manufactured from sustainable forestry in which at least two trees are planted for each one used for paper production.

To Julia (Olivia), Hélène, Margaret, Audrey, Madeleine and Iris, for sustaining my quest for half a century.

Contents

Illustrations		xi
Foreword		xiii
Acknowledgements		xvii

1 Prologue 1

Part I. Evolution: the genetic basis of quest 15

2 Unity and diversity in living organisms 17
    Molecular basis of life 17
    Proteins and DNA 20
    Inheritance 23
    Generation of variant genes 28
    Generation of new species 30
    Generation of a new genus 35
    Variability of form and function 37
3 Plants and microbes: the origin of vision 44
    The beginning of life 44
    Dependency of life on light 46
    Photosynthesis 47
    Phototropism 51
    Heliotropism 52
    Circadian rhythm 53
    Microbial movement 53
        Bacteria 53
        Protoctista 57
    Molecular unity 60
    Conclusion 61
4 Animals and man: development of human attributes 69
    Migration 70

CONTENTS

Evolution of man   73
  Dating techniques   74
  Australopithecus   76
  Early *Homo* species   78
  Recent *Homo* species   81

**Part II. Domination: the consequences of
          human quest**   103

5 Out of Africa: exploration and expansion   105
     Migrations of early *Homo*   105
     Homo sapiens on the move   111
     Modern explorers   117
       Conquerors and navigators   117
       Contemporary heroes   128
     Recent migrations   131
6 The ladder: adversity and achievement   138
     The challenge of adversity   140
     Inheritance of human potential   149
     Rulers   152
     Back to the neolithic   158
7 Civilisation 1: towns and temples   163
     Mesopotamia   164
     Egypt   166
     India   171
     China   172
     Crete   174
     Central America   175
     South America   178
     Elsewhere   181
8 Civilisation 2: communication and culture   187
     Language and literature   187
     Scholarship and art   200
     Quality of life   211
     Conclusion   215
9 Technology: war and welfare   223
     Stone Age technology   227
     The legacy of China   231

CONTENTS

	Islamic technology	233
	Instruments of war	235
	Leonardo da Vinci	238
	Technology and wealth	242
10	Religion: belief and dogma	249
	Early beliefs	249
	The Old World	251
	The Americas	257
	Contemporary faiths	259
	Hinduism	260
	Judaism, Christianity and Islam	261
	Buddhism, Confucianism and Daoism	268
	Conclusion	272
11	Science: explanation and experimentation	277
	The ways of science	279
	Scientists	282
	Archimedes	282
	Galileo	283
	Newton	285
	Einstein	288
	The foundations of medicine	291
	Molecular biology	296
	Finale	298

Part III. Controversy: current quest 305

12	Tinkering with genes 1: GM foods	307
	Risk	309
	The need for novel foods	313
	Risks to health of eating GM foods	315
	Risks to the environment from growing GM foods	318
	Resistance to antibiotics	324
	Foreign genes	328
	Conclusion	331
13	Tinkering with genes 2: GM people	335
	Gene therapy	336
	In vitro fertilisation	340
	Cloning	343

CONTENTS

Xenotransplantation   349
Summary   353

Part IV. Speculation: a glimpse into the future   359

14 Extinction or survival of *Homo quaerens?*   361
       The next century   362
       The next milioneum   375

15 Epilogue   381

Bibliography   391
Glossary   396
Index   403

Illustrations

Figure 1.1   The genetic make-up of chimpanzees and humans
Figure 2.1   Molecules that are the same in all organisms
Figure 2.2   Molecules that are slightly different in all organisms
Figure 2.3   Chromosomes
Figure 3.1   Searching for light by plants
Figure 3.2   Bacterial chemotaxis (*Salmonella typhimurium*)
Figure 3.3   Searching by protoctista (A) Self-aggregation by
               Dictyostelium discoides. (B) Avoidance of toxicity by
               Stentor
Figure 4.1   Upright gait
Figure 4.2   Flexible hand
Figure 4.3   Voice box
Figure 4.4   Cortical neurons
Figure 4.5   Panbanisha
Figure 6.1   The birth of primary civilisations
Figure 8.1   Ancient Mediterranean scripts
Figure 8.2   Ancient Chinese scripts
Figure 9.1   Stone Age symbols
Figure 9.2   Leonardo's helicopter
Figure 11.1   The bending of light
Figure 12.1   Bt toxin technology
Figure 13.1   Therapeutic cloning and stem cell technology

Plate 1   Explorers of the modern era
Plate 2   Egyptian pyramids
Plate 3   Meso-American pyramid
Plate 4   The Rosetta Stone
Plate 5   The lake at Hanghzou
Plate 6   Galileo Galilei
Plate 7   Newton's major works: *Optics* and *Principia*
Plate 8   Albert Einstein

'Pasternak is an intellectual eclectic, and he writes with seductive fluency and splendid authority across an impressively broad landscape. In enjoying this book, historians will come to understand more biology, physicists will come to appreciate more anthropology, and all of us as questing H. sapiens will learn a great deal about who we are and how we got here.'

Dr Jeremy Knowles, lately Dean of Arts and Sciences, Harvard University

Foreword

*C*harles Pasternak has written a book of compelling interest on questing, one of the most perplexing characteristics of humans and, possibly, other animals. The approach is that of modern biology based in large part on the principle that has guided it for at least the past century – that biology can be explained in terms of chemistry and that chemistry can be explained in terms of physics. But, it is recognised that an analytical explanation of the component chemical processes alone will not provide a satisfactory or operational explanation, that is, an explanation that can lead to application and intervention. There must also be an understanding of the complex interactions, over time, of the separate processes with each other and how the total organism interacts with the enormous richness of its environment and with other like and unlike organisms that it encounters. Georges Perec, in his curious novel *Life, A User's Manual* (translated by D. Bellos, Collins Harvill, London 1988) describes the jigsaw puzzle in a form that allows a useful metaphor for the pitfalls of totally reductionist science. Careful study of a piece of the jigsaw puzzle does not give a clue as to the whole pattern. It is only after the entire image is realised that the contribution of a single part can be appreciated.

Science is a major means for human questing. By its very nature, the scientific venture assures that there will always be mysteries to unravel; the process of answering questions generates new data of which new questions may then be asked. When a hypothesis is formulated, new data must be collected to test it. This data can then be used to determine if the hypothesis is supported or rejected. But the new data has an additional use. It has the inherent property – because of its newness – of stimulating questions that could never have been asked before. Usually, there are more questions asked then are answered. As more and more is known, more and more unknowns will be disclosed. The Romantic poets and writers of the

18th and 19th century were concerned that science would remove mystery from the world because of its relentless problem solving capability. They need not have feared; science has and will reveal more mysteries of the universe around us – the subject matter for questing – than humankind can answer between now and the end of its time in the cosmos. Victor Frankenstein in Mary Shelly's long enduring novel committed the sin of creative arrogance when he tried, successfully in part, to solve the mystery of life by creating the Monster. But, *Frankenstein* was fiction and we still don't know how life originated on Earth or elsewhere in the Universe and it is not for lack of trying.

The scientific paths of questing and discovery are often convoluted and have unexpected turns and twists. They have the same qualities that make fictional adventure stories interesting and readable. Consider the unpredictable events that occurred during the voyage of Ulysses and his men returning from Troy, and the busy day filled with unexpected if mundane predicaments experienced by Leopold Bloom in his travels around Dublin in James Joyce's version of the Ulysses adventure. Despite the rich creative imaginations of novelists, real stories of exploration and scientific discovery are often stranger and more unpredictable than any fiction. The research that my colleagues and I did on the discovery of hepatitis B virus is an example of this unpredictable character of scientific research. We had started with an interest in inherited and other biochemical variation in humans that differentially affect susceptibility to disease and in particular to the responses to infectious agents. As part of our research strategy we used the serum of transfused patients to see if they had developed a reaction against serum proteins that they had received in the transfused blood but which they themselves had not inherited or acquired. We did find such differences, but we also identified the hepatitis B virus that was present in the blood of the donors, even though they did not, at the time have symptoms of disease. This discovery resulted in the protection of the blood supply against transmission of HBV, the development of the vaccine against HBV and the initiation of one of the world's largest vaccination programmes. It also made it possible to determine that HBV is the major cause of primary cancer of the liver, a very common cancer particularly in Asia and sub-Saharan Africa. (Hepatitis C is also an important cause). The HBV vaccine is the first cancer prevention vaccine and the worldwide vaccination program has already begun to decrease the incidence of this deadly cancer. The wholesome outcome could not have been predicted at the beginning of the apparently meandering scientific adventure.

Pasternak makes the point that many animals are searchers while at the same time proposing that searching distinguishes man from chimpanzees and other animals. What is the resolution of this apparent paradox? It is, he notes, the increased ability of *Homo* to quest that makes the difference. This is very apparent in modern science. The availability of instruments of great accuracy and reliability and with remarkably rapid measurements allows for the efficient accumulation of vast amounts of data. The space science programme is an especially good example of humans' ability to increase their capability for the quest. In the past few decades satellites and space ships of previously unimagined versatility have been launched and even more exciting ones are planned. Robotic missions have visited all the planets in our solar system save Pluto, human landings have been made on the Moon and kilogrammes of specimens have been returned to earth for study, several satellites have orbited Mars and others have landed and returned pictures and measurements. An intensive Mars Lander programme is planned with a major goal of determining if water and life exist or have existed on the planet now or in the remote past. A human mission to Mars is under study although the actual mission awaits the results of research that will make this potentially hazardous mission safe. Earth observing satellites have provided a remarkably detailed understanding of the dynamics of weather and the conditions of land and sea. There has been a human presence in near-Earth orbit for many years on the Soviet/Russian Mir Space Station and now on the International Space Station. The NASA 'Living With a Star' project will include a flotilla of satellites to study the Sun, our own star, and determine the effect it has on Earth's weather and communications and the hazards that Sun storms may present to satellites, to the power grid, and to humans in near and distant space flights. It is fascinating to think of this as a great step forward in the human desire to understand the nature of the life-giving centre of the solar system, the *Sol Invictus* – the Unconquered Sun – proclaimed by the Emperor Aurelian in 274 as the universal Godhead.

Three of the so-called NASA Great Observatories are in orbit; the redoubtable Hubble Space Telescope, (an even larger optical telescope, the James Webb Space Telescope will be flown within a decade or more), the Compton Gamma Ray Observatory, and the Chandra X-Ray Observatory. The Space Infrared Telescope Facility is scheduled for orbiting in 2003. All these, and many other scientific instruments for heretofore-impossible observations are examples of humans' capabilities to extend the range of their adventuring. These devices allow for an enormous influx of new ideas for additional exploration based on observations that were not made before. They could not have been made before the present because the high platforms were not available.

What is the motivation for these visionary but expensive searches and travels? There are, of course, important commercial 'spin-offs'. The transmission of messages, images, and data via satellites, navigation using the Geographic Positioning System, and remote monitoring of patients in Intensive Care Units, are examples of important applications of the space programme. It is likely that the countries engaged in space will be the leaders in the commercial world of this and following centuries. Although the space endeavour needs to focus on engineering and technical problems in order to fly the devices, the goal is to enrich the scientific understanding of nature and to accomplish basic science projects that were not previously possible. But a major reason for the space programme, and others similar to it, is to satisfy the driving force of curiosity that impels questing humans and may, as the author noted, serve to distinguish them from the other living beings with which we share the Earth.

Baruch S. Blumberg
June 2003

Acknowledgements

$\mathscr{I}$ am indebted first and foremost to John Ellis, Arne Petersen and James Rogers for reading large chunks of the book and for their constructive comments. Many other colleagues checked particular sections and provided useful pieces of information. They include Lesley Abdela, Leslie Aiello, Roy Anderson, Vincent Ang, Wallace Arthur, Richard Asser, Francoise Barbira-Freedman, Lindsay Bashford, Dot Bennett, Baruch Blumberg, Nigel Brown, Stuart Brown, Paul Ciclitira, Prophecy Coles, Richard Dawkins, Noel Dilly, (Sir) Richard Doll, Gabriel Dover, Donald Edmonds, Mark Fisher, Mickey Gaitonde, Frank Hay, Adrian Hill, (Sir) John Krebs, Stuart Knutton, Robert Kruszynski, David Jones, Chris Leaver, Stephen Matlin, Anne McLaren, (Lord) Robert May, Dennis Mitchison, Richard Moxon, Steve Nussey, Govindarajan Padmanaban, (the late) Roy Porter, Mark Ridley, Ian Robinson, George Rowland, Richard Rudgely, Charles Shaw, Christopher Stringer, Keith Thomson, (Sir) Alan Walters, Denis von der Weid, Anne and Christopher Widnell, Endymion Wilkinson, David Winterbourne and Lewis Wolpert. Naturally I take full responsibility for any errors of fact or interpretation that I have overlooked.

To Anthea Morton-Saner of Curtis Brown and Kirk Jensen of the Oxford University Press in New York, I am grateful for convincing me not to write a book on Science in Developing Countries, and turning my mind elsewhere. It was David Smith of Annette Green Authors' Agency and Sally Smith of John Wiley & Sons Ltd who took up the challenge of *Quest* and are responsible for bringing this work to fruition, aided by Lesley Winchester's admirable copy-editing.

I appreciate the tolerance of successive Heads of Department at St George's—first Mike Clemens, then Lindsay Bashford—in allowing me continued use of my office, the other functions of which were ably looked after by Stefanina Pelc while I was working on *Quest*. The assistance I have received from the staff of the British Library,

ACKNOWLEDGEMENTS

The London Library, Kensington and Chelsea libraries, St George's Medical School library and Imperial College library has been invaluable. The same is true in regard to the maintenance of my ageing lap-top by Nick Ramsay.

To Helen and Bill Ramsay I owe an enormous debt: for providing tranquility at their Spanish home whenever I needed it.

London and Almeria, 2003

CHAPTER ONE

Prologue

We're all of us guinea pigs in the laboratory of God.
Humanity is just work in progress (Tennessee Williams)[1]

Scientists have unravelled the human genome. It is time to take stock. What really makes us human? Philosophers and scientists have long argued about it. I believe it is our innate propensity for quest.

The word is derived from the Latin verb *quaerere*, to search, to seek. From it we have query and inquisitiveness on the one hand, conquest on the other. Together the words describe the qualities that have made us masters of life on earth: we search for new horizons, we seek explanations for the phenomena around us, but we also strive to dominate our fellow creatures.

Yet to search is a fundamental quality of all living organisms: it is as integral to life as growth and reproduction. Plants search and so do microbes: we all know that plants have a tendency to grow towards the light—the sun is their only source of energy—and some microbes swim towards a source of food. So it is not surprising that animals, sharing a common ancestor with plants and microbes, also search: primarily for food and a mate, and in the non-aquatic animals for water and shelter also. As animals have become more highly developed over the past half billion years, so has their capacity to search. It has reached its peak in *Homo sapiens*. Not only do we search for food and water, for a mate and for shelter, but we also search for no apparent reason at all: it is curiosity alone, not need, that has led men to seek the source of the Nile and to unravel the origin of the stars.

Pedants may argue that I am using the word 'search' in two different senses. Plants and microbes respond to light and food in an involuntary, preprogrammed, manner: it is simply a question of being attracted to a source of light or a concentration of nutrients. Man's search is voluntary and variable. Some of us are curious about the origin of thunderstorms and earthquakes, others are no more interested in their causes than in the way an automobile or a computer works, but might like to find out why the most popular star of the day has abandoned her boyfriend and what the zodiac holds in store for them this month; they search the media and surf the Internet for the answers. You are searching for something— entertainment, knowledge—at this very moment of holding *Quest* in your hand.

Physiologists and biochemists, however, have taught us that there is little fundamental difference between an involuntary act like the beating of one's heart and a voluntary one like the raising of an eyebrow, between an involuntary feeling like fear and a voluntary one like deciding to read this book: the underlying mechanisms are virtually the same. I will not go into details at this stage, except to point out that all life—whether that of a bacterium or a plant, an animal or a human—depends on chemical reactions between the fundamental units of matter called molecules.

Two types of molecule are the most important for anything that is alive: genes, which biochemists also know as DNA, and proteins. Genes are related to proteins in the way that an architect's blueprint is related to the building he will construct: it defines its shape and its size. A gene is a set of instructions for making a protein: it specifies its size and its shape. What proteins do is to endow matter with life: with movement and growth, with reproduction and an awareness of the environment, with the ability to search. It is the proteins underlying the voluntary and involuntary responses of animals that are similar. Moreover, we now know that some of the genes involved in the responses of plants and microbes—their search for light and food—have been retained in animals and man: in other words, some of the proteins that enable us to search are structurally related to proteins possessed by much simpler, and older, forms of life.

If there is a continuity of function, and of the underlying molecules, from ancient bacteria to fish and to birds and to mammals, what is it that distinguishes one primate—*Homo sapiens*—from all other organisms, and especially from that primate's nearest relatives, *Pan troglodytes*, the common chimpanzee, and *Pan paniscus*, the bonobo or pygmy chimpanzee? Could it be something as subtle as a heightened propensity for quest?

For 150 years, since Darwin's time, anthropologists have tried to identify the qualities that identify man's unique behaviour, but they have failed. As each suggested characteristic is sought among non-human primates, it has been found: the use of simple tools, an ability to reason, the feeling of misery or joy, consciousness and an awareness of self, the appreciation of humour, the comprehension of words and an understanding of language.[2] The quality may be expressed only to a very minor extent, and merely in one or other species that has been taught by humans, but it leaves us unable to pinpoint a defining feature of man. Attempts to do so, by writers as recent as Kenan Malik (2000) in *Man, Beast and Zombie*, fail to convince. They have merely fudged the issue by ascribing man's uniqueness to some non-genetic behavioural trait, like the development of 'memes', a subject to which we shall return in the Epilogue.

So, in *The Rise and Fall of the Third Chimpanzee*, the biologist Jared Diamond rightly describes man as just another primate, to be classified in the same genus as the bonobo and the common chimpanzee: provocatively, he calls that genus *Homo* rather than *Pan*. Desmond Morris had done much the same in his book, *The Naked Ape*, 30 years earlier.[3] No single feature, it appears, characterises *Homo sapiens*: wisdom (*sapientia*) is certainly not one. If no discrete attribute explains the essential difference between chimpanzee and man, we must look for a number of features— none of which is unique to man—that in combination have somehow resulted in his altered behaviour, in his increased ability for quest. What might those features be?

Hundreds of characteristics distinguish man from chimpanzee. The most obvious to a casual observer are less body hair, a different type of face, much shorter arms, an upright gait. To a specialist the features he focuses on are those connected with his particular discipline. An anatomist will describe in detail the shape of the jaw and the pelvis as well as every other bone in the body, a nutritionist will examine the diet in regard to the consumption of animal as opposed to vegetable protein, an anthropologist will focus on the earlier onset of reproductive ability and the shorter life span, a sociologist will observe the mating behaviour in terms of the duration of sexual urge and number of partners, a statistician will note the relative differences in height between male and female and might comment on the larger breasts of human females and the longer sexual organ of human males.[4]

We will concentrate on just four features that have accompanied the evolution of man from other primates. The first is a change in the spine that makes him walk upright. This increases his view of the horizon and simultaneously frees his hands: you may be able to wipe the sweat off your brow and to peel a banana walking along, but a chimpanzee does so sitting down. The second is a modification in the relative length of thumb and fingers and in the muscles that control their movement. We can bend our thumb and move it past each of our finger tips better than a chimpanzee: our precision grip allows us to sense the shape of objects and to fashion these in a superior way. Some of us can learn to play a violin or take out an appendix; a chimpanzee would perform clumsily at either of these tasks. The third distinguishing feature is the vocal cord. It lies within the larynx, through which all primates breathe; the cord is positioned lower down in humans and made into an intricate voice box through just two small pieces of cartilage. The result is that we can produce an enormous diversity of sounds—just listen to the range of Luciano Pavarotti's voice or the recordings of Maria Callas—whereas a chimpanzee can merely grunt. Yet we are born with a primitive vocal cord high up in the larynx, just like an ape. Babies can only whimper and cry, although like chimpanzees they are able to breathe and swallow at the same time: adult humans cannot. So a slight lowering of the vocal cord at around a year or so of age is all it takes to endow a human with the power of speech. The fourth attribute relates to the millions of neurons or nerve cells that are responsible for thought and memory, for the power of reasoning. They are contained in the region of the brain known as the cortex. Their function is precisely the same in chimpanzees and humans: the only difference is that we have three times as many.

I believe that it is the combination of these four attributes that has enabled man to search more widely—both physically and mentally—than any other animal. In stressing that it is a combination of qualities that characterises man, I am doing no more than adapting to a species the definition of individuality formulated by the immunologist Peter Medawar: 'One individual differs from all others not because he has unique endowments but because he has a unique *combination* of endowments.'[5] On the other hand, man's heightened ability to search depends so much on his use of language that I might have chosen to focus on the attribute of speech alone. In a beguiling book entitled *Grooming, Gossip and the Evolution of Language*, the anthropologist Robin Dunbar has done just that. He suggests that gossiping among humans is an extension of grooming among apes and that it is gossip that has led to the evolution of language and thence to man's complex behaviour. But while speech undoubtedly contributes to man's superior ability for quest, it alone does not account for the emergence of civilisations and the development of culture. Chattering does not produce the great pyramid of Cheops, neither does it lead to the Mona Lisa or the theory of relativity. Quest does.

The four anatomical differences between man and chimpanzee on which I have focused—upright gait, agile hand, sophisticated vocal cord and greater quantity of cortical neurons—have arisen gradually over the past 5 million years or so. Their appearance was pure chance; their retention is due only to the fact that their owners—successive species of primate—outbred others of their kind. None represents a sudden and dramatic change of form, any more than does the evolution of terrestrial animals from fish, or of birds from reptiles. Each of the four anatomical features is specified by a number of genes. As yet these have not all been identified, but it is probable that they belong to families that are similar in humans and chimpanzees. As we shall see in Chapter 4, the genes responsible for human characteristics are homologues of genes specifying comparable functions in other primates: so far as searching is concerned, it would appear unnecessary to postulate the existence of 'human' genes in order to define the essential differences between man and ape.

This conclusion applies to all other functions of humans and chimpanzees as well, and sits easily with the fact that our genetic make-up resembles that of a chimpanzee by 95%.[6] But a difference of 5% might still mean that more than 1000 genes are uniquely

DNA of related organisms: 95% similarity

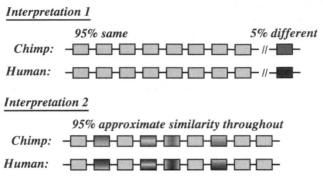

Figure 1.1 The genetic make-up of chimpanzees and humans. See text and Note 24 to Chapter 2 for details.

human as opposed to chimpanzee-like, and those who subscribe to this view continue to search for characteristically human genes. I do not believe they will find them. My interpretation, which is shared with many molecular scientists, is different. To us, the '95% similarity' implies that *all* the genes of chimpanzees and humans are *on average* 95% similar and 5% different: some genes, like that for the alpha chain of haemoglobin, are identical; other genes, like that for insulin, are almost identical; yet other genes differ by more than 5%, but even these belong to the same gene family, specifying the same function, in humans and chimpanzees. There are no 'human' as opposed to 'chimpanzee' genes at all (Figure 1.1).

To summarise the gist of this book. All living organisms, from bacteria to plants and to animals, search. In humans, the propensity for quest is amplified; in other primates, it is constrained. Man has come to dominate the world and every creature on it; the chimpanzee is in danger of extinction.[7]

***

Quest is divided into four parts. In the first, we consider the genetic basis of searching. In order to do so, the molecular nature of life has to be appreciated. There is both unity and diversity. All organisms are made up of the same *kind* of molecules, but no two organisms, even of the same species, are exactly alike: they differ in the fine structure of their constituent DNA and proteins. As a result, one shrub grows taller than its neighbour, one amoeba swims faster than its mate, one pigeon coos louder than its sibling, one human being is more inquisitive than another. It is such subtleties of molecular structure that also underlie the emergence of new species: of us humans from an ancient bacterium, as explained in Chapter 2.

I have alluded to the search by plants for the light of the sun and by microbes for food. Because these are relatively simple systems, many of the molecules that underlie the search have been defined. It turns out that several of them, proteins as well as smaller molecules like vitamins, play a role also in the physiological processes that underlie searching by higher organisms. As will become apparent in Chapter 3, vision—which is crucial to an animal's ability to search—is based on a mechanism that has its origin in the responses of plants and certain microbes to light.

As aquatic organisms moved on to land 400 million years ago, the search widened. As mammals began to replace reptiles some 65 million years ago, the search widened yet again. And as the forerunners of modern man began to evolve from other primates around 5 million years ago, the ability to search increased even further: the advantages of the attributes I have identified when looking for food and water, a possible predator, or a new environment in which to settle, are clear. The benefits of successful searching in terms of survival and passing on one's genes—the concept of the selfish gene[8]—are obvious. Recently discovered molecules related to human quest are introduced in Chapter 4.

The second part of the book traces the quest of modern man, of *Homo sapiens*. It is essentially the story of the last 100,000 years, analysed in terms of man's unceasing search. Each of the topics I describe is a measure of the behavioural differences between human and chimpanzee: each stems from nothing more than man's superior means to engage in the primeval act of quest. His brain questions and dreams up new challenges: his hands respond. What, then, have the consequences been? Man's search for new environments has taken him beyond his African origins to Asia and to Europe, and subsequently to every part of the globe. In most places except the polar ice caps, arid deserts and snow-capped mountains, some members of the species decided to settle, and in many cases their descendants are there to this day. The exploratory drive of humans, from walking out of the Great Rift valley in east Africa to landing on the moon, is illustrated with appropriate examples in Chapter 5.

Ten thousand years ago men began to feel more secure in keeping predators at bay. They began to cultivate their own crops and to domesticate animals for food and work. As the nomadic life was abandoned for that of a settled community, some groups were not content to remain where they were. They searched for fresh places in which to settle and they began to look for novel ways in which to carry out their daily lives: not just more comfortably in buildings and palaces made of stone, not merely more hygienically, with piped water and drains, but surrounded by pleasing objects also. Civilisations emerged. Their birth, and the part that heredity plays in producing leaders and men of culture, are examined in Chapter 6.

The achievements associated with those civilisations—in Mesopotamia and Egypt, in China and India and Crete, in central and southern America—are compared with the relative dearth of accomplishments elsewhere in Chapter 7. The development of language, which is the forerunner of the written word, and the basis of scholarship and art, constitute Chapter 8.

From the shaping of the first flint stone and the lighting of a fire more than a million years ago, man has worked with his hands. The technologies of the stone age, of China and Islam, have defined the way we lead our lives. But every improvement is accompanied by a new instrument of war. Chapter 9 is devoted to these topics and to an assessment of the relationship between technology and wealth. It closes with the innovations of one man: Leonardo da Vinci. No one has been able to match Leonardo in combining dexterity of hand with ingenuity of mind.

Early man must often have been frightened by the natural world around him: by thunder and lightning, by hurricanes and floods, by volcanic eruptions and earthquakes. He searched for explanations. And the best explanation all came up with, whether in Sumeria,

Egypt, India, China, Crete, Central or South America, was religion: belief in some supernatural beings that are ultimately responsible for events that the people do not understand and cannot control. The explanations proved so satisfactory that the faiths that developed —Hinduism, Buddhism, Judaism and its offspring Christianity and Islam—are practised throughout the world to this very day: by millions of educated men and women of every profession, in temples and shrines, in mosques and synagogues, in churches and in the home. Yet when pressed, few admit to ascribing natural phenomena to some sort of deity any more. What do they seek? An answer is attempted in Chapter 10.

Divine origins for physical events started to be questioned by Greek philosophers seeking alternative interpretations 2000 years ago. Attempts at scientific reasoning then stagnated until explanations for events such as the transition of day into night, winter into spring, began to emerge in the sixteenth century (although we still use terms like 'sunset' and 'sunrise'). A scientific explanation differs from all others in having universal validity: the concept that the earth moves round the sun and not the other way round is as true in Rome as it is in Krakow. Science—questioning beliefs through experiments that lead to a hypothesis, or a hypothesis followed by experimentation—is the same wherever it is practised. Scientists are explorers, too: they search for stars that are trillions of light years away, for particles that are billions of times smaller than a molecule of sugar; for the traces of animals that have been extinct for millions of years, for strains of virus that are only now appearing. Chapter 11 recounts the contributions of some scientific geniuses and asks a simple question: will we soon have discovered all there is to know, or is the search unending?

The third part of this book focuses on current controversy regarding science and technology. The knowledge that we have gained during the last two decades regarding the manipulation of genes—of plants as well as of animals, including man—is leading to enormous changes in agriculture and medicine. The search to generate crops that are resistant to drought, to cold or to pests, that produce a higher yield of wheat or maize or sugar beet or sweet potato, leads to obvious economic advantages that are especially important for the underdeveloped countries of the world. Yet there is much heated debate over genetically modifying foods, and the dispute over doing the same for people is at boiling point. Should human cloning be permitted? Should genes that cause disease be replaced by healthy versions? Should organ transplants from animals be encouraged? Should people be allowed to freeze their body cells in order to have access to them if the need arises? Do the benefits of tinkering with nature outweigh the risks? Is unrestricted quest by scientists acceptable? An objective view is attempted in Chapters 12 and 13.

In the final part we look into the future. Where will man's quest lead him in the next 100 years, where in the next million? Of course, we can only speculate. In the short term I predict that a waning of inquisitiveness — 'dumbing down' — that is occurring in Western societies today will lead to their decline compared with the cultures of eastern Asia. Overall, though, humans will be as stupid and as inventive, as kind and as cruel, as they now are: the experience of past events has proved to have little impact on man's behaviour, and a century produces but an imperceptible alteration of his genes. To consider evolutionary change in humans, we need to think in terms of millions of years, not centuries. Over such a time scale, will man's quest lead to the appearcncc of a new species of *Homo*? Or will his searches result in his own destruction, in the extinction of *Homo quaerens*, before then? A guess is presented in Chapter 14.

***

As the idea for writing this book grew in my mind, I began to wonder why no one else had considered quest as a quality that is both distinctive of humans and yet fundamental to all forms of life. Was this idea rubbish or was it self-evident? I spoke to scientific colleagues and approached anthropologists: they listened politely, smiled and suggested that I talk to someone else, as this was not really their field. Others reacted in similar vein. The important point is that no one was able to refer me to an article or a book where it had all been said before. That, at least, was encouraging.

Then Richard Dawkins came to the rescue. He thought that the late Sir Alister Hardy, Professor of Zoology at Oxford half a century ago, had suggested something along these lines. He recalled an article somewhere, but could not remember the exact reference. Perhaps Arthur Cain, a former colleague of Hardy's who had moved to Liverpool but was now retired, could help? By the time I was able to track him down, he had, sadly, died. I resumed my search. Another Oxford zoologist, Mark Ridley, thought that the elusive article might be in one of the Gifford Lectures that Hardy had delivered shortly after his retirement. Success! As the following quotation shows, my idea was neither foolish nor obvious. On the contrary, by writing this book I seem to have answered the question that Hardy posed. Listen to his own words:

Nevertheless, out of this process of evolution, from *somewhere* has come the urge, or love of adventure, in Man that can drive him to risk his life in climbing Everest or in reaching the South Pole or the Moon. Is it altogether too naive to believe that this exploratory drive, this curiosity, has had its beginnings in some deep-seated part of animal behaviour which is fundamental to the stream of life?[9]

* * *

To write this book I have chosen to delve into subjects like religion and anthropology, history and art, in which I have received no formal training: I am but a humble biochemist. But the search for expression of my thoughts is in my genes. Was not my grandfather an artist, his wife a musician, my uncle a writer and my mother a philosopher? The reader must forgive my errors in what follows. I have written as a scientist, but have allowed my thoughts to wander.

In my mind's eye I see, now, a group of our earliest ancestors walking upright along the Olduvai Gorge in northern Tanzania, looking for food; now, Archimedes at Syracuse, pondering how to measure the relative amounts of gold and silver in King Hieron's crown; now, Christopher Columbus standing in the bow of the Santa Maria, scanning the western horizon in the search for land; now, Claude Monet in his garden at Giverny, striving to depict the sunlight as it falls upon the water lilies; now, Adolf Hitler and

Heinrich Himmler in the Berlin chancellery seeking faster ways to annihilate an entire people; now, Mother Theresa in the slums of Calcutta, endeavouring to let a few starving souls die with dignity; now, a group of white-coated scientists in their laboratory trying to insert a frost-resistant gene into a tomato plant. I see humans but I know that I am witnessing nothing more than the expression of a fundamental quality of living matter: the ability to search. Since I began writing, the sequence of the human genome has been unravelled. It will still be a long time before the function of all the proteins specified by our genes, and the complicated cross-talk between them, is identified. But if you believe, as I do, that such molecular interactions are the basis for our complex behaviour, for our heightened propensity for quest, then join me in a journey of 3.5 billion years that I will try to tell you in just under 400 pages.

Notes

1. From *Camino Real* (1953).
2. See, for example, Carl Sagan and Ann Druyan, op. cit.; a useful summary is on p 399. Good accounts of tool technology and social customs in chimpanzees are given by Frans B. M. de Waal and by A. Whiten *et al.*, in *Nature* **399**: 635–636 and 682–685; 1999 respectively. For a discussion of the chimpanzee's mind in relation to our own, see Steven J. Mithen, op. cit., especially pp 73–94; see also Jane Goodall, op. cit.
3. Jean-Jacques Rousseau, in 1753 (100 years before Darwin's *Origin of Species*), even classified chimpanzees and humans as members of the same species; the power of speech, he presciently suggested, was at the beginning 'not natural to man'. From Carl Sagan and Ann Druyan, op. cit., p 273.
4. But chimpanzees have bigger testicles—producing more sperm—and are able to copulate once an hour throughout an entire day (with different females). Bonobos are particularly fecund; they are also the only species of primate, apart from man, that mates in the 'missionary position'. See Carl Sagan and Ann Druyan, op. cit., p 310.
5. See Peter Medawar, *The Uniqueness of the Individual*, 2nd edn. Dover Publications, New York, 1981, p 134.
6. For over two decades the figure was assumed to be 98.5%. See Roy J. Britten, 'Divergence between samples of chimpanzee and human DNA

sequences is 5%, counting indels', *Proc. Natl Acad. Sci. USA* **99**: 13633 – 13635; 2002.

7. In 1996 there were around 10,000 bonobos in the wild (all in the Congo); 4 years later the number had shrunk to half. See *Nature* **405**: 262; 2000.

8. The hypothesis was stated with clarity by Edward O. Wilson (1975) loc. cit., p 3 ('The Morality of the Gene') and enriched by Richard Dawkins' use of the word 'selfish' in *The Selfish Gene*, op. cit. For a spirited critique of the concept, see Gabriel Dover, 'Anti-Dawkins', in *Alas, Poor Darwin*, Hilary and Steven Rose (eds), op. cit., pp 47 – 66.

9. Hardy compared evolution to a stream: the former starts at a single point and branches out, the latter begins at many locations and finishes up at one mouth; evolution loses entropy as it progresses, a stream and its tributaries gain entropy during their downward flow. See A. C. Hardy op. cit.

PART I

Evolution: the genetic basis of quest

CHAPTER TWO

Unity and diversity in living organisms

Molecular basis of life

*A*ll life—indeed, the entire universe—is made up of molecules: molecules of hydrogen and helium in the sun and other stars, molecules of water in the rivers and oceans of our planet, molecules of aluminium silicate in its outer crust, molecules of nitrogen and oxygen in its atmosphere, and molecules of nucleic acid (DNA and RNA), protein, carbohydrate and fat within every organism that lives on its surface. The last-mentioned group of molecules are sometimes called organic, to distinguish them from the non-living, inorganic molecules that make up rocks and sand, sea and air. Microbes, plants and animals are nothing more than a conglomeration of organic molecules, together with some salts and water.

Molecules are all extremely small: molecules like water, oxygen or carbon dioxide are less than a billionth of the size of the point of a needle; carbohydrates like glucose and fats like cholesterol are 10 times larger; proteins and carbohydrates like starch are a 100 times larger, and DNA—the biggest molecule of living matter—is a million times larger (but still visible only with an electron microscope).

Since living organisms consist of nothing *but* molecules, it follows that there are a very large number of them in any one microbe, plant or animal: some thousand million million million

million (10^{27}) molecules of water, a hundred thousand million million million (10^{23}) molecules of protein and ten thousand million million (10^{16}) molecules of DNA in an adult human being. These molecules constitute the organs—liver, kidneys, brain—and the tissues—muscle, fat, bone—that make up our bodies.

Organs (and some tissues) are divided into small structures called cells. These are delineated by a membrane which is, of course, also made up of molecules: mainly protein and fat with some carbohydrate. Cells of plants and animals are of similar size (approximately one hundredth of a millimetre in diameter, just too small to see with the naked eye), irrespective of whether they are part of a daisy or a beetle, a giant sequoia or an elephant, a month-old foetus or a 20 year-old man. Microbes are single-celled organisms, and are even smaller: less than one tenth the size of a plant or animal cell. Hundreds of infectious bacteria like *Mycobacterium lepri*, for example, can live inside a single human cell. Viruses are smaller yet again: they grow even within bacteria, and tens of thousands can populate an animal cell before it bursts.

The number of cells in an organism depends on its size: an adult human being contains some hundred million million (10^{14}) cells. A quick calculation shows that any one cell contains around ten million million (10^{13}) molecules of water, a thousand million (10^9) molecules of protein and about a hundred (10^2) molecules of DNA.

Molecules, then, are the smallest units of which all matter is composed. They differ from one another not only in size, but also in composition. Water, for example, consists of two atoms of hydrogen (H) linked to one atom of oxygen (O): H_2O. Glucose consists of six atoms of carbon (C), 12 of hydrogen and six of oxygen: $C_6H_{12}O_6$ (Figure 2.1). Atoms do not exist as discrete entities (except at very high temperatures). It is molecules and the reactions between them that make up the chemistry of life. The interactions are complicated, because some of the molecules are complicated. Proteins and DNA illustrate this particularly well. In contrast to water or glucose, which are the same wherever they occur, proteins and DNA differ slightly from organism to organism.

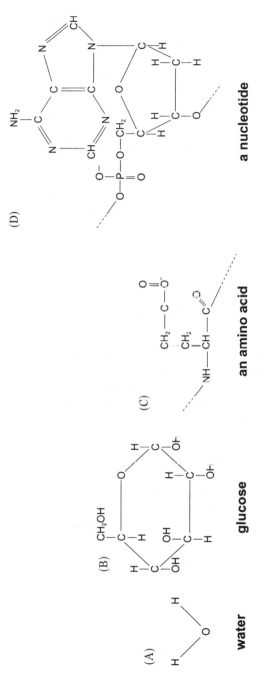

water   glucose   an amino acid   a nucleotide

Figure 2.1 Molecules that are the same in all organisms: (A) water; (B) glucose; (C) an amino acid; (D) a nucleotide. The amino acid illustrated is called glutamate. The links that join it to adjacent amino acids in a protein are indicated by the broken lines. The nucleotide illustrated is called adenine deoxynucleotide: the upper ring structure containing N atoms is the adenine part, the lower ring is called deoxyribose and the group of atoms to its left, containing a P atom, is called phosphate. All deoxynucleotides (sometimes called nucleotides for short) contain deoxyribose and phosphate; it is the N-containing ring that varies between the four nucleotides, referred to for simplicity as A (shown), C, G and T. The links that join adenine nucleotide to adjacent nucleotides in a molecule of DNA are indicated by the broken lines. All nucleotides are negatively charged (indicated by the ⁻ on one of the oxygen atoms (O) linked to the phosphorus atom (P). The NH_2 group on adenine is sometimes positively charged, sometimes not; here it is shown in the uncharged form. Some amino acids are positively charged, some are uncharged (neutral) and some—like the glutamate shown in (C)—are negatively charged.

19

Proteins and DNA

Proteins consist of hundreds of atoms of hydrogen, oxygen, carbon, nitrogen (N) and some sulphur (S), all linked together in long chains: each chain is made up of a series of much smaller units, called amino acids (Figure 2.1). Imagine a metal link chain, containing hundreds of links: if the chain corresponds to a protein, then each link corresponds to an amino acid. Just as a link chain can be folded into a smaller structure, by throwing it into a bucket for example, so a protein becomes folded into a similarly coiled structure in cells (Figure 2.2). The amino acids that make up a protein are not identical. There are 20 different types of amino acid, and any one can be linked to another. The length of the chain is variable: some proteins are made up of relatively short chains, others consist of longer chains. Insulin is an example of the first type, haemoglobin of the second. So when a molecule is referred to as being a protein, that defines merely its composition: lots of amino acids linked together in a chain. The fine structure varies from protein to protein.[1] Because the structure of a molecule determines its function, proteins can carry out an immense variety of activities: proteins, in fact, are nature's catalysts.

In the human body there are over 100,000 different types of protein, each with a specific function: insulin promotes the absorption of sugar from the blood stream to muscle and liver; haemoglobin carries oxygen through the blood stream; actin and myosin constitute the contractile filaments of muscle; other proteins catalyse metabolism, helping to break down the food we eat and then enabling us to use the energy released in order to pump blood round the body and to run and jump and fight; yet other proteins make our eyes blue or dark, our hair fair or black, curly or straight, our stature large or small, our thoughts gloomy or joyous, our mental capacity agile or dull. Every feature we possess is determined by proteins. How are those features passed from one generation to the next, as many of them clearly are? Not by the proteins themselves, but by the molecule that is the blue print for every protein in our body, namely DNA.

(A)

(B)

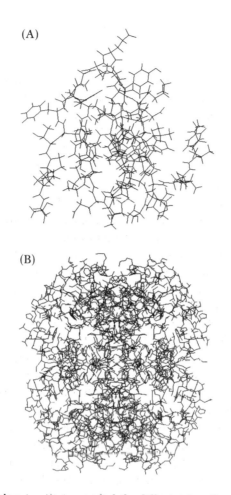

Figure 2.2 Molecules that are slightly different in all organisms. Two proteins are shown: (A) human insulin and (B) human haemoglobin. The lines correspond to the bonds between atoms as in Figure 2.1, at lower magnification (actual atoms are omitted). The structures are three-dimensional models based on X-ray crystallography. Haemoglobin appears to be symmetrical because it is actually composed of four separate chains of amino acids: two alpha chains and two beta chains. Both images are reproduced from the SwissProt database (insulin: **http://ca.expasy.org/ cgi-bin/niceprot.pl?po1308**; haemoglobin: **http://ca.expasy.org/ contact.html**) of the Protein Data Bank: see H. M. Berman *et al.*, 'The Protein Data Bank', *Nucleic Acids Res.* **28**: 235–242; 2000.

DNA consists of atoms of hydrogen, oxygen, carbon, nitrogen and phosphorus (P), linked together in even longer chains than proteins. Again, the chain consists of smaller units, that in this case are called nucleotides (Figure 2.1); just four types of nucleotide make up DNA: adenine nucleotide (called A for short), cytosine nucleotide (C), guanine nucleotide (G) and thymine nucleotide (T). The extent of a DNA chain is quite remarkable. The length of a molecule of human DNA, if it was stretched out, is some 2 metres. Yet it is accommodated within cells that are just 10 micrometres wide. Since a micrometre is a millionth of a metre, this is a reduction of 500,000-fold. To achieve this, DNA within cells is wound round and round itself many times. That is not all. During cell division, DNA becomes packaged into chromosomes, which are even smaller: compared with its highly compacted structure in chromosomes, DNA during interphase (the period between successive cell divisions), is relatively 'unwound'. Each molecule of DNA is actually a closed circle, like a necklace made up of small beads.

To illustrate the enormous length of DNA, imagine the necklace to be a 100 times thinner than a human hair (a strand of DNA is actually much narrower than this); its length would then be equivalent to a mile-long circular race track. A chromosome would be the size of a pin head, and each bead of the necklace—the individual nucleotides—would be a thousandth of the size of a pin head. The beads come in just four colours: amber (A = adenine), cream (C = cytosine), green (G = guanine) and turquoise (T = thymine). In fact the necklace (DNA) consists of two strands wound round each other, with every amber (A) or turquoise (T) bead on one strand opposite a turquoise (T) or amber (A) bead on the other strand, and every green (G) or cream (C) bead on one strand opposite a cream (C) or green (G) bead on the other strand. I am unable to depict a necklace of these dimensions, not least because this book does not have colour illustrations; but I am sure that any questing reader who likes a challenge and is able to reproduce such a necklace, will find the publishers of biochemistry texts and CD-ROMs falling over each other to purchase his creation.

It may be wondered how the two strands of DNA come to line up so accurately opposite each other. It is because their structures are complementary: the strands attract each other. The situation may be compared to that by which two magnetic bars stick together: the north pole of one bar binds to the south pole of the other bar, and the south pole of the first bar binds to the north pole of the second bar. The attraction between the two bars is magnetic; the attraction between the strands of DNA is chemical. It involves a relatively weak force known as a hydrogen bond.[2] Life on our planet could begin only once the temperature had dropped sufficiently to maintain the integrity of hydrogen bonds that hold DNA together.

The sequence in which A, C, G and T are assembled along a part of a DNA strand specifies the sequence in which the 20 different amino acids of a protein are linked together. You might wonder how four different entities can specify 20 others; surely there need to be at least 20 different nucleotides in DNA to specify each one of 20 different amino acids? The answer is that it is not single nucleotides, but groups of three, that specify each of the amino acids: the code by which the nucleotides of DNA determine the amino acids of a protein is a triplet one. Any of the four nucleotides can occupy any of the three positions in a triplet; there are therefore $4 \times 4 \times 4 = 64$ different possibilities—more than enough for 20 amino acids. Some of the triplets specify additional signals like 'start' and 'stop', the punctuation marks in DNA that tell the cellular machinery where a protein begins, and where it ends. So ATG, for example, indicates 'start a new protein', GAG specifies the amino acid glutamate, GTG specifies the amino acid valine, TGA indicates 'end of protein' and so on.

Inheritance

Molecules may exert a life-time's fascination for a biochemist or neuropharmacologist, but are rather heavy going for the traveller who has picked up this book at an airport (especially if he is under the impression that *Quest* is a novel form of dating agency). However, the reader who is still awake at this point will have noted a discrepancy. How can a molecule of DNA code for a specific protein when there are only around 100 molecules of DNA in a cell, yet more than 100,000—perhaps as many as 300,000—

different proteins to choose from in any one cell? The answer is that one molecule of DNA codes not for one but for several thousand different proteins: one stretch of DNA codes for one protein, the next stretch codes for another, and so on. A molecule of DNA is millions of times longer than a protein.[3]

The part of a molecule of DNA that codes for a single protein is called a gene, and there are therefore more than 1000 genes, arranged end-to-end, in each molecule of DNA.[4] A molecule of DNA is also called a chromosome, and there are 23 different chromosomes, comprising DNA of varying length, in every human cell. The total number of chromosomes is actually 46, because each chromosome is present as a pair (Figure 2.3).When a cell is about to divide, the number of DNA molecules, in other words the number of

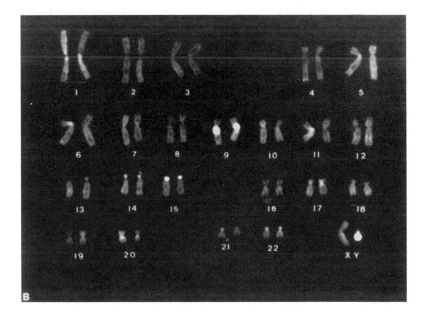

Figure 2.3 Chromosomes. The chromosome pairs in a male human cell at metaphase (just before cell division) are shown. They have been been stained with a fluorescent dye and sorted according to size. Reproduced from Ram S. Verma and Arvind Babu, *Human Chromosomes. Principles and Techniques*, 2nd edn, McGraw-Hill, New York, 1985 with permission of The McGraw-Hill companies.

chromosomes, doubles to 92, so that after a cell has split in half, the two daughter cells will again contain 46 chromosomes (23 pairs) each. Hence the approximation of 100 molecules of DNA per cell, that was made at the beginning of this chapter, is not so far out. Why are chromosomes present as pairs? The answer is simple. One set of 23 of the chromosomes is inherited from one's mother, the other set of 23 from one's father.

The confusion about names like 'gene' and 'chromosome' is due to the fact that they were coined years before their chemical composition (namely DNA) was known. 'Gene' refers to a functional unit of inheritance (from the Greek and Latin word for 'birth'), 'chromosome' (Greek for 'coloured body') alludes to a structure that is visible by light microscopy in cells stained by a dye just before they are about to divide. We owe the concept of the gene to Gregor Mendel, a Moravian monk, quietly crossing different strains of sweet pea in a monastery garden at Brünn (now Brno in the Czech Republic) 100 years ago. He carried out the first *scientific* experiment on cross-breeding, which man had been practising for 10,000 years. He was searching for nothing less than the mechanism by which certain features are passed on from one generation to the next. What he found was that characteristics of the sweet pea plant, like tallness or shortness, presence or absence of colour in the blossoms, wrinkled or smooth appearance of its seeds, are inherited independently of each other, in a predictable manner. From this he deduced that the characteristics are transmitted as separate elements. He called them genes. With just pride can the Austrians (or the Czechs) acknowledge Gregor Mendel as one of their greatest scientists to date. Chromosomes have been known to be involved in the inheritance of particular characteristics for almost as long as genes. Only subsequently, within the last 50 years, has the chemical nature of chromosomes and their constituent genes been recognised as being simply a very long strand of DNA.[5]

By 1950, then, the composition of hereditary material— chromosomes and their constituent genes—was generally accepted as being a single chemical entity called DNA. The discovery of the way it functions came by chance, as a result of establishing its structure. In Cambridge, William Bragg and his son Lawrence had pioneered the technique of X-ray crystallography for determining the structure of crystals. The Braggs elucidated that of salt (NaCl), one of the simplest chemicals in nature. Could the same technique be employed for DNA, the most complex molecule on earth, that is not even a proper crystal? A junior scientist at Cambridge, Francis Crick, was tempted to try. A young post-doctoral research fellow from the USA named James Watson, who was in the department at the time, had a similar idea. Determining the structure of DNA seemed a suitable, if highly challenging, project for their collaborative efforts. In fact, Crick was still without his PhD because his studies had been interrupted by the war. He was actually supposed to be working under Max Perutz for his thesis on the structure of haemoglobin, while Watson had been offered a place in the same laboratory to join John Kendrew in his studies on myoglobin. It says much for the tolerance of Perutz and Kendrew, as well as for the relaxed atmosphere in which they were working —the Cavendish Laboratory, the most distinguished physics department in Britain—that Watson and Crick were allowed to indulge their enthusiasm for DNA at all, instead of applying their energy to the structure of proteins. But the importance of DNA as the likely genetic material was recognised, and Linus Pauling in the USA, who had shown that the backbone of many proteins is in the form of an alpha helix, was said to be about to crack the structure of DNA (he thought it was a triple helix). Kendrew, Perutz and the head of the department—now Sir Lawrence Bragg —were certainly not averse to the possibility of the precocious young duo securing this discovery for England.

The rest of the story has become as well known as Archimedes' cry of *Eureka!* as he leapt from his bath, and has been admirably told by James Watson in *The Double Helix*. Although there is actually no evidence that Archimedes did run naked through the streets of Syracuse, the details of *The Double Helix* are all factually correct. So, did Watson and Crick manage to crystallise DNA? No, they did not even try. Instead they sought X-ray photographs of pseudo-crystalline DNA prepared by others, which they would interpret. They found them an hour and a half away, at King's College in London. Another young research duo, Rosalind Franklin and Maurice Wilkins, had obtained photographs that might just be good enough to attempt a structural interpretation. This they proved to be, and Watson and Crick published the results in 1953. Their article described DNA as being a double helix, held together by bonds between A and T and between C and G.[6] At the end of their paper is a casual remark: 'It has not escaped our notice that the specific pairing we have postulated immediately suggests a possible copying mechanism for the genetic material'. The import of that sentence was instantly recognised, and Watson and Crick, together with Maurice Wilkins, were feted at every scientific meeting. Rosalind Franklin, the only person to have actually handled DNA and who isolated the material from which its structure was deduced, was largely ignored. By the time that Crick, Watson and Wilkins (but not Chargaff) received their Nobel prize in 1962, she had succumbed to cancer: she was just 37.

A child may resemble its parents in certain features and mannerisms, but it is not an exact replica of either of them. The mechanism of inheritance is essentially the same in all organisms — plants and microbes as well as animals — so we may continue to use humans to illustrate the process. Why, then, is a baby girl not a copy of her mother, a boy a copy of his father? It is because the chromosomes — the entire repertoire of genes, sometimes referred to as the genome — that are inherited from each parent are not identical throughout. Each set of genes corresponds to a part of each pair of chromosomes: one maternal and one paternal. A pair of genes codes for a pair of proteins of similar function. Some gene pairs are identical, as a result of which the pair of proteins for which they code are also identical. An example of this situation is the gene for the protein insulin: it is the same in the maternal and paternal chromosome, and only one type of insulin is made. Other gene pairs are not identical, but merely similar, and therefore code for proteins that are slightly different; while each of the two proteins carries out the same function, one may do so better or worse than the other. The result is that the expression of that gene pair is a mixture of two activities. An example will be given shortly. First, we need to focus on what precedes the combination of maternal and paternal chromosomes during the fertilisation of an egg by a sperm.

In order that each cell of the developing embryo has the requisite number of chromosomes — two sets of 23 — the number present in egg or sperm needs to be halved, so that each contains a single, not a double, set of chromosomes. This halving of chromosome pairs takes place in the germinal tissues: ovaries in females, testes in males. During this process the cells—that will mature into egg or sperm—contain mixtures of the 23 chromosomes. Some chromosomes in a germinal cell are those that the individual has inherited from the father, some are those inherited from the mother.[7] You have only to look at a family reunion to appreciate the situation: 'James has his mother's eyes, but he is tall, like his father'; 'Yes, but look at his nose, it's an exact replica of grandfather Frederick's'; 'True, but in his scholarly ways, he's much more like his grandfather Leonard'. So genes themselves do not change from generation to generation, as Mendel found, but are retained within a family grouping. Extended to an entire population, we find that the overall pool of genes remains more or less the same for hundreds and thousands of years.

Generation of variant genes

The mechanism I have described accounts for the mixing of genes at each generation. But how do variant genes arise in the first place? The molecules within an organism—proteins, DNA, lipids and so forth—are constantly being modified by interacting with molecules present in the environment: the food we eat, the air we breathe, the molecules generated by sunlight and other radiations that fall on our skin. Life is a continual interaction between the molecules we inherit and those we acquire. Some of the latter are of a kind known as 'free radicals', that tend to oxidise the molecules with which they come into contact. If a molecule of protein (or lipid) becomes damaged in this way, it does not matter much, because there are some 10,000 copies of any one protein in a cell, and the 9999 unaffected molecules are sufficient to maintain the functions of that cell. Even if all 10,000 molecules in a cell were affected, the consequences might still not be serious, as there are trillions (10^{12}) of cells in any one organ, such as the liver.

Where function is dependent on far fewer clusters of cells, as in particular sensory pathways in the brain or in the 'pacemaker' muscles of the heart, a deterioration of function does become apparent (rarely is the function of proteins improved). This underlies certain diseases and is part of the ageing process. However much our proteins become damaged, though, we do not pass the defect on to our offspring; not merely because procreation generally occurs well before significant damage has occurred, but because very few of the proteins just mentioned are present in sperm or egg. In any case, proteins do not self-replicate, so that a molecule of defective protein in an embryo would soon be diluted out by the millions of new protein molecules synthesised.[8]

DNA, on the other hand, is replicated at every cell division, whether in an adult human being or in a fertilised egg. Any damage to DNA is therefore maintained. The nature of the damage may result in the alteration of a nucleotide: a C may become a T, for example. Such change is called a mutation. If it occurs within a region of DNA that codes for a protein, in other words within a gene, it will generate many millions of modified protein molecules, in millions of cells. The activity of a modified protein may be unaffected, or it may be reduced; very occasionally it is improved. Depending on the exact position of the mutated nucleotide, it may also result in no protein being made at all—if it introduces a 'stop' at the start of a protein sequence, for example.

A person in whom such a mutation has occurred will contain two versions of that protein: the original, unmodified version, and the modified one. If the mutation occurs in a cell that is not within germinal tissue, that is the end of the story, once the person dies.[9] If the mutation occurs in sperm or egg, however, there is a 50% chance that the modified gene will be passed on to the next generation. Those who inherit the modified version—plus an unmodified version from their other parent—may be, so far as the function of that particular protein is concerned, unaffected, slightly worse off, or slightly better off.

'Worse' and 'better' are relative terms: a 'worse' variant of a protein may actually be advantageous in certain circumstances. Possessing a variant form of haemoglobin called 'sickle cell' haemoglobin, for example,[10] confers an advantage to those living in a malarious environment, for the parasitic microbe *Plasmodium falciparum*, that enters the blood stream of an individual bitten by a *P. falciparum*-carrying mosquito, survives less well in red cells that contain 50% sickle cell haemoglobin and 50% normal haemoglobin. Such a person may be subject to minor vascular problems because sickle cell haemoglobin causes red cells to become deformed—sickle-shaped—and hence to pass less well through capillaries; but he is less likely to die of malaria. Where 100% of a person's haemoglobin is of the sickle cell variety, the vascular problems tend to outweigh any advantage associated with resistance to malaria. So variant genes become concentrated within populations in certain geographical regions. As the environment changes over thousands of years, such mutations may very gradually be lost, or concentrated, within a particular group. This is the mechanism by which different versions of a protein become associated with different racial groupings: skin colour is the most obvious example, simply because metabolic differences, like the possession of sickle cell haemoglobin, are not discerned from a person's outward appearance.

Generation of new species

Caucasians, Asiatics, Africans and Australian aborigines are all variants of the same species, *Homo sapiens*. Chimpanzees are of different species, *Pan troglodytes* or *Pan paniscus*. What constitutes a species, and how do new species arise? The answer to the first question is, surprisingly, less clear than that to the second.

Two organisms are generally defined as belonging to separate species if the offspring of a coupling between them is sterile. A horse mates with a donkey: the offspring, a mule, is sterile. Hence, horse and donkey are separate species.[11] On the other hand, wolves, coyotes and dogs are considered to be separate species, yet the offspring of matings between them are mostly fertile.[12] The criterion of sterile issue appears not to hold. So should wolves, coyotes and dogs be considered as belonging to a single species? Are the three types of animal merely variants of one another? Not necessarily.

The point is that wolves, coyotes and dogs happen to have the same number of chromosomes— 39 pairs—whereas horses and donkeys have a different number. Hence, meiosis[7,11] in the offspring of inter-canid matings is more easily achieved than in the progeny of horse – donkey pairs. Perhaps the surest definition of a species is the following: 'the set of all individuals between which there can be gene flow'.[13] This evades molecular mechanisms but takes into account geographical and behavioral reasons for the absence of gene flow. Zoologists debate these matters. For us, the important point is that the distinction between variants and species is imprecise. Darwin himself was cautious: at no point in *The Origin of Species* does he actually define what he means by a species.

I have mentioned the duplication of certain genes. This occurs when a particular gene is copied twice instead of once during the synthesis of DNA. Such an event means that two identical genes are now present —end to end—on the same chromosome. These errors, like mutations within genes, are generally repaired during a process termed 'proof-reading'. But if the proof-reading mechanism itself is impaired, mistakes may be retained and passed on to the next generation (if the mutation occurs in a germ cell). Possessing multiple copies of genes generates an opportunity to produce proteins with differing efficacy through subsequent mutations.[14] So gene duplication and mutation are continuously producing variant proteins. If those that possess them are at a disadvantage, the variant genes will gradually be lost from the gene pool. But if they prove to be advantageous, they will be retained. As more and more such variants within a population accumulate, they will eventually endow their owners with attributes that set them aside from their predecessors. That, in outline, is how a new species emerges.

A novel species, whether of man, ape, elephant or butterfly, does not simply appear at a point in time. All organisms[15] are constantly changing in the subtle ways I have described. Of all the variant forms that are generated, some find themselves better suited to the environment of the time than others, and therefore breed faster. The well-suited ones continue to flourish, the others gradually die out: the sheer numbers of the successful ones means that they win out in the competition for food and shelter, water and a mate; they may also be better at avoiding predators. This is essentially what Charles Darwin and his forgotten contemporary, Alfred Russel Wallace,[16] meant by proposing that the evolution of species occurs through natural selection: through 'survival of the fittest', as Herbert Spencer—the nineteenth century social reformer and follower of Darwin's evolutionary theory—put it. By the mid-nineteenth century, the principles of slow geological change—the formation of valleys through erosion by glaciers and rivers, for example—were coming to be recognised and accepted by many scientists of the day.[17] What had not yet occurred to anyone, save Darwin and Wallace in England, and Jean-Baptiste Lamarck half a century earlier in France, is that living creatures may also change slowly with time. Where Lamarck differed was in his belief that characteristics acquired during the life of an organism are passed on to its progeny; Darwin and Wallace preferred to think that nature throws up a number of different forms, of which those best suited to the environment of the time survive. Lamarck's view has subsequently been shown to be incorrect, although in the Soviet era it was revived by the biologist Trofim Denisovich Lysenko. His results purporting to show the inheritance of acquired characteristics appealed to Josef Stalin: the values of Marxism would rub off on people for generations. Moreover, Lysenko's claim, that seeds exposed to low temperature would be better able to produce crops in a cold climate, found particular favour with Stalin, as it would transform agricultural yields throughout Siberia. The result was rather different: millions of people died of starvation (but Lysenko became Director of the Institute of Genetics and President of the V. I. Lenin All-Union Academy of Agricultural Sciences). The important point is that in 1850, whether in England or France, there were few who did not accept that all species of animal and plant owe their origin to a one-off event of divine origin.

Darwin had been sitting on his results, suggested by subtle differences between the finches found on the different Galapagos Islands situated to the west of Ecuador, for more than 15 years. When he became aware that Wallace was thinking along similar lines, his work *On the Origin of Species by Natural Selection, or the Preservation of Favoured Races in the Struggle for Life* was rapidly published by John Murray, on 24 November 1859. Murray had sent parts of the manuscript out for review and, although it received damning comments from some, sufficient scientists of stature— the geologist Sir Charles Lyell and the botanist Sir Joseph Hooker were among them—backed Darwin's views forcefully enough to encourage Murray to take a gamble. He printed 1250 copies; they were immediately sold out and a second edition of 3000 was printed to meet the demand. The book became the talk of cultured circles throughout England and was soon published in America; translations into German and French followed. The overall reaction, however, was mixed: few understood what Darwin was trying to say, and those who thought they did, condemned it on religious grounds. Ridicule was added to the attack: 'Mr Huxley, I beg to know, was it through your grandfather or your grandmother that you claim to have descended from a monkey?' Thus Bishop Samuel Wilberforce tried to discomfit Thomas Huxley, when that gentleman was expounding Darwin's hypothesis on the origin of species at a meeting of the British Association for the Advancement of Science in Oxford in 1860.[18] This quip of 'Soapy Sam' Wilberforce—son of the social reformer William Wilberforce, who, through his forceful arguments in Parliament, had been responsible for the abolition of slavery in Britain 25 years earlier —infuriated Huxley. On the other hand, the illogicality of Wilberforce's attack gave Huxley the opportunity for a vigorous riposte: 'I am not ashamed to have a monkey for my ancestor; but I would be ashamed to be connected with a man who used great gifts to obscure the truth'. Huxley was applauded; Wilberforce was booed.

Apart from an innate bias by people against the hypothesis that species are constantly changing, the problem was that Darwin could provide no plausible explanation for the way that variation is achieved. More than a century was to elapse before the necessary evidence began to emerge. Only when living organisms were considered in molecular terms, did the mechanism by which subtle changes in form and function are brought about become apparent. How Darwin would have appreciated the scientific discoveries of the 1950s and 1960s, the innate simplicity of DNA duplication and the triplet code!

If the generation of a new species is slow, the dying out of an existing one, less able to cope, is usually even slower. Over the past billion years or so, new species have appeared faster than living ones have become extinct, creating an ever-increasing variety of living organisms. Today there are probably some 10 million different species of plants and animals on the globe, of which only a million and half have so far been described. Species that will eventually become extinct coexist with those that will survive. Long after the appearance of modern man, for example, there were still species of earlier hominids around. The time scale for evolutionary change to become manifest, in the case of primates like the higher apes and man, is in hundreds of thousands of years. Of course, sometimes the second half of the process, that by which species die out, is greatly speeded up.

The probable impact of an asteroid from outer space 65 million years ago so altered the environment that dinosaurs, for example, became extinct within a relatively short time.[19] The asteroid is believed to have measured 6 miles across and to have struck with an impact equivalent to a billion nuclear bombs. As a result it produced a crater—in the Gulf of Mexico—100 miles in diameter. This led to the emergence of a dust cloud that may have lasted anything from several months to as long as a decade, virtually stopping all photosynthesis. A gradual lack of green vegetation would have had a major effect on the food chain, which would have affected the dinosaurs directly—many were vegetarian—or indirectly, by reducing the animals on which they preyed. Another consequence would have been global warming, since without photosynthesis, carbon dioxide in the atmosphere is not absorbed by the leaves of trees. The result is that the additional carbon dioxide in the atmosphere creates an insulating barrier around the earth—the 'greenhouse' effect. Such a warming might have adversely affected the breeding efficiency of dinosaurs. This is because we know that the sex of certain new-born reptiles (a class of vertebrate related to that of dinosaurs) is partially determined by the temperature at which the egg matures. If this was true of dinosaur eggs also, perhaps the ratio between males and females shifted too much for any dinosaur species to survive. And then again it is possible that it was toxic fumes from the crater that killed them off.

Before all dinosaurs became extinct, however, certain species had already begun to evolve into the antecedents of today's reptiles, like crocodiles and turtles; others, most likely, evolved into our current repertoire of birds. What is generally accepted is the notion that the Age of Reptiles came to an end around 65 million years ago, with the gradual replacement of dinosaurs by mammals, which had begun a precarious existence towards the end of the dinosaurs' reign. The resulting Age of Mammals has lasted right through until the present day. Other organisms, such as some foraminifera,[20] were wiped off the face of the earth together with the dinosaurs. The fact that turtles and crocodiles have been around for more than 100 million years might lead one to regard them as highly successful in evolutionary terms. Alternatively, you could consider success to be measured by the number of different species that are representative of any one class. In that case, insects (over a million named species, with probably another 9 million still to be discovered) easily outstrip all others: mammals, for example, comprise less than 5000 distinct species.

Since the emergence of man, species have been dying out faster still as a result of his actions: through hunting and farming, and through continual encroachment on forest and savanna, as man's numbers increase at the expense of the plants and animals around him. It has been estimated that during the last 300 years the rate of extinction of birds and mammals has increased some 5–50-fold over the 'natural' rate, which is roughly one species every 4 years; put another way, the total lifetime of any one species is, on average, very approximately a million years. Within the last decades of the twentieth century, the extinction rate rose a further 20-fold: we are now losing roughly one species of animal or plant every day.[21] One way or another, more than 99.9% of the species that have ever lived on this planet are extinct.

Generation of a new genus

If the generation of one species from another involves no more than the accumulation of variant genes, is this also true of the generation of a new genus, of *Homo* from *Pan?* The genes of man resemble those of chimpanzees by 95%. What does this actually mean, and how is the figure derived?

A high degree of similarity means that the DNA of man is composed of almost, but not quite, the same numbers of A, C, G and T along its two strands.[22] Although the total length of DNA in a chimpanzee is about the same as that in a human, the number of chromosomes, surprisingly, is not. Chimpanzees have 24 pairs of chromosomes, compared to the 23 of man. What appears to have happened at some stage during the evolution of *Homo* is that one of the 24 ancestral chromosomes became fused to chromosome 11, making it much longer in humans than in chimpanzees. So the number of chromosome pairs in any particular organism—18 in the red fox, for example, but 25 in the arctic fox, 32 in the Saharan fox, and 37 in the hoary fox of north-east Brazil[23]—is of little significance compared with the overall number of genes that are contained within them.

The figure of 95% similarity comes from a method called hybridization.[24] As mentioned in the previous chapter, my interpretation of the 5% or so genetic difference between man and chimpanzee is that it reflects the degree of variability among genes that belong to similar families in the two organisms, and therefore have more or less the same functions. Specifically 'human' as opposed to 'chimpanzee' genes do not exist.[25] In this I differ from scientists like Jared Diamond, who appear to believe that it is in the 5% genetic difference between humans and chimpanzees that specifically human genes are to be found.[26] However I must be cautious. Although we now know the precise sequence of most of the DNA in man, the genome of the chimpanzee has not yet been sequenced (the project is now in hand). We cannot therefore be sure that there is indeed homology—gene for gene, with some identical, some almost identical, some merely similar—along the entire length of the respective DNAs.

As to the function that each gene specifies when it is translated into proteins, we do not even know this for man. One cannot at present deduce the function of a protein merely from the sequence of its constituent amino acids, which is all the information that a gene contains. Some proteins of similar sequence have turned out to have different functions, and some proteins of dissimilar sequence have turned out to have the same function. Sequencing the DNA of man took less than a decade; understanding the functions of all the proteins that are specified by those genes is likely to take at least as long again. Until the functions of all the proteins of chimpanzee and man are clarified, one will not be sure whether any of them play a quite different role in chimpanzee and man. Whatever the outcome, though, one can be fairly certain that the mechanism described above for the generation of new species in terms of a gradual accumulation of variant genes, applies to the generation of a new genus as well.

Extending this argument further, I would predict that there are no primate as opposed to simian genes, no mammalian as opposed to bird or reptile genes, no vertebrate as opposed to invertebrate genes, and so on. We cannot recognise a human being or a chimpanzee, a monkey or a pigeon, a crocodile or a wasp, by its genes alone. It is only the intact organism that is clearly recognisable as belonging to one or other species, genus, family, order, class or phylum. For over 40 years I have been telling biochemistry and medical students that if they were presented with a suspension of homogenised liver, it would be extremely difficult to tell whether it came from an elephant or a human being: analysis of the constituent molecules does not reveal the source. Yet if the appropriate creature walked into their living room, there would be little difficulty in recognising one from the other. The fact that we share 50% of our genes with a banana rather emphasises this point of similarity of molecular structure between all living forms—of no more than a gradual variation from the first microbe to man.

Variability of form and function

Outside my office window grow two well-proportioned horse chestnut trees (*Aesculus hippocastanum*). In late summer they are indistinguishable: each is laden with the fruit that as children we called conkers. In spring, however, I note that the appearance of leaves, and subsequently of flowers, is delayed by several weeks on the tree to the left, compared with the one on the right. Most probably, both trees are from the same stock; they are siblings, of whom the one on the left is a 'late developer'. We referred earlier to the fact that no two offspring of an organism are exactly alike. Even identical twins begin to diverge slightly from each other as the environment starts to affect their genes differentially (to cause cancer in one, but not in the other, for example).

So it is that in a group of, say, 100 people all descended from a single set of parents, the members will differ not only in their outward appearance, but will also behave in a wide variety of ways. A few of the 100 will be more aggressive than the others, a few more docile. Some will be cleverer, some more stupid. A number will be better at fashioning objects with their hands, others more clumsy. Some will be more inquisitive, others less so. The spread of attitudes and skills is enormous.[27] These features include, of course, the qualities identified in the previous chapter as being typically human: the ability to work with one's hands, the power of speech, increased cerebral function. So there will be those in whom the urge to search is heightened: to fashion novel tools, to wish to explore new horizons, to articulate their intentions more clearly, to seek solutions to problems keenly and effectively. The members of the group who possess one or more of these characteristics are the ones who will lead the others to new adventures. It is they who will be responsible for the consequences of human quest that are described in Part II.

If we now compare such a group of 100 humans with a group of 100 chimpanzees descended from a single set of parents, we are likely to find some overlap. Not only will some chimpanzees be more docile than an aggressive human, but we may encounter a chimpanzee more intelligent than a backward person. This is precisely what the experiments conducted by scientists like Sue Savage-Rumbaugh have shown. She and her colleagues have reared chimpanzees from birth in an environment at the Language Research Center in Atlanta, Georgia, in which they were taught simple words, just as a child is taught. The result is that one of her charges has been able to develop a vocabulary similar to that of a retarded child. Had she carried out the experiment with 100 chimpanzees, she might have found one that actually exceeded the learning ability of such a person. And of course, a chimpanzee is likely to be better at peeling a banana than a paraplegic who has trouble with his hands. I am emphasising an earlier point: the genes of a chimpanzee and a human are so similar that it should not surprise us if there is occasionally an overlap between the functions that they specify, such as an ability to carry out certain tasks. We are both, after all, closely related descendants from a common ancestor. Some members of that species, around 6 to 8 million years ago, proved better at tree climbing and evolved into the present day *Pan troglodytes* and *Pan paniscus*; others proved better at walking upright and searching for predator or prey, and evolved into *Homo sapiens*; yet others[28] turned out to be less proficient at either of these skills and died out. It is the combination of many attributes that distinguishes man from chimpanzee; pick only one, and you may find an overlap.

Notes

1. A chain of 100 amino acids, for example, can come in 20^{100} different forms; I will not attempt to put this number into words, but merely note that 20^{10} is already over 10 trillion (10 million million). Although many possible combinations—such as a protein made up entirely of a single type of amino acid—do not occur in nature, the calculation shows the enormous variability of structure that proteins can adopt.

2. Whenever an A of one chain finds itself opposite a T on the other chain, two bonds are formed between them, because A and T fit so well together (and the total energy of the system is decreased); whenever a G of one chain finds itself opposite a C on the other chain, they too form a tight pair, in this case held together by three bonds. The bonds are called hydrogen bonds, because a hydrogen atom is always at the centre of the bond. Compared with the bonds that hold the atoms *along* a strand of DNA together, hydrogen bonds are relatively fragile: little energy is needed to break them apart. Heating to a temperature of around 60 °C is sufficient. Hydrogen bonds underlie not only the attraction between complementary strands of DNA: they also keep the chains of proteins—and of DNA—wound round each other: heat a protein or DNA, and the chains unwind.

39

3. In fact less than 10% of the DNA of animals codes for proteins at all: the rest specifies regions that control the switching on and off of protein synthesis—in other words, the trigger for translating a particular stretch of DNA into a protein—as well as long stretches that have no apparent function; these may merely represent stretches of DNA from viruses that have become incorporated into the DNA of the host as a result of an infectious episode.

4. The total number of genes in all the chromosomes does not equal the total number of proteins, because some genes code for more than one protein of similar but not identical structure, as a result of molecular rearrangements called 'splicing'; thus, a total of around 30,000 different genes in a human being specifies up to 300,000 different proteins.

5. Although certain proteins are attached to DNA, and are therefore part of chromosomes, they play no direct role in the process of information transfer from DNA to protein.

6. Their proposal of such a fixed relationship between pairs of the bases in DNA owed much to an earlier observation by an American biochemist, Erwin Chargaff: he had found that the content of A plus G always appeared to be the same as that of T plus C, and in particular that the amount of A seemed to equal that of T, with the amount of G equalling that of C.

7. During the halving of the chromosomes, before each pair of chromosomes becomes separated, there is in addition an interchange of genes between respective chromosome pairs, just before they separate to generate the haploid cells (containing only a single set of chromosomes, not a pair) that will become sperm or egg. As a result of this rather complicated process called meiosis, genes become shuffled at each generation in a totally random manner.

8. A special type of protein that is present in very small amounts, called a prion, does appear to replicate itself. Such proteins are responsible for the transmission of BSE in cattle—'mad cow disease'—and of Creutzfeldt – Jakob disease (CJD) in humans.

9. Although death may occur sooner than expected: cancers arise because unfavourable mutations have occurred in that individual.

10. In sickle cell haemoglobin a glutamate residue is replaced by a valine residue, as a result of an A to T mutation in DNA (GAG codes for glutamate, GTG for valine).

11. The probable explanation of this result in molecular terms is the following. The number of chromosomes in a horse and donkey are the same. The chromosomes are also sufficiently similar that pairing between them, when a sperm fertilises an egg, takes place as normal. The subsequent duplication of the DNA every time a cell in the mule divides, throughout the growth of the foetus and the maturation of the new-born animal, is also normal. Where matters go wrong is in

the germ cells. During the process of meiosis (see Note 7 above) there is much interchange of DNA between each of the chromosome pairs. In order for the exchange to occur, the two chromosomes (one paternal, one maternal) must be precisely aligned. If there are slight discrepancies between the DNA of one chromosome and that of its partner, it does not matter. For example, if one chromosome has the gene for normal haemoglobin opposite the gene for sickle cell haemoglobin on the other chromosome, it is of no consequence. But if the difference between two genes is much greater (not merely a T in place of an A) and there are in addition extra copies of certain genes, precise lining up—gene for gene—cannot take place. Meiosis is halted, no sperm (or egg) is produced: the animal is sterile.

12. See D. C. Dennett, op. cit., p 45.

13. See Steve Mack on *How to Define a Species?* at **www.madsci.org** (1999).

14. One reason why multiple copies of genes are retained is that they minimise the chance of a mutation having a deleterious outcome: possessing three unaffected genes that produce normal protein, instead of just one, helps to counter the adverse effects of a particularly deleterious protein. Multiple copies of genes also introduce variations of function, through the retention of different mutations in separate copies of the original gene. Many of our own genes are present as more than one copy, as a result of duplications that occurred hundreds of thousands of years ago, and that have been retained. The haemoglobin gene is a good example. We have over five genes, each producing haemoglobin with a slightly different efficacy for binding oxygen. One type of haemoglobin functions during foetal life, another comes into play in adulthood. Each has been retained because its presence optimises the transport of oxygen at the different stages of human development, and therefore leads to a fitter organism.

15. This includes plants and microbes.

16. For a recent biography, see Michael Shermer, *In Darwin's Shadow: the Life and Science of Alfred Russel Wallace*, Oxford University Press, Oxford, 2002.

17. And proposed by Leonardo da Vinci over 300 years earlier. See Sherwin B. Nuland, op. cit., p 103.

18. Since Wilberforce's remarks from the floor were not recorded, various versions exist. See e.g. Walter Gratzer, *Eurekas and Euphorias. The Oxford Book of Scientific Anecdotes*, Oxford University Press, Oxford, 2002, pp 71–73.

19. The view that it was the asteroid collision with earth that caused the dinosaurs to become extinct is not now universally accepted.

20. A class of protozoa—single-celled organisms—many of which live in the sea.

21. For a discussion of this topic, see Edward O. Wilson (1992) op. cit., pp 215–280, and W. Wayt Gibbs, *Sci. Am.* **285**: 28–37; November, 2001.
22. To be precise, the ratio of A + T to G + C in human DNA is similar to that of chimpanzee DNA (recall that A always equals T, and G always equals C, whatever the origin of the DNA). Most importantly, the A – T and G – C pairs do not fall on exactly the same positions along the DNA backbone.
23. See Robert K. Wayne at **www.idir.net/-wolf2dog/wayne2.htm**
24. When a bit of DNA is heated, the two strands that are wound round each other separate: the hydrogen bonds holding A to T, and G to C, are broken. If the temperature is then lowered, the two strands re-anneal. If one now takes a mixture of DNA fragments (the total DNA is far too large to work with)—the DNA of chimpanzee and that of man, for example—and heats them, the strands in each of the DNA fragments will separate; when cooled they will recombine. In so doing, some hybrid fragments will be formed: those that have one strand from chimpanzee, the other strand from man. When hybrid fragments are reheated, they separate at a lower temperature than the pure DNA fragments of either chimpanzee or man: because the complementarity is not perfect, it takes less energy to separate the two strands. For every 1 °C of difference in temperature required to separate the two strands of a hybrid DNA, the parent fragments are said to differ by approximately 1%. The temperature at which the strands of a chimpanzee – human hybrid DNA separate was found to be approximately 2 °C less than that at which the strands of either of the parent DNA fragments separate, so the DNA of the two species was said to be 2% different, or 98% similar. This was an early result that has now been asserted to have been in error: the actual difference is nearer 5%, not 2% (see Figure 1.1).

    Hybridization yields a value that represents the *average* difference between the DNA of two species, whether of the same or a different genus. The complementarity between the two hybrid strands may be perfect in some parts along the chain, imperfect at other parts. This leads to a problem of interpretation, since most of the DNA consists of regions that are not genes at all: as mentioned earlier, some of the regions specify the controls that turn the expression of genes on and off, while others are concerned with functions that are as yet unclear. It could therefore be the case that much of the homology between chimpanzee and man lies in this non-genetic region and almost none within the genes themselves. Such a possibility can be tested by isolating and analysing specific genes. This has been done, and we now know that the 95% similarity applies to coding regions of the DNA—in other words genes—as well as to the non-coding regions that make up the bulk of DNA. On the contrary, most genes are much more than 95% similar, even ones that lie at the heart of human – chimpanzee differences (see Chapter 4). This is because selective pressure tends to retain coding sequences of DNA better than non-coding stretches: most mutations are deleterious to gene function, so organisms containing them will gradually be eliminated from the population. Mutations in the bulk, non-coding regions of DNA simply accumulate. The fact that the degree of homology is *roughly* the same in coding and non-coding stretches of DNA should not surprise us, for mutations are random events that happen anywhere along the length of DNA.

25. Because many mutations are 'silent', meaning that the changed units along DNA do not lead to proteins with altered function, a genomic difference (like the 5% discrepancy between human and chimpanzee) may in part reflect no more than the time since the two organisms diverged: the more they differ, the longer ago the ancestral lines separated. As will be seen in Chapter 4, genes that underlie crucial differences between humans and chimpanzees may be altered less than genes that perform an identical function in the two organims. Silent mutations include those that give rise to polymorphism: proteins with altered amino acids, yet without apparent effect on function.

26. '... we do not yet know which chunks of our DNA are responsible for the functionally significant differences between humans and chimps ...': Jared Diamond, op. cit., p 28. As shown in Chapter 4, in the one instance where an extremely significant difference in function has been analysed, the underlying genes are virtually the same, and the responsible proteins differ by no more than two out of 715 amino acids.

27. There are those who consider such subtleties of behaviour to somehow lie beyond the realms of molecular interactions. Yet if we turn to the behaviour of honey bees—whose social interactions are not so distant from those of humans—we find that the difference between one type of bee that quietly stays behind and tends the hive, and one that goes out and actively forages for nectar, depends on the activity of a single gene. This is dormant in the former type of bee, but switched on, i.e. translated into a protein, in the latter. Injecting the protein into the meek bee turns it into an active forager: see Elisabeth Pennisi, *Science* **296**: 636; 2002. Likewise, when a particular species of female wasp is faced with the choice of remaining within the society of the nest or of striking out on her own to start a new nest, her decision depends in part on genetic background and in part on environmental factors that are amenable to analysis: see Raghavendra Gadagkar, *The Social Biology of Ropalidia marginata*, Harvard University Press, Cambridge, MA, 2001.

28. Like *Australopithecus afarensis*, *Homo habilis* and *Homo erectus*; see Chapter 4.

CHAPTER THREE

Plants and microbes: the origin of vision

The beginning of life

*L*ife started on earth around 3.5 billion years ago. A billion years earlier, gaseous matter from the sun had begun to coalesce to form our own planet[1] as well as the others within this solar sytem. The sun itself had been shining for half a billion years before that, although at 5 billion years old it is by no means the most ancient star in the universe: according to most astrophysicists, the Big Bang that formed all matter occurred somewhere between 10 and 20 billion years ago. Once the earth had been formed, although continuously bombarded by meteorites, it gradually cooled down over a period of less than a billion years to reach a temperature at which water is liquid and organic molecules are stable. How these were formed is a matter of debate.[2]

Over a long period of time organic molecules began to assemble into polymers contained within a fatty membrane. By chance, some of these assemblies were able to replicate themselves.[3] Fossilised remains of such structures—the earliest cells—have been found in rocks 3.5 billion years old.[4] Microbes living in waters of high salinity today appear to be their nearest relative and have accordingly been dubbed Archaebacteria, or archaea for short, to distinguish them from most other current bacteria.[5] Some of the latter inhabit hot springs and thermal vents, and have retained the ability to multiply in extremes of acidity (pH 0) and at temperatures in excess of 90°C that their ancestors possessed.[6] Most other bacteria, not to mention plants and animals, cannot survive under such conditions.

From the time of the first living organisms 3.5 billion years ago, it took more than 2 billion years before multicellular organisms — first plants, then fungi, then animals (invertebrates at around 600 million years ago, followed by vertebrates) — began to appear.[7]

There is another hypothesis regarding the synthesis of the first organic molecules. The late astrophysicist Fred Hoyle and his colleague Chandra Wickramasinghe champion the view that self-replicating molecules like DNA were originally synthesised not on earth, but in outer space — perhaps near comets — and arrived here in some particulate form (they even use the word 'cell'), that then took off to produce ancient bacteria. Such particles, they further assert, continue to bombard the earth and thereby introduce — like viruses — new infectious diseases. Their first postulate may be partly correct, in that organic material has been detected (by spectrometric techniques) in outer space. Such molecules, containing carbon, hydrogen, oxygen and nitrogen, might conceivably have seeded earth with the precursors of amino acids and the building blocks of nucleic acids. And it is true that meteorites and dust particles from our own solar system have been found to contain organic compounds that might have contributed to the evolution of the molecules of living organisms.[8] What is difficult to understand is how cosmic matter is supposed to infect current humans. Our cells are derived from the earliest forms of life, and contain the same molecules as they did.[9] Our genes are related to all who came before. Is it really likely that the evolution of such molecules occurred in outer space — in comets and star dust — over a period of three and a half billion years entirely in step with their evolution on earth? Until we find life on another planet we will not know, but my guess is that when we do, the molecules — never mind the actual organisms — will not resemble those on earth at all. Yet listen to the closing sentences of one of the last articles written before Fred Hoyle's death: 'Genetic structures must, therefore, have been supplied to Earth, also we think in cometary material, which serves to relate life here to its cosmic origin. Evolution on Earth through natural selection only serves to fine-tune systems of cosmic origin once they are established here'.[10]

Dependency of life on light

From the time that archaea first appeared, if not before, the light of the sun has been crucial to life on earth. It alone provides the energy that enables plants and some bacteria to undergo photosynthesis, and hence to grow. By eating plants, animals use some of that energy for their own growth and movement, so that indirectly they, too, are dependent for their existence on the light of the sun. The rays of the sun are necessary for another reason: the heat they create keeps water on most of the planet in its liquid state. Water is the universal solvent in which all reactions of living matter take place, and animals that live at sub-zero temperatures survive only because the heat generated by their metabolism prevents the water in their cells from freezing.[11]

But the sun's rays impinge on the earth only during daylight, and it may be wondered how the temperature is prevented from falling precipitously at night. It drops no more than 30–40 °C at best, which may be compared with a change of more than 1000 °C between day and night on the surface of the moon. The underlying cause is the same as that by which the temperature is prevented from rising too much during the day: a layer of gases in the atmosphere that insulates the earth's crust against extremes of hot and cold. The most important of these gases is carbon dioxide.[12] It is the relative stability of temperature—whether near the poles or at the equator—that has allowed life to evolve and to continue doing so.

Photosynthesis shares certain features with the visual process in animals. Vision is crucial to the ability of animals to search. Sightless animals, like the blind goby fish *Typhlogobius californiensis* that depends on the ghost shrimp *Callianassa* to dig it a hole in which to live, have not had much evolutionary success. On the other hand, animals like owls and certain bats[13] that search by night, rely on highly sensitive eyesight to find their prey. Man's quest, even with today's technology to hand, is carried out predominantly during daylight: most of us spend the night asleep. It is true that many animals become aware of a possible prey (or predator) by smell, and reptiles like snakes have very sensitive heat detectors as well.

But most animals have two eyes that allow them to identify objects as part of their quest for food and a mate.

Few have described the importance of vision to man's domination of other forms of life more vividly than John Wyndham in his science-fiction novel, *The Day of the Triffids*.[14] A gigantic fireball from outer space passes by the earth. The flash instantly blinds everyone. Unable to see, people have lost much of their advantage over noxious plants. One such is a giant, man-eating version of the Venus' fly trap: a Triffid. These plants rapidly spread as they devour the sightless, who are unable to avoid bumping into them. Gradually mankind begins to be eliminated off the face of the globe. All is not lost, however. A man who happened to have his eyes heavily bandaged, undergoing surgery in hospital at the time of the fire ball, has retained his sight. So have a few others. Together they set about destroying the Triffids. *Homo sapiens* is saved.

Photosynthesis

Plants use the energy of light to synthesise organic molecules. The reaction, photosynthesis, is essentially the opposite of that, respiration, by which animals oxidise organic molecules in order to obtain the energy necessary for muscular movement, nerve conduction, growth and other processes.[15] Having used the energy of light to synthesise carbohydrate during the day, plants then oxidise some of this, by the same mechanism as that employed by animals, namely respiration, during the night. Although plants obviously need less energy than animals because they do not move, some is still required for growth and other processes: moving the nutrients derived from the soil up to the leaves, for example, which in the case of a 300 foot-high sequoia is no mean requirement.

The sequence of molecular changes underlying photosynthesis —more than a dozen discrete chemical reactions are involved— may be the opposite of those involved in respiration, but the enzymes that catalyse many of the two sets of reactions are essentially the same. It is merely the direction in which material flows that is different: from carbon dioxide and water into carbohydrate and oxygen in the first case, and from carbohydrate and oxygen to water and carbon dioxide in the second case. A funicular railway that consists of two cabins—one ascending, the other descending—is an analogy of sorts, in that the ascending one gradually gains potential energy while the descending one gradually loses it. The ultimate source of energy may be electrical or it may simply be mass, as in the Lynton–Lynmouth railway in North Devon, England: water is added to a tank beneath the cabin that is at the upper station on a cliff at Lynton, sufficient to just exceed the weight of the cabin and its passengers that is waiting at the bottom in Lynmouth. The cabins start to move towards each other, and when the cabin that was at the top reaches the bottom, the water is let out and the operation is repeated. The entire process is fuelled by a loss of water from the summit, just as all life on earth is driven by a loss of light energy from the sun—infinitessimal, of course, compared with the absorption of sunlight by other matter within the solar system.

Animals cannot use the energy of light to synthesise organic molecules, but they do absorb light and turn it into an impulse that is transmitted from the back of the retina in the eye to the visual centre in the brain, where the sensation of light—and hence shape—is registered. The first part of this process, absorption of light, resembles in many ways the absorption of light by plants. An even closer similarity is with a particular type of microbe. This is a photosynthetic archaeal bacterium that derives part of its energy from light and part from the oxidation of organic molecules. The bacteria live in high-salt environments, like those of the Great Salt Lake in Utah and the Dead Sea between Israel and Jordan, and are therefore known as halophilic (salt-loving): *Halobacterium salinarum* is a typical example.

In each case—animals and *H. salinarium*—the light-sensitive molecule is one called rhodopsin. It consists of two units: a small molecule called retinol that is similar in structure to vitamin A (from which it is derived) and a protein called opsin. Retinol is bound to opsin rather like haem is bound to the protein globin in haemoglobin. The chemical structure of its oxidised form, retinal, enables it to absorb light; in so doing its shape (and its colour) change slightly. That modification triggers a subtle alteration within the structure of opsin. In the case of *H. salinarum*, the structural alteration initiates a sequence of molecular reactions that culminate in the synthesis of the energy-transducing molecule, ATP, which is used both for the growth of the bacterium and for its ability to swim towards the source of light. In the case of the retina within the eye of an animal, the modification of opsin leads to an electric impulse to the brain. The impulse is similar to that generated by touch or heat or sound or smell; in no case is ATP generated. On the contrary, ATP is used up during the process of nerve conduction. The opsin of animals is obviously not identical to that of *H. salinarum*, but similar enough to perform the same function of transducing a light impulse into a chemical reaction.

Plants and other photosynthetic bacteria do not use the retinol of animals or *H. salinarum* to harvest light. In plants the chief light-absorbing pigments are chlorophyll, carotene and lutein, each associated with a protein that translates light energy into chemical energy (in the form of ATP). Since archaeal bacteria diverged more than 700 million years before the common ancestor of plants and animals was alive, the possesion of rhodopsin by *H. salinarum* is anomalous. It provides an example of converging, rather than diverging, evolution. What is important here is that the overall function—the ability to absorb light and trigger a chemical reaction—is essentially the same in plants, in photosynthetic bacteria and in the eyes of every type of animal including man.

Of course, many molecules perform a similar function across a range of organisms. ATP itself is but one example.[16] ATP is exactly the same molecule in microbes, plants and animals, and the proteins involved in the various energy-transducing processes, if not identical, are similar enough to perform the same role in all organisms. One begins to see why the genomes of microbes, plants and animals exhibit so much homology.

In order to appreciate the molecular changes that constitute the phototropic response of plants, we need to remind ourselves of some of the physics and chemistry underlying the absorption of light by living organisms.[17] Rhodopsin absorbs light of wavelengths between about 450 and 600 nm, in the middle of the light spectrum—fine for triggering a response in *H. salinarum* or the retina of animals, but it does not explain how the latter also manage to distinguish one colour from another. In fact many animals cannot. The reason why primates like ourselves perceive light as blue or green or yellow or red is because in addition to the main, retinol-containing receptor rhodopsin, we have molecules that absorb light of other wavelengths: one molecule absorbs light maximally at 420 nm, another at 530 nm, and a third at 560 nm. Together they enable us to distinguish one colour from another.[18]

Plants do not merely utilise the light of the sun for photosynthesis. They actively seek it out as avidly as sunbathers on the beaches of the Mediterranean. They do this in two ways: by phototropism and by heliotropism. The words belie their meaning of nourishment (tropism) from light (photo) or sun (helio). In each case the light in natural surroundings is the sun (Figure 3.1). Phototropism is used to describe the process by which plants *grow* towards light, heliotropism the process by which plants *turn* towards the light. To a plant, perception of light is as important as vision is to an animal: it tells the plant where it is in space (shade or open) and time (darkness or daylight).

Figure 3.1 Searching for light by plants. I am grateful to Professor Christopher Leaver for this picture of sunflowers growing towards the sun.

Phototropism

Several mechanisms underly phototropism. As early as 1881 Charles Darwin showed that the major response of plants is to light at the blue end of the spectrum. It took more than 100 years before the main photoreceptor was characterised. This is a light-sensitive component attached to a protein, just as in rhodopsin. The complex has been named phototropin.[19] The light-sensitive part is a yellow molecule called flavin.[20] The protein part transduces the impact of light on flavin into a molecular response, culminating in growth towards the light.[21] Another group of proteins that are sensitive to blue light are called cryptochromes.[19] They contain the same light-sensitive component, flavin, as phototropin, but their protein parts are different. Cryptochromes play a major role in setting the circadian rhythm of plants.

Another photoreceptor that participates in the phototropic response of plants comprises a group of proteins termed phytochromes.[22] The light-sensitive part is a molecule called phytochromobilin, that absorbs light not at the blue end of the spectrum like phototropin or cryptochrome, but at the red end: between 600 and 700 nm. Because the light that is reflected off the leaves of one tree on to the leaves of a neighbouring one is predominantly red light (which is why leaves appear green), the phytochromes maximise the absorption of light in a forest canopy by causing one shrub or tree to grow away from adjacent vegetation; like the response mediated by phototropin, it is a 'shade-avoidance' reaction. As with phototropin also, there are additional consequences of activating phytochromes: they include accelerated flowering and early production of seeds. It is the phytochromes that tell a plant where it is in relation to other plants.

Having identified the molecular structures in plants that sense light, we should consider briefly the processes by which these photoreceptors cause the growing tip of a plant to proliferate in the direction of light, away from the shade. An important component is a plant hormone called auxin. It induces the elongation of those cells in which its concentration exceeds a threshold value. These are the cells on the shady side of a growing shoot-tip. Yet the photoreceptors that sense light, whether this is blue light falling on phototropin or reflected red light impinging on phytochromes, are on the light side of the shoot-tip. The effect of activating phototropin and phytochrome is to reduce the concentration of auxin. As a result there is relatively more auxin in cells on the shady side of a shoot-tip than on the light side. Consequently, it is these cells that become elongated. Because cell division occurs at the same time in the elongated cell as in its shorter neighbour, and because adjacent cells cannot separate from each other, the overall effect is to bend the growing tip away from the longer cell: in other words, away from the shade towards the light.

Heliotropism

The leaves of plants and trees are the major sites of photosynthesis: anything that is green by virtue of its content of chlorophyll is likely also to possess the proteins necessary for photosynthesis. In order to maximise the process, several plants have developed the capacity to turn their leaves towards the sun, so that its rays impinge on as large an area of leaf as possible. This is during the morning and afternoon, when solar radiation is relatively weak. At mid-day, when it is strong, heliotropic plants move their leaves so that they are 'edge on' rather than 'end on'. This is in order to limit the area of leaf exposed to the direct rays of the sun: too much radiation damages cells (as it does those of animals). Sufficient light is absorbed even at an angle in the middle of the day to induce photosynthesis at maximal rate. That, essentially, is what is meant by heliotropism:[23] the search by leaves for light. The mechanism is quite different from that of phototropism. It does not involve irreversible elongation — growth — in a particular direction; instead, leaves move in one direction or another as a result of reversible changes in turgor (pressure) within them. The underlying molecular interactions have not been elucidated, so we do not know the nature of the photoreceptor or its associated proteins. In so far as heliotropism is a repetitive event, it may share some properties with circadian rhythms. The knowledge we have about those events may therefore shed light on the mechanism that drives heliotropism.

Circadian rhythm

Plants, like animals, behave in a circadian manner. As mentioned earlier, during the hours of daylight they carry out photosynthesis. At night they convert part of the carbohydrate so synthesised back into carbon dioxide and water by the reverse sequence.[15] During daylight many flowers are open, at night they are closed. The mechanism used by plants to sense the presence of daylight involves cryptochromes. The protein component of these photoreceptors serves a variety of functions, chief of which is the 'setting' of the circadian clock. I will not delve into details, but instead note that cryptochromes are present in animals as well. The genes that code for this family of proteins have so far been shown to be present in fruit flies, mice and humans. No doubt they exist in all animals that display circadian rhythms.

Like rhodopsin and the receptors of colour vision, cryptochromes of animals are found in the retina, from which they transmit molecular messages through the switching on and off of certain genes. The centre that is in overall control of circadian rhythm is situated within the hypothalamus, a specialised structure in the brain. The centre generates a 24 hour clock; visual impact at the retina sets the clock to the periods of day and night. When an animal or a person moves to a different time zone, signals transmitted from cryptochrome in the retina to the hypothalamus reset the clock.[24] Circadian rhythm is yet another example of a molecular response to light that has been inherited from the earliest plants through to man.

Microbial movement

Bacteria

Like plants, photosynthetic bacteria not only *use* the energy of light, they also seek it out. So, in an archaeal organism like *Halobacterium salinarium*, there are two types of rhodopsin: one that turns light energy into chemical energy[25] and one that senses the intensity of light and causes the bacteria to swim towards it:[26] the first type of rhodopsin triggers the photosynthetic response, the second initiates phototaxis (movement towards light). The energy needed for phototaxis is provided by some of the ATP generated during photosynthesis.

Non-photosynthetic bacteria search for food, not light. They swim towards a source of oxygen (aerotaxis) or organic compounds (chemotaxis, which includes energy-sensing mechanisms). Actually, movement is not always in one direction. Too high a concentration of oxygen is toxic to some bacteria (as it is to animals: recall the deleterious effect of free radicals, that can be generated by too high a concentration of oxygen): accordingly, they swim away from the source. So in a pond or other environment in which there is a gradient of oxygen from the surface downwards, bacteria will settle at the level that is optimal for their metabolism. Different species favour different concentrations. *Bacillus subtilis*, for example, is attracted to a concentration of oxygen not much less than that of a solution saturated with air; for *Escherichia coli*, the optimal concentration of oxygen is 25% of this, and for *Azospirillum brasilense* it is 2%.[27] In the case of organic compounds, some attract, others repel. The main attractants in nature are sugars and amino acids (Figure 3.2), found typically in areas of rotting vegetation and animal remains.[28] In fact, any compound that a particular bacterial species is able to metabolise—turning it into the DNA and RNA, protein, fat and carbohydrate that it needs for growth, as well as using the energy released by metabolism in order to fuel those synthetic processes—is likely to be an attractant. In contrast, non-metabolisable compounds like phenol and other acids repel (except of course in acidophilic bacteria).

I have implied throughout this discussion that bacteria have the capacity to swim in one direction or another. How this is achieved is as follows. Motile bacteria have a tiny flagellum that rotates and therefore drives the cell forward, not unlike the propellor of an outboard motor or a giant tanker. There is one key difference. The flagellar rotor of a bacterium like *Escherichia coli* (which I mention only because it is one of the best-studied of all bacteria) rotates

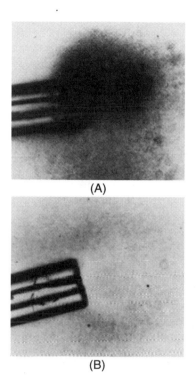

(A)

(B)

Figure 3.2 Bacterial chemotaxis in *Salmonella typhimurium*. Various solutions are released from the end of a pipette (a narrow glass tube) into a suspension of bacteria. These either move towards, or away from, the end of the pipette. (A) attraction by food (the amino acid serine), (B) repulsion by noxious chemicals (phenol). A particular mutant of *S. typhimurium* shows the opposite behaviour: attraction by phenol, repulsion by serine. Note that *S. typhimurium* is a benign relative of the extremely pathogenic *S. typhi*, yet they diverged more than 100 million years ago, a time frame during which the entire spectrum of mammals evolved. This photograph appeared originally in a paper by B. A. Rubik and D. E. Koshland, *Proc. Natl Acad. Sci. USA* **75**: 2820–2824; 1978 from which it is reproduced by permission.

first in one direction (say clockwise), and then after a while it switches to the opposite direction (anti-clockwise). The result is random motion, like a leaf spinning on water, blown first this way and then that. Another difference, of course, is that the energy for rotation of a bacterial rotor is supplied not by the combustion of an appropriate fuel, but by the universal transducer of chemical energy, ATP. But do not think that bacterial rotors are slow: they turn at a rate of some 18,000 revolutions per minute, not bad compared with the propellor of a small motor boat (1800 rpm) or the screw of a battleship (300 rpm).[29] If motion by the flagellar rotor is random, how is movement towards an attractant and away from a repellant accomplished? It is because reversal of the rotor is inhibited or stimulated. The result is that in the first case movement towards the source is favoured, in the second motion away from it.

Chemotaxis occurs not only in aqueous environments but also in the soil. Rhizobacteria, many of which have a symbiotic relationship with the roots of plants, fall into this category. Symbiosis is established because the bacteria are able to 'fix' nitrogen—to oxidise atmospheric nitrogen gas to nitrate, which the plant then uses as its nitrogen source.[30] In return, the plant synthesises organic compounds, on which the bacteria grow. It is those compounds that constitute the attractive stimulus for chemotaxis.

Another type of movement is triggered by the magnetism of the earth. Bacteria such as *Magnetospirillum magnetotacticum* swim along magnetic lines: in the northern hemisphere they swim towards the north pole, in the southern hemisphere towards the south pole. The magnetic field causes their random movement to be changed into swimming in one direction only. But they also seek out the concentration of oxygen that is optimal for their growth. In a lake or ocean they will therefore accumulate in that layer below the surface in which the oxygen is at the right level. The movement of such bacteria has accordingly been termed magnet-aerotaxis. Here, then, we have another link in the searches of microbes and animals. Birds like pigeons, fish and bees, like magnetotactic bacteria, all use an internal compass—actual molecules of iron oxide (magnetite)—to orient themselves during their respective journeys.

Many types of bacteria also seek something else: a surface on which to grow. One example is provided by the archaea that inhabit the hot, salty water along a particular part of the coastline in western Australia: they literally form a series of mats, one above the other. In this instance their own surface provides the stimulus. Another example is that of the bacteria that infest our lower intestine. Not all are pathogenic: on the contrary, the excessive use of antibiotics is sometimes counter-productive by eliminating harmless bacteria that normally prevent the establishment of pathogenic colonies. The surface to which intestinal bacteria attach is the mucosal layer of epithelial cells. Scientists are currently researching ways to encourage harmless bacteria, like most strains of *Escherichia coli*, to attach and so to prevent adherence of pathogenic variants like *E. coli* O157.[31]

Protoctista[32]

One of the most striking examples of self-attraction is provided by the organism called *Dictyostelium discoides*. This is a type of fungus, commonly known as a slime mould. The organism has a life cycle made up of two phases. In the first, single cells grow and multiply, just like bacteria. But when their source of food runs out, the second phase commences. A chemotactic stimulus attracts the single cells to form one giant spore of non-dividing cells (Figure 3.3). This undergoes several changes of shape, until eventually it breaks up into individual cells that, once they are blown into a nutritious environment, begin cell division once more. The chemotactic stimulus is a molecule called cyclic AMP. It is derived from ATP and plays a role in signalling pathways, like those that relay the effect of hormones to susceptible cells, in every species of higher organism from fungi to plants and animals.

The source of cyclic AMP that causes aggregation of *D. discoidum* is the organism itself. The first cells to experience lack of nutrient begin to secrete cyclic AMP. This then causes other cells to migrate towards them; eventually the ever-increasing hub of *D. discoidum* cells turns into a structure that is made up predominantly of spores. Chemicals that attract one organism to another are well known in the animal world. Various molecules, collectively called pheromones, mediate the attraction between male and female in most animals: from insects to cats and dogs, tigers and lions, and

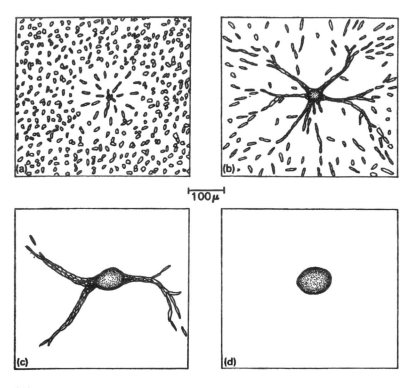

(A)

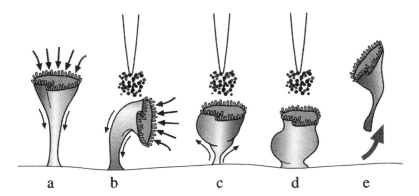

(B)

even ourselves (at least until the advent of deodorants and frequent washing of the sexual organs). Vision provides as powerful an attractant as smell: the gathering of predators around a kill or water-hole, the aggregation of humans at the sight of an accident or a street acrobat. The sound of a busker or an open air concert provides a similar stimulus for humans to assemble—as indeed does the peal of church bells or the cry of the muezzin. The behaviour of humans surely has much in common with that of slime moulds.

Other protoctista carry out different forms of search. Protozoa like *Stentor* seek to avoid noxious stimuli in the way that bacteria do. They use their cilia to move themselves away from danger to a new position (Figure 3.3). During their quest, certain protoctista change shape. An amoeba-like cell called *Physarum polycephalum* does this while it searches for food. The authors of the relevant article go so far as to conclude that, 'This remarkable process of cellular computation implies that cellular materials can show a primitive intelligence'.[33]

Figure 3.3 Searching by protoctista. (A) Self-attraction by *Dictyostelium discoideum* (a type of amoeba also called a slime mould). (a)–(c) As organisms growing on a synthetic medium run out of nutrients, they stop dividing and instead begin to aggregate, eventually forming a single ball of cells, seen from above in (d); if viewed sideways, the ball is seen to consist of two regions: a stalk and a cap or fruiting body (which will ultimately release spores, ready to begin growth and division as single cells once more). For further details, see text and C. A. Pasternak, *Biochemistry of Differentiation*, Wiley-Interscience, New York, 1970, from which this illustration is reproduced by permission.

(B) Avoidance of toxicity by *Stentor* (a type of ciliated protozoa). (a) When feeding, *Stentor* anchors itself to a surface by its stalk; beating cilia along its exterior sweep particles into the mouth region. (b) If a suspension of carmine particles is applied from a pipette, the organism turns away from the objectionable stimulus. (c) If the stimulus is continued, the cilia reverse their motion so that water is expelled. (d) If this manoeuvre still fails to eliminate the noxious particles, the organism contracts, detaches its stalk from the surface and (e) swims to a new position. Redrawn by permission of the author from D. Bray, *Cell Movements*, Garland, New York, 1992.

Molecular unity

I have described the search for the means to thrive—be it light or organic molecules—among organisms from which we are descended. Light-sensing molecules like retinol and flavin have been retained throughout evolution. The same is true of many proteins. Within the photoprotein of plants is a sequence of some 270 amino acids that occurs also in proteins of other organisms. In photosynthetic bacteria, in which a protein containing the 270 amino acid sequence is coupled to flavin as it is in phototropin, the consequence of activation by light is movement towards its source. In non-photosynthetic bacteria, the same 270 amino acid sequence is involved in their response to a source of food: organic molecules and oxygen.

Bacteria are not the only organisms that sense oxygen. Animals respond to the concentration of oxygen in their tissues[34] and they, too, possess proteins that contain the 270 amino acid sequence. Some of these proteins react to the concentration of oxygen, others perceive the voltage difference across the membrane of cells; the membrane potential plays a crucial role in the propagation of nerve impulses from one area of the body to another.[35] For this reason the 270 amino acid sequence of the phototropin molecule that is common to bacteria, plants and animals has been called the LOV domain: able to sense light, oxygen, and voltage. Recently, the acronym PAS has replaced LOV.[36]

The protein component of phytochromes also contains a PAS domain. Not just in the phytochrome of photosynthetic plants and bacteria, but in proteins of non-photosynthetic bacteria and fungi as well, where the PAS domain senses organic compounds—both nutrients and toxins—in addition to temperature, acidity and other environmental conditions. So far, phytochrome-like proteins have not been reported to be present in animals. But now that four animal genomes have been sequenced—the worm called *Caenorhabditis elegans*, the zebrafish, the mouse and the human—it should be possible to examine this possibility.

All in all, more than 200 proteins containing the PAS domain have been identified.[37] The molecular consequences of activating these proteins are the same, whether they function in bacteria, plants or animals. In each case a stimulus impinges on a receptor, which is the PAS-containing protein. The stimulus can be light (in which case it is sensed initially by the photoreceptive component) or any of the conditions just mentioned; further stimuli may yet emerge. A slight alteration in the shape of the PAS protein ensues. In some cases the activated PAS protein now acts like an enzyme: it adds a phosphate group to a second protein, termed the receptor. In other cases the activated PAS protein simply binds to the receptor. Either way, the receptor now itself undergoes a subtle change of shape, which initiates the biological response. Such protein–protein interactions play a crucial role in the transmission of virtually every type of biological signal. In many cases the switching on (or off) of specific genes, thus changing the concentration of the relevant proteins, underlies the response. In so far as this embraces the mechanisms by which organisms execute their search—for light, for nutrients, through vision—the PAS domain represents a molecular structure that lies at the very heart of the theme espoused by this book: the commonality of quest from microbe to man.

Conclusion

The genetic advantage of being able to turn towards the light, when the rays of the sun are your only source of energy, is obvious. Plants that have the capacity to undergo phototropism and heliotropism will outgrow relatives that lack these mechanisms: they will develop faster, produce more flowers and seeds, and thus compete more successfully for light and space. Microbes that can sense a source of food or light and then propel themselves towards it will outbreed those that have not developed these faculties so well. In each case faster growth and reproduction lead to a selective retention of the appropriate genes. The same is true of vision. Animals that are better able to glimpse predator or prey outlive those with poorer eyesight; colour vision in primates confers further advantages.

The fact that the proteins underlying the awareness of light have homology, from a *Halobacterium* to a hibiscus, from a herring to a human, illustrates the commonality of quest.

All the mechanisms I have described could fairly be interpreted as a passive response to certain stimuli, like light and food. They do not constitute an active search in the sense of that carried out by animals and man. But we should not be constrained by words like active and passive that have become associated with the actions of the animal world. Is the capture of a fly by the Venus' flytrap (*Dionaea muscipula*) really so passive a process? Remember that the plant is not just fending off the fly: it goes on to eat it, as a lion would a gazelle. An inanimate object like a small pebble or twig does not trigger the entrapment process: the plant distinguishes between living and dead matter; it is a genuine carnivore, looking out for prey. You will retort that the lion truly searches for his quarry before attacking it. But the fly would not come to rest on a leaf if the plant did not in the first place secrete the nectar that attracts it. A unique species of the Borneo pitcher plant, *Nepenthes albomarginata*, goes one further.[38] Unlike other species of *Nepenthes*, *N. albomarginata* distinguishes between one source of food and another: ants, beetles or flies leave it cold, but termites are devoured in their thousands at a single sitting. How does the plant achieve this? Because it provides the termites with a source of food that they—in contrast to other insects—find irresistable: the white rim hairs in the peristome or 'mouth' of the plant. Having eaten the hairs, the termites lose their hold and are unable to climb out: they fall into the pitcher and become digested by the plant's powerful enzymes. In other words, the pitcher plant trades some of its hairs for a nutritious meal of termites.

From a reductionist point of view, which is how scientists like myself regard the world, the difference between active and passive acts, between voluntary and involuntary responses, becomes blurred. I am not denying the existence of free will: in common with most animals, we choose which actions to perform. What I am talking about are the molecular interactions that underly those activities, many of which involve the same PAS domain within the relevant proteins. A plant senses light and grows towards it: the response is mediated by one type of molecule (auxin). A bird senses the dawn and wakes up; the response is mediated by another hormone (melatonin) that is involved in circadian rhythm. A chimpanzee and a human begin their search for food when they are hungry: the response is mediated by a change in the concentration of a molecule called leptin. Animals and humans search for a mate: the response is mediated by hormones (testosterone in males, oestrogen in females). Even the curiosity-driven search by man is almost involuntary: some people cannot help wanting to solve a crossword puzzle as soon as they open a newspaper or magazine, others automatically search every pocket of every garment they are wearing when they realise they have not seen their travel documents for a while (they are in their purse after all), some instinctively flick on every channel of the television set the moment they enter a hotel bedroom,[39] others compulsively go over in their mind every possible question they may be asked at tomorrow's interview (and are unable to get a decent night's rest as a result). Are the responses of humans to a stimulus really so different to those of plants?

Notes

1. An early impact with extraterrestial material catapulted a huge chunk off the earth to form the moon.
2. The most likely explanation is that the gases that were swirling around the earth's crust at that time—carbon dioxide and nitrogen, with lesser amounts of methane and ammonia—were turned into more complicated molecules through the catalytic properties of inorganic surfaces, such as aluminium silicate, that exist within the cracks of rocks or in thermal vents below the ocean surface. Gradually, molecules related to the building blocks of proteins (amino acids) and RNA (nucleotides) were formed; also some simple carbohydrate and fat. DNA came later. The energy required to drive those synthetic reactions forward must have come from lightning, from the impact of extraterrestial particles bombarding the earth's surface, or from volcanic eruptions above ground or on the sea bed.
3. Exactly how self-replication began is one of the most intriguing, but unanswered, questions in developmental biology. Some computer simulations that address this problem are described in Gerald F. Joyce, 'Booting up Life'. *Nature* **420**: 278–279; 2002 and Peter Szabo

et al., 'In silico simulations reveal that replicators with limited dispersal evolve towards higher efficiency and fidelity'. *Nature* **420**: 340–343; 2002.

4. Not everyone accepts that what appear to be fossilised microbes, found in rocks dated at 3.5 billion years old, really *are* the remains of living cells: see e.g. Henry Gee, 'That's life?' *Nature* **416**: 28; 2002.

5. But archaea are not, in fact, the precursors of today's bacteria: they appear to have diverged after their common ancestor lived, perhaps 2.5 billion years ago. By comparing proteins that carry out a similar function in bacteria, archaea, plants, fungi and animals, Russell F. Doolittle has produced a 'tree of life' that shows the origins of these five kingdoms appearing in the sequence mentioned. See Russell F. Doolittle *et al.*, 'Determining divergence times of the major kingdoms of living organisms with a protein clock.' *Science* **271**: 470–477; 1996; and an updated version in John Maddox, op. cit., p 262.

6. Certain archaea live happily at 113 °C.

7. The common ancestor of plants and animals was some type of primitive cell that had acquired the characteristics of a nuclear structure within it. The nucleus, which disappears before every cell division and is then reformed in the two daughter cells, accommodates most of a cell's DNA. As the nuclear membrane breaks up, the DNA becomes packaged into chromosomes. Once a complete set of chromosome pairs has been incorporated into each of the two daughter cells, the DNA is again (partially) unwound. Nucleated cells encompass fungi like yeast (whose DNA has 60% homology with that of man), in addition to the cells of animals and plants. Nucleated cells are known as eukaryotic, in distinction to smaller cells like bacteria that lack a nucleus, called prokaryotic. The first eukaryotic cell appeared some two and a half billion years ago, and is the common ancestor of the cells present in today's plants, fungi and animals.

8. Mark A. Sephton, 'Life's sweet beginnings?' *Nature* **414**: 857; 2001, George Cooper *et al.*, 'Carbonaceous meteorites as a source of sugar-related organic compounds on the early Earth'. *Nature* **414**: 879–883; 2001 and Everett H. L. Shock, 'Seeds of life?' *Nature* **416**: 380–381; 2002.

9. Amino acids in proteins, A, C, G and T in DNA, A, G, C and U in RNA, and so forth.

10. Fred Hoyle and Chandra Wickramasinghe, 'Cosmic life: evolution and chance', *Biochemist* (published by the Biochemical Society of the UK), **December**: 11–18; 1999. But note a rebuttal of their ideas by Athel Cornish-Bowden and Maria Luz Cárdenas, 'Life on Earth: probability of a cosmic origin', *Biochemist* **April**: 35–38; 2000.

11. They also contain molecules that act as natural anti-freeze.

12. Because it absorbs the infrared radiation emitted from earth when sunlight falls on it. As a result, the radiation does not escape back into space but remains locked within the earth's atmosphere, which

warms up in consequence. Originally much higher, by 3.5 billion years ago carbon dioxide levels had fallen to almost the trace levels present today, and the temperature on earth has not, since then, fluctuated up or down by more than about 10 °C, at a mean rate of around 1 °C every 1000 years. These changes, of course, are averaged out to allow for diurnal and geographical differences: the temperature at the poles drops to below −40 °C at night, and that at the equator rises to more than +40 °C during the day. Nevertheless, it takes no more than a 10 °C drop for the polar ice caps to extend sufficiently to constitute an ice age. One of the earliest ice ages was exceptional. Even the equator was frozen and life survived only in the waters below the ice sheet. At present we are between ice ages, the last one having tapered off some 12,000 years ago. Excessive heat is as inimical to the molecules of life as cold. The hydrogen bonds that keep the strands of DNA together break down at temperatures above 60 °C; by around 80 °C proteins, too, begin to unravel. This, in essence, is what we do when we sterilize surgical instruments or boil food: we kill any microbes that may be present by destroying the structure of their DNA and proteins.

13. The insectivorous bats—there are over 900 species of bat—use ultrasound to locate their prey.
14. Michael Joseph, London, 1951.
15. Plants – photosynthesis:

$$6CO_2 \text{ (carbon dioxide)} + 6H_2O \text{ (water)} + \text{light energy} \rightarrow$$
$$C_6H_{12}O_6 \text{ (carbohydrate)} + 6O_2 \text{ (oxygen)}$$

Animals – respiration:

$$C_6H_{12}O_6 + 6O_2 \rightarrow 6CO_2 + 6H_2O + \text{chemical energy}$$

16. ATP (the A being the same A as the adenine base in DNA and RNA: see Figure 1.1) is a small molecule that acts as a transducer of energy in every cell of every living organism, from grass (photosynthesis) to gorilla (respiration). It is the key intermediate not only in the conversion of light energy into chemical energy in plants and photosynthetic bacteria (and in the opposite direction in light-emitting animals like fire flies), but also in the conversion of chemical energy into electrical energy in the nervous system of animals. This, of course, includes the visual process. In animals like the electric eel, that has an amplified arrangement of neurons for generating an electric impulse, the voltage produced—some 750 volts—is sufficient to stun even the largest prey. ATP is also pivotal in the conversion of one form of chemical energy—for example carbohydrate—into another form of chemical energy—for example fat.
17. Visible light, whether considered corpuscular or wave-like, is a mixture of emanations travelling at slightly different speeds. A

glance at a rainbow reveals the differences in terms of colour. Blue light, for example, travels faster than red light. This is because its wavelength is shorter and hence its inherent energy greater; green and yellow light travel at wave lengths that are intermediate between those of blue light and red light. The spectrum of light that we are able to apprehend stretches from purplish blue light at around 400 nanometres (nm) to dark red light at 750 nm. To place visible light in the context of other radiations, we remind the reader that 1 nm is 1 billionth of a metre; ultraviolet light, which we cannot perceive with our eyes but which interacts with molecules in our bodies (like DNA and proteins) in generally deleterious ways, has a shorter wavelength (around 100 nm). X-rays and gamma-rays are of even shorter wavelength—down to less than 1 nm—and are therefore of even higher energy; they are also more destructive. In contrast, infra-red and microwave radiations are of longer wavelength (from a millimetre to a metre), and radio waves are longer yet again (up to thousands of metres).

18. The reason why objects appear coloured in the first place is because the molecules at the surface of an object absorb light of one but not another wavelength. The reflected light that impinges on our retina is therefore devoid of some of the components of visible light: we absorb only what is left. The leaves of plants, for example, appear green because they contain chlorophyll. Chlorophyll absorbs light at both the blue end and the red end of the spectrum: consequently the only light that reaches us is the remainder, green. Carrots appear orange because they contain carotene, tomatoes red by virtue of the lycopene plus carotene within them. Wearing blue-tinted sunglasses may be fashionable but carries a risk for drivers: the blue colour absorbs red light, so that it is easy to miss a traffic light set at stop. Objects that do not contain colour-sensitive molecules are perceived as merely white (all light reflected off them), black (no light reflected off them) or grey (in between). Because chlorophyll and other light-sensitive molecules like carotene enable plants to absorb light across a wide range of wavelengths, up to 30% of the energy of sunlight is utilised.

19. Winslow R. Briggs and Eva Huala, 'Blue-light photoreceptors in higher plants', *Annu. Rev. Cell Dev. Biol.* **15**: 34–62; 1999.

20. Flavin plays a role also in the reactions of photosynthesis and respiration (see Note 15), metabolic changes that are fundamental to the life of plants and animals.

21. Phototropin also regulates processes like the germination of seeds, the development of leaves, the extension of stems, and the induction of flowers.

22. See Harry Smith, 'Phytochromes and light signal perception by plants—an emerging synthesis', *Nature* **407**: 585–591; 2000.

23. Until the beginning of the twentieth century, 'heliotropism' was the name used to describe phototropism. It was then realised that the growth of plants towards the light of the sun is different from the turning of leaves to follow the rays of the sun throughout a day, and the word 'heliotropism' was retained to describe the latter process.

24. For details see Michael Young, 'Biological clocks' *Sci. Am.* **282** (March): 46–53; 2000; Karen Wright, 'Clocks in the brain', *Sci. Am.* **287** (September): 43–47; 2002; or Steven M. Reppert and David R. Weaver, 'Coordination of circadian timing in mammals', *Nature* **418**: 935–941; 2002. Recent research indicates that possessing the molecular circuitry for circadian rhythm may be of advantage in preventing cancer: mice in which certain genes involved in circadian rhythm were mutated were far more prone to developing cancers than their litter-mates: see Michael Rosbash and Joseph S. Takahashi, *Nature* **420**: 373–374; 2002.

25. Via the movement of H^+ and Cl^- ions across its membrane and the ensuing synthesis of ATP.

26. John L. Spudich, 'Archaeal rhodopsins use the same light-triggered molecular switch for ion transport and phototaxis signalling', in *Microbial Responses to Light and Time*, M. X. Caddick, S. Baumberg, D. A. Hodgson and M. K. Phillips-Jones (eds). *Soc. Gen. Microbiol. Symp.* **56**: 57–68; Cambridge University Press, Cambridge, 1998.

27. Barry L. Taylor *et al.*, 'Aerotaxis and other energy-sensing behavior in bacteria', *Annu. Rev. Microbiol.* **53**: 103–128; 1999.

28. Where cellular components like carbohydrates (cellulose, starch and glycogen) and proteins are degraded to sugars and amino acids, respectively.

29. The larger the vessel, the lower the rpm of the propellor: if the rotational speed of the propellor is too high in relation to its translational speed, cavitation—the formation of air bubbles—ensues.

30. By reducing it all the way back to ammonia in order to synthesise amino acids and the building blocks of nucleic acids.

31. See also Marina Chicurel, 'Slimebusters', *Nature* **408**: 284–286; 2000.

32. Single-celled organisms that display features characteristic of both plants and animals.

33. Toshiyuki Nakagaki *et al.*, 'Maze-solving by an amoeboid organism', *Nature* **407**: 470; 2000.

34. We ourselves switch from oxidising glucose to carbon dioxide and water by respiration, to metabolising it only part of the way—to lactic acid—when oxygen supplies are low (as in our leg muscles when sprinting). A prolonged lowering of oxygen in the bloodstream leads to an increased synthesis of haemoglobin (as in those who live at

high altitudes). In each case, a protein containing the 270-amino acid domain senses such changes in oxygen concentration in the cells within our bodies.

35. Since voltage-sensitive proteins play a role in the transmission of all the different impulses in animals—sight, hearing, smell and touch, as well as those underlying thought and memory, mood and behaviour—proteins that contain the 270 amino acid sequence represent a family that is fundamental to their function.

36. The LOV sequence in a protein is also known as the PAS domain (an acronym for some rather cumbersomely named enzymes). See Barry L. Taylor and Igor B. Zhulin, 'PAS domains: internal sensors of oxygen, redox potential and light', *Microbiol. Mol. Biol. Rev.* **63**: 479–506; 1999.

37. One way in which a common amino acid sequence like the PAS domain becomes incorporated into many diverse proteins, each having a different function, is through the fusion of genes: the gene for PAS, for example, becomes aligned next to the gene that codes for another portion of the phototropin, phytochrome, cryptochrome, or other type of protein. The result is that a single protein molecule, containing the PAS sequence within it, is 'read off' during translation of an RNA that is complementary to the fused gene.

38. See M. A. Merbach *et al.*, *Nature* **415**: 36–37; 2002.

39. See Robert Kubey and Mihaly Csikszentmihalyi, 'Television addiction', *Sci. Am.* **286** (February): 62–68; 2002.

CHAPTER FOUR

Animals and man: development of human attributes

*I*n the previous chapter we saw that vision in animals, which is a fundamental ingredient of their ability for quest, has much in common with the sensing of light by microbes and plants. Some of the photoreceptors are identical, and the proteins that process the impact of light into a signal leading to altered growth (plants) or movement (microbes) belong to families of proteins that are also found in animals. In the case of bacteria, some of those proteins enable them to seek out food as well as light, and in animals they play a role in processes like nerve conduction that are central to their behaviour. In short, the genes that code for such 'sensing' proteins have been inherited from the earliest microbes through to man. At the molecular level they function in similar ways. It is the consequences of their action that vary from one organism to another: searching for light in plants, seeking nutrients and avoiding noxious molecules in microbes, seeing what lies around them in animals.

Vision, however, is not one of the characteristics that distinguishes humans from chimpanzees. In this chapter we return to those attributes that do, and that underlie man's unique ability to search: an upright gait, an agile hand, the power of speech, a greater number of cortical neurons. First, I would like to draw attention to the migratory habits of animals: in humans these have caused their expansion across the globe, a subject we shall examine in the following chapter.

Migration

Migration involves search. Animals are able to move and can look, individually or *en masse*, for new sources of food and water when present supplies have run out or are dwindling. Locusts will search for new ground once they have stripped an area of all vegetation; with up to 40 billion per swarm, they devour 100,000 tons of food at one go. Reindeer in the Arctic or wildebeest[1] in Africa do not wait so long: they are constantly on the move. Climatic conditions often trigger the return to familiar ground. Wildebeest breed near the water holes in the Serengeti of equatorial East Africa (in south-east Tanzania) between December and April. As the pools dry up, they move north-westwards towards Lake Victoria, where they stay until July. They then trek north-eastwards to the Kenyan border to await the early rains. By November they are ready to begin their return journey south. Zebras, Thomson's gazelle, elephants, lions and other animals within the Serengeti follow similar strategies as water holes empty at the end of one season and become replenished at the start of another. Within the northern and southern hemispheres, migrations are triggered by the periods of autumn and spring. The grey whale, for example, swims 12,000 miles from the arctic waters of Alaska, round the tip of Baja California, to breed in the warm waters of the Gulf of Mexico during the autumn months. By the time the return journey is made in the spring, the females are pregnant. They do not give birth until they are back in the warm waters the following year (the gestation time is 13 months). Many species of bird migrate southwards so as to avoid the cold northern climate during the winter (and those of the southern hemisphere do the reverse). Some, like swallows and swifts, travel from Europe all the way to South Africa in the autumn and make the return journey in the spring. The arctic tern does the same, flying more than 12,000 miles each way between the Arctic and the Antarctic regions. Other birds, like cranes and cuckoos, fly only a part of the way: they winter in the milder regions of southern Europe or North Africa. Some birds remain in the air for even longer than a year: swifts can spend 2 years in flight and the albatross has been known to fly 200,000 miles at an average speed of 40 mph.[2]

Insects also migrate. One that flies further than most is the monarch butterfly (*Danaus plexippus*). This orange, black-striped butterfly spends its summer in Canada, around Toronto, whence its name—monarch—originates: the Scottish Presbyterian settlers named it after their favourite King, the Protestant William of Orange. I said summer rather than summers deliberately: they live for only one season. As the autumn nights draw in, the young butterfly leaves Canada and begins a long migration south, to the pine forests along the San Andrés mountains of Michoacan in Mexico, 3000 miles away.[3] It navigates by the use of an internal magnetic compass and by following the sun, flying up to 100 miles a day. Since this is its first journey, it has to find its winter location largely by instinct alone. As it approaches the forests, it looks out for other members of its species, and it finds them. Here are some 50 million of its own kind, all of whom spend the winter, attached to the bark of pine trees, in a kind of hibernation; they have stopped feeding. Come February, and they begin the return journey north. The butterflies will have mated on the way down, and the females are now carrying up to 400 eggs each. As they reach Texas, the most important search begins: they have to find a milkweed plant, on which to lay their eggs. The leaves of this plant are the only place on which the eggs will develop into caterpillars. The butterflies continue their journey north, laying eggs wherever they find a milkweed among the spring meadows; north of Toronto, milkweed dies out, and this limits the travels of this remarkable butterfly. But they have in any case come to the end of their lives; exhausted by their long journeys to and from Mexico, they fall prey to any marauding predator. For their offspring, the journey is about to begin. Once hatched, the caterpillars feed on the milkweed leaves, and eventually metamorphose into butterflies. These then commence the journey north to Toronto, and the cycle of migration is repeated.

The migration of plankton, from one layer of the ocean to another according to the clarity of the water (they derive their energy from sunlight through photosynthesis) provides a good example of the overlap in the behaviour of plants and animals: all plankton migrate, yet some (phytoplankton) are classified as plants, while others (zooplankton) fall within the animal kingdom. On the other hand, there are those who consider even land plants to undergo a kind of migration to reach new germination sites.[4] No species of animal, however, has migrated as extensively as man. He has encompassed the entire globe. Unlike the sperm whale in the Pacific, the antelope in the Serengeti or the swallow travelling between Europe and South Africa, man does not migrate for climatic reasons: curiosity is the main stimulus. Escape from persecution and a desire to improve his economic situation are other triggers. Together they form the substance of the next chapter.

You may say that some of the migrations just described are not really searches, as the animals have been pre-programmed, by their genes, to troop or swim or fly from one place to another at the appropriate time. I include such responses to environmental conditions—the triggers for the search—in the same way that I justified the responses of plants and microbes to an environmental stimulus as a form of ensuing search: the organisms seek to maximise their chances of survival and to breed. And in the case of animals and man, vision is a common thread.[5] Moreover, there is surely also an element of active search in the migration of animals. First, their forebears must have sought out the appropriate journeys to make: those who succeeded survived, the others perished. Second, when climatic conditions alter, the migrating species respond accordingly: they change their strategy. Third, most migrants find their way back to precisely their point of origin: swallows return to the same corner of the same farmhouse they left 6 months ago; turtles have been known to leave Australia, swim to California and back (a distance of 15,000 miles) and still find the beach from which they departed 30 years earlier.[2] It is difficult to accept that their directional mechanisms are accurate to such an extent; it seems more plausible to assume that the last part of their journey involves an active search for their previous home. Sometimes, of course, they fail to find it, having been blown off course by a strong wind or current. There is an imprinting mechanism in the brain of animals— just as there is in ours—that helps successful migrants to remember where they have been. Offspring may follow their parents initially, but thereafter they too remember the route of their journeys. We call it memory: remembering places, events, thoughts.

Memory, of course, is not transmitted to the next generation. A recent study in the USA—not on recognizing migratory destinations, but on identifying possible predators—provides a good example of the need to learn about predators afresh at each generation, in the way that human children need to be taught to avoid dangerous situations like touching hot stoves or sharp objects, eating dirt or drinking unclean water. It is the animal equivalent of cultural transmission from parent to offspring through language. What the scientists did was to compare the response of moose in Yellowstone National Park to those of moose in Alaska. In Yellowstone, the natural predators of moose, the grizzly bear and the wolf, have only just been reintroduced after an absence of 50 years; in Alaska they have been present continuously. The researchers found that moose in Yellowstone were 50 times more likely to be killed by a grizzly bear or wolf than those in Alaska: they had forgotten how to recognize their enemies. Since no genetic change could have occurred in such a short interval of time—just a few generations—it is clear that moose need to learn about the dangers of predators afresh at each generation. So it is likely that knowledge about migratory routes is taught to the young by their parents or by older animals who have made the journey before: the knowledge is not innate.

Evolution of man

The evidence that man evolved from a common ancestor of the higher apes is overwhelming: we have seen that 95% of our genetic make-up is the same as that of today's chimpanzee. The ancestor lived around 6–8 million years ago, probably somewhere in Africa; until recently, no fossil remains had been found. In 2001, however, a joint team from France and Kenya decided that bones they had located in the Tugen Hills of Kenya, and dated as being 6 million years old, belonged to just such a contender: they named the genus *Orrorin* and the species *tugenensis*.[6] Although *O. tugenensis* is indeed a likely ancestor of man, the evidence that it was also a precursor of today's African apes is less secure. What is undisputed is that from around this time onwards the lineages leading on the one hand to man, and on the other to today's chimpanzees (*Pan troglodytes* and *Pan paniscus*), diverged. The lines culminating in today's gorilla and orang-utang separated even earlier. Man is a closer relative of the chimpanzee than is a gorilla or an orangutang.

Dating techniques

How is the age of a piece of bone or a stone tool assessed? In the case of fossilised remains, it is generally the surrounding strata of rock or limestone in which the specimens are found, rather than the fossils themselves, that are dated. As dust and dead vegetation settle on the ground, some animal remains become fossilised, provided they are left undisturbed; a new layer then forms above that, and so on. The hardness of fossils, which is what preserves dead organisms, is due to the minerals in the water that runs over the ground. As the water evaporates, it leaves behind a crystalline layer that retains the shape of organic remains like bone. Most fossils of early man have been found along river beds or in caves; corpses on open ground do not survive long enough to become fossilised.

Organic, carbon-containing remains like wood (that may have been used for a tool), charcoal (from fires), bones (from skeletal remains), shells (from sea and land animals) or peat (from erstwhile vegetation), can be dated by measuring the proportion of a radioactive isotope of carbon—^{14}C as opposed to the stable isotope ^{12}C—that is present.[7] While plants and animals are alive, the fraction of carbon that is present as ^{14}C reflects that of the surrounding atmosphere. This is because the ^{14}C content of the carbon dioxide in the air equilibrates with the carbon dioxide within the cells of living plants and animals. When they die, equilibration ceases and the proportion of ^{14}C gradually decreases as the radioactive ^{14}C isotope decays: the less ^{14}C that is present, the longer ago the organism died. The technique can date objects that are between 200 and 50,000 years old, within an error of 1–5%. For something dated at 50,000 years old, the accuracy is therefore between plus and minus 500–2500 years. But carbon dating is clearly of no use for objects as old as a million or more years. Nor, for that matter, is analysis of DNA, assuming that a suitable sample can be isolated: the molecule is unstable after about 100,000 years,[8] although decomposition through enzymes shortly after death often leaves little intact material for analysis anyway.

For rocks that contain iron, it is possible to date them by assessing the orientation of the magnetic field within a sample. This is because the magnetic axis of the earth changes orientation every so often as the molten iron deep within the earth shifts around. By knowing when such shifts of magnetic axis occurred and by measuring the orientation within a sample of rock, the latter can be dated to one or other 'window' of time.[9] In order to pinpoint during which particular window the laying down of the rock occurred, other dating methods have to be employed. One that has found favour, and that is useful for time periods from around 300,000 years ago to more than 10 million years ago, is also based on the decay of a radioactive isotope, in this case an isotope of K (potassium).[10] Another radiometric method, that spans the gap between radiocarbon dating (useful up to 50,000 years ago) and radiopotassium dating (useful from 300,000 years ago onwards), depends on the proportion of radioactive ^{238}U to stable ^{235}U in uranium-containing pieces of rock (the reader will recall that it was the isolation of ^{238}U from such ores that led to the production of the first atomic bomb in 1945). As ^{238}U decays, it leaves a track in the sample of rock: the length of track is proportional to the amount of ^{238}U that was present at the time the rock was laid down. The two radiometric methods just described are particularly effective for dating rocks in areas of high volcanic activity (during each of which the 'clock' is reset to zero). Since the Great Rift Valley is just such a region, the techniques have proved useful for dating the layers of rock in which most of the fossil remains of *Homo* and his antecedents have been found.

The methods described[11] depend on the analysis of an actual sample. Alternatively, the date at which a living organism first made its appearance can be inferred from molecular analysis of its descendants. One approach is to analyse stretches of DNA. Another is to sequence particular proteins. A third is the hybridization technique explained in Chapter 2 (note 24). Each method depends on comparing the DNA or protein of one species with that of another: the more they differ, the longer ago they diverged. Since the disparities are due to mutations, knowing the rate at which these occur would give one an actual time scale; by making certain assumptions, this is precisely what molecular scientists have achieved. The result, depicted as a tree with branches indicating the forks within kingdom, phylum, class, order, family, genus and species, bears remarkable resemblance to such trees of life drawn—largely on the basis of intuition alone—100 years ago. In both, *H. sapiens* takes top position. But if the extremity of a branch is supposed to indicate how recently that species evolved, should not a virus like HIV take pride of place?

Australopithecus

Our direct ancestor first began to walk upright in a sustained manner more than 5 million years ago,[12] having lost the splayed toes of tree-climbing primates and instead acquired an arch to the soles of his feet. The advantages of walking upright on only two limbs, instead of bent on four, are obvious: better vision to search for predator or prey across tall grasses (a four-fold increase in the distance to the visual horizon), and hands free for carrying objects such as food or babies. An increase in the sensitivity of the hand and upper limb means that those possessed of two-footed gait can explore in the dark and in places where the eye cannot see: the ability to sense texture and weight have played an important role in man's exploratory progress. Being able to carry tools or weapons has been cited as another of the genetic benefits of walking on two feet, but this is unlikely to have been a factor, since bipedalism preceded the use of tools by almost 2 million years. What is clear is that once the forelimbs had been freed from bearing the weight of the body, the development of handy crafts became possible. It is for those reasons that I consider the upright gait to be one of the four features that has enabled man's quest for new technology to be realised: so long as his arms were used to support his movement, the fingers on his hands could not evolve into appendages capable of fashioning tools. The trade-off in developing bipedalism in contrast to quadrupedalism is slower movement: four-footed animals like gazelles and leopards, horses and dogs, move faster than man. But compared with other primates, man has lost nothing in speed: he can easily outrun a gorilla or a chimpanzee.

The fossil remains of an upright-walking creature, which has been termed *Australopithecus afarensis* and called Lucy for short (it was a female), were found a quarter of a century ago in the Middle Awash valley of Ethiopia, and dated to be 3.2 million years old; note that the term *Australopithecus* does not imply an Australian origin: it merely means 'southern ape'. Finding Lucy was important for two reasons: first, because up to 40% of her skeleton could be accurately re-assembled; second, because when this was done, the structure showed her to be a forerunner of modern man (although some palaeoanthropologists now doubt whether *Homo* species are directly descended from *A. afarensis* itself). A few years ago, a probable descendant of Lucy, termed *Australopithecus garhi*, was found in the same valley, and dated at 2.5 million years ago. He was taller than Lucy (who was exceptionally short), had more human-like teeth, but still had rather long arms and a relatively small brain. Skeletal remains of other creatures that are likely ancestors of man have been found all along the wide valley known as the East African rift, that runs from Ethiopia and the Red Sea in the north, through Uganda and Kenya, down to Tanzania and the other countries that border Lake Malawi in the south (Lake Malawi is a misnomer: the explorer David Livingstone, who named it in 1859, misunderstood the gestures of the locals who pointed at the waters and said 'malawi': the word merely means 'lake'[13]). It is in this long valley region, also, that the earliest remains of a new genus, defined as *Homo*, have been found and dated to around 2.5 million years ago.

During the writing of this book, another potential ancestor of *Homo* was identified on the basis of a skull found in the East African rift, this time near Lake Turkana in northern Kenya. The fossilised pieces, when reassembled, showed the owner to have had a brain the size of a chimpanzee, but a much flatter face and smaller teeth, more like those of a human. It was dated at between 3.5 and 3.2 million years ago, in other words during the period of *Australopithecus afarensis*. The distinctive features of facial flatness and small molars has led the team, that included two members of the Leakey family who have been fossil hunters in this part of Africa for more than a generation, to consider the remains to be not only a new species, but one belonging to a genus different from *Australopithecus*: accordingly they have named it *Kenyanthropus platyops* (flat-faced human-like being from Kenya).[14] Although *Kenyanthropus* existed at the same time as *Australopithecus*, both are considered by some to be ancestors of *Homo*; this would imply that *Kenyanthropus* is a descendant of *Australopithecus* (or vice versa). The fact that each had developed an upright gait has led both genera to be included in the family Hominidae, alongside the genus *Homo*.

Early *Homo* species

Many attributes distinguish *Homo* from his predecessors. The shape of the jaw and teeth—more gracile (meaning light and small) in *Homo*; more robust (meaning heavy and large) in *Australopithecus* —for example. Another is the size and complexity of the brain. This characteristic plays a vital part in our story: without it *Homo* would have remained just another genus of primate; with it, he has been able to refine an innate capacity for curiosity into the intellectual search that started with the first species of his kind and grew steadily to become one of the distinguishing features of present-day man.

Leslie Aiello, of London University, has an interesting hypothesis about the evolution of the *Homo* brain, and indeed of *Homo* himself. A hominid (be it *K. platyops*, *A. afarensis*, or whatever primate proves to be the immediate ancestor of *Homo*) comes across the skeleton of a prey—say an antelope—that has just been killed and eaten by a predator. There is no meat left; but wait, perhaps the head will yield something edible? It picks up a piece of rock to smash open the skull. Indeed there is soft tissue which it sucks out voraciously. This is its first taste of meat and to its liking. Meat satiates it sooner than the fruit and berries it is accustomed to eating. It continues, like a vulture, to forage dead animals. This switch to a high-fat, high-protein diet by a group of primates leads to their faster growth and reproduction, and to better development of the brain, which in turn leads to superior tools and their use for hunting, which in turn leads to a the maintenance of a richer diet, and so on. The shift from the vegetarian gatherers (although they probably also ate small mammals and insects, as do today's chimpanzees) to the omnivorous hunter-gatherers is occurring: the evolution of *Homo* beings from their immediate ancestors is slowly taking place.[15] The fact that some of us may have reverted to a strictly vegeterian diet does not mean that our brain function has become impaired.[16] Once a particular function has been selected for by the evolutionary process, it remains: the genes that underlie the function do not need 'nourishing' by the original stimulus. In common with most non-ruminant mammals, for example, we have no use for our appendix, but the genes underlying its formation have not disappeared. Male mammals have nipples, but they serve no purpose.

Other features distinguish *Homo* from his primate relatives: among them we may mention his predominant right-handedness, the fact that on average males are not much taller than females, and the advent of the menopause in women.[17] More pertinent to the message of this book is the development of the agile hand. It is around this time, 2.5 million years ago, that the fully rotating thumb begins to make its appearance. The significance of manual dexterity to human development cannot be over-emphasised.[18] Because 2.5 million years is also the age of the oldest stone artefacts fashioned by a living creature, the new species of primate has been termed *Homo habilis* (skilful or handy man). Another species of *Homo*, who probably walked more upright than *H. habilis*, (who himself had a straighter posture than *Australopithecus*), and who is called *H. erectus*, has been dated to some 0.5 million years later, around 1.8 million years ago. The most complete skeletal remains of a member of this species were found 15 years ago by Richard Leakey, son of the anthropologists Louis and Mary Leakey, on the western shore of Lake Turkana in northern Kenya, and dated to be some 1.5 million years old. When the fragments of skull and the many pieces of bone were assembled, it became clear that its owner had been a boy who had died at around 9 years of age. His youth and the place of his demise have caused this specimen of *H. erectus* to be known as Turkana boy.

Australopithecus, *Kenyanthropus* and *Homo* probably coexisted in the East African rift valley and elsewhere for many thousands of years. From the types of stone implements found alongside skeletal remains, it appears that some *Australopithecus* were able to hold primitive stone tools in their hands. The difference between *Australopithecus* and *Homo* is that the former merely used what they found lying around, whereas the latter actually shaped stones—with other stones—to be used for cutting or chopping branches and meat, as well as for killing prey: man's search for new technology had begun. But it has to be admitted that most of the details concerning our origin are largely speculative.

First, the reader must appreciate that linking the use of objects to particular skeletal remains found nearby is based on no more than the fact that both are present in the same layer of earth or rock below the surface: the older the specimens, the lower down they will be buried, as explained above.

Second, attributing skeletal remains—often no more than a few bones, a skull if one is lucky—to one or other genus like *Homo*, *Australopithecus* or *Kenyanthropus*, let alone to a particular species like *H. habilis* or *H. erectus*, is not an exact science and is influenced very much by the prejudice of their discoverer. A Canadian anatomist called Davidson Black, who was appointed professor of neurology and embryology at the newly-founded Peking Union Medical College in 1919, made his name 8 years later through the finding of a single tooth that he claimed to be the oldest human-like fossil in Asia; he named its erstwhile owner *Sinanthropus pekinensis* or Peking Man. He was probably right in his assumption of great antiquity, and a dozen other fossilised bones found since in the same region have caused anthropologists to assign Peking Man to the species *Homo erectus*, with an approximate age of 500,000 years. Recent attempts by Davidson Black's grandson to view the bones of Peking Man have been unsuccessful. The bones were originally kept in Peking Union Medical College, but when the Japanese invaded China in 1937 it was decided to remove them elsewhere for safe keeping. They are said to have been transferred to the American Embassy and to have been included in a shipload of items that were transported to the USA a few years later, when war between Japan and the USA broke out. Apparently they never arrived at their destination. Another version of events is that they were taken to Japan on the orders of the Emperor, but endeavours by Davidson Black's grandson to locate them there have failed.

Perhaps they are still in China after all, or maybe—the worst and yet the most likely explanation—the carefully wrapped contents of a small brown box were simply discarded by someone as so much rubbish. Thus have the bones of China's oldest human taken on the mystery that surrounds a lost painting by a great master or a missing manuscript from the library of an ancient monastery.

To summarise. Some 2.5 million years ago there coexisted various primates with skeletal structures somewhere between today's chimpanzees and humans. As a result of their capacity to grasp with their hands stones and other materials they found lying around, some of these early hominids had learnt to manufacture primitive tools. More than 2 million years were to elapse before the emergence of man as we now know him. One cannot be precise about dates for the reasons already mentioned. In any case, one can only date what has been found, and there is a paucity of remains. Attributing a particular artifact, the cut-up remains of a slaughtered animal, or a drawing on the wall of a cave, to one or other species of *Homo* is largely a matter of speculation, especially as the evolution of one species from another is a very gradual process, with both being present together for a long time. There is therefore considerable argument among palaeoanthropologists regarding the identity of their finds. They also dispute—with the fervour of mediaeval theologians—one another's right to be excavating in a particular region at all: intrigues, sackings and lawsuits alleging unlawful arrest, false imprisonment and malicious harassment are not unknown among the fossil hunters of the East African rift. They search as much to foil their competitors as to discover the bones of their ancestors.

Recent *Homo* species

In August 1856, at about the time that Charles Darwin was slowly putting the finishing touches to *The Origin of Species*,[19] a village schoolmaster named Dr Johann Karl Fuhlrott was handed the skull and some bones of a cave bear. Workmen quarrying along the banks of the Düssel River in the Neander valley, which leads into the Rhine near Düsseldorf, had found the remains while blasting one of the caves 60 feet above the river. Knowing that Dr Fuhlrott's hobby was natural history, they thought he might be interested to have them. They were right. The schoolteacher immediately realised that the bones were not those of a bear, but of some primitive man. The skull resembled that of a human more closely than anything found before. The brain was actually larger than that of current man, although other features were rather heavier. Dr Fuhlrott rushed back to the cave and began digging around for further traces of human occupation, but by this time limestone fragments and debris had obliterated all traces of the erstwhile inhabitant of the grotto. Fuhlrott guessed that he was on to something significant and consulted Hermann Schaffhausen, Professor of Anatomy at Bonn University. Schaffhausen agreed that the specimens appeared to be of great age (they have since been dated to 40,000 years), and announced the discovery 6 months later at a meeting of the Lower Rhine Medical and Natural History Society in Bonn. This engendered none of the interest and excitement that Darwin's publication was about to create, and Fuhlrott's discovery remained unnoticed for a number of years.

It was only later that the skeletal remains described by Fuhlrott and Schaffhausen would be linked to other fossils found in Europe: these included a skull that had been discovered in Forbes' quarry on the rock of Gibraltar in 1848. From the outset, scientists like T. H. Huxley were doubtful that these skeletons represented the elusive 'missing link' between ape and man. Subsequent discoveries in the Near East and in central Asia have confirmed that view. To mark the German finding, these hominids have been termed Neanderthal Man ('thal' being German for valley) or *Homo neanderthalensis*.[20] This species of *Homo* appeared some 250,000 years ago, and was still living as recently as 30,000 years ago, well after the emergence of *H. sapiens*, who by this time had himself reached Europe. Because the timing of *H. neanderthalenis*'s existence coincides with that of the last Ice Age, there is good ground for believing that Neanderthal Man had mastered the art of keeping warm by sheltering in caves and by the fabrication of garments from the skins of animals like bison or bear. No remains of *H. neanderthalensis* have been found north of the line that marks the extent of permafrost at that time, nor for that matter in Africa or southern Asia. Despite the reservations of some anthropologists, the overall similarity between *H. neanderthalensis* and *H. sapiens* is so striking that many consider the two to be variants of the same species (*H. sapiens neanderthalensis* and *H. sapiens sapiens*). Some go further, and suggest that Neanderthal Man is the precursor of modern man. Molecular biology, however, tells another story, as will shortly be explained.

What is clear is that Neanderthal Man was possessed of three of the attributes necessary for human quest: upright gait, agile hands and a reasonably-sized brain. Whether his larynx was sufficiently developed to enable him to speak, we do not know. The problem relates to the detailed anatomy of the pharynx, the tube that starts at the back of the mouth and then divides into the larynx, through which animals including man breathe, and the oesophagus, through which animals and humans swallow. Within the larynx is the vocal cord, which consists of two elastic membranes stretched across its interior. The membranes vibrate when air from the lungs is exhaled past them, producing sound. The membranes function somewhat like the strings on a violin: they can be shortened and lengthened by the contraction and relaxation of tiny muscles that also control the opening and closing of the space between the membranes. The muscles are anchored to two small cartilaginous structures, the thyroid cartilage at one end and the arytenoid cartilage at the other end. It is the precise positioning of all these pieces of cartilaginous, elastic and muscular tissue relative to the larynx that allows one organism to modulate sounds through an enormous range of possibilities, whereas another can no more than grunt. Unlike bone, all the structures we have described, namely cartilage, elastic tissue and muscle, are degraded when an animal dies. There are therefore no remains—fossilised or not—to settle the issue of whether or not the owner was possessed of a sophisticated vocal cord. There *is* a small bone (the hyoid bone) that is attached through muscles somewhat differently to the back of the mouth in a human and a chimpanzee; this structure contributes to the power of emitted sound. Even if the hyoid bone were routinely found alongside other bones, which generally it is not, it would not help much, as its shape is very similar in the two species, and the precise attachments will have been degraded. It is for these reasons that we do not know whether or not *H. neanderthalensis* was capable of human speech.[21]

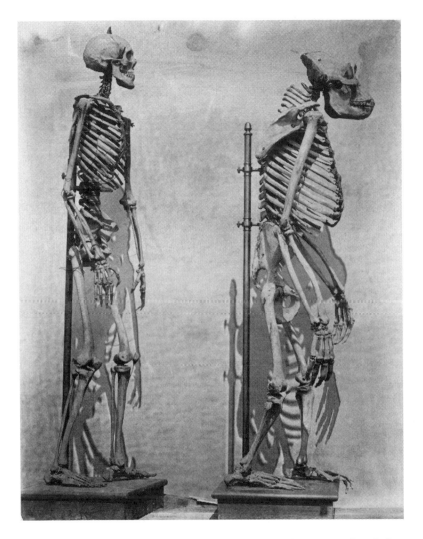

Figure 4.1 Upright gait. The skeleton of a human (left) compared with that of a gorilla (right). The latter skeleton is shown in the bipedal position (on two feet), although gorillas normally walk quadrupedally (on four feet). Reproduced by permission of the Natural History Museum, London.

A few hundred thousand years after Neanderthal Man was making his appearance in Europe, a new species of *Homo* had arrived on the plains of Eastern Africa. He walked upright easily and well (as a result of modifications to pelvis, femur and foot; Figure 4.1) and had mobile thumbs and shorter fingers (Figure 4.2) that allowed him to grasp tools much better than any of his predecessors: not just with a power grip (object held between thumb and clenched fingers), but with a better precision grip (object held between thumb and extended finger tips). More important, his brain was considerably larger[22]—three times the size of that of *A. garhi*—and he had developed the voice box just described (Figure 4.3), through which he was able to converse with others of his kind in a much more sophisticated way. The top layer of his brain, the cortex, contained three times as many

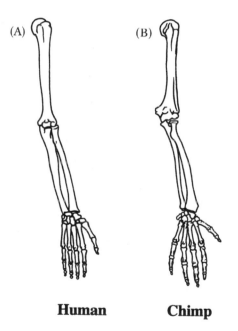

(A)   (B)

Human   Chimp

Figure 4.2 Flexible hand. The forelimb of a human (A) compared with that of a chimpanzee (B). The latter has been reduced in length for easier comparison. Adapted from J. Z. Young, *An Introduction to the Study of Man*, and reprinted by permission of Oxford University Press, Oxford, 1971.

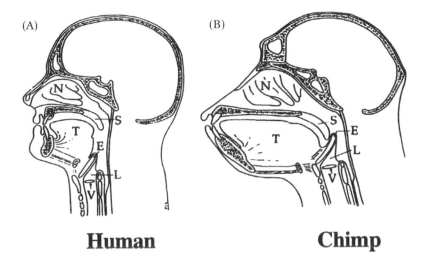

Human   Chimp

Figure 4.3   Voice box. The larynx of a human (A) compared with that of a chimpanzee (B). E = epiglottis; L = larynx; N = nasal cavity; S = soft plate; T = tongue; V = vocal cord. The larynx extends downwards to the trachaea, which leads to the lungs. The pharynx (not marked) is behind it (to the right) and extends downwards to the oesophagus, which leads to the gastrointestinal tract. See text for further details. Adapted by permission from Roger Lewin, *Human Evolution. An Illustrated Introduction*, 3rd edn, Blackwell Scientific, Oxford, 1993.

neurons (nerve cells) as a modern chimpanzee (Figure 4.4). He was more inquisitive, intelligent, ingenious, creative and ambitious than his predecessors. He was the being we now call *H. sapiens*, the first representative of the species to which all humans living on the earth today belong. The relatively subtle difference between the gait, hand, larynx and brain of a human compared with that of a gorilla (Figure 4.1) or chimpanzee (Figure 4.2–4.4) are compatible with my earlier assertion that specifically human genes do not exist: the genes are merely variants of those possessed by the common ancestor of humans and chimpanzees. Through mutations within homologous stretches of DNA, proteins of slightly altered function are produced; a change merely in the timing of when a particular protein is made probably accounts for differences like the elongated fingers of chimpanzees and the extended thumb of humans.

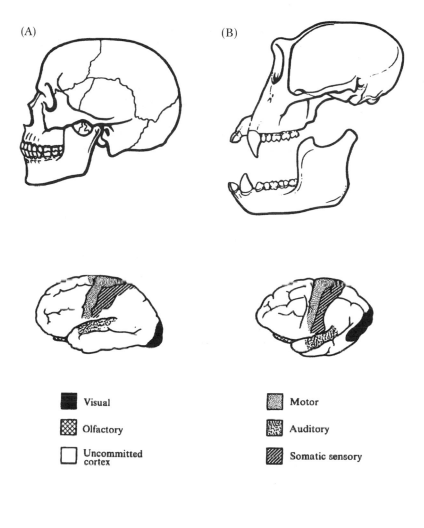

Human   **Chimp**

Figure 4.4   Cortical neurons. The brain of a human (A) compared with that of a chimpanzee (B). The various areas of the brain, and their functions, are indicated. It is within the unshaded area (uncommitted cortex) that neurons (nerve cells) involved in thought and memory, consciousness and mood, are located. The neocortex (see Chapter 8) is the top left (frontal) part of the cortex. Adapted from J. Z. Young, *An Introduction to the Study of Man*, and reprinted by permission of Oxford University Press, Oxford, 1971.

Biologists have long pointed to an analogy between the stages of embryonic development and the stages of evolution. This is particularly evident in regard to the formation of the human larynx: a new-born baby has the same type of larynx as a chimpanzee; it can produce primitive and limited sounds only. Like the adult chimpanzee, though, it can swallow and breathe at the same time. From around 1.5 to 2 years of age onwards, a subtle change takes place in the larynx of humans: the upper end gradually grows downwards away from the opening of the oesophagus. As a result, the larynx has to be closed while solids or liquids are being swallowed, to prevent them entering the trachea (and thence the lungs); on the other hand it now becomes possible to emit a far greater variety of sounds. The lowering of the larynx continues until it reaches its final position around 14 years of age.[23] Because overall the larynx of a chimpanzee resembles that of a human remarkably closely (see Figure 4.3), it is likely that the genes controlling their formation are all variants of genes that were present already in their common ancestor 6 million years ago. No more than a subtle change in a few proteins has resulted in an enormous difference in function between chimpanzee and man.

The consequence of possessing a voice box capable of developing speech, in conjunction with neuronal processing, is enormous: as pointed out earlier, certain anthropologists consider it to be the most important attribute of humans. Some years ago it was discovered that 2–5% of all children have a severe speech and language disorder. Their grammatical ability is badly impaired, they have difficulty in articulating words, and they are unable to control the muscles around their mouth properly. The condition is hereditary, and persists throughout life. A gene called *FOXP2* has been identified as lying at the heart of the problem. Now a group of scientists from Leipzig and Oxford have shown that in chimpanzees and other apes, the *FOXP2* gene is different from that in humans.[24] But within all healthy humans studied, including individuals of African, Asian, European, South American, Australian aboriginal and Papua New Guinean descent, the gene is identical. Moreover, it appears not to have mutated over the entire time span (some 200,000 years) that *H. sapiens* has been around. In short, it is the first molecular marker for the development of speech and language to be identified. One might therefore suppose that the protein coded by the *FOXP2* gene is significantly different in chimpanzees and humans.[25] Indeed, genes like *FOXP2* might account for much of the 5% disparity between the genomes of chimpanzees and humans. Far from it. The dissimilarity between the chimpanzee and human *FOXP2* gene is just 0.03%, and the FOXP2 protein of humans differs from its counterpart in chimpanzees by a mere two amino acids out of a total of 715.[26] Proteins that perform essentially identical functions in chimpanzees and humans are considerably more diverse.[27]

The results of the analyses of FOXP2 proteins are entirely consistent with the hypothesis enunciated in Chapter 1: there are no 'human' as opposed to 'chimpanzee' genes. The 5% difference between the two respective genomes does not indicate the existence of a number of genes that are crucially different in chimpanzees and humans. It may do little more than reflect the number of 'silent' mutations that have accumulated in chimpanzees and humans, since their common ancestor was alive 6–8 million years ago. We mislead ourselves by equating genetic differences with alterations of function. The similarity between the FOXP2 protein of chimpanzees and humans reinforces the thrust of my argument, that very minor changes in anatomy underlie the very much increased capacity of humans for quest. Just as the PAS domain lies at the centre of the *similarity* between the ability of microbes, plants and animals to search, so the FOXP2 protein illustrates one *difference* between the ability of chimpanzees and humans to exercise that search. Other differences will surely emerge, now that sequencing of the chimpanzee genome is under way.[28] The identification of developmental genes that underlie the formation of thumb and larynx, and those that determine the number of cortical neurons produced,[29] is eagerly awaited.

Of the four differences on which I have focused, that of posture is probably the most distinctive (cf. Figure 4.1 with Figures 4.2–4.4). This is to be expected, since an upright gait preceded the other attributes by several million years. There was therefore more time for mutations to accumulate and to accentuate the contrast. For the other differences, it is the interaction between the use of hand, vocal cord and cortical neurons that has enabled a relatively slight

(A)

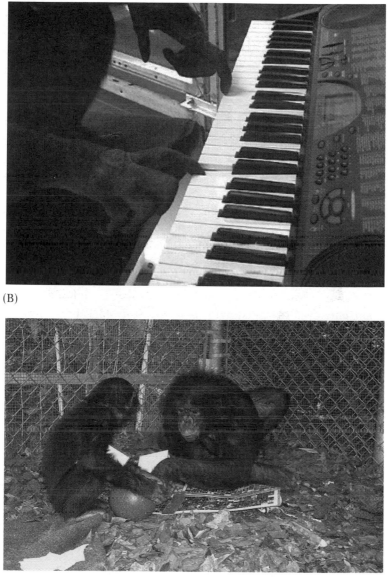

(B)

(C)

Figure 4.5   Panbanisha: (A) with her lexigram keyboard; (B) at the 'piano' (musical keyboard); (C) teaching her 4 year-old son, Nyota. See text for further details. Pictures by courtesy of Dr Jared Taglialatela of the Language Research Center, Georgia State University, Atlanta, USA.

modification of each to lead to such an enormous change of function when combined: to the difference between a primate whose inquisitiveness has led him to tinker with his own genes and one whose curiosity is unfulfilled; to one that has voyaged to the moon and one that has remained within the confines of its forest home.

There are those who express surprise that a sub-Saharan African, a Chinaman, a European or an Australian aborigine, whose visages seem so different to one another, are all of one species. But outside appearance is misleading. Metabolic pathways like the digestion and oxidation of foodstuffs, the control of these processes by hormones, the ionic changes that underly the nervous system, contribute much more to the definition of a species than does the external aspect (which in any case is determined by less than a dozen out of 30,000 genes in the case of humans). One mutation in a single gene can result in the offspring of a typically dark-skinned, dark-haired, black-eyed Pakistani family being a fair-skinned, blond, blue-eyed girl indistinguishable from a Swedish or Norwegian child.[30] Most butterflies seem pretty similar to us: there are actually 20,000 different species around the world today.

The description of our own kind as *Homo sapiens*—Latin for 'thinking' or 'wise' man—was coined by the Swedish naturalist Carl Linnaeus in the middle of the eighteenth century, at a time when other primates were considered to be incapable of much conscious thought. We now know this to be untrue: even if their overall intelligence is less than ours, chimpanzees, gorillas and orang-utans are as capable of reaching rational decisions as we are. It is only the lack of a sophisticated vocal cord that prevents communication between them, as the following experiments have shown. Panbanisha is a 14 year-old bonobo chimpanzee; bonobo means pygmy, but at 160 lb you would not describe her as slight (Figure 4.5). She lives on the campus of Georgia State University in Atlanta, USA. She is a good student, with a vocabulary of 3000 words. When asked by a visiting reporter if there is anything she would like, she responds with 'coffee, milk and juice with ice'; as she sips the coffee, she says 'good coffee', and then 'more'. To be accurate, she does not actually say it, as her voice box is unable to emit human-type sounds. But she uses a portable electronic keyboard with a voice synthesiser; the keys—there are 384 of them, assembled in a folder rather like a stamp album—represent objects like coffee, milk, juice and ice, as well as concepts like good, bad, yes, no, with, without, and so on. Panbanisha was born in captivity and has been brought up, as if she were just another child, by Sue Savage-Rumbaugh of the Language Research Center.[31] She has learnt well, and is now teaching her offspring: how such 'language competent' bonobos pass on their linguistic skills is of considerable interest to the researchers.

Koko is a lowland gorilla who was born in San Francisco zoo 30 years ago. Since then she has been raised by Francine Patterson of the Gorilla Foundation in the Santa Cruz mountains of California. She has been taught by sign language and is just able to move her little fingers sufficiently to carry out a normal conversation. She has a vocabulary of 1000 words and understands a further 1000. Her IQ is said to be around 80, typical of that of a slightly backward child. She does not use a voice synthesiser, as she broke the first one that was tried; a more robust one is being built for her, but her skill at sign language makes this unnecessary.[32]

What does all this mean? Apart from clues that it may give us regarding the evolution of human languages, it confirms two points. First, primates like chimpanzee and gorilla are perfectly capable of logical thought. Second, they are intelligent enough to learn a human language like English. Presumably they might just as easily have been taught Chinese; its symbolic language might make it easier for them to learn to write. Whatever else, the intelligent use of vocabulary seems not to be one of the differences between ape and man. It also shows that the early twentieth century writer H. H. Munro ('Saki') was a man ahead of his time:

'And do you really ask us to believe', Sir Wilfred was saying, 'that you have discovered a means for instructing animals in the art of human speech, and that dear old Tobermory has proved your first successful pupil?'.

'It is a problem at which I have worked for the last seventeen years', said Mr Appin, 'but only during the last eight or nine months have I been rewarded with glimmerings of success … with Tobermory, as you call him, I have reached the goal'. …

'Hadn't we better have the cat in and judge for ourselves?' suggested Lady Blemley.

A sudden hush of awkwardness and constraint fell on the company. Somehow there seemed an element of embarrassment in addressing on equal terms a domestic cat of acknowledged mental ability.

'Will you have some milk, Tobermory?' asked Lady Blemley in a rather strained voice.

'I don't mind if I do', was the response, couched in a tone of even indifference. A shiver of suppressed excitement went through the listeners, and Lady Blemley might be excused for pouring out the saucerful of milk rather unsteadily.

'I'm afraid I've spilt a good deal of it', she said apologetically.

'After all, it's not my Axminster', was Tobermory's rejoinder.

Another silence fell on the group, and then Miss Resker, in her best district-visitor manner, asked if the human language had been difficult to learn. Tobermory looked squarely at her for a moment and then fixed his gaze serenely on the middle distance. It was obvious that boring questions lay outside his scheme of life.

'What do you think of human intelligence?' asked Mavis Pellington lamely.

'Of whose intelligence in particular?' asked Tobermory coldly.

'Oh, well, mine for instance', said Mavis with a feeble laugh.

'You put me in an embarrassing position', said Tobermory, whose tone and attitude certainly did not suggest a shred of embarrassment. 'When your inclusion in this house party was suggested, Sir Wilfred protested that you were the most brainless woman of his acquaintance, and that there was a wide distinction between hospitality and the care of the feeble-minded. Lady Blemley replied that your lack of brain-power was the precise quality which had earned you your invitation, as you were the only person she could think of who might be idiotic enough to buy their old car'.[33]

It is likely that other species of *Homo* preceded *H. sapiens* along the lineage leading to it from *H. habilis* through *H. erectus*: *H.*

ergaster, followed by *H. heidelbergensis*, have been suggested as intermediates, although they may prove to have been no more than variants. All were able to fashion increasingly intricate objects with their hands; the size of their brains, particularly the part (the neocortex) associated with higher cerebral function, gradually increased.

The age of *H. sapiens* has been put in the region of 140,000 years. The first study attempting to determine our antiquity was based on molecular analysis of a particular set of genes within five distinct groups of today's humans: those from sub-Saharan Africa (group 1), those from China, Vietnam, Laos, the Philippines, Indonesia and Tonga (group 2), those of aboriginal Australian descent (group 3), those from North Africa, the Middle East and Europe (group 4), and those of aboriginal New Guinea descent (group 5). The analysis revealed three things.[34] First, all current humans, as represented by the five groups, are fairly closely related. Second, the variation within any group is greatest for group 1, suggesting that Africans have been around the longest. Third, by assuming a constant rate of mutation at 2–4 nucleotide bases (the A, C, G and T residues of DNA) out of every 100 per 1 million years, the convergence of all humans backwards in time can be computed to around 200,000 years. It has to be said that since that analysis was carried out, more than a decade ago, some criticism of it has been raised, and it is clear that certain assumptions were incorrect. More recent studies have led to the revised figure of 140,000 years ago as the time at which our common ancestor lived. Even this number, it should be noted, is only a calculated average: we can say with 95% confidence merely that the age of *H. sapiens* is between 63,000 and approximately 383,000 years. Where all molecular biologists agree, is in the conclusion that the present species of *Homo* is neither 1 million nor 30,000 years old (an earlier twentieth century guess), but that it emerged somewhere in between, with 140,000 years as the most reasonable current estimate.

The genes that provide this information are not, in fact, located within one of the 23 chromosomes at all. They are within a separate, small cluster of genes called mitochondrial DNA.[35] Mitochondrial DNA is passed from one generation to the next only by females.[36] It is for that reason that our 140,000 year-old ancestor has been dubbed 'Eve'. It would be nice to know that one arrives at the same figure if mutations in the DNA of some of the 23 chromosomes in the nucleus of cells are measured. The problem here is that because of a jumbling up of maternal and paternal genes at every generation, it is difficult to obtain meaningful data, with one exception—the DNA of the Y chromosome.[37] If it were possible to isolate the Y chromosome away from all the others, it would provide an unambiguous record of paternal ancestry, in the way that mitochondrial DNA specifies maternal descent. This has now been achieved and the results confirm the close relationship between current human populations and their common origin within sub-Saharan Africans.

There is only one discrepancy. The time of Adam's first appearance appears to be approximately 59,000 years ago, not 140,000. If correct, it means that the men—presumably *H. sapiens*—with whom Eve and her descendants mated for around 80,000 years left no male heirs to carry on an uninterrupted line into modern times. It would have been a chance coupling 59,000 years ago that produced a son from whom all of today's men are descended. What the timing of Adam shows (if the data are confirmed) is that our male ancestors were still in Africa 59,000 years ago; their migration into Eurasia would therefore be more recent than previously thought.[38] Taking all the current evidence —based on skeletal remains as well as on molecular analyses— into account, we may settle for 140,000 years ago as the approximate time at which modern man appeared. For the purpose of this book, our exact age is not so important as the generally accepted view that we are all descended from a single group of ancestors, comprising perhaps 10,000 individuals, who lived originally in Africa.

The analysis of mitochondrial DNA and of Y chromosomal DNA extracted from the bones of various specimens of Neanderthal Man reveals little similarity with that of humans: a European is closer to a sub-Saharan African than to a Neanderthal. It is therefore pretty clear that Neanderthal Man is not a precursor of modern humans. Some 14 different species of hominid (a grouping that includes the genus *Australopithecus*) are said to have lived over the past 5 million years: all bar ourselves have died out. Why? Is it because the lineages leading to *H. sapiens* killed the others, competed more successfully for food and shelter, were better adapted to the climatic conditions of the time? Or is it simply luck, of being in the right place at the right time, the others having been wiped out by impacts of small asteroids, as some scientists believe? At present we do not know: let anthropologists and palaeontologists, geologists and astrophysicists search for the answer. For our part, we will move to the next section of this book and consider how the quest of man has enabled him to dominate the world in which he lives.

Notes

1. A type of antelope, known to scrabble players as 'gnu'.
2. We know this because they were tagged.
3. Others winter at places like Pacific Grove in California.
4. See Hugh Dingle, *Migrations: the Biology of Life on the Move*, Oxford University Press, Oxford, 1996.
5. Unlike many animals, humans are not well attuned to using scent or magnetism to guide their quest.
6. Leslie C. Aiello and Mark Collard, 'Our newest oldest ancestor'. *Nature* **410**: 526–527; 2001.
7. When the 90-odd different elements found on earth today were produced by nuclear explosions from hydrogen and helium within the sun 4–5 billion years ago, some, like ^{12}C, have remained the same ever since; but others, like a heavier version of carbon, namely ^{14}C, are not stable. [^{14}C differs from ^{12}C in that its nucleus contains two extra neutrons: instead of six protons and six neutrons, the atomic nucleus comprises six protons and eight neutrons. ^{14}C resembles ^{12}C in that its six protons are balanced by six electrons outside the nucleus. Since chemistry—the bonding between different atoms—is dependent on electronic interactions, not on nuclear structure, molecules containing ^{14}C undergo the same reactions as molecules containing ^{12}C]. Unstable atoms continuously emit radiation in the form of particles, electrons or gamma rays: they are said to be radioactive. ^{14}C emits electrons and these can readily be measured with an appropriate instrument.
8. Quoted by Tomas Lindahl in his review of Martin Jones, 'The Molecule Hunt: Archeology and the search for ancient DNA'. *Nature* **413**: 358–359; 2001.
9. At present, the magnetic north is the same as the geographic north. Between 20,000 and 30,000 years ago it was reversed (the needle of a

compass would have pointed south); between 30,000 and 690,000 years ago it was the same as now; between 690,000 and 890,000 years ago it was reversed; between 890,000 and 950,000 years ago it was the same as now; between 950,000 and 1,610,000 years ago it was reversed, and so on. As rocks form—from volcanic eruptions or as dust that settles—they are laid down according to the magnetic orientation at that time, indicating a 'window' of time (i.e. between 20,000 and 30,000, or between 690,000 and 890,000, or between 950,000 and 1,610,000 years ago if the polarity is the opposite of today's). See also Sarah Simpson, 'Headed South? Earth's fading field could mean a magnetic flip soon', *Sci. Am.* **287** (November): 12; 2002.

10. The proportion of radioactive ^{40}K relative to the amount of stable ^{39}K in potassium-containing rocks indicates their age. Because ^{40}K decays to ^{40}A (argon), which is an inert gas, all of it is expelled at every volcanic eruption; thereafter, the gradual accumulation of ^{40}A in a sample, relative to the amount of ^{39}K that is present, reflects its age. In order to avoid having to take two samples for analysis (one for gaseous ^{40}A and one for solid ^{39}K), a single sample—as small as one crystal of rock—is irradiated with neutrons, which converts all the ^{39}K to ^{39}A. The sample is then heated, and the $^{39}A/^{40}A$ ratio of the expelled argon is determined.

11. For more details, see Roger Lewin, *Principles of Human Evolution*, op. cit., pp 83 *et seq.*

12. But he still walked on his knuckles, like today's chimpanzees. See *Nature* **404**: 339, 382; 2000. A skull found recently in the Djourab desert of Chad, which has been dated to 6–7 million years ago, belonged to an ape that also probably walked upright. See M. Brunet *et al.*, 'A new hominid from the Upper Miocene of Chad, central Africa', *Nature* **418**: 145–151; 2002.

13. A similar story is told about the origin of the word 'kangaroo', which means 'what is he referring to?'

14. See Maeve Leakey *et al.*, *Nature* **410**: 433–440; 2001.

15. For a discussion of the 'feeding ecology', see Haim Ofek, op. cit. pp 62–83.

16. Whether vegetarian or meat-eater, some 25% of our nutrient intake is channelled towards the brain.

17. For other differences between current humans and chimpanzees, see Chapter 1 and David Cyranoski, 'Almost human ...'. *Nature* **418**: 910–911; 2002.

18. As the German philosopher Immanuel Kant put it in the eighteenth century, 'Die Hand ist das äussere Gehirn des Menschen' (the hand is the exterior brain of man).

19. It was in the autumn of 1855 that Darwin had learnt of Alfred Wallace's hypothesis, 'On the Law Which Has Regulated the Introduction of New Species'. Devastated by this article, Darwin

returned to the opus on which he had been working for the past 18 years with renewed vigour. Two years later he received a letter from Wallace referring to the publication and adding that it was '... of course but preliminary to an attempt at a detailed proof of it, the plan of which I have arranged, and in fact written ...': Irving Stone, op. cit., p 621. It was this missive that finally spurred Darwin on to complete his work (although it took him another 2 years) with the expanded title of *The Origin of Species by Natural Selection, or the Preservation of Favoured Races in the Struggle for Life*. He received a letter from Alfred Wallace a year later, in which it was apparent that he and Darwin had reached similar conclusions.

20. See Eric Trinkaus and Pat Shipman, op. cit., for more details.

21. See Richard Leakey, op. cit., p 131, for more anatomical details; but note that he himself believes that even *H. erectus* was capable of speech.

22. Brain size is estimated by filling the hollow skull with water and measuring the volume: that of a current chimpanzee (and probably also of the common ancestor 8−6 million years ago) is 450 cc; *Australopithecus afarensis* (4−2.5 million years ago) 400−500 cc; *Homo habilis* (2.3 1.6 million years ago) 500 800 cc; *H. erectus* (1.9 million − 300,000 years ago) 750−1250 cc; 'archaic' *H. sapiens* (400,000−100,000 years ago) 1100−1400 cc; 'early' *H. sapiens* (130,000−60,000 years ago) 1200−1700 cc; Cro-Magnon *H. sapiens* (45,000−12,000 years ago) 1300−1600 cc; current *H. sapiens* 1000−2000 cc (mean 1350 cc) [cc = ml]. From Steven Pinker, op. cit., p 198.

23. Note that the vocal cord of females is thinner and shorter than that of males, as a result of which the sounds emitted are higher.

24. Wolfgang Enard *et al* 'Molecular evolution of FOXP2, a gene involved in speech and language'. *Nature* **418**: 869−872; 2002.

25. Because the difference between the power of speech and its lack is so dramatic and therefore likely to involve many mutations.

26. An asparagine instead of a threonine at position 303 along the protein chain, and a serine instead of an asparagine at position 325. Because serine is a favoured site for phosphorylation reactions, like those mentioned in Chapter 3 that are involved in the transmission of signals from the PAS domain of proteins that sense the environment, the consequences of the serine at position 325 (coupled with the lack of a threonine at position 303) may be considerable.

27. Although the overall structure of a protein does determine its function, amino acid differences along the protein chain do not necessarily indicate an altered function: as mentioned in Chapter 2, many mutations are 'silent', meaning that a change in amino acid at that site does not affect the activity of the protein. The fact that the

FOXP2 protein is the same in all healthy human beings, and has not diverged for more than 100,000 years, shows that its efficacy is very sensitive to even the slightest change. Where such mutations have occurred—as in children with speech and language disorder—the consequences are so dramatic that the affected genes do not spread across the human population, but are confined to a few families only; gradually the genes tend to be eliminated, as affected individuals die without progeny.

28. There was considerable debate among scientists whether to embark on the genome of the chimpanzee (because it is our closest relative) or on that of the rhesus macaque (because it is a model for research on human brain function, HIV vaccines, and so forth). The chimpanzee won over the macaque: *Nature* **418**: 910–912; 2002.

29. An approach similar to that used to identify the *FOXP2* gene might yield interesting information regarding the mind of humans and chimpanzees. Autism, for example, has a strong hereditary component and appears to be linked to intellectual abilities that are typically human (see e.g. Christopher Badcock, 'Mentalism and mechanism', in *Human Nature and Social Values: Implications of Evolutionary Psychology for Public Policy*, Charles Crawford and Catherine Salmon (eds), Lawrence Erlbaum, Mahwah, NJ, 2003). Hence, mapping genes that underlie the autistic state should provide dividends not merely for neuropsychiatry, but for anthropology as well.

30. The girl in question is an albino and the gene responsible is known as P or OCA2. See Richard A. Sturm *et al.*, 'Human pigmentation genetics: the difference is only skin-deep', *BioEssays* **20**: 712–721; 1998.

31. S. L. Williams *et al.*, 'Comprehension skills of language-competent and non-language-competent apes', in *Language Commun.* **17**: 301–317; 1997.

32. See **www.koko.org**

33. From H. H. Munro, 'Tobermory', in *Saki*, The Bodley Head, London, 1963.

34. R. L. Cann *et al.*, Mitochondrial DNA and human evolution, *Nature* **325**: 31–36; 1987.

35. Mitochondrial DNA is part of a sub-cellular structure called a mitochondrion. Mitochondria are present in every one of our cells, except the red cells (the same is true for all animals). Mitochondria play a very important role: it is within mitochondria that much of the overall process of respiration (see Note 15 of Chapter 3) is carried out. That is, conversion of the energy contained in food into a form (ATP) that is able to drive all the energy-requiring processes in our body: muscle contraction (which includes the beatings of the heart and the writhings of the intestines), pumping salt across the membranes of

one cell into those of another (which underlies the passage of all nerve impulses) and the synthesis of all internal molecules like DNA, protein, carbohydrate and fat. It is the genes responsible for the synthesis of ATP that lie largely within mitochondria.

36. During the fertilisation of an egg by a sperm, the mitochondria — and hence the mitochondrial DNA — of the sperm are left behind and do not enter the egg. The mitochondria of a newly-fertilised egg are therefore derived solely from the mother, and none from the father. Mitochondrial DNA is therefore inherited only through the female line.

37. It will be recalled that all chromosomes are present in pairs: one inherited from one's mother and one from one's father. In humans for 22 of the chromosomes the pairs are very similar, but for the 23rd pair, called the sex chromosomes, they resemble each other only in females, where they are designated XX. Males possess only one X chromosome; its partner is a different and much shorter chromosome called Y (see Figure 2.3).

38. But as discussed in the next chapter, the most recent large expansion out of Africa seems to have occurred around 100,000 years ago. My guess is that this comprised H. sapiens, and that the Y chromosomal data for the appearance of Adam may need to be revised.

PART II

Domination: the consequences of human quest

CHAPTER FIVE

Out of Africa:
exploration and expansion

'*C*uriosity killed the cat'[1] but for humans it is key to their behaviour: from the first wanderings of man beyond his habitat to the exploration of the planets, from experimenting with a flint stone to transplanting a gene, the quest of man has been driven by an innate curiosity. Look at your 1 year-old son as he probes every item of furniture in the room, every object he can pick up. Listen to your 3 year-old daughter as she incessantly asks you questions: 'why this?', 'why that?'. Can you honestly say that curiosity, expressed through hands and voice and mind, are not at the heart of their development? If inquisitiveness is such a general feature of man's behaviour, is it not then a consequence of the expression of certain genes? Were we too hasty in our assertion that human genes do not exist? I do not believe so. For all we know, a chimpanzee wonders as much as you or I about the world around him. He merely lacks the attributes we have identified—agile hands, power of speech and complicated neural network—to gratify his ponderings.

Migrations of early Homo

Between 1 and 2 million years ago, groups of *Homo* began to explore what lay outside their immediate home in the African bush. Most likely they were *H. erectus*, but we cannot be sure, as *H. erectus* must have co-existed for hundreds of thousands of years with his predecessor *H. habilis* (assuming they were indeed separate species, and not just variants of one another). From the point of illustrating the exploratory drive of our ancestors, though, it does not really matter whether they were *H. habilis* or *H. erectus*. The exact geographical origin of these early groups of *Homo* is not known either, and different bands probably started from different places. Many must surely have originated from the lower parts of the Great Rift Valley, along which the richest finds of hominid activity have been made. The tools nearby their remains were still very primitive: no more than a pointed stone fashioned by scraping one piece against another, a process termed 'flaking' by archaeologists. Only later were such implements inserted into wooden shafts to make primitive axes and spears.

The wanderers must have realised very early on that the fires that occasionally arise from lightning pose no danger provided one keeps at a safe distance. On the contrary, fires drive potential predators away, and cooking the animal one of their group has managed to kill makes it a lot easier to chew and improves its taste. But how to start a fire on one's own? It must have been a chance observation that the sparks produced by flaking can set alight dry sticks and other vegetation. This single act of deliberately starting a fire is one of man's distinguishing characteristics: no chimpanzee has ever lit a fire. As groups of *Homo* wandered further north into Eurasia, the heat generated by the flames of a fire at the entrance to a cave must have become a very welcome addition to the skins of animals they had learned to cast around their bodies: Zhoukoudian (Chou-K'ou-tien) in north-east China can be a cold place in winter.

The roamings of *Homo* did not follow a single route, like those of migrating animals. They were expansions, in the way that a circular ripple created by tossing a stone into a pool of water gradually moves outwards; and like waves in a pool, one expansion followed another, albeit over a time scale of thousands of years. As a group moved to new ground, it may have remained there for centuries or more. Then, perhaps because the members of a community had exhausted the berries and fruit on the bushes and trees in their vicinity, they extended the boundaries of their daily searches for food a little more. *Homo*, as we saw in the last chapter, gradually added scavenging of dead animals, and later hunting, to merely living off the vegetation around him. These people were hunter-gatherers; farming would not be developed until the holocene era 10,000 years ago. Perhaps climatic changes threatened their source of water: the group moved on. Perhaps the danger from predators was less in another region. There is another reason for expanding into new territories. Throughout the animal kingdom there is a never-ending struggle between the leader of a group — generally the strongest, most aggressive male — and young upstarts. If a challenger wins the fight for domination of the group, he takes over. But if he loses? The most probable outcome, from insects to mammals, is that he will move away. Juveniles and young adults are the most likely to be found wandering beyond the periphery of a group. It is such migrants who extend the territories of a species. As the American biologist Edward Wilson puts it, 'The wanderers are the ones most likely to pioneer in new habitats, to experiment with new forms of adaptation, to learn more quickly and to adjust the cultural capacity of the species by genetic assimilation'.[2] If this form of emigration applied to early *Homo*, it would provide an explanation for his expansion.

Gradually the migrants spread across Africa. There are *H. erectus* remains at Ternifine in Algeria, and at Swartkrans in South Afica. But how did they expand north-eastwards into Eurasia? They certainly did not have boats. The construction of a boat requires considerably more technical know-how than was possessed by early *Homo*. The answer is that they did not need boats. The Mediterranean basin had largely dried up during an ice age at this time. When the waters of the Arctic freeze, the sheet of ice that is formed effectively locks up much of the earth's surface water, and levels everywhere fall. Ice ages come and go, because the earth's orbit around the sun is not constant.[3] As a result the earth cools or warms over the millennia; the temperature in the northern hemisphere during successive summers is a particularly important factor in regulating the level of the oceans. The Mediterranean did not refill until around 450,000 years ago, by which time *H. erectus* had walked as far as the eastern shores of Asia. His remains have been found at Ubeidiya in Israel (dated around 1.4 million years ago), in Georgia (a skull dated to be 1.75 million years old makes it the oldest specimen outside Africa), in an area between the Caspian and the Aral Sea, in India at Narmada (perhaps 500,000 years ago), at Zhoukoudian and Lantian in north-east China (Peking Man, 500,000 years ago) and in Java, along the Solo river at Trinil (Java Man, 500,000–750,000 years ago) and at Sangiran and Modjokerto (said to date back more than 1 million years). At that time, the whole of south-east Asia was one large land mass. In a westerly direction he had penetrated as far as Boxgrove in southern England (500,000 years ago, at which time Britain was still linked to Europe), while other remains have been found at Bilzingsleben in Germany (400,000 years old) and Ceprano in Italy (800,000–700,000 years old).

The cerebral functions of *Homo* a million years ago were still limited. He used fire and tools, but most likely could communicate only in grunts and cries. Even such primitive sounds, however, can be made in different ways, to indicate a variety of environmental scenarios. Vervet monkeys that are common throughout Africa make a different warning cry if they see a leopard, an eagle or a snake; their fellows recognise the sound and take appropriate action. We know this because zoologists have recorded the cries of one troop and played them back, unseen, to another troop: at the sound for leopard the second troop will climb a tree, at that for eagle they try to hide in bushes, and at that for snake they stand upright, the better to see the enemy in the grass on the ground. Nevertheless, there was probably little discussion among a group of *Homo* as to when to move, and in what direction. Instead, they just followed their leader. Every community or group has a leader. Among troops of modern apes it is generally the dominant alpha male who leads, although the decision when to move is often taken by a female. With early *Homo* we do not know to what extent the expansion into new territory was the result of male or female influence. In any case, as mentioned earlier, migration may have been triggered by the losers of contests for leadership.

Whatever the migrants were seeking, they moved further away from their habitat than any other primate then, or since. Because no skeletal remains of the forebears of today's chimpanzees have been found, inside or outside Africa, it is not possible to state categorically that such journeys were not made; all we can say is that if they were, they were unsuccessful. I am speaking here of relatively recent events. Over millions of years, during which climatic conditions fluctuated, many animals moved from one location to another and then remained in their new habitat. The motion of continents through tectonic shift that gradually separated the northern land mass (North America and Eurasia) from the southern one (South America, Africa, India, Australia and Antarctica) around 135 million years ago, followed by the dissociation of the southern mass into its present continents and the fusion of India with Asia 70 million years later, means that many fauna and flora became separated. As a result, different species emerged in different locations. Simians are one example: the monkeys of South America (platyrrhines, having a flat nose) are different from Old World monkeys of Africa and Asia (catarrhines, having a dropped nose). Elephants are another: the Indian elephant is distinguished from the African bush elephant in that it is smaller and the females have no tusks. Of course, geographical separation does not need to be as dramatic as that between continents. The two current species of chimpanzee (*P. troglodytes* and *P. paniscus*) both live within central Africa and, as Darwin noted, distinct species of turtles and finches live on the different Galapagos islands. All that is required for a new species of animal (or plant for that matter) to appear is that it should not have an opportunity to mate with other descendants of its ancestor. The point I am making is that the wanderings of *Homo* are not uncommon among animals. What is unique is that early man deliberately expanded out of a favourable, warm climate into one less so: he sought to adapt to colder conditions once he had arrived in central Asia and Europe through his ingenuity, his thirst for quest.

The American economist Haim Ofek thinks that some form of trade may have been taking place among *Homo* as early as 1.5–2 million years ago. By exchanging, perhaps, one type of flint stone for another, unrelated individuals were making contacts that led to mating and an exchange of genes. Such genetic flow, Ofek believes, sets hominids apart from other animals, and explains why, in contrast to his ancestor *Australopithecus*, so few distinct species of *Homo*—a single one for the past 30,000 years—have coexisted at any one time.[4]

The migrations out of Africa all took place, wave after wave, within the last 2 million years. The first probably occurred some 1.7 million years ago, followed by further major expansions around 600,000 (between 420,000 and 840,000) and 100,000 (between 80,000 and 150,000) years ago.[5] By half a million years ago, *Homo* had expanded his territory, albeit sparsely, from less than 10,000 square miles to more than a million square miles. Some of those who reached Europe and the Near East became the ancestors of Neanderthal Man (*H. neanderthalensis*), perhaps by way of Heidelberg Man (*H. heidelbergensis*). Others were living in Asia, or had remained in Africa. None survived. By 30,000 years ago all had died out, and been replaced by the new species of *Homo* that had appeared 140,000 years ago between the Awash valley of Ethiopia and the mouth of the Klasies river in South Africa. At the time that *H. sapiens* was making his way out of Africa, the Mediterranean did constitute a formidable barrier. But it was still feasible to walk across the isthmus at the point where the Red Sea comes close to the Mediterranean (the site of the present Suez Canal); in any case, *H. sapiens* may have been able to construct simple boats.

The story I have told, which is based on a mixture of molecular and fossil evidence, is not universely accepted. Some anthropologists, notably Milford Wolpoff of the University of Michigan in the USA, argue vehemently against it.[6] While agreeing that the earliest form of *Homo* appeared in Africa, they do not accept the evidence that modern man originated entirely in Africa. Instead they postulate an Asiatic and a European origin, in addition to an African one, for the root of today's humans. They do not concede that all the earlier *Homo* species who were living in Asia and Europe died out: on the contrary, they are said to be our direct ancestors. This 'multiregional' hypothesis implies that modern Africans are descended through an African line of *Homo*, with an admixture of Asian and other genes, while modern Asians are descended through an Asian line of *Homo*, with African and other genes thrown in, and modern Europeans are descended through a European line of *Homo*, again with other genes present. The similarity of genetic make-up among all living humans is ascribed to intermingling and interbreeding over more than a million years. The 'solely out of Africa' proponents for the origin of *H. sapiens* agree that descendants of the original *H. erectus* migrants might well have come across other species of *Homo* in Asia and Europe, but disagree in so far as interbreeding with them is concerned. The argument would be resolved if *H. erectus* and *H. sapiens* turn out not to be separate species but merely variants, or if the offspring of different human species were fertile:[7] these are possibilities we cannot now test. I note that the proponents of the multiregional hypothesis are careful not to commit themselves as to precisely which species of *Homo* they are talking about.[8] The latest molecular study,[5] in which genes other than those of mitochondria or the Y chromosome were analysed,[9] points to a situation that encompasses both points of view: all modern humans are largely, but not entirely, of African stock. On the other hand, the molecular evidence that modern Europeans are more closely linked to modern Africans than to *H. neanderthalensis* seems not to be in dispute.

Homo sapiens on the move

One way or another, modern man was in the continents of Africa, Asia and Europe by 50,000 years ago. One of the arguments for multiregionalism is that there was insufficient time for him to have walked from his supposed birthplace in Africa all the way to eastern Asia within some 90,000 years. I do not understand this assertion. After *H. sapiens* crossed from Asia into northern Canada— probably in two waves between 16,000 and 12,000 years ago[10]—it took him little more than 1000 years to expand throughout the Americas: human remains in Patagonia, at the southern tip of South America, have been dated to 10,500 years ago,[11] (although as we shall shortly see, their origin is not without dispute). If man was able to extend his environment by 8000 miles, from northern Canada to southern Chile, within 1000 or so years, why should a similar expansion, out of Africa into Eurasia, not have been feasible during a period 100 times as long?

The kind of life that *H. sapiens* was leading at this time was not so different from that of his *Homo* ancestors. He was still a hunter-gatherer, wearing the skins of animals in northern Europe and

Asia, but probably going about naked in the tropical zones of Africa and southern Asia. It is not clear when modesty in regard to the display of sexual organs appeared. Whenever explorers of the nineteenth and twentieth century came across a community of primitive people who had been isolated from the rest of the world—in Africa, New Guinea or Amazonia—men and women appear to have had their sexual organs covered.[11a] In the case of men, some kind of tie to prevent a dangling penis getting in the way of hunting and other activities, surely preceded a garment worn merely for reasons of delicacy. Modesty may have reached its heights among Europeans during the nineteenth century, but it is disappearing fast. Nudist colonies and total exposure on certain beaches are a feature of our time. Cyclical changes in attire illustrate man's incessant search for novelty.

Where *H. sapiens* differed from earlier species of *Homo* was in the power of speech. The development of a sophisticated vocal cord made it possible for members of a group to converse among themselves. As groups settled and became isolated in the various parts of Africa and Eurasia into which they had expanded, their languages developed into distinct varieties. Unlike technology, which exemplifies a considerable unity of form and function among different peoples, language has remained discrete. It provides a good indication of the extent to which different communities have interacted: throughout much of Eurasia on the one hand (witness the common features of all Indo-European languages), not at all in others (consider the 1000 languages spoken in New Guinea, at least 10 of which have quite distinct roots). It is a subject to which we shall return in Chapter 8.

The settlers in south-east Asia were not all content to remain there. By 50,000–40,000 years ago some had moved on and had reached Australia,[12] and by 30,000 years ago they were in the Solomon Islands. At that time many of the Indonesian islands were still joined together ('Sunda Land'), and New Guinea, Australia and Tasmania were also one land mass ('Sahul'). Nevertheless, some eight sea crossings were necessary to move from the south-eastern tip of the Asian mainland to Sahul. The art of building a simple boat must therefore have been achieved by these voyagers. The crafts were probably canoes made from hollowed tree trunks or animal skins, with every member of the crew using a shaped wooden paddle—much as some of the Polynesian islanders do to this day; or they may have been rafts of logs held together by saplings. The stretches of water they had to cross were not great—the longest was some 54 miles, or twice the width of the English Channel— but it was still a tremendous feat. Remember, these were simple hunter-gatherers, who set off into the sea without any idea of where they were going, for reasons unknown. While the chances of survival by expanding into new territories on land are mixed, those of surviving on the seas in the expectation of reaching land are slim indeed. Of all the explorers who ever lived, the antecedents of the Australian aborigines and of the Solomon Islanders surely showed the greatest fortitude in their quest for venturing into new domains. From this period of history onwards, *H. neanderthalensis* had died out in Eurasia, and *H. sapiens* was the sole human species on earth; I will therefore drop the cumbersome Latin tags and refer to ourselves simply as humans.

Between 16,000 and 12,000 years ago, groups of people whose ancestors had settled in Siberia many thousands of years earlier, and who are grouped together as belonging to the Mongoloid race, began another expansion. They extended their habitat in the direction of the north-eastern tip of Siberia. At that time the most recent ice age was already coming to an end, but Asia and America were still linked by land in this region. From there, groups of Mongoloid people spread into what is now northern Canada, probably in two waves. Within 1000 years or so, the waters of the sea had risen and the land bridge had vanished: turning back would have required boats.[13] Even now, 10,000 years after the ice age, northern Canada is an inhospitable place in winter, so it is not surprising that the settlers there, to whom I shall now refer as Amerindians, soon began to expand southwards. Those who remained in the north are the present Inuits (Eskimo) and Aleuts of Alaska, Canada and Greenland. Others of their kind spread into every one of what are now the United States of America. Here they hunted the woolly mammoth (to extinction): large numbers of stone spearheads capable of mortally wounding a mammoth have been found at many sites. Expansion by these explorers, termed Clovis people by archaeologists,[14] continued into central and southern America. Within 1000 years they had reached Patagonia.

That migration is not the only one that has been proposed for the appearance of man in the Americas. Three additional routes, each involving journeys by boat, have been put forward.[15] One is from eastern Asia into western Canada, hugging the coast lines as much as possible; this migration might have continued all the way down to the western tip of South America. Another postulated coastal journey is from the Iberian peninsula northwards, following the ice sheet and arriving at the eastern edge of Canada. The third (and even more improbable, as it involves the longest journey across open water) is from the eastern shores of Australia right across the southern Pacific to the south western coast of South America. The arguments in favour of these migrations run roughly as follows. First, the stone implements that have been found at some sites are of different shape to those found at other sites; this suggests—at least to some archaeologists—that peoples other than Clovis hunters populated certain parts of the New World. Second, some artifacts at a camp site dating to almost 15,000 years ago have been found at Monte Verde in southern Chile; would Clovis people really have had time to work their way all the way down from Canada to Patagonia in less than 1000 years? They are unlikely to have crossed the Bering land bridge any earlier than 15,000– 16,000 years ago, as it would still have been covered by an ice sheet. Third, the fact that migrants from New Guinea managed to reach Australia by boat 50,000–40,000 years ago shows that man had mastered the art of simple boat building by this time.

It is difficult either to refute or to accept these suppositions, because there is simply not enough evidence. Molecular studies certainly confirm a Mongoloid origin for many present Amerindians, but because of interbreeding over the years, an admixture from small pockets of people who may have originated in western Europe or eastern Australia cannot be ruled out. Since archaeological remains are largely restricted to implements made of stone, alternative modes of life by different groups, such as fishing rather than hunting, are difficult to trace. Some evidence of occupation in southern Greenland has certainly been found, but it seems that this particular group of settlers died out and never made it into America.

The argument about the speed of migration is contentious: Jared Diamond considers 1000 years more than enough time to account for a journey from Alaska to Patagonia. In any case, since travelling along the coast by canoe is faster than hacking one's way through the dense rain forest and along the mountains of central and South America, why could not some of the original migrants from Siberia have done this themselves? They must have developed boats, for there are signs that many of the large rivers in North America were settled on both banks. So far as the thrust of my main argument is concerned, such speculations only strengthen it: wherever man has found himself, his curiosity about what lies beyond, and his search for the technology to take him there, has resulted in migrations across the entire globe.

At the other end of the world, in south-east Asia, seafarers were on the move once more. The islands of the Pacific began to be settled by people of Asiatic origin. By 3600 years ago they were in Fiji (2000 miles south-east of New Guinea), 2000 years later in Hawaii (3000 miles north-east of Fiji), and by 1000 years ago in New Zealand (1500 miles south of Fiji). A few millennia is not a long time for racial characteristics to change, and Hawaiians, Fijians and New Zealand Maoris are all rather closely related. Until the molecular evidence of mitochondrial DNA was worked out, it was thought that the inhabitants of the Cook Islands and Tahiti, to the east of Fiji, not to mention those of Easter Island that is situated even further east, arrived from South America, not from south-east Asia. Easter Island, named by a Dutch explorer called Roggeveen because he found it on Easter Day 1722, lies only 2500 miles off the west coast of Chile, whereas it is double that distance from Fiji and five times as far from the mainland of south-east Asia. Since the Norwegian anthropologist Thor Heyerdahl had shown that it is possible to sail a small raft, his *Kon-Tiki*, some 6000 miles in a westerly direction from the west coast of the South American mainland (Peru to Tahiti), it was naturally assumed that this was the direction from which the Easter Islanders had come.

No-one thought that these people were clever enough to have sailed more than 10,000 miles against the prevailing wind. Their folly in using up all their natural resources, including the trees on which they depended for the construction of boats in which they might have left the island to seek a new life elsewhere (or at least used to provide food by fishing), and that decimated their numbers almost to the point of extinction by the eighteenth century, was surely proof enough. But sail across the entire Pacfic Ocean is precisely what they did. For the Oxford geneticist Bryan Sykes has analysed the mitochondrial DNA of the islanders: like the DNA of the other Polynesian settlers, it resembles that of south-east Asians, not that of present day Amerindians in South America (or Central and North America, for that matter).[16] Since mitochondrial DNA traces only the relationship between females,[17] it is possible that a group consisting solely of male Amerindians made the journey westward from Chile or Peru (but how, then, did the womenfolk get there?). Sykes has ruled out this situation, at least as far as the Cook Islands are concerned, by analysing DNA within the Y chromosome. Although there is an admixture of European Y chromosomes—the islands were after all explored by Captain James Cook during the 1770s and have been visited by Europeans ever since—the predominant lineage is of south-east Asian origin, with no trace of Amerindian ancestry. Thus can molecular biology quickly answer questions that have kept anthropologists and historians arguing with one another for centuries. Easter Islanders were clever for another reason. Their island is famous for the 10 metre high statues of human heads, lined up along one of its shores. How the original inhabitants, using only primitive tools, managed to carve these enormous statues—never mind transport them several miles and erect them on to pedestals—is amazing; the techniques they used elude us to this day.

By 1000 years ago, the early migrations of humans had largely ended. Wherever he settled, man generally stayed. There was little interchange between one group and another, and over time the racial characteristics—like the languages—of different groupings developed. The fact that the present inhabitants of Europe, the Middle East and North Africa are genetically, as well as linguistically and culturally, related shows that in this region there *has* been much movement and interbreeding. I referred in Chapter 2 to the fact that DNA is continually changing slightly as a result of random mutations; the way that mitochondrial DNA and the DNA of the Y chromosome can be used to trace human populations bears this out. There is also a high variability among the genes, and hence among the proteins, within the immune system.[18] Another set of proteins, functionally part of the immune system, shows a similar degree of variability. In this instance it is a person-to-person variation, rather than a 'recognition of one foreign molecule versus another' variation within the same individual. Among the proteins that underlie the person-to-person variability are molecules (called human leukocyte antigens, or HLA) that have a slightly different structure in every individual except identical twins. This is the system that is responsible for the rejection of a skin or organ graft from all but the most closely related. It is the system that gives us much of our individuality and it underlies our relative resistance, or susceptibility, to different diseases.

Mutations within the HLA system provide a plethora of different molecules that characterise not only individuals but also racial groupings. One version of a particular protein may prove to be of advantage in one type of climate, another version is advantagious in a different one; one variant of a protein offers protection against an infectious disease that may be prevalent in one area, another variant protects against a pathogenic microbe present elsewhere. Over time, people possessed of the favourable molecular configurations will outbreed the others, and their descendants will bear those molecules for many generations. Having mentioned the advantages of possessing one or other type of protein molecule, and therefore the gene to maintain its production in our offspring, I must reiterate an earlier point: many molecules, like those involved in the formation of the appendix, are simply there: they are neither beneficial nor detrimental. What benefit they might offer relates to a much earlier period of human, or indeed mammalian, life.

Modern explorers

Conquerors and navigators

The exploratory spirit of man did not die out 50,000 or 1000 years ago. As civilisations developed in some parts of the world but not in others—a topic examined in the following chapter—their rulers wished to know what lay beyond their boundaries. Expeditions were sent out and these often reported the presence of a foreign community. Depending on the warlike nature of the ruler, he would dispatch an army in order to conquer his neighbours and extend his territory into theirs. Alternatively, he might merely widen his economic base through new trading partners. Both types of expansion are a recurring theme in the history of man.

In the case of Alexander the Great in the second half of the fourth century BC, for example, the first aim was to reclaim the land taken by the Persians in Anatolia (now Turkey). Next, he enlarged the Greek Empire by defeating the Persians in Egypt, Syria and Mesopotamia (now Iraq). After that, his goal was to capture the elusive Persian king, Darius III, himself. Alexander entered Persia and took Persepolis, the ancient capital of Xerxes. He burned the palace and the rest of the city—the most cultivated and magnificent in the world at that time—to the ground, ostensibly in order to avenge the earlier defeats of the Greeks by the Persians. It was an act of desecration that sits uneasily with Greek values of civilised behaviour. He had no need to seize Darius: the Persian king had been deposed, then stabbed to death, by one of his own men. Alexander was now ruler of the largest empire in the world: 'Great King' and 'Lord of Asia'. Yet he pressed on, heading for central Asia. From this stage, Alexander became more the explorer than the general: half the time he did not know where he was going. Nevertheless, he expanded the territory of the Greeks eastward as far as the Punjab, a distance of 2500 miles. He spent 11 years on his campaigns, virtually his entire reign. He led an army of whom most had marched all the way on foot. But like subsequent leaders—Napoleon in 1812 and Hitler's generals in 1941 during their respective attempts to conquer Russia—he had overstretched himself. Land that is taken by force tends to revert back to the original inhabitants. It is for that reason that the cultural and linguistic characteristics of a people often survive periods of domination by a foreign power. Alexander did not live to see his empire crumble. He did not even make it back to Greece. On his way home he died of a fever—probably typhus—in Babylon. He was just 33 years of age.

If the sea-going peoples of south-east Asia 50,000 years ago were the greatest explorers of their day, Christopher Columbus, or Cristobal Colon as he liked to be called, was one of the most persistent of modern times. Believing what he had read—in the apocryphal biblical Second Book of Esdras, in the writings of Ptolemy[19] and the contemporary Florentine cosmographer Paolo Toscanelli—that the earth is actually round, not flat, and that the land distance from the western edge of the world (Spain) to the eastern edge (the Indies and Cathay) is very long, this Spanish sailor of Genoese origin argued that the distance from Spain to Asia in a westerly direction must therefore be relatively short: 3900 miles from the Canaries, according to his calculations (he was not far out: the distance across the Atlantic at the point of his crossing is indeed around 4000 miles). By sailing west instead of east, one should arrive at the fabled lands that Marco Polo had been able to reach only after a long overland journey across central Asia 200 years earlier. Columbus was searching for something else as well: the mythical island of Antillia—called Atlantis by Plato and described by him as the oldest civilisation on earth—that was said to lie 'beyond the Pillars of Hercules' (the Straits of Gibraltar), in other words straight in Columbus' path.

He badgered the King of Portugal, the Duque de Medina-Sidonia, the Conde de Medina Celi and the rulers of Spain, King Ferdinand and Queen Isabella, for funds. All refused. Columbus was a driven man: after 6 years of pleading with the Spanish royal couple, he managed to persuade them to change their minds. On 3 August 1492 he set off (Plate 1). We all know that Columbus made landfall not in Asia, but in America; he, of course, believed that he had reached the Indies. The island of Antillia—thought to be as large as the continent of Europe—he did not find either. But in honour of his quest, some of the islands of the Caribbean have been termed the Antilles. What is less well known is that Columbus was not the first European to find the Americas.

The Vikings had been there 500 years earlier. They too had set off—in this case from the fjords of Norway—in a westerly direction. What they were looking for is not clear: were their fishing grounds being depleted, or were they escaping taxes—against which their fellow Europeans were to rebel in New England 700 years later?

Erik the Red landed in Greenland in 982, having been banished from Iceland for murder; he tried to encourage others to follow him by naming the new country 'green land' (which apart from the coastal areas in the south, is something of an overstatement). By the eleventh century Leif Erikson had brought Christianity from Norway to Greenland, and other Norsemen made it as far as the mainland of Canada. A site near present-day L'Anse-aux-Meadows on the northern peninsula of Newfoundland was established: the first Europeans had landed on American soil. However they left no lasting settlements. Neither, for that matter, did the colonists of Greenland, even though they had come into contact with indigenous Thule Inuits and had gone so far as to establish a bishopric in 1126. The conditions close to the Arctic Circle proved just too harsh for these men of European blood: they probably all perished from lack of food and shelter. Several thousand miles further south the climate was more equable, and the Spaniards lived to tell of their discoveries.

These began not on the mainland, but on the islands of the Caribbean. Although they subsequently turned out not to be in Asia, the entire region has been called the West Indies as a mark of Columbus' belief. It is a measure of his perseverance that he reached land at all. After being at sea for 2 months, the expedition was beginning to run low on food and water. Morale was sapping. His lieutenants on the three ships that made up his small fleet—the *Santa Maria*, the *Nina* and the *Pinta*—begged him to change course and return to Europe. Columbus refused. His tenacity was rewarded within a matter of weeks: he made landfall on an island which he appropriately named San Salvador. He continued in a south-westerly direction and reached the northern shore of Cuba (which he thought was Japan, then called Cipango). He changed direction and veered eastwards, landing on an island that he called Española or Hispaniola (now Haiti and the Dominican Republic). By this time his main vessel, the *Santa Maria*, had run aground and been abandoned. A detachment of men was left behind on Española while Columbus returned to Spain early in 1493 on the *Nina*, accompanied by the *Pinta*. His welcome was ecstatic.

Nevertheless, he did not dally and in October of that year sailed westwards once more: the spirit of quest—for no reason save curiosity and the discovery of a new trade route with Cathay — was in his blood. He discovered and named Guadalupe (Guadeloupe) and then Puerto Rico on his way to Española. There he found that his men had been massacred; he moved to another site and established the town of Isabella, the first European city of the Americas. He sailed west and now reached the southern coast of Cuba, which he took to be the mainland of Asia. Turning south he reached another island, which he named Santiago (later Jamaica). Eventually he returned to Spain, now on the first ship ever built in the Americas. His reception was not quite as enthusiastic as he had hoped, and by 1498 he was off again. This time he took a more southerly route and made land at the island he called Trinidad. The mouth of the river that lay to his port, he later assured his backers, was the delta of the Ganges (it was the basin of the Orinoco in Venezuela). On his return to Española, things started going seriously wrong. The men mutinied and Columbus was arrested by Francisco Bobadilla, sent out by Ferdinand and Isabella to sort out problems in what was by now called the New World (Mundus Novus): King Ferdinand and Queen Isabella had come to the conclusion that Columbus was a great admiral but a poor governor. This time Columbus returned to Spain in chains.

Undeterred, he managed to recover some of his dignity and departed yet once more in 1502. From Española he sailed to Santiago, then veered south-west and sighted land in what is now Honduras. He followed the coast all the way south to Panama ('Mango' province), where he founded the town of Belen (Bethlehem). There he left his brother Bartolome with a contingent of 80 men. He himself turned north for Española and by 1504 was back in Spain. Now 53 years of age and racked with arthritis, Cristobal was a truly disappointed man: he had not received the honours or the wealth that he felt was due to him. Two years later, in Valladolid, he died. To the end he believed that he had found the western route to the Indies (and were it not for the narrow strip of land that connects the continents of north and South America he might well have been successful). It was his compatriots who had grown sceptical. They did, however, honour his discovery by transferring his bones to Española, where they lie in the Cathedral of Santo Domingo to this day.

Columbus may have been the most inquisitive and persistent navigator of the modern era, but he was by no means the earliest. The Portuguese had started exploring the coast of Africa almost a century before, in 1418, while at the other end of the world a Chinese admiral, one Zheng He, was searching the eastern oceans for new lands with which to trade.[20] What Columbus' exploits epitomize are the determination and tenacity of some men to find what they are looking for against all odds. Such journeys show that the search for new horizons needs to be accompanied by a lot of guts, a human quality I have so far not emphasised; the necessity for bravery applies, of course, to all explorers before or since, on land as well as on sea. In so far as bravery depends not on higher cerebral functions—some might argue the opposite—nor on the use of a voice box or manual dexterity, it falls outside the qualities I have identified as typically human. Are chimpanzees ever brave? I leave that to the ethologists to argue over.

Is bravery allied to a search for something? Sometimes. Those who believe in an afterlife, and strive to attain it in paradise rather than in hell, often commit acts of bravery out of choice. They seek eternal redemption for their earthly sins. Religious martyrs across the centuries have faced torture, dismemberment, burning, beheading and hanging for adhering to their creed. But others commit acts of bravery without seeking spiritual reward. What was the motivation behind those in The Netherlands and France who sheltered Jewish children and Allied airmen from the Nazis during the 1940s? They were ordinary men and women who acted simply out of compassion, despite the knowledge that if they were caught—as many were—they would face torture and death. Their actions define the extent of what we term humanity. And yet risking one's life to protect another, including of course one's own family, is something that we share with other animals: altruism is not a uniquely human quality. Indeed, it is difficult to discern a truly genetic benefit of altruism among humans[21] at all. In common with many animals,[22] our altruism is sometimes expressed by devoting resources to relatives like grandparents. Well past child-bearing age themselves, they nurture their grandchildren to breeding age and thus ensure the continuity of the line; scientists use this argument to explain longevity (living beyond the age by which one's own children still require attention) as well as the genetic profit of altruism. If bravery in humans is sometimes driven by spiritual aspirations, the opposite, cowardice, at times underlies material pursuits: in men who use others to do dangerous work for them in order to gain riches. Acquisitiveness is surely a facet of quest, as the word implies, and I return to the subject of wealth in Chapter 9. So far as courage is concerned, its possession defines the extent of our inquisitiveness. Like other qualities — the degree of a person's intellectual prowess, for example — valour merely modulates the outcome: it is not an essential ingredient of quest.

The name of Columbus is associated with places not just in Central America, but with towns and rivers — even a university — within the USA. Recently, some native Americans objected to this veneration of a man they consider a usurper of their lands. Their anger and the use of Columbus' name are equally misplaced: so far as we know, Columbus never even sighted the coastline of North America, let alone set foot upon it. It was another Spaniard, Juan Ponce de Leon, who did so in 1513: he named the land Florida, to reflect his discovery during the Easter celebrations (Pascua Florida) and the fact that the countryside was indeed lush with floral vegetation on account of the tropical rains. Ponce de Leon had landed on the eastern shore near a spot that subsequently grew into a useful port. The French established a settlement in the area, but in 1565 were thrown out by the Spaniards, who now founded a proper town on the site of the harbour: they called it San Augustin. Although this is the oldest city in the USA, it is the French name, St Augustine, that has stuck.

Another small army of Spaniards had arrived in 1528. Their goal was not to settle the land. Like most explorers of the Americas at this time, their aim was to find gold. Starting from Cuba, they sailed up the west coast of Florida. A group of men was dropped off to begin the search. They wandered into the swamps and made contact with the Seminole Indians, who are there to this day; they did not come across their compatriots, who were living many miles away across the other side of the peninsula. Neither did they find gold. Suffering from fever and attacked by alligators, they moved north to the rendezvous with their boats, near present-day Tallahassie. A further set-back: the fleet had sailed off without them. The land group, now down to 300 men and led by one Cabeza de Vaca, decided to try to reach Mexico, which they thought was relatively close. They built small boats and set off into the turbulent waters of the Gulf of Mexico. After 6 weeks at sea, during which most perished, the remainder made land on what proved to be an island: they had reached not Mexico but Galveston Island off Texas. The local Carrangua Indians were not unfriendly and the survivors stayed for several years. By this time, Cabeza de Vaca had lost all but three of his men: most had perished to disease, as had the Carranguas. Lacking any immunity against infections brought by the Europeans, the entire tribe died out over the following two centuries. Indeed, of the 5 million Amerindians living in North America, Mexico and the Caribbean islands at the end of the fifteenth century (some put the figure two to five times higher), most succumbed to the microbes, not the bullets, of the invaders: 95% of the Aztecs were killed by measles and smallpox alone. In South America the situation was the same; it continues to this day, as eager but foolish researchers try to 'improve' the lives of isolated Amerindians living in the Amazonian rain forest.

On the shores of Texas in 1530, Cabeza de Vaca and his companions were learning the language of the Carranguas and following their life styles. Combining his Christianity with the beliefs of the Indians, Cabeza de Vaca had become a kind of shaman who preached to his neighbours and tried to cure their diseases. But he had not given up on his original quest. Eventually he and his comrades left, walking in a south-westerly direction, looking for gold. They reached the highlands of northern Mexico and found iron-containing minerals—pyrites or fools' gold—which the local Indians, settled in villages and towns, were smelting. Cabeza de Vaca may have had the 'head of a cow' but he had the stubbornness of an ox: he was after gold and he meant to find it. Turning northwards along tracks that had probably been followed by the original migrants coming down from Alaska 10,000 years earlier, the group eventually found themselves walking along paths strewn with shells. They followed these westwards until they were within sight of the sea: they had walked more than 2000 miles across the southern part of North America, the earliest Europeans to have traversed the continent.

Before they could take their first dip in the ocean for almost 5 years, they were set upon by a patrol of Spaniards who mistook them for natives and were about to shoot them down on sight: Cabeza de Vaca and his men had reached European civilisation. On his eventual return to Spain, Cabeza de Vaca wrote an account of his travels. He tried to persuade the authorities to change their attitude to the Indians and to treat them as ordinary human beings, but he failed in this, as he had done in his search for gold: Cabeza de Vaca died a pauper.

Apart from the settlements in Florida, Europeans did not colonise North America during the sixteenth century. In Central and South America[23] the picture was different. Hernando Cortés landed in Mexico in 1519, and Francisco Pizarro in Panama in 1531. These conquistadors were, as the name given to them implies, much more than explorers: their aim was to steal the land from its inhabitants in the name of Christendom and bring back gold. 'I and my colleagues have a disease of the heart which can be cured only by gold', Cortés explained to Montezuma.[24] He defeated the Aztecs in Mexico, Pizarro the Incas in Peru. If the natives were prepared to convert to Catholicism, they might be spared; if not they were slaughtered.

The conquerors considered themselves missionaries, although the resemblance to true followers of God is difficult to see. Missionaries like St Augustine, sent by Pope Gregory in 596 to convert the English to Christianity, or Albert Schweitzer, who established a mission hospital for lepers and other diseased natives in Lambarene in French Equatorial Africa (now Gabon) in 1913, or Mother Theresa, who founded the Order of Missionaries of Charity for the destitute and dying in Calcutta in 1948, do not engage in bloodshed; moreover, in the last two cases their quest did not involve religious conversion at all. Genuine missionaries seek to help others, materially as well as spiritually. They seek to better human lives, not to destroy them.

Throughout the sixteenth century, seafaring explorers from the Iberian peninsula continued to delineate the coastlines of the continents. The southern coast of Africa was explored by the Portuguese navigator, Vasco da Gama, in 1497, although another Portuguese sailor, Bartolomeu Dias, had sighted the high promontory of Table Mountain near the southern extremity before him in 1488. Dias named it the Cape of Storms (which it certainly is), but the name was subsequently changed to a more optimistic one: Cape of Good Hope.[25] Nine years later Dias accompanied da Gama on his more thorough expedition. On the other side of the Atlantic, Ferdinand Magellan, a Portuguese in the service of Spain, sailed through the archipelago of Tierra del Fuego (land of fire) that is situated at the southern tip of the American continent in 1519; the waters through which he steered now bear his name. Magellan became the first European to sail across the Pacific—the Polynesians, of course, had traversed much of it from the opposite direction several thousand years earlier—and eventually made land in the Philippines in 1521 (named after Prince Philip of Spain, later Philip II). In contrast to the conquistadors who followed Columbus to the Americas, Magellan's quest was neither for land nor for gold. He was searching for a commodity of equal value that was known to be found only on a small group of islands in the east: spices. Previous Portuguese explorers had reached the Molucca islands, which had become fabled for their content of nutmeg, cloves and pepper, by sailing around Africa and eastwards across the Indian ocean. Magellan, like Columbus, was convinced that a shorter route to the Indies could be found by sailing westwards: in his case, he found it (although it proved to be considerably longer). Magellan was killed in a skirmish with natives on the Philippine island of Mactan, but the survivors of his expedition made it to the Spice Islands, loaded up with nutmeg and cloves, cinnamon and mace, and managed to return to Spain. Their voyage represents the first-ever circumnavigation of the globe. This, as much as anything else, was the final proof that the earth is indeed round, not flat.

The sixteenth century, then, was one of exploration. Long before its close, pretty accurate maps of the coast line in most parts of the world had been drawn. The Flemish cartographer Gerardus Mercator,[26] living in Germany, produced such a map in 1569. Although it showed the lines of longitude as parallel to one another, which of course they are not, this depiction was useful to navigators, as compass lines—like due north—are indeed straight lines. Parts of Mercator's map were accurate due more to guesswork than to factual information: he anticipated the existence of the

Bering Straits between Asia and America by almost 200 years. We probably owe to Mercator the very word 'Atlas' (taken from the name given by the Greeks to one of their mythological giants): he used it as the title for his maps of part of Europe in 1585.

Among those who sought a new route to the Spice Islands was a particularly persistent English navigator named Henry Hudson. His first attempt was to sail due north, and in 1607 he got to within ten degrees of the north pole, where he thought the waters would suddenly become warmer: they did not, and he was forced back by ice. Knowing of his arctic exploits, the Dutch East India Company commissioned Hudson to find the 'North East Passage' that they and their English counterparts were sure would cut thousands of miles off the lengthy journey around Africa. Previous attempts, including one by Hudson himself, had got no further than Novaya Zemlya on the northern coast of Russia, but the Directors of the Company felt that Hudson's perseverance and knowledge of arctic waters would lead to a successful outcome. The expedition finally set off in 1609. What his backers did not know was that Hudson had no intention of sailing eastwards at all. His aim was to find the 'North West Passage', not the eastern one. He reached the west coast of Nova Scotia, but icy winds and snow, not to mention a rebellious crew, made him turn southwards. He sailed past Cape Cod and reached the wide opening near the island called 'Manna-hata' by the natives, that a navigator named Giovanni da Verrazano had sighted almost a century earlier. This waterway, Hudson felt, would lead him to the Pacific ocean and thence to the Spice Islands. Alas, it was not to be. He sailed up the broad waters as far as present day Albany, but at this point realised that he was merely progressing up a river that was leading nowhere. Reluctantly he turned back. Had he known that subsequent inhabitants of these shores would name the river after him, he would not have been consoled: his goal was to find a westerly route to the Pacific, not leave his name to posterity. Aware that his Dutch paymasters might not be too pleased with his results,[27] he returned not to Amsterdam but to London. From here he set off once more in search of the North West Passage, this time with backing from the English King James I. He sailed past Newfoundland, through the strait between Baffin Island and the northern shore of Quebec, and into the bay that now—together with the strait—also bear his name. It was snowing hard and once more there was trouble on board. Two members of the crew seized Hudson, forcing him and seven of his supporters into a small boat without provisions. They were then set adrift. Henry Hudson was never seen again.

Most of the English and the French who set out to explore North America in the seventeenth century did not behave so differently from their Spanish predecessors in Central and South America: any attempts by the local inhabitants to resist appropriation of the land on which the newcomers had set their sights were brutally crushed. This was not true of the Pilgrim Fathers, who had left England in 1620 to *escape* religious persecution.[28] They sailed from Plymouth for Virginia, which had been settled by Europeans in 1607, but because they left without maritime maps, they landed over 400 miles further north at Cape Cod in Massachusetts. From that day on Bostonians and other New Englanders have prided themselves on their liberal attitude towards ethnic minorities like American Indians and the less well off. Francis Cabot founded the world's first textile mill at the beginning of the nineteenth century and, in contrast to the factories of Lancashire and Scotland, the working conditions were exemplary. Other Cabots used their wealth to promote institutions like the Massachusetts General Hospital and the Boston Symphony Orchestra. The Lowells[29] were a similarly philanthropic family, but the rest were less altruistic. Well over half of the 1.5 million native Americans who at the beginning of the seventeenth century were living across what is now Canada and the USA, died at the hands of the new settlers: the English and French from Europe, the Spanish from Mexico.

Contemporary heroes

Once the outline of the continents had been delineated by European (and Chinese[20]) explorers, and the interiors colonised through conquest by their equally adventurous compatriots, human quest took on more chivalric overtones. Men searched not merely for new sea routes, for precious metals or for new territories in which to settle, but because any part of the world where they had not been—the more inaccessible the better—became a challenge. We begin with the frozen wasteland of the polar ice caps, and end on the even less hospitable surface of the moon.

The difficulty of reaching the North Pole is two-fold: it is many miles away from the nearest point approachable by boat, and the snow melts into pools of water that make the going by sledge tricky. There is also the danger of the ice near the edge melting and cracking away. All this is in summer; no one has been foolish enough to attempt the quest in winter, when the temperature can plunge to −70°C and it is dark for 24 hours of the day. The American naval officer Robert Peary was not deterred. He made eight Arctic voyages, and on his ninth he succeeded. Pulled by a team of dogs, he and his American companion Matthew Henson claimed to have reached the pole on 6 April 1909: the first men to do so. I am talking here of the geographic North Pole. The magnetic north pole, to which all compasses point, is over 300 miles to the south-west in the Canadian Arctic, and would not be reached until 1926, by Richard Byrd, another American, in an aeroplane and by the Norwegian explorer Roald Amundsen in a dirigible.

The South Pole offers a different challenge. It is even further away from a navigable approach and is 9816 ft (2922 m) above sea level, making the ascent through huge boulders of ice, especially with a team of dogs, an arduous one. Undaunted, Amundsen attempted it. He succeeded on 14 December 1911. A British expedition led by Robert Scott, that had started out the previous year, reached the pole in January 1912, just one month behind Amundsen. You can imagine their dejection.[30] Worse was to follow. Violent storms beset the return journey and their food had just about run out. All five members of the expedition perished.[31] A search party sent out from their base ship *Discovery* found their remains 8 months later. Among the diaries that were recovered was a series of beautiful watercolour sketches painted by the expedition's doctor, Edward Wilson.[32]

The highest mountain in the world, at 29,028 ft (8848 m), is a natural challenge to man. For one, the air is so thin that it is difficult to reach it without a supply of oxygen (although it has been done); for another, steep rock faces, large ice fields and deep crevasses make the going onerous and dangerous. Situated on the border between Nepal and China, Sagarmatha (Nepalese) or

Qomolangma (Chinese) is known to Europeans by the name of the surveyor-general of India in the nineteenth century, Sir George Everest. Attempts to scale it by parties during the first half of the twentieth century all failed. In the spring of 1953 a British party led by Colonel John Hunt succeeded. Two of the team, the New Zealander Edmund Hillary and the Nepalese sherpa Tenzing Norgay, stood on the summit on the 29 May 1953. Four days later a new head of the British Commonwealth was crowned, and the scaling of Everest seemed to mark the beginning of a new Elizabethan age of exploration. The only problem was that there was nothing left to discover. The British consoled themselves with being the first to circumnavigate the world single-handed (Francis Chichester in *Gypsy Moth IV* in 1967) and the first to do so largely on foot (Ranulph Fiennes and Charles Burton between 1979 and 1982[33]).

The Russians and the Americans had loftier goals. The Soviet Union led the way into space in 1957 with the launch of *Sputnik 1* into an orbit around the earth; the USA followed it with *Explorer 1* in 1958. The Russians were first on the scene again in 1961 when Yuri Gagarin became the first man in space. He was less successful nearer the ground and he died while testing an aeroplane some years later. In 1962 John Glenn was blasted off into space; he was luckier than Yuri Gagarin, and was able to repeat his astronautical experience some three decades on. The real goal, of course, was a manned landing on the moon. One should not underestimate the technical achievements involved. First, to blast a space capsule safely into the atmosphere; well, the Russians had shown it could be done, and the Americans had repeated the feat. Then, however, to accurately pin-point the target 240,000 miles away and gently land a lunar module, while leaving the command module in orbit around the moon. And that is just to get there. By 1969 they were ready, and three astronauts were blasted into space. On arrival near the surface of the moon, Michael Collins remained on board the command vehicle, while Neil Armstrong and Edwin (Buzz) Aldrin landed in the lunar module (Plate 1). They carried out their allotted tasks, which included picking up pieces of rock for subsequent analysis: this proved the moon to be about the same age (4.3 billion years) as the earth (4.6 billion years). Further experiments showed that seismic tremors occur, similar to those on earth. Apart from being about an eightieth of the mass of the earth, and the pull of gravity at the surface therefore being only a sixth, it would seem that there is but one significant difference between moon and earth: the lack of any life whatsoever. With no water and temperatures varying between 100 °C during the lunar day and −200 °C at night, none of the molecular interactions that constitute living organisms on earth are able to take place. It is only because the earth has been surrounded for the past 4 billion years by an atmosphere of gases that insulate its surface against diurnal extremes of temperature that life here ever took off.[34] Armstrong and Aldrin climbed back into the module; would the rockets needed to propel them off the surface of the moon ignite? If not, they were doomed to a rapid death once their oxygen supplies had run out, and the falling temperature during the lunar night froze them to death. American technology prevailed: the first men on the moon were able to rejoin their colleague and make it safely back to earth. I asked Buzz Aldrin recently whether that mission had really represented the most memorable moment of his entire life: 'without a shadow of doubt' was the instantaneous reply.

Recent migrations

Let me end this short narrative of human quest and conquest where I began: with an account of man's migratory instinct. Four examples, each illustrating the movement of a cohesive group of people in recent times, will suffice.

The gypsies, so called because of the mistaken impression that they hail from Egypt, actually originated in northern India. Their language—Romany, a name by which they are also known because of their long sojourn in Romania—is derived from Sanskrit and therefore falls within the Indo-European group of tongues. They are essentially nomadic, and have moved gradually westwards into Europe and North Africa; some have even made it into North and South America. They probably began their wanderings as camp followers to Indian armies: the crafts that they practice to this day, namely horse-trading, metal-working, basket-weaving and wood-carving, would have been useful to an army on the march. And then there is their music. Influenced by Moorish dancing, itself derived from that of northern India, the gypsies of fifteenth century Spain developed the mournful yet defiant style that has come to be known as flamenco (meaning Flemish, another misnomer). They had reason to be sad. Together with the Moors, they were persecuted relentlessly by 'their most Catholic majesties', Ferdinand II and Isabella I of Spain. Oppression has marked the travels of gypsies throughout most of their history: the Nazis managed to exterminate half a million between 1933 and 1945, and since then they have been hounded in countries like Romania, first by President Ceaucescou and then by his successors. And yet they have maintained their identity: dispersal across the continents has not diminished their values of brotherhood. Like the other groups I shall discuss, they seek merely to be allowed to go about their traditional ways.

In the seventeenth century a group of Dutch farmers decided to emigrate to southern Africa in order to escape the religious persecution they were experiencing at home: they were adherents of the strongly-reformist and Protestant faith named after John Calvin, the French theologian who had founded the Presbyterian movement in Geneva in the middle of the previous century. The Boers, as they came to be known (the word is Dutch for farmers), settled on the east coast of what is now South Africa in 1652. Later they were joined by Calvinists from Germany and France, although their language—Afrikaans—has remained essentially Dutch. At first the Boers intermarried with the native Khoikoin (or Hottentots); subsequently they forced them off their land and employed them only as labourers. In the 1830s a group of Afrikaners, as the Boers had become known, set off on another migration, north into the interior: their aim was to escape the interfering British who had established a colony in the same area, then known as the Cape Colony, in 1806. During this Great Trek, they did not hesitate to massacre any natives in their way: 3000 Zulus lost their lives at the Battle of Blood River. The migrants reached the Transvaal, where the capital Pretoria was eventually established by Marthinus Pretorius. Some battles against the British were won, but others were lost, notably the second Boer War in 1902. The antipathy of the Afrikaners to those of other origins living in their midst continued. At the height of their xenophobia, following the election of the right-wing National Party in 1948, the Afrikaners discriminated against all non-whites with a truly religious zeal. Yet to this day, most Afrikaners remain devout Christians. From persecuted to persecutor,[35] they continue to retain some of the bonds and values that have united them over a period of 350 years.

In 1830 one Joseph Smith founded the Church of Jesus Christ of Latter-Day Saints in New York. Smith was inspired by divine revelation and claimed to have found the lost Book of Mormons, that descibes the migration of a group of Hebrews into North America some 600 years before the birth of Christ. His followers, the Mormons, consider themselves to be heirs to that group of people. Smith also preached polygamy as a way of life.[36] In 1847 his successor as leader, Brigham Young,[37] decided to move their base westwards in search of their own Zion. Five thousand Mormons followed him on a trek across hundreds of miles of largely unexplored territory. When the expedition arrived at a large salt lake in what is now Utah, Young knew that he had found the spiritual home of the Mormons. He built a great church that has remained their central place of worship. The Mormons are a devout sect, now spread across much of the American continent and beyond: there are said to be over 5 million members of the Church in the USA alone, with an equivalent number abroad. They practise what they preach (they have no clergy): helping one another, donating a proportion of their income to the Church (as high as 15%), and missionary work. Many other movements—the Church of Christ Scientist, established by Mary Baker Eddy in Boston in 1879 is but one example—have sprung up in the USA: its relaxed atmosphere to innovative ideas provides fertile ground for the cultivation of religious sects.

The State of Israel was founded in 1948. Zionists had sought to establish a homeland for Jews for many years, and had been partially successful in 1917, when the Balfour Declaration decreed Palestine to be the Jewish national home. I say 'partially' because Palestine was a mandate under overall British rule for the following 30 years. Millions of Jews (4.5 million between 1948 and 1994) have migrated to Israel. Their reason is not religious fervour, neither is it predominantly to avoid persecution, although for those emigrating from Europe, oppression has certainly been the major stimulus. The common cause of the migration is something else: the desire for a sense of identity, of belonging; for a life in which a Jew can honestly say that he is living in *his* country. The quest of these people has not been without hardship: often relinquishing well-paid jobs in comfortable surroundings in order to begin life as a farm labourer, as a conscript in an army on a war footing, as a civilian facing the threat of a bomb on a daily basis. In common with gypsies, Jews too were persecuted by Ferdinand and Isabella and suffered extermination at the hands of the Nazis in Europe (6 million died).

I could have chosen other examples of modern migrants—the Huguenots, who were persecuted on and off throughout the sixteenth and seventeenth century by their French masters because of their adherence to Protestantism; the million Irish who left their homeland in 1845, when the potato harvest failed due to blight, and the large number who emigrated to the USA because of persecution by their British masters for being Presbyterian. I could have referred to the migrations of the Jamaicans to Britain after World War II, to the expulsion of the Asians out of Uganda by Idi Amin in 1971, to the Vietnamese who fled their country after the fall of Saigon to the Viet Cong in 1975, to migrants from China, eastern Europe and North Africa to western Europe, Canada and the USA in recent decades (for economic as well as political reasons). But the four examples I have chosen illustrate well enough the point I am making. That man's search for a better life involves not just individuals, but often a cohesive group of people, motivated by common ideals. Quest first took man out of Africa a million years ago; it is continuing to move him from one country to another before our very eyes.

Notes

1. Early twentieth century proverb.
2. Edward O. Wilson, *Sociobiology. The New Synthesis*, op. cit., p 290.

3. Latterly, ice ages—defined by a sustained fall in average temperature of around $5-10\,^{\circ}C$—have lasted around 60,000 years: between 290,000 and 240,000 years ago, between 190,000 and 130,000 years ago and between 70,000 and 12,000 years ago.
4. Haim Ofek, op. cit., pp 118–121.
5. Based on molecular analysis that traces numerical as well as geographical expansions. See Alan R. Templeton, 'Out of Africa again and again', *Nature* **416**: 45–51; 2002.
6. See e.g. M. H. Wolpoff *et al.*, 'Multiregional, not multiple, origins', *Am. J. Phys. Anthropol.* **112**: 129–136; 2000. For a good discussion of these contrasting views, see J. H. Relethford, op. cit.
7. See Chapter 2.
8. The term 'archaic' *H. sapiens*, as opposed to 'current' or 'modern' *H. sapiens*, is used by some anthropologists to fudge this issue (in the way that *H. sapiens neanderthalensis* and *H. sapiens sapiens* are sometimes used for Neanderthal Man and current humans).
9. That is, genes on the other 22 chromosomes. Although the information is not as clear cut as that derived by analysis of mitochondrial DNA (tracing female ancestry) or of Y chromosomal DNA (tracing male ancestry), some overall conclusions can be reached.
10. Although some put it as early as 30,000–20,000 years ago. See e.g. Vincent H. Malmström, op. cit., p 16.
11. Jared Diamond, op. cit., p 306.
11a. Not so the Australian aborigines, who were still completely naked in 1788, when Europeans first came across them in Botany Bay. See Robert Hughes, *The Fatal Shore*, Vintage Books, New York, 1988, p 85.
12. Some archaeologists put the arrival of humans in Australia as early as 75,000 years ago. Peter Kershaw of Monash University goes even further. He believes that man was lighting fires there 140,000 years ago, but so far the evidence for this is slim. See Richard Rudgley, op. cit., p 245–247.
13. The channel that was created was discovered by a Danish explorer called Vitus Bering; he had been encouraged in 1740 by Peter the Great of Russia to investigate whether Asia and North America were linked. Bering found that they were not, and the strait was named after him. On one of his return journeys (he made several trips) his ship was wrecked. He sought refuge on an island where he perished, and this too bears his name as well as his remains.
14. After a site particularly rich in stone implements at Clovis in New Mexico.
15. Sasha Nemecek, *Sci. Am.* **283** (September): 62–69; 2000.
16. Bryan Sykes, op. cit., pp 96–107.
17. See Note 36 to Chapter 4.
18. As a result of which we are able to fight off infections—whether of viral, bacterial or protozoan origin.

19. Pythagoras (580–500 BC) and Eratosthenes (c. 275–194 BC) preceded Ptolemy (c. 90–168 AD) by many centuries in proposing that the earth is round. Eratosthenes even came up with a value for the circumference of the earth that is within 2% of the actual figure (24,911 miles).

20. Zheng He is credited by some with far more dramatic feats than his well-documented exploration and trading voyages between China, India and the Middle East during the 1420s. A maverick naval officer turned scholar, one Gavin Menzies, has Zheng He reaching the Americas 70 years ahead of Columbus and discovering Australia and New Zealand more than 300 years before James Cook. See the *Daily Telegraph* (UK) of 4 March 2002, and Menzies' forthcoming book, *1421*.

21. Ernst Fehr and Simon Gachter, 'Altruistic punishment in humans'. *Nature* **415**: 137–140; 2002.

22. See Edward O. Wilson, *Sociobiology. The New Synthesis*, op. cit., pp 106–129.

23. The name of the continent had been introduced by a German geographer, Martin Waldseemuller, in 1507. Waldseemuller was apparently unaware of Columbus' voyages and decided to honour the claims of an Italian explorer, Amerigo Vespucci, to have been the first to sight the shores of South America in 1497. Vespucci was more interested in trading than in warfare, in sharp contrast to the Spanish navigators who crossed the Atlantic ocean with small armies several decades later.

24. Quoted, for good reason, by Sterling Seagrave in *The Marcos Dynasty*, Macmillan, London, 1989, p 15.

25. By the Portuguese King John II, or possibly by Bartolomeu Dias himself. The most southerly point of Africa is actually Cape Agulhas.

26. See Nicholas Crane, op. cit.

27. Although his description of rich vegetation and useful game on 'Manna-hata' contributed to the subsequent purchase of the island by the Dutch from the natives for just 60 guilders' worth of trinkets.

28. Moving from one's home to seek a better life elsewhere, of course, is not a particularly human form of quest. We share it with other animals, as illustrated by the accounts of migration in Chapter 4 and at the beginning and end of Chapter 5.

29. *And this is good old Boston,*
    The home of the bean and the cod,
    Where the Lowells talk to the Cabots
    And the Cabots talk only to God (John Collins Bossidy, 1860–1928).

30. Unwisely, as it proved, they were using ponies instead of dogs, and were carrying heavy scientific equipment for future research.

31. For a recent account, see Susan Solomon, *The Coldest March: Scott's Fatal Antarctic Expedition*, Yale University Press, New Haven, CT, 2001.

32. They can be seen at St George's Medical School in London, the hospital at which Wilson received his medical training.

33. They left Greenwich on 2 September 1979, crossed the South Pole on 15 December 1980, crossed the North Pole on 10 April 1982 and returned to Greenwich on 29 August 1982, having completed a trek of 35,000 miles (56,000 kilometres). See *Guinness World Records,* 2003.

34. For further details, see Chapter 3.

35. Until President Botha's retirement in 1989.

36. Although officially now illegal, polygamy is still practised by many Mormons, predominantly those living in Utah. Despite banning polygamy on joining the Union in 1896, the state turned a blind eye to the practice for over a century; only now is it toughening up on those — some 30,000 — who continue the custom.

37. Young practised what he preached. He had over 20 wives and fathered 47 children.

CHAPTER SIX

The ladder: adversity and achievement

Let me begin with an analogy to illustrate how man's thirst for new ways to live his life, and his resulting achievements, have led to the development of civilisations and cultures. It is a simple enough concept: a ladder. With each successive invention, be it a technological advance or a better form of governance, man climbs a step up the ladder. It is not an individual step, but that of a community. You may be the cleverest, most inventive, person in the world, but if you live in hermit-like isolation on a mountain top or in a cave at the shores of the ocean, your ingenuity helps no one; it is not even noticed. In order for your wisdom to make an impact, it needs to be expressed within a community that is receptive to your thoughts, and able to integrate your contribution within its life style. The community has to be a certain size. A single family is not enough, but 100 families begins to achieve critical mass. They are able to make things happen. In Chapter 2 I considered biological variability in human terms, and pointed out that in a group of, say, 100 individuals there will be a mix of skills; some will be brighter, others more persistent; some will be better at hunting, others at fashioning a garment or a bowl; some will be more suited to leading, others to following. If we imagine that each of these individuals is part of a family, we have our 100 families, that as a community is able to advance a step or two up the ladder.

By 10,000 years ago, the hunter-gatherer was being replaced by the farmer in many areas of the world: most notably in the 'fertile crescent' of the Middle East, that runs from the area between the

Euphrates and the Tigris in present-day Iraq in the north to the upper reaches of the Nile in the south.[1] Agriculture leads to a more settled life; the newborn are more likely to survive and as a result communities grow in size, even though the close proximity to animals may have a detrimental effect on life span through the transmission of infectious diseases.[2] The counter-argument, that increases in numbers led man to abandon the nomadic life and turn to agriculture in order to feed his burgeoning families, is less convincing: can you think of a single example of the human spirit reacting to overpopulation by a remedy as dramatic as intervening in nature by propagating the seeds of edible plants and taming animals for domestic use? The contraceptive pill is not a good example. The people who benefited from its development 40 years ago were in North America and Europe, where population size is not a problem. Its adoption by overcrowded countries like India has so far been a failure, and in China a simpler remedy was adopted to keep its population in check: eradication of a second child. Whatever the reasons for the development of agriculture, it enabled communities to reach the critical mass defined above. I am not saying that *no* progress was made during the first 2 million years of *Homo's* existence: he learnt the value of fire, he constructed simple tools. And after *H. sapiens* had arrived, some 140,000 years ago, he eventually began to farm the land. These were crucial advances, several steps up the ladder of achievement. But they were slow in coming when we compare them with accomplishments achieved within a matter of centuries from around 6000 years ago onwards: the construction of towns and cities, the framing of laws, the development of writing, the growth of art. These represent an ever-expanding quality of life. Through the combination of manual dexterity, speech and sophisticated cerebral function, man has been able—within the right community—to climb several steps up the ladder. He has climbed further than any of his predecessors. Indeed, there is little evidence that chimpanzees, or other animals for that matter, climb the ladder at all: their way of life changes little from generation to generation, and is unlikely to have altered much over the past 5 million years.

I would now like to introduce another concept, that attempts to explain why some communities proved superior at launching a civilisation[3] than others: better able to climb up the ladder of cultural progress. It is one that was made half a century ago by the English historian Arnold Toynbee. Present-day scholars do not have much time for Toynbee's views: they are not 'modern' enough. I agree that Toynbee's analysis of recent historical movements, say over the last 1000 years, is too simplistic. But his analysis of the events we are considering here, namely those that occurred roughly between 4000 BC and 1000 AD, during which the first civilisations were born, I find compelling. Judge for yourself. The hypothesis is straightforward: it is that communities respond better to a challenge of adversity than to an opportunity for an easy life.

The challenge of adversity

In considering the fate of our ancestors, wandering through Africa, Europe and Asia, reaching Australia and the islands of the Pacific, working their way down from the north to the south of America—historians call it *Völkerwanderung* ('the wandering of folk' in German)—an obvious question arises. What triggered the emergence of sophisticated communities in some parts of the world but not in others? Why in Mesopotamia (now Iraq) and Egypt, in China and India, in Greece (Crete, to be precise), in Central America (the Yucatan peninsula in particular) and in South America (the high Andes of Peru), but not in northern Europe, central and southern Africa, Australia or North America (Figure 6.1)? There are essentially three views. The first is that of 'race'.

It implies that some groups of *H. sapiens* are somehow cleverer, more entrepreneurial, than others. There is a belief, popularly promoted by those of European descent, that some races—as defined by physical characteristics such as skin colour—are less endowed with intellectual skills than others. Yet there is no scientific evidence whatsoever that physical attributes are linked to cerebral qualities like intelligence, and are therefore inherited concurrently. On the contrary, I have several times made the point that it is individuals, not communities, who vary in such qualities as mental ingenuity. Furthermore, given that the Maya of central

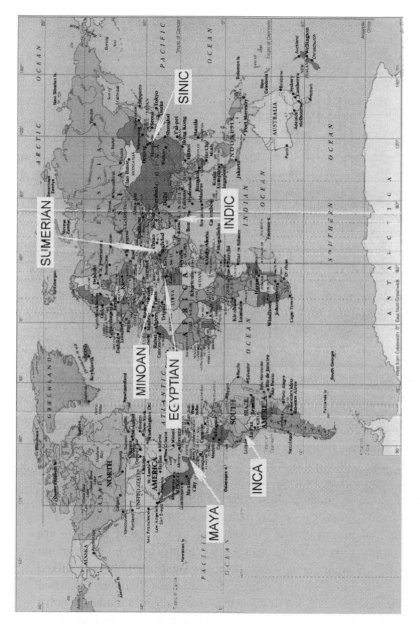

Figure 6.1   The birth of primary civilisations.

America and the Incas of Peru, both of whom established flourishing civilisations, are related to the Amerindians of North America and the Caribbean Islands, few of whom developed much beyond tribal settlements, the proposal that race determines the successful establishment of civilisations seems shaky. The same difficulty arises in relation to the sophisticated culture of the Minoans on Crete, compared with the simple life of their kind elsewhere in the Mediterranean basin. It is true that the mainland Greeks (Mycenians) subsequently developed one of the most successful societies yet seen on earth, but they stole their ideas from the Minoans, just as the Romans took theirs from the Greeks, and the rest of the Europeans eventually copied, or had thrust upon them, the culture of Rome.

Such arguments can also be advanced in respect of the civilisations founded in Mesopotamia and Egypt, India and China. In each case some groups built cities and developed a sophisticated culture, while others of the same racial background did not. It must be appreciated that I am talking here of *primary* civilisations that arose in isolation, in the absence of contact with any existing culture. Just as the Christian civilisaton of Europe can be traced back to the Minoan, with input also from the cultures of Egypt and Mesopotamia, so the Islamic civilisation has its roots in the cultures of Mesopotamia and Egypt, with input also from the, by then, Roman civilisation. In the same way the cultures of Korea and Japan developed from that of China,[4] and that of the Aztecs from the Maya. There is a school of thought that attributes the rise of the Gupta Empire and the emergence of Hinduism around 1600 years ago to the influence of the Sumerians of Mesopotamia and subsequently to that of the Greeks, but to most Indians the Mauryan Empire established 700 years earlier, which reached its peak under Ashoka, represents the continuation of a civilisation that arose in the valley of the Indus. The point I am making is that primary cultures arose independently, alongside primitive settlements populated by the same ethnic group, and only thereafter was there much borrowing and interchange of ideas among communities of similar racial background.

So much for race. The other explanations for the appearance of a civilisation in one part of the world but not in another are based on the quality of the environment; they differ only in being exact opposites of one another. The first proposes that it is favourable environments — the lush valley of the Nile in Egypt, the fertile area between the Tigris and the Euphrates in Mesopotamia (the word is Greek for 'between rivers'), the banks of the Yellow River in China, the plentiful supply of food from the sea in Crete, the forests rich in game and edible plants of Yucatan — that led to a settled life and the development of stable societies. Men simply moved in where living seemed easy and stayed there. I cannot deny that opportunism, exploiting an advantageous situation, is a very human quality. It is also, like searching, one that characterises all living organisms: plants exploit a favourable environment and so do microbes; the latter rapidly multiply in a person whose immune function is compromised. But there is a downside to this. Bacteria that are parasites of animals, like staphylococci and streptococci — the cause of much human disease — have become so dependent on their hosts that they have lost the capacity to grow anywhere else. their requirement for preformed nutrients is greater than that of man. Of the 20 different amino acids that are required to make a protein, we humans can synthesise all but a few from glucose and ammonia through our own metabolism; staphylococci and streptococci require every one of the 20 amino acids to be present in their dietary soup.

You will remind me that I said in an earlier chapter that some of the genes we carry are a left-over from much earlier predecessors. So why did staphylococci and streptococci not retain the genes of *their* ancestors, by which they were able to make all 20 amino acids from glucose and ammonia themselves? The answer is that over a long enough period of time we do lose certain genes. The common ancestor of plants and animals that lived three billion years ago was probably photosynthetic: it used the energy of the sun to turn carbon dioxide and water into carbohydrate and oxygen. We have lost the genes that specify the proteins necessary to accomplish this reaction. How? Through the gradual extinction of some ancestral species, and the evolution of others. This process is much slower in animals than in bacteria. Man reproduces approximately once every 20 years, a staphylococcus every 20 minutes: a difference of 500,000-fold. So does opportunism in man have a downside? Over the time scale during which civilisations emerged—a few thousand years at best—genetic change is imperceptible. That does not mean it is not happening, but the effect is miniscule. On the other hand, a change in human behaviour does not necessarily imply a genetic alteration at all: the fluctuations in fashion to which I referred in an earlier chapter have no genetic basis, and neither does the development of culture.[5] For my part, I believe there is a negative as well as a positive side to opportunism in man, whether it is genetically defined or not: in the short term it is undeniably beneficial, but in the long term it leads to complacency, which is brother to lethargy. Listen to the nineteenth century English poet Alfred Tennyson as, following Homer's *Odyssey*, he describes a group of toiling fishermen who have stumbled upon an island of people made indolent by eating water lilies:

We have had enough of motion,
Weariness and wild alarm,
Tossing on the tossing ocean
Where the tuskèd seahorse walloweth

This is lovelier and sweeter,
Men of Ithaca, this is meeter,
In the hollow rosy vale to tarry,
Like a dreamy Lotos-eater, a delirious Lotos-eater!
We will eat the Lotos, sweet
As the yellow honeycomb,
In the valley some, and some
On the ancient heights divine;
And no more roam,
On the loud hoar foam,
To the melancholy home
At the limit of the brine,
The little isle of Ithaca, beneath the day's decline.
We'll lift no more the shattered oar,
No more unfurl the straining sail;
With the blissful Lotos-eaters pale
We will abide in the golden vale
Of the Lotos-land, till the Lotos fail;

We will not wander more.
Hark! how sweet the horned ewes bleat
On the solitary steeps,
And the merry lizard leaps,
And the foam-white waters pour;
And the dark pine weeps,
And the lithe vine creeps,
And the heavy melon sleeps
On the level of the shore;
Oh! islanders of Ithaca, we will not wander more.
Surely, surely slumber is more sweet than toil, the shore
Than labour in the ocean, and rowing with the oar.
Oh! islanders of Ithaca, we will return no more.[6]

A community that lives opportunistically is less inventive, less progressive, than one that faces a challenge head-on. The demanding activity of hunting, in the long run, proved more beneficial to man than the facile one of scavenging.

The second proposal that relates to the environment, then, is that it is the challenge of harsh conditions that brings out the ingenuity of man, his quest for ways to tame the environment to his bidding. It was adversity, not ease, that resulted in the emergence of civilisations. Even at an earlier time, 50,000 years ago, was not man responding to a challenge when he set out from what is now Indonesia and started paddling in an easterly direction to reach the shores of New Guinea, then linked by a land bridge to Australia? Access to water is an essential element for any community—especially an agricultural one—and the fact that the Sumerian, the Egyptian, the Indic and the Sinic civilisations all emerged along a river is no accident. But Toynbee points out that the grassland adjoining the Nile, and that between the Tigris and Euphrates, actually underwent a period of desiccation following the end of the last Ice Age, during which the surrounding land turned from grass to desert. Yet this is the very period—around 6000–4000 years ago—during which the cultures of Egypt and Sumeria (in Mesopotamia) reached their height.

It happened because those groups who between them possessed a greater determination, a heightened urge to search for answers to

145

new challenges, chose to move from the disappearing grassland around the Euphrates and the Nile into the swamps of the rivers themselves, which were shunned by peoples of lesser appetite for adversity.[7] Through having to cope with marshland, the adventurers worked out ways of drainage and irrigation of their crops that have lasted to this day. The less inventive either stayed where they were and perished, or moved to areas that could continue to support their lives of primitive agriculture and hunting without much effort. They were not the ones who built the pyramids of Giza or the city of Babylon; they did not invent the wheel or the cuneiform script, they did not elaborate trinkets and vessels made of gold, they did not define the points of the compass from the position of the stars.

What challenge did settlers in the valley of the Yellow River have to overcome? Perhaps it was the variation of temperature with the seasons: extreme winter cold fluctuating with intense summer heat. The peoples further south, in the valley of the Yangzi, in which the weather remains warmer throughout the year, did not have to face this challenge; according to Toynbee it was not they who were the founders of the Sinic culture.[8] However, we now know that the weather in northern China was considerably warmer in neolithic times, so other factors may have played a part. Moreover, since Toynbee's day, excavations within the Yangzi River basin have revealed sites of settlements as old as those along the Yellow River: perhaps the challenge to their founders were the floods that regularly spill over the banks of swollen Yangzi.

The forests of the lowlands of the Yucatan may be rich in natural resources, but their very rapid growth presents a continuing challenge of keeping nature at bay: constant cutting down of bushes and felling of trees in order to preserve the clearings in which the Maya chose to settle. Those living on the highlands — who eventually formed the Aztec Empire — had an easier life. Their forebears did not found a primary civilisation, but remained hunters and primitive farmers, until they eventually absorbed the culture of the people who founded Teotihuacan in the north and that of the Mayan builders of Palenque and Chichen Itza in the south east. The Incas in Peru had to face two kinds of challenge: on the high Andes it was the bleak climate and a poor soil; along the coast it was an almost complete absence of rain and a ground that was nothing but desert, as it is to this day. Nevertheless, they managed to overcome both challenges and to found an empire that lasted for 300 years.

In the case of the Minoan civilisation (and there are those who do not consider it a primary one anyway) it is more difficult to discern a challenge posed by life on Crete. The argument that Arnold Toynbee advances is that the challenge had already happened by the time the island was settled, and it was in fact the sea. Ethnological evidence suggests that the earliest settlers came not from Europe or Asia, but from the more distant shores of North Africa. It appears that the dessication of the grasslands not only drove the founders of the Egyptian civilisation into the swamps of the Nile, but also propelled another group of men, ready to face a different challenge, to cross the sea to Crete.

Of the three explanations for the emergence of primary civilisations that I have discussed—race, a favourable environment or an unfavourable one—my preference is largely for the third.[9] That it is a challenge, the challenge of the unknown, that has a special appeal for man because it is in his nature to search: for ways to overcome adversity, to succeed where his ancestors have failed. We have seen that man's appetite for exploration has led him to settle in all parts of the world, from the frozen tundra of Alaska and Canada to the deserts of Africa and Asia, from the steppes of Siberia to the jungles of Borneo and Brazil. No other primate has ventured from the environment of its forebears; if it had, it would have perished from the cold or the heat, or the lack of food and water. It is the ingenuity of man, the search for ways to overcome the restrictions imposed by the environment, that has enabled Inuits to clothe themselves and live in their igloos at temperatures that fall below −40° (at which the Centigrade and Fahrenheit scales coincide) and the Berbers to adjust to the drought and heat of the Sahara through the detection and conservation of every available drop of water. Yet neither Inuit nor Berber founded a civilisation: if the challenge is *too* harsh, a group will simply not be able to overcome it. The balance between challenge and the ability to meet it is a delicate one. I have dismissed differences of racial background as a cause for the emergence of civilisations, but concede that the extent of man's ingenuity, his quest for novel ways of living, is relative:

some have it more than others. And *all* groups of *Homo sapiens* clearly possess more of the exploratory instinct, as well as the ability to exploit that characteristic through the use of language and the manipulations of their hands, than any other primate.

To return to the ladder. Not all groups ascend. Some remain where they are; sometimes they slip further down. I referred in the previous chapter to the Polynesians of Easter Island. Having advanced far enough up the ladder to get there in the first place, and then to build the most extraordinary statues, they slipped down several rungs when they used up all their resources without a thought for the morrow. Was it because, being isolated, they were not challenged enough by outsiders? Was this also why the Mayan civilisation within the dense rainforest—at its peak between the fourth and eighth centuries AD—declined over the following seven centuries? Another reason for sliding down the ladder is the opposite to lethargy: destruction from without or within. The Roman Empire, at least that in the west, collapsed because of internal decay that made it unable to repulse successive invasions by Vandals, Goths and Franks. One contributing factor was the rise of Christian values, which proved incompatible with rule by the emperor (subsequent rulers, whether in Italy or Spain, learned well enough how to cope with the problem of Christian humility and tolerance: they ignored it). Another factor may have been disease: for example, there is evidence that malaria was brought to Sardinia and thence to the mainland by marauding Vandals, who brought infected mosquitoes with them from the shores of North Africa.[10] The remnants of the Empire in the east, although declining in influence and size, held on for another 1000 years before being finally overrun by the Ottomans. In our own time, the example of China under Mao Zhedong shows how the annihilation of culture from within can diminish a civilisation. Few societies stand still for long. Just as the value of the stock market rises and falls but rarely remains static, so the fortunes of cultures either improve or deteriorate, but seldom remain constant. What, after all, is the value of the stock market but a reflection of financial successes and failures? A few steps up or down the financial ladder?

The ladder of achievement itself is not stationary. It is a moving staircase, an escalator, and it is moving in one direction only:

upwards. Civilisations may decline, but it is a temporary slip. The Chinese tradition of pride in workmanship and knowledge may have been abrogated for a generation or two during the second half of the twentieth century (together with the loss through starvation or suicide of 55 million innocent Chinese citizens—more than Stalin's and Hitler's victims put together—during Mao's Great Leap Forward) but it is not lost and is being revived even as I write. Most people on earth today lead better lives than they would have done 5000 years ago. If the poverty-stricken slum dwellers of Mexico City or Mumbai (formerly Bombay) are worse off today than their ancient forebears were, it is because their attempt to improve the quality of their lives by moving from village to city in search of work proved to be in error: there were no jobs. The quest was there, but the road they followed was the wrong one.

Inheritance of human potential

If the skills learned by previous civilisations are not lost, does this mean that we are getting cleverer as time goes by? Yes, in so far as cleverness refers to our ablity to build a better house, dam, boat, acroplane or rocket, or our capacity to communicate with each other by telephone, wireless or Internet. The technology achieved by one generation is the starting point for that of the next: knowledge is an ever-increasing asset. And because successively more people are involved in the quest, because one technology spawns several new ones, our acquisition of skills increases at an exponential rate. We have acquired more technology in the past 100 years than in the previous 10,000. No other species changes its habits in this way: the life style of the animals around us is much the same as it was a million years ago. What does not change is man's capacity to invent something new, his intellectual prowess. Individuals, as I have stressed, are possessed of intellectual ability to varying degrees, but these remain the same over thousands of generations.

Physical attributes like the shape of one's face or the agility of one's limbs, and mental qualities like mood or ingenuity, kindness or cruelty, the urge to explore or to create works of art, are determined by a network of interacting genes and other stretches of DNA. Together they specify a combination of many proteins that act in concert. The end result is influenced also by the environment: by factors such as a healthy diet on the one hand or an unhealthy level of pollution or microbial infection on the other. Intelligence, for example, seems to be determined roughly equally by our genes and by our environment. Moreover, it appears not to change greatly with age: our IQ is about as high at 7 as at 70 (in the same way that our character—weak or strong, mendacious or truthful—remains much the same throughout our life). It is our knowledge—learning —that increases with age, just as the skills acquired by successive cultures are cumulative. Our ability to use that knowledge—well or badly, fast or slowly—does not alter, any more than does the capacity of societies to create a culture, or their will to destroy one. If intelligence does not vary with age, it means that the environmental influence—nutrition, pollution, infection—must act very early on, perhaps already during conception. This is not so surprising, for we know that most of our brain cells are assembled by the age of 3 or so. During subsequent childhood, our behaviour is moulded somewhat further by environmental factors; as much, probably, by our peer groups as by our parents. Once we reach adulthood, we remain as clever or dull, as honest or devious, as aggressive or docile, as we were when young. That is why creative men and women who have achieved success in their field—Nobel Prize-winning scientists and writers, for example—continue to work into their 70s and 80s. Why do they do it? Can they not rest on their laurels? They cannot. The search for new ideas, the urge for creativity, is in their blood.

We must remember something else. The environment may influence the way that genes act, but it does not alter their composition—except, as mentioned earlier, over a time scale of tens of thousands of generations, and then in a totally random manner. A person living at high altitude may adapt to it over time by increasing the amount of haemoglobin he produces,[11] but this ability is not passed on to his progeny, who have to re-adapt from birth. Equally, living in an intellectually rich culture does not rub off on one's children. Knowledge may be cumulative, but the qualities required to generate or utilise that knowledge cannot be absorbed and passed on to the next generation. If they were, the descendants of Socrates and Plato, of Aristotle and Archimedes, would by now have created a country of geniuses; a few hours spent at Athens airport, or in the city's traffic jam, illustrates the folly of such a suggestion. Although intelligence does sometimes run in families — it is after all partly genetically determined — the shuffling of genes at every generation, as well as environmental factors, makes it an unpredictable quality. None of Darwin's children was a genius,[12] and nor I believe is Einstein's daughter (she will, I trust, forgive me this remark). On the other hand, it is true that Irene Curie, the daughter of Marie Curie, won a Nobel Prize in 1935 for her discovery of man-made radioactivity. Her mother had won two: the first in 1903 (with her husband Pierre Curie) for the discovery of radium, and the second on her own in 1911 for its isolation. In 1915 William Bragg shared a Nobel Prize with his son Lawrence Bragg for developing the technique of X ray crystallography, on which the subsequent elucidation of molecular structure has depended. The Nobel committee showed remarkable foresight on this occasion, as it was able, 50 years later, to bestow its honour on the discoverers of the structure of DNA (Francis Crick, James Watson and Maurice Wilkins) and of proteins (myoglobin by John Kendrew, haemoglobin by Max Perutz and insulin by Dorothy Hodgkin), all achieved by X-ray crystallography.

The same uncertainty regarding the passing on of talent is true of artistic creativity. Liszt's daughter Cosima married Richard Wagner, but none of their descendants — most of whom have been involved with the Bayreuth Festival in one way or another — actually *composed* music. Four of Johann Sebastian Bach's sons, on the other hand, did: Wilhelm Friedemann wrote for the keyboard, as did his more prolific brother Carl Philipp Emanuel, one of the originators of the sonata and symphony style of music; Johann Christoph Friedrich composed chamber music, concertos and symphonies, and Johann Christian did likewise, becoming known as the 'English Bach': he was music master to George III's family and gave a notable performance of a sonata with Mozart (aged 8) in London.

Yet is it really all a genetic, and not also an environmental, influence that accounts for an offspring's achievements? Irene

Curie's husband, Jean-Frederic Joliot, with whom she shared *her* Nobel Prize, was Marie Curie's assistant, and both Jean-Frederic and Irene must have been influenced very much by Irene's parents and by the environment of the institute in which they all worked. Bragg father and son were close collaborators. J. S. Bach taught composition to all four of his sons (despite the distractions of producing 16 other children and composing more than 600 canons, cantatas, concertos, fugues, masses, oratorios, preludes and suites) and the environment of the Bach household cannot be said to have been anything other than strongly musical. To show an unequivocal genetic link between geniuses and their offspring we have to look for examples where a child is separated from its parents at an early age and yet develops outstanding qualities in philosophy or science, scholarship or art. Unfortunately none springs to mind.

To reiterate. The qualities that distinguish us from chimpanzees are distributed equally among all peoples of the world. Skin colour and other physical attributes may differ among various racial groupings, but there is no evidence that the cerebral qualities we have been discussing are expressed to a greater extent in some races than in others. The chances of finding in any one community a clever person or a stupid one, a leader or a follower, an artist or a vandal, an honest person or a crook, a tyrant or a saint, are the same in Amsterdam, Addis Abbaba and Adelaide, in Boston, Bogota and Beijing. They are more or less the same today as they were 10,000 years ago. What is different is the use to which different communities have put this blend of attributes. What we call culture and the quality of life will be considered in the following two chapters. First, the gist of the present discussion—that attributes like genius are rarely passed to one's progeny—will be extended to the quality of leadership.

Rulers

Within a group of animals there is always one who dominates the others. The ruler is generally the strongest, most aggressive of the males, but sometimes—in vervet monkeys or hyenas, for example—it is a female. Likewise, in social insects like wasps, bees and ants, it is the queen who rules. Dominance is not the same as leadership when animals move from one place to another. In a troop of primates, the alpha male may be leader in a battle, but a female often takes the decision when and where to move on; this is because the limiting factor for females in so far as reproductive success is concerned is finding food, whereas for a male it is finding a female. In common with 97% of all mammals, male primates do not invest time in caring for their progeny; instead they hunt for females. Leadership in an animal community may be as short-lived as that in a human one: when the dominant male within a group loses a fight with a challenger, the latter takes over. And as the leader ages, he is replaced by another member of the community. The new leader emerges naturally, as being the strongest and the most dominant. Only in a few cases is the new ruler selected. An example of this is afforded by the hierarchical system within the social insects: when a queen bee dies, the workers choose her successor by picking the female that is likely to produce the largest number of offspring (only the queen is allowed to have sex in a hive of bees). Never, however, is the *offspring* of a leader selected to follow in his parent's footsteps simply by virtue of birth. The instinct of animals serves them well: qualities like leadership are seldom inherited by progeny. Yet humans, in societies throughout the world, have chosen to follow just such a course, by electing a close relative, usually the first-born son, of the former leader to succeed him. How well has the hereditary principle worked?

During the flowering of Greek culture throughout the fifth and fourth centuries BC, when men like Aeschylus, Sophocles, Euripides, Socrates, Democritus, Aristophanes, Plato and Aristotle were laying the foundations of Western philosophy and drama, when the world's first University (the Academia) was being established, Athens was governed by its own citizens. The concept of democracy (government by the people)—championed throughout his lifetime by Pericles—owes its origin to this very period; and if those who govern are the most able, the best-educated, so much the better. There was no element of hereditary succession in aristocratic (government by the best) rule at this time. On the contrary, the achievements of the age show that environment is a stronger influence than kinship in passing on intellectual prowess: Socrates was Plato's mentor, who himself taught Aristotle.

We may also take note of how China was then being ruled. Although the emperor always had the last word, government was essentially enacted by a well-educated bureaucracy; even the army was kept in second place. From the time that China was unified under the Qin dynasty in the third century BC, scholars trained in the art of government formed a meritocracy under which advancement was strictly by talent, not by birth; the examination system by which future administrators were selected was one of the most rigorous ever devised. This form of rule must surely have contributed to the stability of the empire and its continuity for the next 21 centuries.

Moving to Roman times, it was under the Republic (around 500– 27 BC) that its greatest accomplishments occurred (and the word 'king' became one of abuse). During the first century BC, in particular, Rome expanded its boundaries through the victories of Julius Caesar; it began to introduce the legal system that is used to this day throughout most of Europe, and was home to orators like Cicero and poets like Virgil. The Republic was ruled by two Consuls and the Senate, whose membership (of 900 at this time) included not just the landed aristocracy (patricians), but also some plebeians (the common people).[13] Leaders like Julius Caesar were given their commands by the Senate, and acted on its orders. It is true that when, in 49 BC, Caesar was told to relinquish his command, he ignored the order and took his army, quartered on the northern banks of the Rubicon near the present-day republic of San Marino, south. By crossing this stream, he committed himself to the course of action that determined the rest of his life: he chose to enter Rome and govern it on his own. He achieved his aim (he generally did) and, although he ruled as a dictator, he did so with wisdom and innovation. On his assassination 5 years later, power passed to Octavian, whom Caesar had adopted as his son; Octavian's link by blood was no more than that of great-nephew. The practice of naming a distant relative as son—and therefore as successor— shows that the Romans appreciated the weakness of the hereditary principle. Although Octavian nominally restored government to the Senate, who bestowed on him the title of Augustus (meaning venerable), he governed very much as an emperor from 27 BC onwards. Under him Rome reached its zenith in terms of novel administration and blossoming culture; it was also largely a time of peace ('Pax Romana'). So successful was the Augustan Age that its name has been bestowed on early to mid-eighteenth century France and England, when writers like Corneille, Racine and Molière, like Pope, Addison, Swift and Steele—all of whom incidentally admired the Roman values—flourished.

At Augustus' death in 14 AD, the crown passed to his step-son (he had no son) Tiberius, whom Augustus had named as his adoptive son, and the custom of naming one's successor continued throughout the years of empire. As might be expected, the adoptive son sometimes proved worthy of the task, sometimes not. Tiberius' adopted son (his great-nephew) Caligula was a disaster for Rome, whereas *his* successor, Claudius (actually his uncle), managed to retrieve the situation somewhat. Claudius' own adoptive son, Nero (Augustus' great-granddaughter's son from an earlier marriage) turned out worse even than Caligula: when he died his reign was officially struck from the record by the Senate. With the death of Nero, the dynasty stretching back to Julius Caesar came to an end. New blood was introduced through the choice of Flavian emperors like Vespasian and Rome recovered. One of its most successful periods began when the Antonine dynasty, which followed the Flavian one, petered out. A rank outsider—the first and probably only adopted son totally unrelated to his 'father'—was chosen; he was not even from Rome, but a provincial from Spain. He was Trajan, who proved to be one of the best rulers of the empire, expanding its boundaries even further, as did *his* successor— another Spaniard—Hadrian. The conclusion one may draw is simple: during the Republic and in the first years of Empire, a period in which no ruler was appointed solely by virtue of his birth, Rome was at its peak. Thereafter, when emperors were chosen largely through kinship (and their reigns curtailed by murder), Rome began to decline.

A self-appointed leader, like Caesar or Augustus, is not necessarily worse than an elected one, provided he is a man of talent. When in 1653 Oliver Cromwell in England appointed himself Lord Protector of the Commonwealth, he initiated many benefical reforms; it was his son Richard, who inherited the title at Cromwell's death in 1658, who proved unequal to the task. As a result, the monarchy was soon restored in preference, but with one important proviso: from now on it was Parliament, not the crown, that took the important decisions of state.

During the the Middle Ages the only power outside Asia that compared with the Ottoman Empire—the dominant force from 1300 AD onwards—in culture and civilisation was a small city state situated on a number of islands within a lagoon that is less than 100 miles from one end to the other. Yet Venice matched the Empire of the Ottomans—stretching 5000 miles from India in the east to Portugal in the west—in trade and outstripped it in art. The Republic of Venice lasted almost 800 years, and at its height (from the fifteenth to the eighteenth century) boasted some of the finest artists in Europe: painters like Jacopo Bellini and his sons Gentile and Giovanni, as well as Jacopo's pupils Giorgione and Titian, followed by Tintoretto, Veronese and El Greco. The Republic was home to architects like Palladio and to musicians like Monteverdi and Vivaldi. Yet at a time when most countries in the rest of Europe were being governed by hereditary kings and princes, Venice opted for elected leaders (admittedly only some 1% of the population had the vote); it had specifically banned hereditary succession of the Doges—the rulers of Venice—in 1032. You may say that the dynastic powers of England, France and Spain managed equally well, but weak rulers have limited their country's progress at various times. Venice grew steadily, in the extent of its overseas possessions and in the stability of its institutions. Its power, if not its culture, began to decline only when trade between Europe and Asia switched from being conducted through the Mediterranean (and a long overland journey) to the more convenient ocean route around Africa, that had been opened up by Portuguese explorers at the beginning of the sixteenth century.

We may in passing compare the stability of Papal rule in Rome with that of the Empire outside the Holy City, that was supposed to implement the authority of the Popes: the secular as opposed to the religious side of Christendom. The Holy Roman Empire, although it lasted 1000 years, was riven by conflict between its dynastic rulers and their neighbours; the Catholic Church has survived for twice that time. Since 1059 no Pope has been able to appoint his successor: every one has been elected, through secret ballot, by the College of Cardinals. There is another example one might quote. From 1382 to 1572 Poland was governed by the Jagiellon dynasty: although the rulers were all related, the monarch was elected — albeit by the aristocracy — not self-appointed; a limited form of parliamentary government was even initiated in 1493. During Jagiellon rule, art and science blossomed: the studies of Nicolaus Copernicus, which led to his proposition in 1543 that Earth and the other planets revolve around the sun, not the other way round, revolutionised astronomy and greatly influenced men like Galileo and Newton. Poland expanded to the largest area it was ever to cover: by 1569 it stretched from the Baltic to the Black Sea. The Reformation arrived around 1520; although initially suppressed, by 1552 the Protestant faith was accepted and for the next 130 years Poland was the only country in Europe without religious persecution. Once hereditary rule was reinstituted, the country declined. It never regained the stature it had enjoyed under elected rulers.

Considering the actual governance of a nation, China stands out in that its officials were all appointed on merit, chosen from the ranks of the scholarly bureaucracy. Despite internal conflict and invasion by Mongols and other warring tribes, the empire lasted 2000 years. Compare two similarly sized countries in eighteenth century Europe. France's ministers were mainly men of rank, appointed by virtue of high birth.[14] In Britain, ministers were politicians who had proved their mettle in affairs of state; many sat in the House of Commons,[15] not the House of Lords.[16] France suffered revolution and the Reign of Terror.[17] Britain moved towards the Industrial Revolution and the Reform Acts of the next century.

What, then, of today's monarchies of Western Europe, all based on strictly hereditary principles? It is true that Belgium, Britain, Denmark, The Netherlands, Norway, Spain and Sweden, as well as Thailand and Japan in the east, are among the most stable and economically successful countries in the world. But in no instance is the monarch anything other than a constitutional Head of

State:[18] all important decisions are taken by the government of the day, every one of its members democratically elected. In no case does it matter very much if the monarch is less competent than his predecessor.

The conclusion is obvious: as might be anticipated from the biological principle I have emphasised, namely that talent is inherited randomly, hereditary rulers have by and large performed worse than elected ones. Only if the holder of a hereditary office is no more than a constitutional figurehead does the country fare as well—sometimes better, rarely worse—as a republic whose ruler is elected by its peoples. Civilisations were born not because the rulers were sons of leaders, but because they happened to possess the necessary qualities of initiative and command. Human quest has transformed the world not because its main players inherited inquisitiveness, exploratory drive or a yen for conquest from their fathers, but because they were endowed with these attributes as a result of pure chance.[19]

Back to the neolithic

Growing crops and breeding animals is a more efficient way of producing food than hunting and gathering. As pointed out, it also fosters stability and the expansion of communities. So it is not surpising that the first towns and cities grew out of the settlements that accompanied the practice of farming. The increase in population was dramatic. Prior to the emergence of agricultural communities, the population of the world was increasing but slowly, and around 10,000 years ago may actually have been in decline: *H. sapiens* was in danger of extinction. Yet he survived, and 5000 thousand years later there were a million people living in Egypt alone. Agriculture requires an assured supply of water, and urban growth began along the banks of rivers, as it does to this day. Elsewhere, as in Crete, rainfall is sufficient to foster the growth of most crops. The same is true of Central America, where farming communities grew on the central highlands or within the rainforest itself. In South America, too, the first farmers probably lived in the mountainous region of the Andes, where melting snow if not rain water provides a favourable environment (the challenge came later, when communities moved into the dry coastal area or on to precipices high in the Andean mountains). In the Old World the transition from hunter-gatherer to farmer first occurred some 10,000 years ago, and that from living in primitive shelters to enjoying the permanence of buildings took a further 4000 years, to become evident by around 4000 BC in the earliest civilisations. In America, which was populated only 12,000 or so years ago in the north and 2000 years later in the south, one should not expect to find evidence of settlements that go back in time as far as this. In fact they were only a few thousand years behind, which suggests that the emergence of agriculture occurred at almost the same time in the New World as in the Old. Was a global climatic change, in the dying throes of the last ice age, responsible? It is an unresolved point that attracts hypotheses considerably faster than facts.

The earliest farming communities arose in certain areas only. Elsewhere man continued to live a nomadic life, whether by hunting or by herding tamed animals, for several millennia. Even today, the Kurds in the mountainous regions of Turkey, northern Iraq, western Iran, eastern Syria, Armenia and Azerbaijan, the Basques in the western Pyrenees of Spain and France, and the Nuer in south-eastern Sudan, can be considered to lead a nomadic type of existence in that they move back and forth with their livestock according to the seasons. This, as well as the fact that they continue to live an independent life, speaking their own language, grates on their powerful neighbours in whose domains they now find themselves, and nomadic people are harrassed from all sides. Another type of nomadic life is exemplified by those who move from place to place by trading. The migrations of the gypsies were mentioned in the previous chapter; likewise, the Tuaregs[20] continue to move between the Maghreb in the north of Africa (mainly Morocco and Algeria) and the region south of the Sahara (mainly Senegal, Mauretania, Mali and Niger).

Farming may lead to a more settled form of life but it does not necessarily result in the emergence of towns and cities: there are to this day agricultural communities whose life has not changed very much over many millennia: in the Grand Valley of the Balim River of New Guinea, along the banks of the Orinoco in southern Venezuela, in many parts of Africa. These people have no towns, no cities, no art, no literature, little technology or commerce. Their life expectancy is lower than that of the average citizen in the developed world—although it is probably similar to that of an impoverished resident in today's Moscow or a slum dweller in Mexico City. No civilisation has emerged from their labours. They have not searched as much as others. Do they therefore lead a less fulfilling life than we do? I make no comment, as I have been careful to define man's quest in terms only of his innate attributes and have considered the consequences as merely cultural; I refrain from attributing to human quest the values we call happiness, contentment or success. Instead I draw the reader's attention to a comment made by the psychologist and neuroscientist Steven Pinker,[21] that the human brain is not 'wired up' to cope with the strains and stresses of today's urban life: it is adapted to the neolithic period—preceding even the birth of agriculture—in which man has spent 99% of his existence. Who is to say that curiosity is not sometimes a mixed blessing?

Notes

1.   Others suggest an earlier emergence of agriculture—not the cultivation of crops, but the planting of trees and plants—in tropical forests. See Colin Tudge, op. cit., p 272 *et seq.* Tudge also questions the supposed benefits of farming compared with hunting and gathering. See also Chapter 9 (Stone Age technology).
2.   Richard Rudgley, op. cit., p 8.
3.   I use the term 'civilisation' throughout this book to refer to an advanced stage of social development that accompanies—as its Latin origin implies—the construction of cities. See also Note 22 to Chapter 7.
4.   But note the achievements of the Jomon culture in Japan 13,000 years ago, referred to at the end of Chapter 7.
5.   Read Hilary and Steven Rose's *Alas, Poor Darwin* (op. cit.) for a view as to the limitations of genetic control over our behaviour. Their collection of essays is actually an attack on evolutionary psychology, as its sub-title makes clear.

6. From the original, 1832, version of *The Lotos-Eaters* (*The Poems of Tennyson*), vol 1, Christopher Ricks (ed.), Longman, London, reprinted 1987.

7. There is a view that the builders of the pyramids of Egypt originally lived in what is now known as the western desert, several hundred miles east of present-day Cairo. Some 10,000 years ago, before the end of the last ice age, this area was savannah country: lakes and rivers provided water, and there was plenty of game for food. As the temperature gradually rose, the land became desiccated, and by 5000 years ago the savannah people had migrated eastwards. They were more than simple hunter-gatherers: there is evidence that they had constructed shelters of stone and buried their dead. And when they moved, they took with them the memory of the pyramid-like stone hillocks—formed by natural erosion—among which they had lived. Those features remain, and may be seen in the area today (from *Lost Worlds*, a programme made by Dr Farouk El-Baz of Boston University in 1963 and shown on UK television (Channel 4) on 18 November 2002).

8. The argument that a warm climate does not present a sufficient challenge may also be applied to sub-Saharan Africa, at least within the rain forest, where water is not a limiting factor.

9. But with an admixture of the second. As mentioned at the end of this chapter, farming communities arose where water was not a limiting factor (although the maintenance of crops and the taming of animals provided challenge enough). Of many agricultural settlements scattered throughout the world, only some met the further challenge of urban life successfully.

10. As proposed in *Malaria and the fall of Rome*, shown on UK television (BBC2) on 26 February 2002 as part of the 'Meet the Ancestors' series.

11. More haemoglobin is required when the external pressure of oxygen is low.

12. Of Darwin's surviving children, George Howard became Plumian Professor of Astronomy at Cambridge (and a KCB), Francis became Foreign Secretary of the Royal Society, and Horace—a civil engineer—also became an FRS. But neither they nor their siblings William Erasmus, Henrietta or Leonard (an army major) inherited the intellectual perspicacity of their father.

13. The well-known initials SPQR (Senatus Populusque Romanus = The Roman Senate and People) acknowledge the significance of a separate Assembly of the People.

14. Ecclesiastics like Cardinals Richelieu and Mazarin are obvious exceptions.

15. Like Robert Walpole and William Pitt the Younger.

16. Apart from notable aristocrats such as the Duke of Portland and Lord North.

17. The automatic succession of the weak son of Louis XV illustrates well my point about the disadvantage of the hereditary system: Louis XVI went to the guillotine bravely enough, but had he been a stronger man and better leader he might have been able to prevent some of the carnage inflicted on French men and women during the Reign of Terror.

18. The nineteenth century economist Walter Bagehot defined three rights for British monarchs: to warn, to encourage and to be consulted (David Cannadine, *In Churchill's Shadow: Confronting the Past in Modern Britain*, Allen Lane/Penguin, London, 2002, p 12) and no monarch in recent times has exceeded those prerogatives.

19. The fact that these qualities are not directly inherited implies that their manifestation depends on more than one gene. Such attributes appear instead to be the result of a subtle interplay between the expression of several genes (that are not passed from generation to generation in concert), as well as with the environment. There is no single gene for leadership or creativity, any more than there is a single gene for diseases like cancer, diabetes or heart attack.

20. They are Berbers and follow the Muslim religion, although it is the men, not the women, who wear the veil.

21. Steven Pinker, op. cit., p 42.

CHAPTER SEVEN

Civilisation 1: towns and temples

*L*et us now consider the rise of the seven primary civilisations to which I alluded in the last chapter. The evidence is largely archaeological: finding the remains of stone structures protruding above the ground and then digging down to reveal the foundations (sometimes excavating on a hunch alone). At the same time the soil is carefully sifted to reveal any objects of antiquity buried near by: coins, trinkets, seals, shards of pottery that were once cups or vessels for storage, tablets containing an ancient script. Human skeletons tell us not only about the size of the people who lived at the site, but also about some of the diseases from which they suffered; the remains of animals and crops reveal clues about farming practices and the diet of some of the inhabitants. The age of everything organic that is dug up can be fairly accurately assessed by carbon dating, which, as mentioned in an earlier chapter, is able to define the age of objects that are between 50,000 and 200 years old. It therefore includes the period under dicussion.[1] For bones and objects made of stone, clay or metal, other dating techniques have been employed. Of course, one can only assess the age of what one finds: wooden structures do not well survive the ravages of time and neither, of course, do simple huts made of mud and straw. Yet these are precisely the dwellings in which the mass of the people lived. The same is true right up to a few hundred years ago; if you drive through Europe you will see churches and cathedrals, castles and the mansions of the rich, all built of stone or brick; the cottages of the poor have not lasted. So it is that much of our knowledge of early civilisations is based on palaces and public buildings, on pyramids and temples: the way in which the labourer (generally a slave) who built all these fine structures lived is largely a matter for conjecture.

Mesopotamia

Ur and Uruk are the oldest cities in the world, with habitation going back some 7000 years; the very word 'ur' has come to imply great antiquity. They lay on the Euphrates near present-day Basra in southern Iraq and formed part of the kingdom of the Sumerians. By 3200 BC Uruk had three temples, a palace, a pillared hall and other buildings enclosed within a special complex known as Eanna. Its population, which had been around 10,000 three centuries earlier, had grown to 50,000 by 3800 BC. The arrival of the Akkadians from the north at this time did not diminish the importance of either of the two cities (although an earlier flood at Ur, downstream of Uruk, nearly did), and by 2150 BC Ur had became the capital of a new Sumerian empire. It was taken by the Chaldeans from Arabia at the beginning of the ninth century BC but continued to thrive alongside other city states: some of these, like Abu Salabikh, Kish and Babylon, were up-river along the Euphrates; others, like Lagash and Umma, were built nearby on the Tigris to the east. All these cities finally succumbed to the Persians under Cyrus the Great around 540 BC. Little is now left of Ur or Uruk and much of our knowledge is derived from artefacts found at the site.

This is not true of Babylon. Protracted excavations have revealed the size of the city, and I have walked along its alleys that are now below ground level and have marvelled at the excavated structures on either side; the reader will recall that the lower one finds remains of human activity, the older they are. Like Ur and Uruk, Babylon underwent occupation by Akkadians, Hittites, Kassites and others over the course of almost 2000 years. The Akkadians probably originated in the area—now northern Syria and Iraq—that contained such recently excavated cities as Mari, Tuttui and Tell Cheura near the Euphrates, Assur and Nineveh on the Tigris, and

Nagar and Nabada on the Khabur River in between. I mention all these sites merely to indicate the extent over which the Sumerian civilisation spread.[2] The Hittites came from the high region even further north; their capital was Hattusas (now Bogaskoy, 22 miles east of Ankara). Babylon reached its peak of cultural sophistication under the Chaldeans, who occupied it for about 100 years before it was finally overrun by Cyrus. Like Ur and the other cities, it was subsequently abandoned. Today many of the excavated remains, including the beautifully glazed bricks in the form of a lion's head that embellished the Ishtar Gate to the city, may be seen in the Pergamon Museum in Berlin (a copy greets today's visitor at the entrance to the city). From the terracota plaques, the stone and ivory carvings, the cylindrical seals and other objects, one can derive some idea of the extravagant way in which the Babylonians, and the inhabitants of neighbouring cities, lived. Under the Sumerians medicine as well as architecture and engineering had become professional disciplines, and they were the first to standardise weights and measures, to develop one of the oldest written languages and to lay the foundations of mathematics and astronomy. Their lunar month of 29 days, 12 hours and 44 minutes was within 0.002% of its true value. And they knew that the sum of the squares on the two short sides of a right-angled triangle equals the square on the long side 1000 years before Pythagoras.

They built elaborate stone shrines to their dead rulers in the form of stepped pyramids known as ziggurats; the lower half of one that was built in the third millennium BC still stands in Babylon, and may represent the legendary Tower of Babel: different dialects of Akkadian, as well as Sumerian and other languages, were spoken at the time. The Sumerians were among the first to cultivate land for enjoyment rather than the mere production of food: the Hanging Gardens of Babylon, that were considered one of the Seven Wonders of the ancient world, attest to their innovative skill in bringing water—some 300 tons per day it has been calculated—to the top of a series of terraces that are high above the nearby Euphrates. Our knowledge of the gardens is based on Greek texts written several centuries later, as the exact site, presumed to be adjacent to the royal palace, has never been identified. It is even possible that the gardens were not in Babylon at all, but in Nineveh 200 miles to the north, on the banks of the Tigris (near present-day Mosul). Generally considered to be one of the oldest—probably *the* oldest —of the civilisations that began to emerge 6000 years ago, that of the Sumerians epitomises how a number of interacting communities can develop a cultured way of life and maintain it through long periods of occupation by foreign aggressors. That success, of course, is as much dependent on the conqueror wishing to assimilate the culture, as on the defeated striving to maintain it.

Egypt

The birth of the Egyptian civilisation did not suffer from foreign domination in this way. That came later. Two distinct areas along the Nile began to be developed during the fifth and fourth millennium BC: one near the delta (Lower Egypt) and one 400 miles further south (Upper Egypt). By approximately 3100 BC, King Menes, who united Upper and Lower Egypt, had established his capital near the delta, just south of what is modern Cairo: he called it Memphis. The waters of the Nile provided the means for communication and trade between Upper and Lower Egypt, but below Memphis, the river began to divide into numerous streams and channels that constitute the delta to this day: their contours and depth are constantly shifting, as sand and silt are washed down the Nile; none is suitable for seagoing craft. Memphis was therefore not a seaport: trade with the Mediterranean was conducted across land and thence from harbours along the coast of Palestine. The city that grew into the trading centre of the Upper Nile, Thebes, developed soon after, and by 1500 BC it had become the capital of Egypt.

The earliest pyramids were built at Memphis, around the time of the Babylonian ziggurats. Like them, they were constructed as burial chambers for the ruler and his family. The pharaohs were interred not only with their favoured possessions made of gold and other precious metals, but with food to guarantee a safe journey into the after-life. The earliest pyramid, which was built at Saqqara for the pharaoh Djoser by his architect Imhotep around 2700 BC, has a stepped base, like that of a ziggurat. It is said to be the earliest building constructed entirely of stone. Imhotep became so famous for his works that he was himself deified and came to be worshipped as the patron of architects, scribes and scholars. There is a recent suggestion that the distinctive form of this pyramid (as well as of the later pyramids and the sphinx at Giza) was built to reflect the shape of natural rock formations 300 miles to the south in the Sahara near the Kharga oasis. Five thousand years ago the land here was savanna, not desert, and nomads living in the area may have wandered northwards to bring descriptions of such distinctively shaped features to the peoples of Memphis. But other historians retain their belief that the shape of the pyramids symbolizes the ascent of the pharaos to heaven up their stepped sides.

The three pyramids of Giza—a village south of present-day Cairo—were built at this period of intense workmanship 4500 years ago (Plate 2). The Great Pyramid was the first to be constructed. It is the largest of all the pyramids and contains more than 2 million blocks of stone weighing an average of 10 tonnes each; some are as heavy as 200 tonnes. Until a mere 100 years ago, no building in the world exceeded it in height.[3] When the Greek historian Herodotus visited the site during the fifth century BC, he calculated that a labour force of 100,000 slaves would have been needed to build the Great Pyramid. Recently the remains of many stone buildings near Giza were unearthed and dated to around 2500 years BC. They include some 600 small tombs. These were not royal tombs: they contained no gold and the dead were not mummified. They show that interment of a large proportion of the population was common practice. Could the dwellings have housed the builders of the three pyramids? Archaeologists believe they did, and consider Herodotus to have been wrong on two counts: first, the number of people involved is likely to have been only some 20,000 (but it probably took them around 20 years to complete each pyramid); second, they were not slaves.

The animal bones that have been found at the site indicate that the people were eating food of high quality: fish and the meat of cattle. They brewed beer and baked bread. Their own bones—well-preserved in various tombs on the site—show signs that where they were fractured (manoeuvring 10 tonne stones leaves its mark on the spine), they were carefully reset. Like the ruling class, these people appear to have received the best medical attention. There is even evidence of carefully performed amputations, probably the earliest in the world. But their lives differed from those of the privileged minority: they died on average 10 years earlier. The bones show that half of the population were women, and there was approximately one child to every couple. In short, the inhabitants of this place were well-to-do working families living in stone houses: they were not slaves. So what is the evidence that they were involved in the building of the three pyramids of Giza at all? As mentioned, the remains of some of the vertebrae that make up the spinal column show signs of severe distortions, compatible with having been put under great physical strain. Second, inscriptions found on the tombs link their occupants directly to the building of the pyramids. From individual bones DNA has been extracted (with care to prevent contamination with DNA from those handling the samples). Although the DNA is not in very good condition—it is after all more than 4000 years old—analysis appears to indicate a relationship to present-day Egyptians dwelling in Cairo and further south along the Upper Nile.

The picture that emerges is this. The builders of the pyramids of Giza were construction workers who came with their families from within the entire Nile valley, most probably out of choice, in order to become involved in a national project. They formed a community— a thriving city representing some 2% of the million Egyptians living at that time—devoted to one aim: the construction of the largest mausoleums imaginable for housing the bodies of their kings. Fortunately most of these pharaos lived long enough to see their final resting place completed before their own demise. The Great Pyramid—the northern-most of the three—was built for King Khufu (Cheops in Greek), the second king of the fourth dynasty.[4] The next to be built was the one that now stands in the middle: it was commissioned by Khufu's second son Khafre, who succeeded after a short reign by his elder brother. The reigns of Khufu to Khafre dominated the fourth dynasty: their rule spanned 106 years. The southern-most and smallest of the three pyramids was built for Khafre's son Menkaure. He did not live long enough to see his tomb completed: it was finished by his successor Chepseskef.

How were these monuments built? Construction probably started with the base in its entirety, and the blocks were then dragged by ropes up a specially built ramp running along the outside of the growing structure; when the apex was completed, the ramp was removed. An alternative explanation for lifting the enormous blocks of stone off the ground was recently proposed by American scientists from Caltech: they suggest that kites were used to literally fly the blocks into place. Intriguing as this sounds, it is unlikely to have been the sole method; tethering the blocks to kites in order to lessen their weight is more plausible. Once the blocks were in place, the sides were faced with smooth white stone. Most of these coverings have since been plundered, as have the interiors of the tombs, but the facing near the top of the middle pyramid is still in place. This gives the visitor an idea of what the three pyramids must initially have looked like in the bright Egyptian sunlight: a truly stunning spectacle (Plate 2).

Everything the Egyptians did was innovative. They were the first to introduce written numerals around 3500 BC: these took the form of simple lines for numbers such as 1 and 10; 500 years later numerals were in use by the Sumerians, and by 1200 BC by the Minoans. Written numerals do not appear on Indic or Sinic inscriptions until almost 1000 years later. The Egyptians probably invented glass—for which temperatures of 1500 °C are required to fuse sand and sodium carbonate—during the great dynasties of the third millennium BC. At first they made small beads, but by the third century BC, all kinds of objects were being produced, that even included the first lenses. Glass blowing began a few centuries later, most likely not in Egypt itself but further up the eastern coast of the Mediterranean in what is now Syria (although others assert that it had been practised by the Egyptians all along). Even the mousetrap, powered then as it is today by a simple spring, we owe to Egyptian technology.

For a brief period from the seventeenth century BC Egypt was ruled by the Hyksos (meaning 'rulers of foreign lands'), but the cultural traditions of scholarship and literature, art and music, astronomy and medicine were maintained right through occupation by subsequent Assyrian, Persian, Greek, Roman and Arab invaders. As trade across the Mediterranean increased, Alexandria, the port city named after its Greek conqueror, grew in size and became the capital of Egypt until the seventh century. The Arabs then moved the capital back upstream to just below Memphis, where it has remained ever since (called first Misr, then Cairo). In its heyday, Alexandria was the cultural centre of the Mediterranean, and its lighthouse on the island of Pharos,[5] another of the Seven Wonders of the ancient world, was probably the first of its kind: sailors were guided safely past the rocky coast line by the fire at its pinnacle that burned throughout the night. It was still standing in the twelfth century, 1500 years after its construction, and collapsed only 2 centuries later, for reasons still unclear.

A further innovation resulting from the fusion of Egyptian and Greek culture in Alexandria at this time was the establishment of a centre of learning within the Alexandrian Museum. There was the famous library, a botanical garden, a zoo, an observatory and some rooms for the dissection of animals: Euclid worked here, as did Eratosthenes[6] and the astronomer Hipparchus. The library contained not only Greek documents in the form of some of the earliest books ever produced, but most likely translations of scripts from Mesopotamia and India also; like glass-blowing, the idea of binding documents together in the form of a book probably originated further north, on the eastern shores of the Mediterranean: the Phoenician port of Byblos, with which Egypt had been in contact since the third millennium BC, lays claim to this invention by its very name.[7] The museum and its library survived the earthquake that demolished Queen Cleopatra's palace in the bay of Alexandria, but were partially destroyed during civil war 500 years after their construction; the remnants were finally burnt by Christian warriors a century later. Thus was one of the most complete records of life — perhaps as many as 700,000 manuscripts[8] — within four of the five civilisations of the Old World lost forever.

The Egyptian civilisation, unlike those that began in Mesopotamia, in the valley of the Indus, in Central America or in Peru, is unique in that it has survived in the same place — which has in many eyes become the intellectual capital of Islam today — for over 5000 years. The Sinic civilisation comes close, as does the Minoan if one considers its assimilation and transplantation from Crete to mainland Greece by the Mycenians as a continuum.

India

The fertile valley of the Indus, an area extending some 700 miles from Lahore in the north-east to Karachi in the south-west, was home to agricultural developments from the eighth millennium BC onwards. Wheat and barley were grown, sheep and goats domesticated. A thousand years later cattle of the Indian humped variety were being bred for food and work. By 5500 BC these peoples, referred to as Indic, were building brick walls and storing their cereal crops in specially constructed granaries. Pottery was being produced, copper and ivory were in use; lapis lazuli was mined from the Kvarjeh Mohammed mountain range, as it is to this day. Three thousand years on and urban settlements such as those at Harappa[9] and Mohenjo-Daro[10] began to appear: towns built to a grid-like plan with public buildings and proper drainage systems. Their inhabitants developed a standardized system of weights and measures, and fashioned objects out of bronze as well as copper, ivory and clay. They traded with the communities around them, and eventually extended commercial links all the way to Mesopotamia. But the suggestion that the Indic civilisation is an off-shoot of the Sumerian is probably unjustified. Its language and architecture, its religion and its arts, are distinct; the resemblance between Indic signs and Sumerian pictographs (see Figure 8.1) may be fortuitous. In short, the Indic civilisation developed independently of others, just as did that of Sumeria, Egypt and Crete; trade between all four centres took off only after thriving communities, living in towns and cities, had formed their individual identities. Like the Sumerian civilisation, that of the Indus valley did not last. It began to decline and in 1050 BC fell into the hands of Aryan warriors, after which it gradually disintegrated. Internal weakness is often the prelude to conquest by an outside invader: the gradual loss of the western parts of the Roman Empire to warring tribes of Goths and Vandals is an example. But in the way that the skills pioneered by the Sumerians were absorbed by subsequent middle-eastern cultures, so the many achievements of the Indus people were assimilated by Hindu and Buddhist dynasties that culminated in the Mauryan Empire on the Indian sub-continent to the east. One society may slip down the ladder, but another benefits and climbs up: the totality of human accomplishments progresses unswervingly.

China

~~~~~~

The trade links that developed between the four civilisations I have so far described can have had little direct influence on the culture that blossomed along the Huanghe, or Yellow River, in China 3000 years ago. The arrival of Indo-Europeans and their horses on the north-west frontier around this time may have contributed certain elements[11] and one can discern similarities in early scripts (cf. Figure 8.2 with Figure 8.1), but the cultural and technological achievements of the indigenous people are unique and in several instances pre-date inventions in other parts of the world. Large settlements surrounded by earth walls along the upper, middle and lower reaches of the Yellow River, as well as further south along the Yangzi, had been constructed up to 3000 years earlier, and indicate the time span over which agricultural communities gradually developed into city states. Similar sites have been unearthed as far north as the provinces of Liaoning, Jilin and Heilongjiang[12] and as far south as Guangxi, Guangdong and Fujian—even the island of Taiwan—all of which border on the South China Sea. So there was probably some intermingling through trade along the entire seabord of China. The peoples to the north grew millet; those to the south, rice. Horses, cattle and sheep were the main animals to be domesticated in the northern regions; in the south, chickens, pigs and dogs. According to Chinese scholars, their first dynasty is that of the Xia, who are believed to have ruled from around the twenty-first to the sixteenth century BC. One of the chief towns is said to have been at Erlitou, near the modern city of Yanshi in Henan, where the remains of a palace settlement have been found. The rule of the Xia was followed by that of the Shang, who had begun to burgeon north of the lands of the Xia, and who went on to develop one of the most sophisticated cultures of the time.

Under Shang rule technologies such as the use of the wheel,[13] casting in bronze, carving in jade and ivory and weaving in silk,[14] were perfected. Astronomy was practised, music was played, and vessels made of clay, whose manufacture dates back to between 6000 and 5000 BC, were elaborated in styles and colours distinctive of each region. One of the most significant advances of this time was the development of a written script[15] that has been preserved in the form of inscriptions made on bronze, on stone and on animal remains. The shoulder blades of oxen, sheep, deer, pigs and occasionally even humans were one favoured medium; the shells of turtles (supposed to have magical qualities) were another. These writings refer to many aspects of Shang life: farming and the city; military campaigns and expeditions; astronomy, the calendar and the climate; religious beliefs and sacrifices; personalities and the royal household. The capital of the Shang was probably at Erligang, now modern Zhengzhou in Henan province. The city, which spanned some 25 km, was surrounded by an earthen wall 7 km in length.

The Shang dynasty came to an end with the arrival of the Zhou in 1045 BC. But their civilisation survived, indeed it was under the Zhou that the Chinese script was further developed and the words of Confucius eventually recorded. Towns and palaces, tombs and statues, bear witness to the achievements of the Zhou. The Western Zhou, whose territories stretched beyond present-day Xi'an, ruled until 771 BC. Their jurisdiction was followed by that of the Eastern Zhou, who occupied the coastal region and ruled until 221 BC. Throughout this time there were wars and conflicts, and turbulence subsided—albeit briefly—only when the lands of the Zhou were unified under the Qin; this was the first dynasty of Imperial China, an Empire that was to last for more than 2000 years until the Qing[16] dynasty came to an end in 1911 and was replaced by the Republic of Sun Yat Sen. It is from the Qin that the word 'China', and its adjectival noun 'sinic', are said to be derived.[17]

For their part, the Chinese people called their kingdom by the capital in which the ruler resided: Xia was the capital of the Xia, Shang the capital of the Shang, Zhou the capital of the Zhou, and so on. Beyond the region designated by its capital lay the lands of the feudal lords, and beyond that the lands of the barbarians.

Neither merited the name of the country. During these times the lands of the people to the south was called Han, which had a pejorative meaning. For their part the Han called their northern neighbours 'barbarian weakling' or 'unkempt caitiff'. When the dynasty of the Han succeeded that of the Qin in 206 BC, the name-calling was reversed. Only during the late seventeenth century AD, by which time the Qing dynasty had followed that of the Ming, was the country briefly called by a 'generic' name: Zhongguo, meaning the Royal Centre. If the Chinese considered those living beyond their boundaries to be barbarians—as of course did the Greeks, the Romans and many other nations—they had good reason to do so. Throughout the Middle Ages, while much of European and Middle Eastern civilisation lay dormant, the culture and technology of China flourished. Its history shows, on the one hand, how lack of human movement does not detract from innovative ideas; but on the other hand, how insulation from outside influence eventually leads to its decline.

Crete

The Minoan civilisation dates back to around 3000 BC, which makes it the oldest in Europe. It was revealed by the archaeological excavations of one man, Sir Arthur Evans. He began digging there in 1899 and continued doing so for the next 36 years. It was he who coined the word Minoan, based on the legendary King Minos, who is said to have lived on an island that Evans identified as Crete. The Minoans developed a distinctive style of architecture. Their rulers cared less about their after-life than their present life: they built palaces, not pyramids. Palaces at Knossos, Mallia, Phaistos and Zakro; that at Knossos, near the present-day port of Heraklion, contained beautiful frescoes of landscapes, animal life and other themes. The Minoan was one of the earliest Bronze Age cultures. They worked not only in metal, but also produced elaborate seals and a vast range of pottery. Their culture continued after the arrival of the Mycenians from the northern mainland in the fifteenth century BC, although the palaces were eventually destroyed. The palace of Knossos most likely suffered as much from an earthquake as from the invading Mycenians. But by this time the aggressors had absorbed sufficient of the Minoan culture to make Greece, to which it was exported, the centre of European civilisation for the next 1000 years.

I referred earlier to the destruction of the great library at Alexandria, with the loss of much information about early cultures including those of Greece and Rome. But others remain: the library at Herculanaeum is an example of a collection that is currently being restored. It is part of a villa that once belonged to Julius Caesar's father-in-law, and contains thousands of papyrus scrolls. The villa, and the rest of the town, became buried below lava when Mount Vesuvius erupted in 79 AD, and much of its contents were burned. During earlier excavations many papyri were simply thrown away as being no more than bits of charcoal. Others survived. Some of these are in sufficiently good condition to be read: they describe the life of the people of the time, and the philosophies of its intelligentsia, which included the Greek sage Epicureus. The majority of papyri, however, are too badly burnt even to be unfolded, let alone read: you cannot distinguish characters written in black ink on a background that is charred black. Now, however, new ways to gently separate the layers have been devised, and spectroscopic techniques—developed by NASA to explore distant stars—are being used to reveal characters even against the charred background. Thousands of such papyri still lie buried beneath the rubble, waiting to be retrieved and read.

Central America

We know less about the civilisations that emerged in Central and South America than we do about those in Asia, North Africa and Europe. The oldest culture is probably that of the Olmecs, who inhabited the eastern shores of Mexico near Veracruz 3000 years ago. Enormous heads, expertly carved out of rocks weighing as much as 30 tons, attest to Olmec skill as craftsmen and engineers. The site at La Venta, now in the middle of a marsh near the coast, is

100 miles away from the nearest source of stone. How the Olmecs managed to transport such boulders we do not know, any more than we understand how the inhabitants of Easter Island brought *their* stone heads—which resemble those of the Olmecs in certain regards—to their present site. The Olmecs appear to have practiced human sacrifice—the earliest recorded in the New World—in a particularly gruesome manner: the bones of a baby that had its arms, legs and head cut off and that seems to have been plucked, Macbeth-like, from its mother's womb, have been unearthed in this region.

What is probably one of the largest, as well as the oldest, settlements in all of America is at Teotihuacan, 35 miles north east of Mexico City. It may have housed as many as 200,000 inhabitants. Like the other cities that grew up in Central America—those of the Toltec to the north, the Olmec on the eastern coast and the Maya in the Yucatan peninsula—life centred around ceremonial courts that contained pyramids as well as areas for indulging in the favourite pastime: the ball game. Trading between the cities was extensive, and the cultures of each of the peoples I have mentioned were similar. The pyramids were stepped, like the ziggurats of Sumeria and the early pyramids of the Egyptians, but they were smaller in size. On the top of each pyramid a temple was built, in front of which were elaborate carved statues. The temples were used for the religious ceremonies (that included human sacrifice) in honour of the Gods, the chief of which was Quetzalcoatl, the feathered serpent. At Teotihuacan one may climb the reconstructed temple that was dedicated to Quetzalcoatl, as well as those built in honour of the sun and moon. The city lasted for 1000 years until it was sacked by the Toltecs in 750 AD. Its ruins were rediscovered by the Aztecs in the fifteenth century, just 100 years before the arrival of the Spanish. By that time the Aztecs were masters of most of the inhabited parts of Central America. They incorporated much of what they had found at Teotihuacan into their own capital, which they built on an island in a lake high in the plateau to the south: they called it Tenochtitlan. After their defeat by Hernando Cortés in 1521, the lake was drained and the area became the site of the present capital, Mexico City.

A refined culture, that of the Zapotec, developed in the region that is now the state of Oaxaca. It reached its peak between 300 and 900 AD (Plate 3), after which it began to wane. The arrival of the Mixtec in this area did not prevent the deterioration, and Zapotec society was in sharp decline by the time of the Spanish invasion in the sixteenth century. One of the most advanced cultures in America—that of the Maya—grew up in the Yucatan, which now includes Belize, Guatemala and Honduras, as well as parts of Mexico; the whole region of Yucatan and central Mexico is often referred to as Mesoamerica. The Mayan civilisation, rather like that of the Zapotec, attained the pinnacle of its achievements between the fourth and eighth centuries AD. But it was much more extensive, with a population of 16 million. Similar to the decline of Zapotec culture, that of the Mayans had collapsed—for reasons that are not at all clear[18]— by the time the conquistadors arrived. Nevertheless, pockets of Maya-speaking people survived, and 4 million of their descendants still speak the language today. They continue to cultivate the same crops— corn (maize), beans and squash—that their ancestors grew 3500 years ago. In the south of the region, where the terrain is hilly, agriculture was maintained through elaborate irrigation and terracing. The Mayans were masters of astronomical observation: their calendar is more accurate than the Julian one introduced by Caesar. They built temples, pyramids, palaces, ball courts and plazas. Intricate stone inscriptions and relief carving, from which much of our knowledge regarding the Mayan civilisation is derived, adorn their edifices. Because many of the edifices constructed by the Maya are more recent than those at sites in the Old World, they have not become buried with the passage of time, and are largely above ground. Moreover many buildings, such as those at Chichen Itza, Matapan, Palenque and Uxmal, have been relatively well preserved despite the inroads of jungle vegetation that took over once they were abandoned. The Maya worked in copper and gold and made paper, which they incorporated into books, from the inner bark of the wild fig tree. Of all the civilisations that grew up in the Americas, that of the Maya is unique: they appear to be the only ones to have produced a written script. It was hieroglyphic and has been largely deciphered, as a result of which we know more about the Mayan than about any other culture that had collapsed before the Spaniards arrived in the sixteenth century.

South America

The civilisation of the Incas, with its capital Cuzco situated 11,000 feet high in the Andes of Peru, can have had little contact with those of Central America, and its culture is distinct from that of the Aztecs or the Maya. There is a similarity merely in the fact that the Inca and Aztec civilisations were each at their peak when the conquistadors arrived in the sixteenth century. The Incas are by no means the oldest civilisation in South America. Recent excavations along the arid coastline of Peru are revealing a once great city of pyramids[19] that has been dated to 2600 BC—exactly the time, as it happens, that Khufu was building his great pyramid at Giza. There were settled communities elsewhere. The Chavin people lived in the north-eastern highlands of Peru from about 900–200 BC: at Chavin de Huantar there was built a large temple complex with elaborate carving. Further south along the coastal plain, 100 miles south of present day Lima, the Paracas existed simultaneously with the Chavin further north; their culture lasted even longer, right up to about 400 AD. The Paracas originally buried their dead in caves; at a later date they were interred in specially constructed cemeteries; the bodies were wrapped in fine clothes, some of which have survived to this day because of the dry soil. Like the Chavins, the Paracas produced highly decorative textiles, as well as pottery and objects made of gold. Another coastal people who developed a culture, from about 200–600 AD, were the Mochica of northern Peru. Their most distinctive legacy is a complex of buildings at Moche that includes the remains of the largest pre-Columbian building in South America, called the Pyramid of the Sun. Also in northern Peru lived the Chimu, whose capital was at Chan Chan, and who developed sophisticated metal working in silver and gold, as indeed did most of these Andean cultures. The Chimu and the remains of all the other cultures were finally absorbed by the Incas, who now dominated the entire western lands of the South American continent.

Inca rule lasted, from around 1200 AD, for just 300 years. But during that time they established the largest empire in South America. By 1528 it stretched from northern Ecuador, across the whole of Peru, to Bolivia and down to parts of northern Argentina and Chile, a distance of 3000 miles. To link their vast lands they constructed a road system as advanced as that of the Romans. But no chariots rattled along these highways: they walked, or rode on the back of a llama. The Incas matched the Romans also in irrigation and aquaculture, and were able to feed some 7 million people: the poor received welfare through the taxes paid by the better-off. Recent research in the Baures region of Bolivian Amazonia[20] has revealed a vast hydraulic network of earthen causeways in zigzag form, which together with ponds covered an area greater than 500 square kilometres. Even today these abandoned waterways are teeming with 100,000–400,000 fish per hectare: buchere, yallu, cuñaré, palomota, sábalo and bentón. In prehispanic times such artificial fisheries would have produced hundreds of tonnes of edible snails as well. By the sides of the water, palms (*Mauritia flexuosa*) still grow. Up to 5000 different fruits, rich in vitamins A and C, oil and protein, can be harvested from a single tree, year upon year. The fibres of the palm fronds would have been used—as they are to this day—for baskets, mats, hammocks, bowstrings and thatch. In short, the Incas had developed a technology that, through ingenious retention of rain water, was able to sustain large populations living in a savanna environment. In common with all the civilisations that grew up in Central and South America, they lacked only one amenity: the wheel. This fact alone makes one deeply suspicious of those who propose a cultural link between the Old World and the New: of all the similarities that are presented to indicate such an entry from East to West—stone pyramids, mummified corpses, reed boats— surely the one item of technology a presumptive intruder from the Old World would have found missing and immediately remedied, is the use of the wheel.

Apart from that, Inca technology was extensive: factories and workshops were set up to produce the finest pottery, textiles and metal objects made of silver, gold and bronze. Their architecture included perfectly fitting stone masonry, often erected in the most demanding places. The buildings at Machu Picchu, which include a palace and a temple to the sun perched on a steep hillside in the Andean jungle below Cuzco, attest to the architectural skills of the

Incas. Surprisingly, Macchu Picchu was never found by the Spanish; it was discovered only in 1911 by an American archaeologist named Hiram Bingham.[21] Having survived intact, and lain undisturbed for over 400 years, the influence of modern civilisation has not been benign: a crane that was being used recently to film a beer advertisement toppled over and did more damage to a beautiful Inca stone sundial in 10 seconds than the weather had been able to inflict in half a millennium.

Sadly, the learning and culture of the Incas was not to last: it would be destroyed by an illiterate Spaniard of peasant stock. Francisco Pizarro had left Spain at the age of 23 to spend the next 25 years in what is now Panama, killing the natives and looking for gold. Failing to find the latter, he sailed south along the Pacific coast and reached the frontier of the Inca empire. Here indeed were said to be the riches he had been seeking. By this time, however, Pizarro's unpleasant temper had caused most of his army to defect, and in 1528 he returned to Spain to pick up more men. With Charles V's support he was back in Peru four years later. The following year he captured the Inca leader Atahualpa in Cajamarca. Atahualpa tried to buy the Spaniards off with gold and silver enough to fill two rooms. Pizarro took the precious metals and melted them down, destroying centuries of craftsmanship. He then betrayed Atahualpa by accusing him of treason and burnt him at the stake. The dead man's son Manco was made puppet ruler of the Incas. Pizarro then marched his army 1000 miles south towards the capital Cuzco. At this point he was, like Alexander in Asia 1800 years earlier, deep within enemy territory and cut off from any possible reinforcements. His men were outnumbered by 100 to one. But there was a difference: in 300 BC the armies of Alexander and Darius fought with similar weaponry; in 1537 the Spanish had horses and gunpowder, whereas the Incas had to rely on llamas and bronze age weapons. Modern technology won: Manco's army was defeated and Cuzco fell to the invader. The empire of the Incas was no more.

Toynbee considered the Mayan and Inca civilisations primary. In the light of many archaeological finds since his day, it may be more appropriate to deem the Olmec in Central America and the Chavin in South America as primary and the subsequent, albeit more extensive, civilisations of the Maya and Incas as secondary, in the way that the Minoan culture is the progenitor of the much more developed one of Greece. This is a matter for historians to argue. What is clear is that the civilisations of the New World left their mark on later societies, just as did those of the Old World — Sumerian, Egyptian, Indic, Sinic and Minoan. The culture of the Maya may have petered out, but not before some of their achievements had inspired the Aztecs. Although they, like the Incas, were largely eradicated by the conquistadors in the sixteenth century, certain features of their life, relating to agricultural products in particular, were incorporated into Spanish ways and soon spread to the rest of Europe: the potato and the avocado, chocolate and tobacco, are obvious examples.

Elsewhere

I have so far not described any cultural stirrings in sub-Saharan Africa, for the same reason that I have ignored those of northern Europe or North America: by the criteria I have chosen — the construction of towns and cities, of pyramids and temples, of harbours and roads, the development of literature and art, of technology and commerce — they do not match up.[22] My aim is to show how man's reaction to a challenge, his search for a better quality of life, has transformed the world he inhabits. The stone circles of Stonehenge and Avebury in southern England, the avenues of megaliths at Carnac in Brittany, the acropolis at Great Zimbabwe, the beads of the Pomo Indians of California and the five storey-high cave dwellings of the Anasazi Indians in the Chaco Canyon of New Mexico[23] contribute relatively little to that quest: the construction of public buildings, the principles of irrigation of crops and drainage of urban waste, the invention of a written script, the art of working in precious metals and the granaries of Cuzco and Mohenjo-Daro do. I appreciate that pyramids and palaces did not do much for the common man, who continued to live in simple huts throughout these early times; but soon they were built of wood, and then of stone. If the rulers had not sought self-aggrandisement, the lives of their subjects would have remained static for ever. It is the same today. What were originally the toys of the rich—the telephone and the automobile, the refrigerator and the television set—have become the everyday appurtenances of the masses. If the spread of luxuries from the few to the many has failed to happen in countries like Bangladesh or Brazil, the problem lies with a biased internal economy, not with the innovative spirit of man.

What about the Celts, you say. Did they not have burial chambers —near Hallstadt in Germany and La Tène in Switzerland— as sophisticated as those of the Egyptians? Rulers buried with elaborate ornaments in gold and accoutrements of bronze, with their weapons made of iron at a time, 1000–500 BC, when much of Europe was still dominated by hunter-gatherers? Did the Celts who migrated into the British Isles and Ireland not live in well-thatched wattle-and-daub structures distinct from those found elsewhere in Europe in being round, not square or oblong? Was not the agriculture of Britain so advanced that by 200 BC they were achieving the same yield of cereal crops as their descendants managed in the middle of the twentieth century? Did they not devise a language that is spoken—in slightly different forms in Ireland and Scotland, in Cornwall and Wales—to this day? Were the Celts in England during the first century BC not living lives more sophisticated than those of the Roman soldiery who invaded them? Very true. And yet the influence of Rome and ultimately of Greece is evident in their jewels and weapons, and in other aspects of their life. We must not forget that the culture of the eastern Mediterranean had been spreading westwards through mercantile traders for many centuries before the foot soldiers of Julius Caesar marched into northern Europe. My point is that, just as I have not considered the civilisation of Rome as a *primary* one, so that of the Celts also owes much to the earlier influence of the Minoan and Egyptian civilisations.[24]

There is evidence of man taking a few steps up the ladder, but of failing to continue the ascent, throughout the world.[25] Some examples have been mentioned already. Recently excavated ruins in eastern Europe and Turkey precede the civilisations of Mesopotamia and Egypt. The buildings at Çatal Hüyük near Konya in southern Turkey, said to have housed 7000 people, are 8000 years old; artefacts from the same period have been found at Porodin in Macedonia and at Lepenski Vir on the banks of the Danube in Serbia; a cemetery at Nitra in Slovakia was in use 7000 years ago. More recent sites have been found in south-east Asia and sub-Saharan Africa. Near the temples of Angkor Wat in Cambodia — said to comprise the largest religious monument in the world — was a city the size of London.[26] There is evidence of extensive irrigation from lakes that became replenished at each annual monsoon. Trade with China was initiated. Yet, for reasons that are as unclear as those that underlie the demise of the Maya, the culture of the Khmer slowly perished.

Near Lake Victoria there are structures dating back to 700 BC that show evidence of Iron Age work; the technology was developed in the Middle East only around 500 BC. Manuscripts have been found in Timbuktu that precede the arrival of the Arab caravans in the eleventh century by 200 years. Some 100 remains of stone buildings have been located throughout eastern and southern Africa: at Mapungubwe in South Africa,[27] at Great Zimbabwe in the country that now bears its name,[28] and on Kilwa island off Tanzania.[29] There was trade with China (the Africans brought the giraffe to those lands), with India and with Persia: gold and ivory were exported in exchange for silks and carpets. So why had all such activity ceased long before the European explorers of the nineteenth century came to this great continent (and divided it up between them)? Why did the quest of these people peter out?[30] We do not know. A change in the climate — as elsewhere — may have played a part. The Portuguese in the sixteenth century may have plundered thriving communities, in the way that the Spaniards did in Central and South America.

And then there is the possibility of entire, lost civilisations in the Mediterranean and in south-east Asia that predated all five of the primary civilisations of the Old World. The proof is scanty, but is presented with vigour by writers like Stephen Oppenheimer[31] and Graham Hancock.[32] The argument runs roughly as follows. There is evidence of the cultivation of rice in Thailand more than 7000 years ago, which predates its use in China. So does the pottery of the Jomon culture in Japan: millions of items, many with human figurines, have been recovered. Some of these were manufactured more than 12,000 years ago, earlier than anywhere else in the world. And so on. Why have not more traces of such ancient civilisations been discovered? Because much of the land on which these developments took place is now under water, submerged by the floods that accompanied the melting of the ice caps at the end of the last ice age. More than 10,000 years ago the single land mass of Sundaland covered much of what is now the Gulf of Thailand, the Java Sea, the South China Sea, the Yellow Sea and the East China Sea. Not only did the rising of the waters — the Asian equivalent of the biblical flood — destroy the evidence of man's activities in this region, it drove some of his descendants westwards towards India, Mesopotamia and Egypt and northwards into China. Genetic and linguistic markers testify to such human migrations, and contribute to the argument that the earliest civilisations emerged not in the fertile crescent of the Middle East, the banks of the Indus and the Yellow River, but in south-east Asia.

That large floods occurred globally around 14,000, 11,500 and 8000 years ago, as huge amounts of land-locked ice began to melt, is fairly well documented. And the searchers for lost cities that now lie submerged below the sea are finding them, not just in south-east Asia,[33] but in the Mediterranean too — off Malta,[34] for example. The survivors of the subsequent flood may have gone on to found another city nearby, for on Malta today there are stone circles that are 1000 years older that those of Stonehenge. Plato may have been remarkably prescient when he described the land of Atlantis as being destroyed 9000 years before his time: since he lived 2400 years ago, this places the devastation of Atlantis at exactly the time of the second great flood.

Have I, after all, been wrong in describing the civilisations of 6000 years ago as primary? Perhaps so, but because little of the earlier, potential civilisations survived, we cannot gauge their success by the criteria I have applied to those that survived for thousands of years on dry land. The builders of Stonehenge and Carnac, of Çatal Hüyük and Lepenski Vir, of Mapungubwe and Great Zimbabwe, of the Cliff Palace at Mesa Verde National Park (Colorado) and Pueblo Bonito in the Chaco Canyon, climbed several rungs up the ladder of achievement but then fell off. The architects of cities that became submerged by the rising waters of the Mediterranean and the seas off south-east Asia had also begun the ascent. In their case, the ladder simply broke.

Notes

1. From about 6000 to 1000 years ago.
2. Joachim Bretschneider, *Sci. Am.* **283** (October): 62–69; 2000.
3. The 300 metre high Eiffel Tower, completed in 1889, is twice as tall.
4. 2575–2465 BC.
5. The place name has been retained to mean lighthouse in Greek (*pharos*) and the romance languages: *phare* in French, *faro* in Italian, Portuguese and Spanish.
6. See Note 19 of Chapter 5.
7. *Byblos* = bible = book.
8. See Alison Abbott, 'A temple of knowledge', *Nature* **419**: 556–557; 2002.
9. 300 miles south-west of Lahore.
10. 200 miles north-east of Karachi.
11. Such as the use of the horse; possibly also bronze.
12. Also called Manchuria.
13. One of its earliest uses was in chariots employed for warfare.
14. Its production from silk worms was a jealously guarded secret, kept from the outside world for centuries.
15. The idea for which may have emanated from the Indus valley.
16. Not to be confused with Qin (Ch'in); the Qing (Ch'ing) dynasty is also known as Manchu, after the name of the Tartar people who conquered China in 1644.
17. But this is doubtful. China, previously known as Cathay, entered European languages only during the sixteenth and seventeenth centuries: the word probably comes from the Persian *chini*, which may itself be derived from the Sanskrit *cina*, meaning thoughtful or cultivated; *cina* was certainly already used in India to refer to its north-eastern neighbour in Tang times (618–907 AD). The possibility that *cina* itself is derived from Qin is unlikely, bearing in mind that Qin was pronounced 'dz'ien' in Old Chinese. *Chini* was originally employed merely to describe the delicate porcelain that came from Cathay: not until the nineteenth century was the word applied to the country itself.
18. Eric Thompson considers the collapse of the 'classic' Mayan culture in the Yucatan to be the result of invasion and conquest by the Putun

(also known as Chontal Maya) from the south, living in what are today's states of Campeche and Tabasco. The Putun were traders who navigated, in canoes, right round the coast of Yucatan. They established a base on the island of Cozumel, from where they attacked the mainland to the west. By 918 AD they had conquered Chichen Itza. See J. Eric S. Thompson, op. cit., pp 3–47. But extended drought is another possibility. See Daniel Grossman, 'Parched turf battle', *Sci. Am.* **287** (December): 14–15; 2002.

19. Horizon programme, shown on UK television (BBC2) on Thursday 10 January 2002.
20. Clark L. Erickson, 'An artificial landscape-scale fishery in the Bolivian Amazon', *Nature* **408**: 190–193; 2000.
21. See Max Milligan, *Realm of the Incas*, HarperCollins, London, 2001.
22. I prefer to follow Thomas Hobbes, op. cit., who considered the characteristics of civilisation to include Arts, Letters and Society.
23. See Jared Diamond, 'The trail to Chaco Canyon', *Nature* **413**: 687–690; 2001.
24. But we should note the views of writers like Marija Gimbutas: see Note 33 to Chapter 8.
25. Or, as Fernand Braudel puts it, 'A culture is a civilization that has not yet achieved maturity, its greatest potential, nor consolidated its growth' (op. cit., vol 1, p 101).
26. Today, never mind during the thirteenth century when the civilisation of the Khmer was at its height.
27. Tenth to twelfth century.
28. Twelfth to fourteenth century. It had a population of 18,000, with evidence of settlements going as far back as the third century BC.
29. Fifteenth century.
30. For centuries, since Great Zimbabwe was discovered by the Portuguese in 1488, sites in sub-Saharan Africa were thought not to have been built by the indigenous people at all: it was the Queen of Sheba, it was the Venetians, but never the native Shono or his ancestors who executed such constructions. Recent evidence shows that the egocentric views of white archaeologists need no longer be taken seriously (*Mysteries of the Ancients*, presented by Bettany Hughes and shown on UK television (Channel 5) at 8 p.m. on 24 June 2002).
31. Stephen Oppenheimer, op. cit.
32. Graham Hancock, op. cit.
33. Stone circles off Okinawa and other structures nearer Taiwan.
34. Malta was joined to Sicily and mainland Italy 12,000 years ago.

CHAPTER EIGHT

Civilisation 2: communication and culture

Language and literature

*I*n the Prologue I mentioned the hypothesis of Robin Dunbar, that language in man grew out of grooming in apes: it is the time when family members relax and gossip. The philosopher Karl Popper, in rejecting the view that language arose out of cries for help and warnings of danger, had earlier proposed something similar: 'I suggest that the main phonetic apparatus of human language arises ... from playful babbling of mothers with babies and of groups of children ...'.[1] Such moments are also the time for telling stories, which are the foundations of literature. Without language there is no culture: communication is an essential ingredient of civilisation. As the physicist Niels Bohr put it in regard to science, 'What is it that human beings ultimately depend on? We depend on our words. We are suspended in language. Our task is to communicate ... without losing the objective or unambiguous character [of what we say]'.[2] If *H. neanderthalensis* lacked a properly developed voice box and therefore language, it is one reason why this group—had it survived long enough—would have been unlikely to have started a civilisation. On the other hand, there are those who believe that our direct ancestors were communicating among themselves 500,000 years ago,[3] long before the emergence of *H. sapiens*. By the time that agriculture began to be practised 10,000 years ago, it is probable that most communities around the world were conferring among themselves in some form of speech. Originally some words were probably onomatopaeic, as in the English words hiss and piss, whistle and whisper, groan and moan, hum and drum, cuckoo and macaw, slither, plop, bang, crack, thunder and so on. On the other hand, Karl Popper believed that language owes more to whole statements—as in Chinese characters—than to single sounds or words.[1] I shall restrict myself to describing the languages that were spoken by those communities that developed into a civilisation. Discourse leads to literature, but this is not a prerequisite for the initiation of a culture: the Incas lacked a written script, yet produced a civilisation as sophisticated in other ways as any. On the other hand, writing does greatly assist in the administration of a growing community. The earliest written records appear to be those of the Sumerians 5400 years ago. Edicts and religious texts were the main uses to which writing was put, although accounting soon followed (or the other way round[4]). In that regard we may note that while the Incas did not develop a written script, they did use bundles of strings knotted in various ways for accounting purposes (as did the early Chinese).

Dunbar mentions a figure of around 150 people as the critical size for the beginnings of language: most people know up to this number of friends—rarely more—with whom to have a good gossip. He compares the group sizes of grooming by various genera of primate (monkeys and apes) with the dimensions of their neocortex; this is part of the outer layer of the brain (the cortex) that is concerned with higher cerebral functions like intellect, memory and consciousness. In most mammals the neocortex accounts for 30–40% of total brain volume, but in primates it is higher: from 50% in prosimians (primitive monkeys) to 80% in humans. Dunbar has compared the size of the neocortex with the number that make up a grooming circle. Since brain size is proportional to body mass,[5] larger mammals will have a larger neocortex irrespective of the grooming size. Dunbar has therefore plotted the neocortex *ratio* (its size divided by the body weight) against grooming size. His conclusion is that the two arc related. In chimpanzees, for example, the neocortex ratio is 3 and the grooming size is 70. In humans the neocortex ratio is 4, which extrapolates to a grooming, i.e. gossiping, size of 150.[6]

Is it the growth of the neocortex that allows primates to remember an increasing number of acqaintances with whom to groom or gossip, or does that activity itself induce the formation of more cortical neurons? One would like to think the latter, and there is some evidence for this. In songbirds, for example, it appears that communicating with others leads to an increase in the number of cortical neurons: if a male songbird[7] is kept on its own or together with a female, there is a small increase in the number of his neurons; if it is allowed access to 45 more songbirds, the increase is doubled.[8] So far as the gossiping size in humans is concerned, Dunbar notes that archaeologists suggest a membership of around 150 for the earliest farming communities, and I proposed—rather arbitrarily —at the beginning of Chapter 6 that one might need 100 families to ensure that a wide range of talents is represented among its members: 100 families, or 200–400 people, is therefore the sort of size required for a farming community to turn its thoughts to building an integrated village, that will grow into a town and eventually into a city state, as the number of men with leadership qualities grows. Dunbar mentions the fact that in some primitive villages in Indonesia, the Philippines and South America today, the population is typically around 150: sufficient for a farming community, but insufficient to climb those extra steps up the ladder of cultural achievement?

The Sumerians, who were a hybrid stock that grew out of two different groupings, amalgated their tongues into a language that forms the roots of present-day Turkish, Hungarian and Finnish, as well as of several Caucasian dialects. It is not the precursor of Semitic languages like Hebrew and Arabic, nor of Indo-European ones. The Sumerian script, acknowledged as being the oldest form of writing, is known as cuneiform, meaning wedge-shaped. This reflects the form of the characters, which were produced by using a split reed to make an impression on soft clay; the shape of the characters was retained when chiselling them into stone replaced brushing them on to a soft surface. Some 1000 tablets—most of which contain numerals referring to some ancient accounting system—have survived. Cuneiform writing, a probable precursor of which is illustrated in Figure 8.1, was adopted by the conquering Akkadians, even though they spoke a different language, which *did*

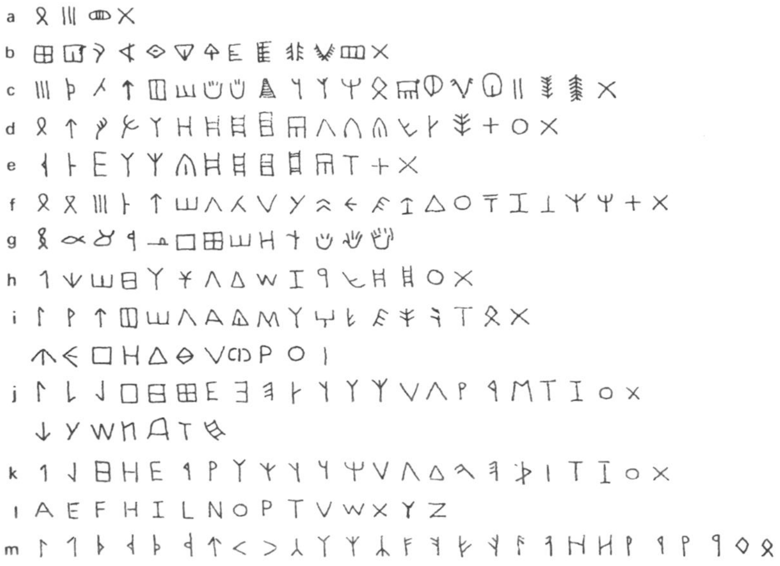

Figure 8.1 Ancient Mediterranean scripts. The signs, characters and letters that are shown formed part of the following languages: a, hieroglyphic determinants (cf. Plate 4); b, Sumerian pictorial writing; c, Indus Valley signs; d, Linear A; e, Linear B; f, Cypriote; g, Proto-Sinaitic (cf. Figure 8.2); h, Phoenician; i, Iberian; j, Etruscan; k, Greek (western branch); l, Roman; m, Runic. The similarity between all these symbols—which were in use throughout a region stretching from the Iberian peninsula to the Indus valley—and their resemblance to some of the marks found on Stone Age cave walls and small artefacts in southern France and northern Spain (Figure 9.1) is to be noted. Reproduced from Allen Forbes and Thomas R. Crowder, 'The problem of Franco-Cantabrian abstract signs: agenda for a new approach', *World Archaeology* **10**(3): 350–366; 1979, by permission of The British Library Document Supply Centre, Boston Spa, Wetherby, West Yorkshire LS23 7BQ, UK.

become what is now known as Hamitic – Semitic (also called Afro-Asian). This represents the first use of a common script for two quite different languages. The Persians refined cuneiform script into an alphabet (Pahlavi), which remained in use until it was superseded by the Arabic script following the conquest of Persia by the Muslims in the seventh century AD. An alphabetic script had been adopted by the Greeks long before Alexander's conquest of Persia, and it remains in use, in the form of the Latin and Cyrillic alphabets, within the Indo-European group of languages, as well as within Finnish, Hungarian and Turkish, to this day. Others ascribe the origin of the alphabet to the Phoenecians around 1400 BC, from whom it passed to the Greeks. Another type of alphabet originated in Canaan (in which the Ten Commandments are said to have been written on tablets of stone) around 1300 BC.

The language spoken by the ancient Egyptians is called just that: Egyptian. It is one of the Hamitic – Semitic group, an offshoot of which is Coptic, spoken by the Christian community from around the fourth century AD onwards. Although largely replaced by Arabic after the seventh century, Coptic remained in use for another 1000 years, and still forms part of the liturgy of the Copts, of whom some 35 million practise this form of Christianity around the world today. In that sense you could say that a form of Egyptian has been spoken continuously for more than 5000 years, longer than any other language. The writing developed by the Egyptians is a hieroglyphic one, meaning the use of pictorial symbols to denote objects and concepts as well as syllables. Chinese is at one extreme of hieroglyphics, with each symbol denoting a whole word, whereas modern Japanese is at the other extreme, with each symbol representing no more than a syllable. Seperate versions of Egyptian hieroglyphics were used for religious manuscripts (Hieratic) and for ordinary documents (Demotic). Egyptian hieroglyphics—on the walls of pyramids and inside tombs—chronicle the lives and achievements of the rulers responsible for their construction. The scripts came to be deciphered as a consequence of war.

When Napoleon invaded Egypt in 1798, his aim was to prevent the English trading with India (partly overland, of course, since the Suez canal was not to be built for another 60 years). Napoleon's mission failed, but a secondary goal was achieved. Alongside his 38,000 troops were 150 scholars, whose task was to interpret Egyptian culture. During excavations near a small town in the Nile Delta, a thick slab of black basalt, roughly a metre long and three-quarters of a metre wide, was picked up. It contained three sets of inscriptions: hieratic hieroglyphics, demotic hieroglyphics, and Greek characters (Plate 4). The significance of the find was immediately obvious. If the Greek version was a translation of the first two sets of writing, it would in principle be possible to decipher the script that had baffled all previous scholars. In practice it was not going to be so easy. First, much of the top part of the tablet, and some from the middle and bottom, had broken off; attempts to find the missing pieces failed. Second, it was not clear which Greek word corresponded to which particular hieroglyph. Nevertheless, such was the importance of the discovery that impressions of the tablet — called the Rosetta Stone after the town of Rashid near which it was found — were immediately made in ink and sent to scholars throughout Europe. By this time Napoleon had left Egypt and the tablet soon found its way to London where, like many another archaeological relic, it finished up in the British Museum. The Greek writing on the stone was rapidly translated by a Rev. Stephen Watson: it turned out to be an edict written in 196 BC, in which the young King Ptolemy V and his works were honoured.[9] Among the scholars accompanying Napoleon had been the mathematician Jean Baptiste Fourier.[10] On his return to France, Fourier showed the Rosetta Stone inscriptions to a precocious young scholar, Jean-Francois Champollion.

By the age of 12 Champollion had been studying Hebrew, Arabic, Syrian and Chaldean (the language spoken in later Babylon); he already new Latin and Greek. At 15 years of age he had entered the School of Oriental Languages in Paris, and within seven years had become Professor of Ancient History at Grenoble. Egyptian hieroglyphics were a new challenge that was to occupy Champollion for the rest of his life. He was, however, competing against an English scientist of wide-ranging interests: the much-respected Thomas Young, who was Champollion's senior by 17 years. Young had already made notable contributions to the study of mechanics[11] and optics[12] and had been the first to propose that light travels in waves, not as corpuscles. Later he would point out that the standard of length,[13] which was the length of a pendulum that swings exactly once every second, depends on the temperature and that this needs to be taken into account in its definition. He also became closely involved in the compilation of the *Nautical Almanac*. All that was in his spare time. His occupation was that of physician at St George's Hospital and Medical School in London.[14] Young managed to decipher much of the demotic text on the Rosetta Stone and made a start on the hieratic script: he identified the symbols denoting the word Ptolemy, and thereby showed hieroglyphics to be in part alphabetical. It was left to Champollion to complete the demotic text and to decipher the main, hieratic, hieroglyphs. The task was not completed without rancour between British and French scholars: the quest for supremacy extends beyond purely military matters.

The peoples of the Indus valley spoke what was probably a forerunner of Sanskrit and therefore one of the Indo-European languages. Sanskrit has been spoken in India, at least by scholars, for 3000 years, right into the nineteenth century. It was gradually replaced by the language of the English, following their arrival as traders[15] in Madras, Bombay and Calcutta around 1700. Local languages, such as Hindi,[16] Bengali and Gujarati, each of which represents a quite distinct tongue, have been spoken by the less-educated for centuries. It is a measure of today's ease of movement from one part of the world to another by people who do not possess Champollion's gift for languages that Hindi, Bengali and Gujarati — as well as Urdu and other Arabic dialects — are now used on official documents like passport applications and hospital registrations forms in the UK, for the benefit of its immigrant communities. The Indic people developed a hieroglyphic script, but as yet it has not been deciphered. We can therefore not say much about their literature. On the other hand, the religion, Hinduism, that had its origins here has left its mark on inscriptions and sculptures on temples, especially in the south of India, in places such as Mahabalipuram near Chennai (formerly Madras) and at sites in Karnataka south of Bangalore.

The language of the Shang who settled on the banks of the Yellow River was what is now referred to as Shanggu Hanyu or Old Chinese. This is one of the Sino-Tibetan group of languages that includes Burmese, Chinese, Nepalese, Thai and Tibetan. Although some seven different dialects (one in the north and six in the south) have developed over the millennia — so distinct that a Mandarin speaker from Beijing cannot understand a Cantonese speaker from Guangzhou — the origins are the same. There is only one script and this has been an important element in maintaining

QUEST

contact and uniformity between all the peoples of China throughout
its history. It dates back more than 3000 years to the Shang.
Compared to the oldest scripts—those of Sumeria and Egypt,
followed by that of the Indic people—it is relatively recent. It is,
however, the only one that can claim to have been in continuous
use, with some adaptations over time, to the present day.

It used to be thought that the origin of the Chinese script is
entirely ideographic, like the cuneiform script of the Sumerians
and the hieroglyphics of the Egyptians, with objects represented
pictorially. This is because ancient pictures carved on stone—
depicting hunting, fertility and other religious rites, stylised forms
of men, women, deer, oxen, horses, snakes, hands, feet, eyes,
mountains and chariots—bear a resemblance to the characters
that define these acts and objects found on bronze artifacts and
bones. Since most inscriptions were based on divination and
fortune-telling, the word 'oracle' is often used to describe the words
found on bones. Recent research suggests that this is only one
origin of Chinese writing; geometric symbols and characters
devised by local scribes and diviners have also played a part
(Figure 8.2). Later, as abstract words came to be included, the
characters became purely symbolic. As in other languages, the
words were originally monosyllabic—mainly nouns—with a single
meaning. Words like those for mountain, water and ox, as well as

Figure 8.2 Ancient Chinese scripts. a, marks on oracle bones from Shang
dynasty (around 1400 BC); b, marks on neolithic pottery (around 4000 BC).
The resemblance to the symbols illustrated in Figures 9.1 and 8.1 is to be
noted. Reproduced from Allen Forbes and Thomas R. Crowder, 'The problem
of Franco-Cantabrian abstract signs: agenda for a new approach', *World
Archaeology* **10**(3): 350–366; 1979, by permission of The British Library
Document Supply Centre, Boston Spa, Wetherby, West Yorkshire LS23 7BQ,
UK.

numerals, have survived from the Shang to the present day. As the culture flourished, polysyllabic words were added. Initially these were part of seven 'core' categories or 'significs'.[17] As time went by, words with extended meanings were placed within the core categories: in the first category (man and parts of his body), for example, the characters for mouth, ears, nose, eyes, tongue, heart, hands and feet. These characters began to be used also for words related to eating, talking and hearing, to smell, sight and taste, to emotions and actions using hands and feet. Other languages show similar adaptations: compare the English 'ear' and 'hear'. Chinese numbers, like those of most other civilisations, are to the base 10; using one's fingers for counting is presumably the origin. Originally there were 13 characters: 1–9, 10, 100, 1000 and 10,000. The larger numbers were probably used to refer to groups such as human population and livestock. We may contrast this aspiration for accuracy with the situation in less advanced cultures. The Ashininca of Amazonia, for example, even today have words only for 1–3: anything larger is either called 'more' or 'many'. In contrast, by Zhou times there were already words for 100,000, 1,000,000, 10,000,000, 100,000,000 and 1,000,000,000.[18] What none of the earliest cultures developed, whether in Mesopotamia, Egypt, China or Europe, was the concept of zero: this remarkable notion we owe to the Indians, who, through the Arabs after their incursion into the sub continent from the seventh century onwards, passed it to the rest of the world.

The deciphering of Shang characters is largely due to a find of oracle-bones around Anyang at the end of the nineteenth century. Peasants digging in the fields were picking up the bones, which they called 'dragon bones', and grinding them up to use in poultices and as tonic infusions. An antique dealer, who had come into the area from Shandong to buy bronzes, spotted this activity and decided that the bones might be of some value. He started digging on his own and in 1899 began to sell his finds. In Beijing he approached a well-known scholar and collector named Wang Yirong, who immediately realised that the writing was similar to that on Shang bronzes, of which he was a collector. He asked a colleague, one Liu E, to help him with the translation. Their efforts did not last long. Wang Yirong was also Chancellor of the Royal Academy and had, reluctantly, agreed to head the Boxer troops who were defending Beijing against assault by the Western allies during the opium war. When resistance failed and foreign troops entered Beijing, Wang Yirong committed suicide: he drank poison and threw himself into a well. His son subsequently sold the bones to Liu, who took rubbings and published them as a collection in 1903. In 1908 they came to the attention of a scholar named Luo Zhenyn, who realised from the inscriptions that the bones indicated the site of a great city: the last capital of the Shang had been pinpointed. Even today, however, 70% of Shang characters[19] remain to be deciphered. As abstract words came to be included, the characters—known as Han after the dynasty that ruled from 206 BC to 200 AD—became purely symbolic. Under the preceding dynasty of the Qin (221– 206 BC), a universal script had been introduced so that people from different regions, unable to understand each other's dialect, could communicate. By the time of the Tang dynasty (618–907 AD), paper and printing had been developed and literature flourished: more than 48,000 poems by over 2000 authors survive from this time. The number of characters continued to increase. By 1066, there were 31,319; today's Zhonghua zihai dictionary contains 85,568. But many of these characters are merely variants specific to Buddhist and Daoist texts (recall the hieratic as opposed to the demotic script of early Egypt), and other alternatives unique to Hong Kong, Taiwan, Singapore, Korea and Japan; moreover, the number of significs under which the 85,000 characters are classified is no more than 200. So is Chinese really such a daunting language to master? To qualify as a scribe in the Han dynasty you had to know 9000 characters, which is no more than the number of words in an average English or Italian dictionary. Today, some 2000–3000 basic characters, representing about 70% of all those used from the Shang times to the present, will enable you to get by. And remember that unlike the Indo-European languages, Chinese is a tonal language: there are no inflexions, declensions or conjugations.

The Minoan language, taken over by the Mycenians, is the prototype for Greek, which has been spoken on the mainland for over three millennia. Although some 400 clay tablets with inscriptions—called Linear A—dating back to 1750 BC have been found on Crete, they have not as yet been deciphered. On the other hand, a second script known as Linear B, found engraved on clay tablets from Knossos and Pylos (in the Pelopennese) that are also 3500 years old, has been cracked. The achievement is due largely to the scholar Michael Ventris, who in 1952 concluded that Linear B is a syllabic script that represents an early form of Greek. It is essentially the alphabet of the Phoenicians, that was adopted by the Greeks around 1000 BC. The Romans followed suit, although the words they developed—Latin—are of course different. Through Roman conquests, the use of Latin spread through much of Europe, and forms the basis of today's Romance languages: Italian, Romanian, Spanish, Portuguese and French, to which may be added English words introduced since the time of the Norman conquest. The Germanic languages—German, Dutch, Scandinavian and English — form another group, as do the Slavonic languages that include Russian, Ukrainian, Polish, Czech, Slovak, Slovenian, Serbian, Croatian and Bulgarian. All are Indo-European languages.[20] A map showing how these languages had spread by the time of the fifteenth century may be found in Jared Diamond's *The Rise and Fall of the Third Chimpanzee*.[21] As might be expected, genetic markers follow the same routes: the dispersal of genes and languages are directly related.[22]

If I have spent more time on the origin of the Chinese language than on that of others, it is for three reasons. First, Chinese provides a good illustration of the way in which the spoken word leads, through pictorial symbols, to writing. Second, it is an example of how our desire to communicate ever more complex matters and thoughts to our neighbours results in the richness of language. Third, the essential elements of speech and script have remained the same for more than 3000 years, and this gives scholars—and readers of this book—an opportunity to trace the influence of man's search for novelty in areas such as literature and technology within a single cultural setting, right up to the present day. The only other society that comes close is that of Greece.

The literature of the Greeks is legendary, in every sense of the word. Story telling, of course, has been around since man started gossiping 100,000 years ago, but for more than 97,000 of the ensuing years the tales were passed on by word of mouth alone. Once writing developed, the events of past and present times soon began to be recorded. In Europe, as we have just seen, this occurred around the eighth century BC. One of the first literary figures to chronicle the history of his country—in verse—was Homer: like another story teller 2400 years later, the English poet John Milton, Homer was probably blind. The epic poems attributed to him, particularly the *Iliad* and the *Odyssey*, are a subtly interwoven mixture of fact and fiction. The minotaur that Odysseus (Ulysses to the Romans) had to fight and overcome is myth, but the site of the palace defended by the minotaur is probably Knossos, the palace of the Minoan king. The gods and the people with whom they interacted—Agamemnon on one side and the Trojans on the other—are legendary, but Troy existed and its ruins (in north-western Anatolia) bear witness to a once great city. And so on. Two centuries later, some of Homer's characters and their exploits were rewoven by poets whose output constitutes the dramatic tradition of ancient Greece. To this day we may see performed the tragedies of Aeschylus, Sophocles and Euripedes, and the comedies of the later dramatist Aristophanes; he satirised fellow poets, politicians and philosophers alike, and his wit is as apt today as it was two millennia ago: in *Birds* Aristophanes invents 'cloud-cuckoo-land', and in *Lysistrata* women withold sexual favours from their menfolk as a protest against war—two themes that have a very modern ring to them. Parody and ridicule of public figures are the very cornerstones of democracy: their suppression in dictatorships pushes a country a few steps down the ladder of achievement.

Greek literature has been the inspiration for much of subsequent European culture: its imprint is visible, for example, in epic poems such as the twelfth century *El cantar de mio Cid* or Dante Alighieri's *La Divina Commedia*, written around 1310. The former recounts the saga of the Spanish soldier El Cid, whose exploits helped to drive the Moors out of northern Spain towards Valencia. The second narrates an imaginary journey by the author: through hell, then purgatory and finally to paradise;[23] in hell he is accompanied by Virgil, in paradise by Beatrice Portinari, the love and inspiration of his life. The legacy of the Greek drama left its mark on European literature for many centuries more, reaching its pinnacle, perhaps, in Shakespeare's plays at the end of the sixteenth century. Shakespeare searched for themes from former times, but it is the freshness of his language that has made his works endure. Like his contemporaries, he wrote in verse. Why did dramatists and bards, from Homer through to the eighteenth century, write in rhyme? Were they seeking to distinguish the words of Gods and imaginary heroes from ordinary speech, because the people would otherwise have felt uncomfortable? Let the literary scholars argue it out. From the point of view of this discussion, I merely note that it was the Augustan Age of the mid-eighteenth century that heralded the use of the vernacular in drama, and with it the birth of the novel.

Since none of the Central or South American civilisations, apart from the Maya, appear to have developed a written script, it is difficult to say much about their language; literature they lacked. Of course we know what was spoken at the time of the Spanish conquest: by Aztecs in Mexico, by remnants of Mayans in the Yucatan and by Incas in Peru. It is through contacts between them and the Spanish invaders that much of their history and legends was able to be chronicled.

By examining the vernacular of our primary civilisations, then, we have been able to trace the origin of the languages now spoken throughout Europe and Asia. These, of course, include today's languages of America: Spanish, Portuguese, English and French. So far as Africa is concerned, the main languages spoken in the north of the continent are Hamitic-Semitic, or Afro-Asian: it includes Arabic, Berber, Chadic, Cushitic, Hebrew and Maltese. More than 20 different tongues are spoken by the Berbers alone, who, prior to the Arab conquest of the seventh century, covered most of North Africa. Their earliest language is Numidian, of which a unique script has been identified; it was in use in Numidia (present-day Libya) 2000 years ago, when much of North Africa was under Roman rule. Chadic is spoken by the peoples living around Lake Chad, which borders on south-east Niger, north-east Nigeria and Chad itself; the predominant dialect is Hausa. Cushitic is spoken mainly in Ethiopia and Somalia. The linguistic groups that are not linked to any so far mentioned are: Niger – Congo, which is the largest group and comprises the languages spoken throughout western, central and southern Africa; Khosian, spoken by the Bushmen and Hottentots of eastern and southern Afica; and Nilo-Saharan, spoken in Uganda and parts of the Sudan, Kenya and

Tanzania.[24] The fact that there are so many languages, each quite distinct, in sub-Saharan Africa testifies to the fact that there are more racially distinct groups here than in the rest of the world put together, and that contact between them up to the present time has been minimal. It is that diversity, as we saw in an earlier chapter, that lends credence to the view that *H. sapiens* originated in Africa.

Scholarship and art

In so far as 'art' is generally defined as a skill, including that of the intellect (as in Bachelor of Arts), it encompasses scholarship as well as technique. And since a stone axe is as much of an artefact as a gold ring, man can be said to have been practising art for over a million years—from the time that he first acquired manual dexterity and a heightened curiosity. But I have chosen to use the word in its more restricted sense, to refer to the creation of works that in themselves serve no useful purpose, and I therefore separate art from technology (Chapter 9). Art and scholarship both involve a search—for beauty and perfection in the first case, for knowledge and understanding in the second. Scholarship, of course, encompasses philosophy and science, and as I shall subsequently devote a little time to the former (Chapter 10), and rather more to the latter (Chapter 11), the present discussion of scholarship will be brief.

Some people consider that art does not depend on intellectual inquisitiveness, but I am not so sure. Most of the great artists have been above average intelligence and, as the pianist Alfred Brendel remarked in a recent interview, the interpretation of art— never mind its composition—requires cerebral curiosity as well as technique for it to attain the highest level. The difference between craftsman and artist may reflect the degree of intellectual input. So far as the quality of art is concerned—good as opposed to bad, great as opposed to trivial—it is essentially a subjective matter which I shall not pursue. What is relevant to this discussion is that the practice of all art, whether it is perceived through sight or sound or touch, results from a process of searching on the part of its originator.

Art preceded agriculture. There is a view, propounded in the eighteenth century, that vocal music is the earliest form of speech,[25] and some go so far as to suggest that Beethoven's 9th symphony is an evocation of the sounds emitted by a troop of baboons.[26] Neolithic cave dwellers used stones and charcoal to depict various scenes on their walls. The clarity with which the lines of animals like bison, mammoth, rhinoceros and horse were executed in the Chauvet cave at Vallon-Pont-d'Arc near Ardèche in southern France, 30,000 years ago,[27] reminds the psychologist Nicholas Humphrey of the drawings produced by some severely retarded children. At 6 years of age an autistic girl called Nadia was unable to speak properly, but her depiction of animals is astonishingly lifelike and bold. Humphrey wonders whether the artists of Chauvet shared a lack of linguistic ability with Nadia, and suggests that the absence of neural connections responsible for language may somehow 'liberate' graphic skills.[28] This may sound like the opposite of Brendel's comment, but intellectual curiosity is not the same as linguistic competence. The reason for mentioning Humphrey's ideas is that they imply that 30,000 years ago the dwellers of Chauvet—who were modern humans, not Neanderthals—had not yet developed proper speech. While it is true that later art, such as that of ancient Egypt or mediaeval Europe, is wooden in comparison to stone age drawings, we should be careful—as Humphrey is himself—in trying to date the advent of language by the disappearance of graphic skills. For later cave paintings, now executed with natural dyes, in places like Altamira near Santander in north-east Spain and Lascaux in the Dordognes region of south-west France, are still remarkably life-like; yet they are only 15,000–17,000 years old, by which time verbal communication was surely extensive. Cave art is not restricted to Europe; I have seen some life-like depictions of animals in the high sierras of California (that must be less than 12,000 years old). The discovery of such sketches in the New World as well as the Old bears witness to the genesis of art as one of the most primitive ways in which man expresses himself.

Why did he do this? It may have been that early man thought it would frighten away predators, or marauding members of their own kind. It may have been because he already subscribed to a belief in unknown spirits whom he held responsible for strange happenings like earthquakes or floods, and whom he wished to appease. There is also an element of magic or myth in the pictures, which included symbolic motifs as well as pictorial representations. Early art was three-dimensional: most of the cave walls were not flat, and the depictions are integrated with the curvature, suggestive of a continuity between nature and art, in the way that some naturally occurring objects, like stones and bones, and even hand axes, have been further shaped for reasons other than utility.[29] But it may also have been because art—the decoration of one's living quarters—is as innate a characteristic of man as the development of useful technologies. Readers may point out that many birds also decorate their nests—the bower bird of New Guinea is a particularly striking example—and that the result can be as elaborate as a painting or a carefully assembled bunch of flowers. The bird may do it for reasons of camouflage, but it may also do it to attract a mate. Does art then perhaps stem from a desire to attract a companion, as much as a means to propitiate the Gods? While the latter reason contributed to the construction of the pyramids of Central America, the temples and shrines of Asia and later the cathedrals of Europe, it is the case that most writers, painters and musicians practise their art in order to gain recognition and applause from their peers. Although this is surely a very human quality—the quest for success—its origins may, after all, lie in the rituals that we perform, like many an animal, in order to attract a mate. In short, the origins of art pervade many species, but only in humans has it reached fulfilment. The peacock is merely *born* with his brilliant display of feathers: men and women have been dressing up, often in direct imitation of a peacock's plumage, for thousands of years. And did not the earliest poems speak of love; were not the primitive sounds of flute (made from animal bones as long ago as 30,000 years) or lyre designed to entice a mate?

There is a theory that art and scholarship are integral to the very emergence of man. The argument, propounded especially forcefully by the scientist and writer David Horrobin,[30] runs something like this. The genes that contribute to creativity are related to those that predispose towards schizophrenia and lesser disorders like manic-depressive psychosis. Horrobin cites Newton, Faraday and Einstein, Handel, Beethoven and Kant, as having been 'schizotypes'—half-way between schizophrenic and normal. He further states that among Icelanders, who are known to be a fairly in-bred population, families with a schizophrenic member are more likely to produce an offspring who is distinguished in the arts or in science than the average (he rather spoils his case by adding politics). Acknowledging that the cause of schizophrenia is only 40–50% genetic, he identifies the non-genetic or environmental contribution as being due to the consumption of animal fat. I mentioned in Chapter 4 Leslie Aiello's hypothesis that man's brain power began to increase when he switched from a purely vegetarian diet to one that included meat. According to Horrobin, it is the content of certain fatty acids in the meat of animals that, in conjunction with the inheritance of certain genes, sharpens up man's wits, while at the same time predisposing him to mental illness. Horrobin is not alone in his views. The link between psychotic disorders and creativity is currently being championed in the writings of Daniel Nettle[31] who, with Horrobin, acknowledges the contribution of Henry Maudsley, one of the founding fathers of psychiatry. In 1871 Maudsley wrote, 'I have long had a suspicion ... that mankind is indebted for much of its individuality and for certain forms of genius to individuals (with) some predisposition to insanity'.[32] Yes, Robert Schumann died in a lunatic asylum at 46, having already contemplated suicide at half that age, and he did write one of the greatest sonatas of all time (*Carnaval*) as well as two operas, 19 choral and 51 orchestral works, more than 100 piano pieces and over 300 songs. Daniel Nettle has no difficulty in rattling off some 70 well-known poets, writers, musicians and artists, each of whom suffered from psychotic illness. Yet molecular links between creativity and mental illness elude him. We have no option but to return to David Horrobin. Are schizophrenia and fatty acids the clue to man's propensity for intellectual quest? If so, it would be nice to learn that chimpanzees do not suffer from schizoid illnesses, and that the fatty content of their neurons is different to that of humans. I also find Nettle's argument, that the genes which predispose us to schizophrenia have not been eliminated by natural selection because they enhance creativity, unconvincing: since when were creative people more fecund—better at finding a mate—than the rest of us? If anything, it has always seemed to me that the opposite is the case.

I have sketched out some of the artistic and scholarly achievements of the seven primary civilisations in this and the previous chapter. Each culture produced decorative art: on buildings in the form of wall paintings, carved friezes and sculpted statues, on the everyday implements like drinking vessels and hand knives or daggers used by persons of quality, and on the garments worn by the wealthy. All civilisations developed astronomy, calenders and mathematics. From these cultures others arose: in Korea and Japan from the Sinic, in south-east Asia from a combination of Indic and Sinic influences (although not if you accept the argument presented in the last chapter, that lost civilisations in south-east Asia and Japan predate the emergence of Chinese and Indian culture by thousands of years). In the Mediterranean basin, the enlightenment of Greece and Rome followed that of Crete fairly rapidly, while the achievements of Islam had their roots in the civilisations of Sumeria and Egypt, as well as in the legacy of Greco-Roman values, which by the seventh century AD included those of Christendom. European art and scholarship[33] were largely dormant for the next 6 centuries or so. Thereafter, its Christian roots re-established themselves and produced ecclesiastical paintings and music, as well as inspiring the poets of the day. Only after that time did the art and scholarship that we associate with France, The Netherlands and England, with Venice, Padua and Florence, with Vienna, Leipzig and Weimar, with Kraków, Prague and St Petersburg, emerge. The different origins of European art gradually became blurred, but the distinctiveness of their product in relation to the culture of other continents has endured. In short, there is no more universality about art than there is about religion. Contemporary Chinese and Japanese art, Indian music and dance, Arab weaving and metalwork, African sculptured figurines, are as characteristic and as prized today as anything being produced in Europe and North America (some would say a great deal more). But just as the religion of one region finds converts in another—Buddhists in San Diego, Christians in Seoul—so the interpretation of art knows no frontiers: some of the world's greatest musicians performing European music, for example, now come from China and Korea and Japan as well as from the Western world.

I am reminded of two instances that illustrate the commonality of cultural accomplishments. The first I learned from a German colleague. As a young student he was visiting Japan for the first time shortly after World War II, when that country was still very much a developing nation, recovering from the ravages of conflict. He arrived with his backpack in Kyoto, still the cultural capital of the country, and made his way to the university dormitories, where he hoped to find a cheap bed. Approaching the run-down huts that housed the students, a strange sound caught his ear. Surely that was a Bach sonata being played—very well—by someone with a violin? He followed the sound and came upon the musician, a young student playing in the yard outside the dormitory. Not knowing a word of Japanese, and the student having no German, they could communicate only in sign language. But somehow the German indicated that he, too, could play the violin. He was actually quite accomplished, as music had been his first choice of study; he took up science at university only, as he told me, because it seemed the easier option. The Japanese student motioned to his German counterpart to remain where he was, and left the scene. A short while later he reappeared carrying a second violin. More sign language. Then the two began to play Bach's concerto for two unaccompanied violins, without score and without fault. It was, my friend said, one of the most moving experiences of his life, and as fresh in his memory when he recounted it 40 years later as the day it took place.

The second instance concerns scholarship. It happened to me when I visited China for the first time in 1992 at the invitation of the Chinese Academy of Sciences. Beijing had been fascinating indeed. My kind hosts had taken me to the Great Wall, the nearby tombs of former Emperors, the Forbidden City and other sites within the region. I had been shown the empty spaces on some of the buildings where during the 'Cultural Revolution', Red Guards had meticulously hacked away every carved ornament that had for centuries testified to genuine culture. My visit to Shanghai, at the beginning of October, coincided with China's National Day, on which the Institute I was visiting, as well as other buildings, would be shut. Rather than leave me kicking my heels in the hotel, my host kindly arranged for me to visit Hangzhou, a city a few hours to the south on the edge of a beautiful lake: the honeymoon city of south-east China (Plate 5). A young man from the Shanghai Institute, who spoke some English, accompanied me. We arrived in the evening and wandered down to the lake as the sun was setting. To my joy I noticed that in the distance stretched green and wooded hills. Although I had been experiencing the rush hour on the London underground for the past 15 years, and had fleeting acqaintance with those of Tokyo and Osaka, the sight of 100 bicycles coming towards one, unswervingly and at great speed, every time one tried to cross a road in Beijing, had unnerved me somewhat and I longed for a few hours quietly walking through the countryside on my own. Here was my chance. Early the next morning I managed — with great difficulty — to dissuade my guide from accompanying me. 'I like to walk long distances, and would not wish to put you to the discomfort of joining me, especially as you do not have appropriate footwear', I said. 'You do not speak the language and have no money', he replied. 'Actually, I do have some Chinese currency, and I will get by', I countered. I do not know what my guide's punishment would have been if he had returned to Shanghai alone, having lost in the hinterland of Hangzhou the professor he was supposed to be accompanying, but he clearly did. Anyhow I managed to get away, with a solemn promise that we would meet outside the restaurant in our hotel for dinner that evening (we did, and I have not seen such relief spread over a man's face since my colleagues and I passed our final exams at university 50 years ago). I had admired a nearby temple and was approaching some rough ground on my way to the hills, when I was accosted by an elderly man, simply dressed, with short, close-cropped grey hair. 'You are German?' 'Actually, British'. 'You will please accompany me to my home — a very humble one I regret — and do me the honour of drinking a cup of coffee with me', he said, switching to faultless English. The day was drawing on, and I was desperate to reach the solitude of the hills, but how could I refuse such a polite invitation?

The pleasure of our meeting proved to be mutual: my host — he turned out to be an 84 year-old heart surgeon — was delighted to be able to converse with a fellow academic from a far-off land and I was

Plate 1 Explorers of the modern era. (Above) Christopher Columbus on board the Santa Maria. Lithograph by M. F. Tobin, 1892; reproduced courtesy of the Library of Congress, USA/Science Photo Library, London. (Overleaf) The first men on the moon. The photograph shows Edwin (Buzz) Aldrin; Neil Armstrong and the lunar module are reflected in his visor. Courtesy of Peter Newark's American Pictures, Bath, UK.

Plate 1 Continued.

Plate 2 Egyptian pyramids. The three pyramids at Giza. See Chapter 7 for details. Reproduced courtesy of Chris Caldicott/RGS Picture Library, London.

Plate 3 Meso-American pyramid. The temple at Monte Albán (Zapotec culture). Like Mayan architecture, that of the Zapotec was much influenced by the builders of Teotihuacan. See Chapter 7 for details. Reproduced courtesy of Chris Caldicott, RGS Picture Library, London.

Plate 4 The Rosetta Stone. See Chapter 8 for details. Photograph courtesy of TopFoto.co.uk copyright © The British Museum, London.

Plate 5   The lake at Hangzhou. The author spent a memorable day there in 1992: in the morning, a fascinating meeting with a Chinese surgeon, scholar and translator; in the afternoon, a search for quietude among the hills. Photograph courtesy of National Oceanic & Atmospheric Administration (NOAA) Photo Library, USA.

Plate 6   Galileo Galilei. Photograph taken by Barney Sharratt and reproduced by courtesy of Ushaw College Library, Durham University, UK.

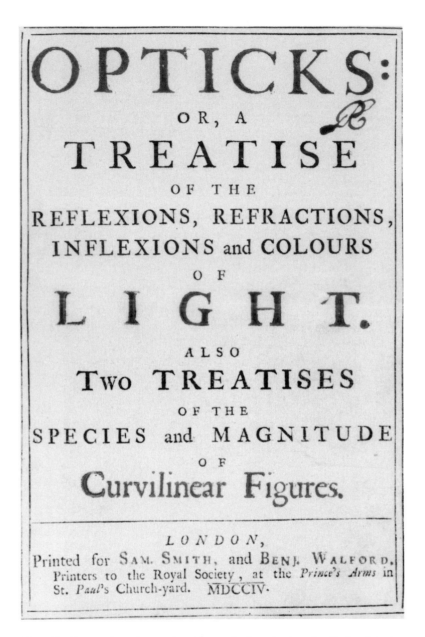

OPTICKS:

OR, A

TREATISE

OF THE

REFLEXIONS, REFRACTIONS, INFLEXIONS and COLOURS

OF

LIGHT.

ALSO

Two TREATISES

OF THE

SPECIES and MAGNITUDE

OF

Curvilinear Figures.

LONDON,

Printed for S A M. S M I T H, and B E N J. W A L F O R D,
Printers to the Royal Society, at the *Prince's Arms* in
St. *Paul*'s Church-yard. MDCCIV.

Plate 7 Newton's major works. Above, the frontispiece for *Optics*, 1st edn, 1704; opposite, that for the *Principia*, 2nd edn, 1713. Both are in the library of Worcester College, Oxford, and are reproduced by permission of the Provost and Fellows of the College.

PHILOSOPHIÆ

NATURALIS

PRINCIPIA

MATHEMATICA.

AUCTORE

ISAACO NEWTONO,

EQUITE AURATO.

Ob: 20 mar: 172$\frac{6}{7}$ ætat: 85.

EDITIO SECUNDA AUCTIOR ET EMENDATIOR.

CANTABRIGIÆ, MDCCXIII.

Plate 7   Continued.

Plate 8 Albert Einstein, painted by Leonid Pasternak (picture owned by the author). For one of the sittings Leonid invited Einstein to tea, and suggested that he bring his violin in order to make music with Pasternak's wife Rosalia, a concert pianist and former child prodigy. At first Einstein demurred, because he felt that his playing was not up to Rosalia's standard, but in the end he was persuaded. The author's mother Josephine, who was present on the occasion when Einstein and Rosalia performed, later described it as one of the most memorable experiences of her life.

privileged to encounter the most fascinating and cultivated person a traveller could meet. Before the Sino-Japanese war he had been in charge of his own hospital in Peking and during the war had become the first person in China—probably in the world—to successfully suture a stab wound through the heart. No, it had not been caused by a Japanese sword, but was a self-inflicted wound by a native resident of the city no longer able to bear the awfulness of war. But bear it he had to, for Dr Ma saved his life.[34] 'What do you think this is?', Dr Ma asked me, pointing to the low table on which our coffee cups rested. 'A sort of coffee table', I ventured. 'No', he said, and with his face creased in a smile of pleasure, he removed the cups and lifted the top of the structure which proved to be hinged to the rest. I was staring at sheets of music, Pleyel and Couperin and Beethoven: we had been taking our mid-morning break off a piano stool. It was one of the few pieces of furniture in that tiny room. 'My wife used to play extremely well'. Now I realised that the handsome young lady playing the piano to a group of children in the oil painting opposite me was the same woman I had passed, washing vegetables at a tap outside the shed—you could hardly call it a house—as we had entered. 'When the Red Guards came —we were living then in another city—they smashed everything of beauty or value, including our piano, before our eyes. The picture, the piano stool and some books are all we managed to save'. The books proved to be lexicons, in German, English and French, which Dr Ma had not only collected (most of his beloved library was destroyed), but had translated into Chinese. Before I left I agreed to send him one of the non-specialist articles I had recently written; when next I heard from him, he had translated it—purely for pleasure, as to my knowledge it was never published —into Chinese. A remarkable and erudite man, witness to the fact that culture is international, and that fortitude outlives evil.

To create a work of art is to search. Even before he has put pen or brush to paper, the writer is searching for the right phrase, the composer for the right notes, the painter for the right scene. The search continues as each work is completed. How many times has Dickens described the plight of children and the conditions of the poor in England during the first half of the nineteenth century —in *Oliver Twist*, *Nicholas Nickleby*, *A Christmas Carol*, *Martin*

Chuzzlewit, Little Dorrit, David Copperfield, Hard Times—but each time looking for a different aspect to illustrate their predicament? How frequently did Mozart use a trill motif to bring an aria or a movement of sonata, concerto or symphony—each of unique melody—to a successful conclusion without apparent reiteration? How often did Monet paint Hungerford and Westminster bridges over the Thames—from the south bank to the north, from the north to the south, at daybreak and at dusk—or Rouen cathedral in different lights—a harmony of brown, of gray, of blue and gold, of white or of blue[35]—or the light falling on to the lily pond in his garden at Giverny—from above, from an angle—in his search to find the most satisfying composition? Of course you could say that each artist was merely experimenting with his chosen form, but what is experimentation if not searching? You could also argue that Dickens hit on the subject that gave him fame, that Mozart could not be bothered to change his endings, that Monet realised that views of the Thames and Rouen cathedral and lily ponds made good pictures. If so, the quest is even more obvious: to ensure that each work is *not* exactly the same as the last: repetition in art is of little appeal. On the other hand, you might say that once an artist finds his metier, he stops searching. Is this not why one can recognise the works of well-known composers such as Mozart, Schubert or Chopin after listening to only a few bars of their music? But none of these masters had time to develop a new style: each died while still in his 30s. It was Beethoven who lived long enough (to the age of 57) to be able to move music from the classical to the romantic style, just as Picasso (who died aged 92) bridged the gap between depictive and non-representational art. Driven to exasperation, you may now say that I have fallen into the error of repetition by my continuing references to man's searches throughout this book. But repetition also serves to emphasise a point. In my case I am striving to convince you that there is virtually no activity that cannot be ascribed to man's unending quest: for novelty as well as for explanations, out of curiosity as well as from need.

The society in which an artist works shapes his style. The cultures of Elizabethan England or seventeenth century Holland, of eighteenth century France or nineteenth century Germany, were conducive to the development of great art. Had someone of Shakespeare's or Molière's imagination been born 4000 years ago he could not have written plays. A person of such talent undoubtedly did live somewhere at the time, and had that been the valley of the Nile, he would have contributed to the art of ancient Egypt. The work of an artist reflects the culture in which he lives. For once, I use the personal pronoun in the masculine sense deliberately. Until very recent times, society was not conducive to the pursuit of art (or indeed any occupation save that of marriage and childbirth, intrigue and housekeeping) by women, which is why very few great female artists have emerged over the years: 'Lack of talent in a woman is a virtue', remarked Confucius[36] (but a seventeenth century writer observed that 'Women do excel men in virtues and rare endowments of the minde, and I think we shall finde that herein also women do farre outstrip men'[37]). It took exceptional grit for writers like Jane Austen, George Sand (Amandine-Aurore Lucille Dupin), the Brontë sisters and George Eliot (Mary Ann Evans) to get their works published in nineteenth century Europe.[38] By 1847, though, some women writers were accepted well enough for a literary magazine to suggest that the young Anthony Trollope might change his surname so as to avoid comparison with his famous literary mother.[39]

There is no evidence whatsoever that the creative potential in women is any less than that in men. It is merely the constraints imposed by societies over the ages that have prevented women of talent from realizing their potential. They seek as hard as men. Any neurological differences that exist between male and female appear to be restricted to a small area of the brain concerned with feelings of sexuality: the range of intellectual ability, from dullard to genius, overlaps that of men. On the contrary, the most important human impact on the world—the practice of agriculture—may have been due to women, as they began to plant seeds in an attempt to guarantee a more reliable supply of food. Of course, the constraints of child-bearing differentiates the sexes, but apart from that women were probably men's equals in neolithic times, as chimpanzees are today (except for the supremacy of the alpha male over all others). Discrimination against women, like the formation of hierarchical social orders and the abuse of the lower by the higher, has been an unfortunate ingredient of most civilisations. Although these attitudes are slowly beginning to disappear, discrimination endures. In the USA it may be no more than the bigotry of excluding Jews and Afro-Americans from fancy golf clubs, and in Pakistan merely a reluctance to educate women, but in countries like Mauretania and the Sudan the slave market continues to flourish.[40] In primitive communities that survive in isolated areas of Asia, Africa and South America, such prejudices have never had much place.

Today, it seems to me, many who consider themselves artists have stopped searching for beauty or perfection. Devoid of the skills necessary to achieve either result, they have traded talent for *chutzpah*:[41] they search merely for ways to shock. It is not an arduous quest. You can achieve it simply by taking down your trousers or exposing your bosom in public, or by peppering your speech with obscenities. And that is precisely what modern art in the Western world is in danger of becoming: pickled animals and foetuses; a dead horse hanging from the ceiling; a load of elephant dung; an unmade bed complete with used condom; a poem about masturbation; a play devoted to explicit swapping of sexual encounters over the Internet; and another that is taken up entirely with two men twisting their penises into different shapes (I assure you I am not making any of this up). Fine for burlesque, but art? And the critics, who are themselves often failed artists, are taken in by it all. It will surprise no one to learn that images created by computer are now sold as art. Does this betoken the decline of man's intellectual curiosity? It is a subject to which I shall return in Chapter 14.

Proper art, that involves beauty and skill as well as originality, leaves a legacy for the next generation. Tolstoy once said to my grandfather:[42] 'Remember, everything will pass away—everything. Kingdoms and thrones, wealth and millions will perish. Everything will change. Neither we, nor our grandsons, will remain and there will be nothing left of our bones. But if our works contain even a grain of real art, they will live forever'.[43] Leonardo da Vinci remarked, rather more succinctly: 'Beauty in life perishes, not in art'. And nor it does. We visit museums and galleries to admire the art of geniuses long dead, we listen to the music of an earlier age and we read the literary works of previous centuries. The pleasure one person derives from art is akin to the solace another finds in religion, or in the enjoyment of nature. It is a thing of the moment, that does not accumulate in the way that knowledge gained through scholarship, technology or science does. What, then, is the contribution that art has made to civilisation and culture? For one thing, it has improved the quality of life, at least for those who are receptive to it. Even the Soviet regime encouraged the pursuit of art, provided it was to its liking; by suppressing other forms, of course, it actually killed the spirit of artistic creativity. And for another thing? I find myself fumbling.[44] The English art historian Kenneth Clark thought, half a century ago in his book (and TV series) *Civilization*, that art is a cornerstone, *the* cornerstone in fact, of civilisation. But his view of civilisation was a rather narrow one: the European culture that arose out of Christianity. I have taken civilisation in its more literal meaning, shared with Jacob Bronowski in *his* book and TV series on *The Ascent of Man*, and have discussed art only because it is an ingredient of a civilised society. Yes, men of genius seek to express their creative instinct. Yes, the desire for beauty is a strong one that we share with other creatures. And yes, these factors are the basis of man's artistic achievements. They are, I believe, brought about through genes that are common to primates and other animals, and to a slight modification of other genes that result in man's manual dexterity, his power of speech and his higher intellect. The pursuit of art is no more than a consequence of man's genetic make-up. For some it allows the fulfilment of their inventive craving; for others it simply gives them pleasure.

Quality of life

If *Homo sapiens* has been ever searching for a better quality of life, what has he achieved? What criteria distinguish the quality of life in the developed world from that of the rest? Few would disagree, if asked to list the necessities of life—those attributes without which no one should have to live—that food and water, shelter and freedom from persecution are the most essential. It is to the shame of our species that there are parts of the world where all four are needlessly denied to the bulk of the population. After a moment's thought, one would probably add education, or literacy at least,[45] and health to the list. While few governments deliberately make their inhabitants ill (although Saddam Hussein tried it by poisoning the Kurds in Iraq), deprivation of literacy is more common. Over 15% of people throughout the world are illiterate, but the rate is much higher in certain areas. In rural Pakistan, for example, 90% are illiterate, and there are villages not 100 miles from bustling Karachi where the illiteracy among 15 year-old girls is 99.7%. The reason is largely the stubbornness of local landowners and overseers to give up their control over the villagers' lives and allow state educators to have a say. In Afghanistan it was the stated policy of the Taliban to deprive *all* girls of proper schooling. We should be careful of complacency: more than 20% of adults in the UK are defined as functionally illiterate, which places the UK—together with Ireland—at the bottom of the literacy league within developed countries. When asked to define UNESCO's role in Latin America a few years ago, its then Director General was in no doubt that education is the most important; science and culture, the other functions of the United Nations *Educational, Scientific* and *Cultural* Organization, Federico Mayor put in second place. He omitted health, not because the UN has assigned that role to the World Health Organisation (WHO), but because he did not need to refer to it: health is the offspring of education.

This was most vividly illustrated some decades ago in the Indian State of Kerala. The State Government, dominated by the Communist Party as it happens,[46] decided to tackle illiteracy at its roots—within the village primary schools. By teaching children not only to read and write, but also the basics of hygiene, two birds were killed with one stone. Remember that cholera, typhus, typhoid fever, dysentery and diarrhoea are readily avoidable diseases if clean water and a modicum of sanitation are to hand.[47] An outbreak of cholera in London in 1854 was halted largely through the sensible approach of a Dr John Snow: he removed the handle of the Broad Street water pump, thus preventing all further access to its supply. Contaminated water, not the air, he argued, was the source of the disease.[48] That the quality of London water, which was obtained from the Thames, left much to be desired is not surprising: 140 sewers were discharging their effluent directly into the river by 1828.

To return to modern-day India. Merely re-folding a sari 10 times and using it as a filter removes over 90% of cholera bacilli: a simple enough technology. But to succeed in their mission, the teachers of Kerala had to overcome a considerable amount of cultural custom and religious belief. To this day, young women in Rajasthan will not accept the introduction of piped water: they smash up any taps that are installed. They prefer to walk a considerable distance each day to the nearest well in order to collect water and bring it back in containers carried on their heads. Why? First, because they say that their mothers will make them work harder at other tasks if they do not have to spend time walking to a well. Second, because the walk gives them a chance to socialise with men: piped water curtails their love life.[49] Attainment of improved living standards is often a question not of wealth, but of cultural idiosyncrasy.

Many in the poorer regions of the world lead lives that resemble those of the peasants in western Europe 300 years ago. They lack most of the amenities the rest of us take for granted, yet they have leap-frogged the centuries in their desire to acquire some of the latest technologies. A few years ago, two colleagues of mine agreed to lecture at a university medical school in a town near Hyderabad in south-central India. The facilities were sparse: no projectors for showing slides or transparencies; the entire university library the size of a large book case (my friends refrained from exploring the washrooms). Their host, a kind and generous man, invited them for a meal. His home was basic: a rat passed several times before their eyes during supper.[50] Afterwards the host asked to have a photograph taken of him with his visitors. They were made to group themselves behind his proudest possession; no, not his wife, who was kept well in the background throughout: his large television set. This situation is typical of many developing and undeveloped countries, especially in the southern hemisphere. Right through much of Africa, people are clamouring to be on the Internet; in many parts of the world e-mail works better than the telephone.

Several years ago I found myself at the University of Ibadan, in southern Nigeria. I had come as external examiner in biochemistry, although in the event I did not set eyes on a single medical student or his work: the university had been closed prior to my visit because of recurring shortages of water and electricity. Lack of water in the heart of the rain forest, of electricity in one of the wealthiest countries in terms of natural resources? It seemed that the adjacent town of Ibadan was growing so rapidly as to soak up every drop of water and every unit of available electricity.[51] During one of our chats—we had little else to do—my host asked me whether I would be kind enough to send him various chemicals for research on my return to England. 'I would be delighted to do so', I said, 'but would there not be a problem in storing them once they have arrived? Your refrigerator will not be able to prevent the compounds deteriorating rapidly if the power supply is not maintained'. 'It is true that we do not have a generator in biochemistry', he answered, 'but they have one in chemistry. All that is necessary is that I send a boy across—with a few naira in his hand—and the operator will switch the electricity over to this department'. The point I am making is simple. The desire for a better quality of life in the most deprived parts of the world is obvious; the intellectual potentiality of the people would allow them easily to achieve their goals.[52] It is culture, not ambition or knowledge, that is holding them back. Wealth, of course, also plays a part. Although much of the money thrown at the poorest countries by the rich and by the World Bank is wasted or misappropriated, we should heed Washington Irving's stricture: 'Until nations are generous they will never be wise'.[53]

What, then, of the criterion of freedom from persecution as one of the necessities of life? Like the concept of freedom or liberty itself—a very human aspiration—its lack is not restricted to the developing world. On the contrary, sociologists will tell you that 'the native resident of Maniapure in the Amazonian jungle has more liberty than the tax-oppressed citizen of Stockholm or Chicago'; that 'there is less freedom in Singapore' (a developed nation) 'where you are arrested for dropping chewing gum on the street, than across the water in Johore Bator' (Malaysia, a developing one); that 'students have fewer rights of protest in Japan or South Korea' (both developed) 'than in India or Brazil' (both still developing). Oppression cuts across much of the world. The fall of communism may have restored individual liberty to eastern Europe, but it lost it again temporarily in former Yugoslavia, and the ending of Mao Zhedong's legacy gave the Chinese people their first taste of limited freedom for centuries (they had never had much of it in the first place). Yet within many African countries—Ethiopia and Somalia, Burundi and Rwanda, the Congo and Sierra Leone spring to mind—honest people live in fear of unwarranted, brutal oppression to the point of genocide. Whether it is their own leaders who deny them a minimal quality of life through their absurd political aspirations, or those of an invading neighbour, is largely irrelevant: the deliberate destruction of their flimsy crops and the misappropriation of much of the aid that is sent to them ensures that they face starvation. It is not the people who need educating, but the rulers. But how to inculcate a sense of decency into a ruthless tyrant? I am afraid it is impossible. The variability of human attributes, to which I allude yet again, means that for every Albert Schweitzer that the world throws up, it produces a Josef Stalin; for every Mother Teresa, an Adolf Hitler. The qualities that define man's greater capacity for quest do not distinguish between virtue and villainy. Containment of evil men is the only solution.

Conclusion

Let me pause before proceeding to the next chapter. The achievements I have described in the last three chapters show a remarkable unity and at the same time a considerable diversity. The Sumerians built temples for worship and so did the Maya, but the structures were not the same; the Minoans built palaces for their rulers as did the Egyptians, but their decorations were of different design. Most of the earliest forms of writing were hieroglyphic in character, but Egyptian hieroglyphics are not the same as Chinese pictographs; the cuneiform writing of the Sumerians differs from the 'Linear' characters of the Minoans (see Figure 8.1). The mathematics developed by the Sumerians was based on 60 (from which we derive the 60-minute hour and 60-second minute), that of the Maya on 20, while those of most other cultures was based on 10, although some of the oldest tribes in Australia, Papua New Guinea, Africa and South America use a system to the base of two to this day. Everywhere artisans carved in stone, but the figures they depicted are different; all civilisations understood the art of metalwork, but the shapes of the objects they produced varied from one culture to another.[54] The Egyptians valued gold and silver, the Chinese bronze and jade. The theme of unity and diversity in human accomplishments should surprise no one: it is the result of the unity of human attributes — manual dexterity, speech and intellect — coupled to the diverse ability of individuals to use them. But why did seven isolated civilisations produce such similar results?

There are those who believe in an ancient civilisation that preceded all others and that was their inspiration: the lost continent of Atlantis. Here were pyramids and palaces, cities and harbours, inhabited by a people of remarkable intelligence and peaceful disposition. Plato thought this land lay in the Atlantic, others have placed it in South America — perhaps the entire continent was Atlantis — in the Antarctic, in Scandinavia. Some believe that it lay in the Aegean itself, and was destroyed only 3500 years ago by a giant volcanic eruption, equivalent in force to the explosion of 100 hydrogen bombs, on the island of Santorini (Thera).[55] No one doubts that the Minoan civilisation, probably extending to Santorini, subsequently influenced the Mycenian culture on the mainland of Greece. But that a civilisation elsewhere, at a much earlier period in time, flourished and had links with primary cultures in both the Old World *and* the New is nothing other than fantasy: there is simply no evidence for it. Plato was probably influenced by what happened to a city called Helike, to the west of Athens in the Gulf of Corinth. This disappeared without trace when an earthquake struck in 373 BC. An ensuing tidal wave may have created an inland lagoon — since evaporated — which submerged all the remains; only today are coins and pottery, fragments of walls and buildings, being unearthed.[56] So far as the similarity between the fruits of Old and New World civilisations is concerned, I suggest a simpler explanation. There are only so many ways to build a boat that floats or a building that resists the elements, to fashion a jug that holds water or a bowl to contain rice, only certain animals that can be tamed,[57] only some plants that grow fast enough to be harvested within a season, a limited number of ways to catch a fish. Equally, there are only so many ways by which order can be maintained in a society—autocracy or democracy, feudalism or bureaucracy—or by which subjects can demonstrate obeisance to their rulers: by bowing, by courtseying, by walking backwards, by shuffling on one's knees, by prostration on the ground.[58] Yet the similarity of pyramids in Egypt and the Americas—even though the former were built to commemorate its rulers, the latter to appease the Gods—continues to engage cultural speculators.

Thor Heyerdahl repeated his *Kon-Tiki* expedition from Peru to Tahiti with one from the shores of Africa to America, to prove that a reed boat, as used by today's fishermen in Africa and South America and, according to his view, common to the Egyptians, Incas and Aztecs, could have made the journey across the Atlantic. He examined reed boats on lakes in Africa[59] and on Lake Titicaca, which lies between Bolivia and Peru. Heyerdahl concluded that there was a similarity not only between the versions in current use, but also with those depicted on the murals and reliefs of ancient Egypt. If he succeeded in his mission, it would be a telling piece of evidence in favour of the theory that explorers from the Old World could have reached the New World thousands of years ago, and thereby introduced the concept of the pyramid across the Atlantic Ocean. By 1969 Heyerdahl had built himself a papyrus boat modelled on those used by the Egyptians more than 4000 years earlier: he christened it *Ra*[60] and with an international crew of six (plus a monkey for good measure), he set off from Safi in Morocco. They sailed south-west along the African coast as far as the Cape Verde Islands and then turned due westwards to pick up the prevailing current. They managed to reach the Caribbean off Barbados after 8 weeks at sea.[61] Heyerdahl felt he had proved his point. Unfortunately, molecular evidence[62] indicates that he was as wrong over this proposal, as he was over the earlier one in which he suggested a migration westwards from the coast of South America to Polynesia. What he proved is that he was a most innovative, persistent and intrepid man, with a strong urge for quest.

Others go further in their conjectures than Heyerdahl. Not only the shape of the pyramids but their exact positions relative to each other, in both the Old World and the New, shows that they share a common origin that involves an image of certain stellar configurations; the builders of these monuments are said to belong to a 'lost' tribe of innovative people. We are back in Atlantis. My response is more mundane; if you wish to construct a monument of stones as high as you can by piling one on top of the other, what do you finish up with? A cone: a pyramid is merely a cone with straight sides. I repeat an earlier point. The focus of an Egyptian pyramid was a royal tomb *below* it. The central point of an American pyramid was a platform *above* it (see Plate 3), on which statues were erected and religious ceremonies performed; burial of rulers inside a tomb was not the major purpose. What was similar was the intention of the pyramidal form: to reach towards the sun, the donor of light and life. I also refer the reader to my earlier comment regarding the wheel: if some early travellers were so intent on transmitting Old World knowledge to the New, why did they not tell them about the use to which a wheel[63] could be put? It is generally accepted that agriculture developed independently, yet along similar lines, in the Old World and the New: so why not the construction of cities and palaces, the building of temples and pyramids, the evolution of language and writing, the development of astronomy and mathematics?

Throughout these three chapters we have witnessed an interplay between the attributes of manual dexterity, speech and neuronal capacity. For the construction of buildings and artifacts, for painting, sculpture and the use of musical instruments, the bendable thumb and precision grip are crucial. For language and literature and song, the vocal cord is paramount. For mathematics and astronomy, law and governance, the neuronal connections in the cortex of the brain are vital. But as I stressed in the opening chapter of this book, what defines the difference between humans and chimpanzees, what leads to a greater ability for quest is not one or other attribute, but a combination of all three: it is through the interaction of hands, voice and brain that man has been able to ascend the ladder of achievement.

Notes

1. Karl Popper, from a 1982 article quoted by Arne Friemuth Petersen, entitled 'On emergent pre-language and language evolution and transcendent feedback from language production on cognition and emotion in early man', in *Language Origin: a Multidisciplinary Approach*, J. Wind *et al.* (eds), Kluwer Academic, Dordrecht, pp 449–464, 1992.
2. See Philip Morrison, *Nature* **413**: 461; 2001.
3. For a rather erudite, mathematical analysis of the relation between language and grammar, see Martin Nowak *et al.*, 'Computational and evolutionary aspects of language'. *Nature* **417**: 611–661; 2002.
4. See Chapter 9 and Notes 19 and 21 therein.
5. An elephant has a larger brain than a human.
6. Robin Dunbar, op. cit., pp 55–80, 106–131.
7. It is the males who do all the singing.
8. Scientists from Rockefeller University in New York reported at the American Association for the Advancement of Science (AAAS) Annual Meeting in February 2002 that they had developed a method of tracking the formation of new neurons in songbirds.
9. By this time Egypt was part of the Greek Empire.
10. He subsequently devised a mathematical system known as the Fourier transformation, which is now used in the interpretation of X-ray crystallographic data in order to work out the structure of molecules like DNA and proteins.
11. Young's modulus.
12. Young's theory of colour vision.
13. The yard in England, the metre in France.
14. Having first accepted, and then resigned, the Professorship of Physics at the Royal Institution in London: he felt it would be detrimental to his professional life. His patients and students were of a different mind: they would have preferred him to have made physics, not physic, his main occupation.
15. Well, that is what they were initially.
16. Another Indo-European language.
17. These covered (1) man and parts of his body, (2) four-footed animals, insects, reptiles and their pelts and skins, (3) trees, plants, wine and food, (4) housing, clothing, utensils, equipment and weapons, (5) sun, moon, topography and the elements, (6) Gods and divination and (7) metrological units.

18. It is difficult to imagine to what use the last three numbers were put, for the total population was below 10 million. One might think that they were beginning to record the number of stars in the sky, were it not for the fact that the telescope would not be invented for another 2000 years. Surely they were not just counting grains of rice.

19. 4000–5000 Shang characters have been identified on more than 150,000 inscriptions.

20. For a 'tree' showing the relationships among the Indo-European languages, see Cavalli-Sforza, op. cit., p 164.

21. Jarad Diamond, op. cit., p 228; see also p 243.

22. See e.g. Cavalli-Sforza, op. cit., pp 133–172.

23. Note that the word 'paradise' is derived from the Persian word for 'walled garden': King Cyrus, who built Persepolis during the sixth century BC and made it the most splendid city of the day, loved his garden of fruit trees and cool running water so much that he used the word to signify supreme contentment. It is that meaning that has stuck with the Judaeo-Christian-Muslim religions to this day.

24. See Richard Rudgley, op. cit., p 37, and Cavalli-Sforza, op. cit., p 135, for maps showing the distribution of the languages spoken across the globe.

25. Charles Rosen, 'The future of music', in *The New York Review of Books*, 20 December 2001. The relationship between music and speech (music is perceived by most people in the right hemisphere of the brain, whereas language is processed predominantly in the left hemisphere) is discussed by Alison Abbott, in *Nature* **416**: 12–14; 2002.

26. William Benzon, *Beethoven's Anvil: Music in Mind and Culture*, Basic Books, New York, 2001.

27. H. Valladas *et al.*, 'Evolution of prehistoric cave art', *Nature* **413**: 479; 2001.

28. Nicholas Humphrey, op. cit., pp 132–161. See also Note 29 to Chapter 4.

29. Personal communication from Richard Rudgley. See also David Lewis-Williams, op. cit.

30. David Horrobin, op. cit.

31. Daniel Nettle, op. cit.

32. Ibid, p 135.

33. Writers like Marija Gimbutas (op. cit.) try to persuade us that European civilisation owes little to the influence of Mesopotamia, Egypt and Crete. It developed independently, alongside agriculture, 9000 years ago but was destroyed 3000 years later by repeated invasions from the east. Save folklore and mythology, little remained.

34. This is not his real name, but he had asked me not to mention his name or my visit to anyone in the region; even in 1992 he was still afraid of the consequences of a visit by a foreigner such as myself, and I respect his wishes to this day.

35. And those refer only to the pictures in the Musée d'Orsay. Monet painted Rouen Cathedral 30 times, the other paintings being scattered around the art galleries of the world. The role of Monet's brain in processing the impact of Rouen Cathedral on his eye is discussed by Semir Zeki, op. cit., pp 209–215.

36. Quoted by George Walden in his review of *The Good Women of China* in the *Sunday Telegraph* of 21 July 2002.

37. From a manuscript entitled *Woman's Worth* that recently came to light (see the *Daily Telegraph*, 20 April 2002).

38. Jane Austen and Charlotte Brontë also resorted initially to male pseudonyms. Amandine-Aurore Lucille Dupin (who married Baron Dudevant) and Mary Ann Evans (who lived with the writer G. H. Lewes) kept them for life.

39. Victoria Glendinning, *Trollope*, Pimlico Press, London, 1993, p 166.

40. See John Adamson's review of *Islam's Black Slaves: A History of Africa's Other Black Diaspora* by Ronald Segal in the *Sunday Telegraph* of 14 February 2002.

41. Cheek.

42. The Russian impressionist painter Leonid Pasternak, who illustrated some of Tolstoy's works; Tolstoy liked one of the illustrations for *Resurrection* so much that he decided to change the story slightly in order to better reflect the artist's picture.

43. Quoted on the back cover of *The Memoirs of Leonid Pasternak*, translated by Jennifer Bradshaw, Quartet, London, 1982.

44. Boris Pasternak had no such reservations: 'Art always serves beauty, and beauty is the joy of possessing form, and form is the key to organic life since no living thing can exist without it' (from *Dr Zhivago*, Part 2, Chapter 14, 1958, translated by Max Hayward and Manya Harari).

45. I am referring, of course, to cultures that have a written tradition.

46. Others ascribe its success to the fact that the region is unique in being a matriarchy.

47. World-wide, 1 billion people lack clean drinking water and 3 billion do not have adequate sanitation (from *The Statesman's Yearbook 2003*, Barry Turner (ed.), Palgrave Macmillan, Basingstoke, 2002).

48. Snow came to this conclusion because he noted that most of the victims dying of cholera in that part of London (Soho) obtained their water from the Broad Street pump: inmates from a neighbouring prison, which had its own well, suffered far fewer deaths despite the fact that conditions were much filthier and the air fouler.

49. See K. S. Jayaraman, *Nature* **397**: 9; 1999.

50. Many Asians lack the typically European horror of rodents.

51. I suspect that corruption may also have played a part: in a nearby internationally funded research institute to which my host took me, there was water and power galore. Rainwater was efficiently conserved and the force of the adjoining river converted its energy into electricity.

52. It was in order to help scientists eager to put their intellectual expertise to good use in relation to better health in the developing world that I launched the Oxford International Biomedical Centre 10 years ago. See **www.oibc.org.uk**.

53. Washington Irving, from his *Journals & Notebooks*, 1824.

54. Cultural differences can be remarkably stable: to this day Sinic societies eat their food with chopsticks, Europeans with knife and fork.

55. That such an event took place is not in dispute: it buried a city below the present village of Akrotiri, and the accompanying earthquakes devastated parts of Knossos and other sites on Crete 70 miles to the south.

56. *Horizon* programme shown on UK television (BBC2), 9 p.m., Thursday 10 January 2002.

57. 90% of potentially useful large mammals lack the necessary attributes.

58. All used to this day in different parts of the world.

59. Lake Chad, Lakes Zwai and Tana (source of the Blue Nile) and a lake in Ethiopia.

60. The Egyptian word for sun, as well as for the sun-king from whom the Pharaohs were said to be descended.

61. But only just. *Ra*'s steering gear had broken, the boat had almost split in two and by the end they had to abandon their sail and merely drift with the current.

62. It has often been stated that all true Amerindians—from Alaska to Patagonia—are blood group O. Although the remains of some prehistoric Amerindians have been found to be of group A as well, the very high predominance of group O (67–80%) and paucity of group B in current Amerindians is not in doubt. Yet group B has been fairly well distributed in Egypt for at least 5000 years as judged by analysis of mummies. See P. J. d'Adamo, 'ABO blood group polymorphisms', (in *The Townsend Letter for Doctors and Patients*, Consolidated Press, Seattle, WA, 1990) and **www.dadamo.com** (which provides a continuing update on these matters) for details.

63. Attached merely to children's toys in pre-Columbian Central America.

CHAPTER NINE

Technology: war and welfare

Technology is the result of man's quest to improve the quality of his life and to overcome the inhospitable conditions of the environment in which he finds himself—whether or not of his own choosing. The combination of manual dexterity and an agile mind has produced staggering results. None of the developments described in the last three chapters could have taken place without technical know-how. For buildings, the assembly of stone walls, the use of lintels for entrances and windows, the construction of struts for roofs and the shaping of gutters, were essential. To manufacture weapons, tools and artefacts like drinking vessels and ornaments, metalworking was introduced: the smelting of minerals found in rocks to produce bronze (an alloy of copper and tin) was a major step forward.

Little copper or tin occurs naturally; mainly they are found in combination with other elements.[1] Heating in the presence of carbon produces the free metal. Presumably early man noticed one day, after a particularly hot fire had been built on some stones or a rock, that a metallic glitter appeared. Intrigued, he repeated the exercise on a larger scale and found that he could beat the metal into different shapes. The period of discovery that occurred between 3500 and 3000 years ago in the fertile crescent of Mesopotamia and Egypt, in eastern Europe and in south-east Asia, has been termed the Bronze Age. In America, working in bronze did not occur until the fifteenth century, when it was introduced by the Aztecs.

Essentially the same process of heating in the presence of charcoal or coke underlies the production of iron, which also occurs naturally not as the free metal, but combined with other elements like oxygen or sulphur. The only difference is that much higher temperatures are required to produce iron. The Iron Age began in northern Mesopotamia (current Anatolia), where its manufacture was introduced by the Hittites between 1500 and 1200 BC. Slowly it spread westwards, gradually replacing bronze for the manufacture of the sturdiest weapons and tools. In China, working in bronze, and then in iron, probably began independently of events in the eastern Mediterranean. In sub-Saharan Africa, the age of iron preceded that of bronze. In the Americas, no iron production at all took place until the arrival of the Europeans. The technologies mentioned so far, as well as those to be described shortly, resulted from trial and error alone. Science played virtually no part in the development of new technology until well into the eighteenth century.

On the contrary, attempts to emulate the techniques used by early man to move huge stones from place to place with the hindsight of twentieth century engineering science have proved elusive. Teams of enthusiasts have tried to recreate the feats of their forefathers in transporting the blocks of Egyptian pyramids, the plinths of Stonehenge, the giant statues of the Olmecs and the Easter Islanders, using only materials available at the time. In each case they barely managed to shift replicas a few metres along the ground.[2] Carving features on to boulders similar to those elaborated by the Olmecs and Easter Islanders proved as frustrating as their transportation and erection: chiselling away for hour upon hour left barely a mark. For hauling the large stone blocks (subsequently carved into the shape of fearsome animals) that flank the steps leading to temples within the Forbidden City, the Chinese came up with a more ingenious solution. A canal leading from the quarry to Beijing was dug and filled with water. Come the winter, and it froze over. Sliding the blocks along its surface required little effort (and predated elucidation of the principles of friction by more than 1000 years).

During the eighteenth and nineteenth century Britain and Germany led the world in the field of new technology. The steam engine, developed by the Scotsman James Watt in 1769 from the earlier beam engine designed by Thomas Newcomen in 1712 to pump water from mines, led to steam locomotives and steamships at the beginning of the nineteenth century. By 1829 George Stephenson and his son Robert had built the first locomotive, the *Rocket*, in Lancashire. Railways dominated travel—whether in Europe, Asia or the Americas—for the next 100 years. The first synthetic dye, mauveine, arose by accident in 1856. William Henry Perkin, a notable organic chemist, was trying to synthesise the anti-malarial quinine (previously isolated from the bark of the cincona tree) from aniline: a darkish blue mess appeared in his reaction vessel instead. He realised the significance of his discovery and, out of this scientific breakthrough, the synthetic dye industry was born.

An example of a technology that arose directly out of a scientific discovery is provided by the development of synthetic fertilisers.[3] It was in 1909 that Fritz Haber, a professor of physical chemistry and electrochemistry at the Technische Hochschule in Karlsruhe, together with his colleague Carl Bosch, produced the first synthetic drops of liquid ammonia. The demonstration that nitrogen (a relatively inert gas that makes up 80% of the earth's atmosphere) could be made to combine with hydrogen in the presence of an electric spark to produce ammonia was a scientific *tour de force*. Any residual oxygen in the nitrogen would have had a disastrous effect: the entire apparatus would have blown up. Haber and Bosch did more. Knowing that from ammonia, fertilisers like ammonium phosphate are readily produced, and that enriching the soil in this way would revolutionise agriculture, they scaled up the process sufficiently to indicate the feasibility of commercial production. Carl Bosch approached the company BASF, who appreciated the potential and invested in the process.

Today ammonia is produced globally at a rate of 150 million tonnes a year; 80% of this is utilized for fertilisers consisting of ammonium salts and urea (which is derived from ammonia and is readily absorbed by plants). The use of such fertilizers has revolutionised agriculture. Prior to the invention of the Haber – Bosch process, the nitrogen that plants require was derived from three sources: from the fixation of atmospheric nitrogen by *Rhizobium*,[4] from the recycling of crop residues, and from the urea in animal manure. At present these sources account for only half the global need, not just in the West but throughout the world. In countries like China and Indonesia, virtually the entire source of nitrogen on their fields is from synthetic fertilisers.

As the twentieth century dawned, technological exploration shifted to the USA. One innovation that stands out among all others is the production of plastics. These are polymers[5] composed of carbon, hydrogen and oxygen, with some containing nitrogen as well. It is Leo Hendrik Baekeland, a Belgian who emigrated to the USA in 1889, to whom we owe the production of the plastic that has since been named after him: bakelite. Baekeland was a truly creative entrepreneur: prior to plastics, he had already invented a type of photographic paper that he sold on to Eastman, originators of the Kodak camera. By adapting the synthetic reactions leading to hard plastics, researchers in commercial ventures like Du Pont developed synthetic fibres, which have become part of every garment from socks and stockings to head-scarves and hats. Another notable innovation was that based on the combustion of liquid fuels: cars, pioneered by Henry Ford through the Model T in 1909, and aeroplanes, shown to work by Orville and Wilbur Wright in 1903. Frank Whittle, an Englishman, may have invented the jet engine in 1930, but it was American firms like Boeing that made inter-continental travel an everyday event following World War II.

Nowadays the rewards of organic chemistry have been largely played out. It is once more physical chemistry, the borderline between physics and chemistry, that has contributed to what many regard as the greatest invention of the twentieth century: electronics and the silicon chip. The science underlying the technology lay in the demonstration that electrons 'hop' along chemically-modified pieces of silicon,[6] rather in the way that electrons 'nudge' one another along a metal wire to produce an electric current. As with the synthesis of ammonia, commercialisation quickly followed the invention. Silicon-based microchips underlie computers and e-mail, digital television and satellite communication. Englishmen like Charles Babbage in 1835 and Alan Turing in 1937 may have laid the foundations of computing, but it was American firms like IBM and Microsoft that turned computers into a trillion dollar business. The fact that in 1999, most countries in the world were concerned about the possible breakdown of essential services like hospitals and shops, banks and aeroplanes, at the moment of transition from 1999 to 2000, shows how much every aspect of our lives has come to depend on the silicon chip.

Western technology was not always in the lead. For over 1000 years before, the wind of innovation blew from the east, and it was from China that it blew the strongest. Yet even before that, the fruits of man's ingenuity were already being put to good use.

Stone Age technology

The Stone Age, which preceded the epochs of bronze and iron, stretches back to the very birth of man. Stone tools, made by whittling away one piece against another so as to produce a point or a sharp edge, have been in use by *Homo* for some 2 million years, for stunning prey and butchering it as well as for the occasional attack on others of his own kind. The hardest materials were of quartz, chert or volcanic rock like basalt or obsidian; once man was in Europe more than a million years later, his tools were predominantly of flint, and he had learnt to start a fire. Soon he began to fashion handles from fallen branches, into which a pointed or edged stone could be inserted; winding pliable saplings around the two parts would hold such a primitive spear or axe together. The sight of branches and the occasional tree trunk floating down a river cannot have escaped his attention. First he probably just sat on a log and paddled with his hands in order to cross a river. Only much later did he begin to lash logs together to make a raft, and to hollow out a suitably sized log to make a boat. There are indications of early man—probably *H. erectus*—chipping the reddish pigment known as ochre off iron-containing ores like haematite:[7] at Terra Amata in France,[8] at Beçov in the Czech Republic[9] and at Hunsgi in southern India.[10] Whether he used the ochre to rub over his body as a cure for sores and bites, or whether the red colour had a symbolic meaning, perhaps of blood, we do not know.[11] What is clear is that *H. sapiens* subsequently used ochre for the cave paintings scattered throughout southern France and northern Spain that date back between 15,000 and 30,000 years ago.

The next major advance was the use of fire for hardening simple vessels moulded out of wet clay: ceramic technology is at least 26,000 years old. The propagation of crops only began some 15,000 years later. Some anthropologists wonder why it took so long. Was this the period during which the voice box was perfected and communication through language became possible,[12] or was an increased versatility in the function of the brain, that enabled man to express himself through art and religion,[13] the pivotal event?[14] We do not know. But then, is 15,000 years really such a long time, bearing in mind that the previous technological advances occurred over a million, not tens of thousands, of years? To me, the surprising thing is that both pottery and agriculture emerged in distant places at similar times: there are fragments of clay artefacts from the Amur River region of eastern Siberia and from a site at Zazaragi in the Miyagi Prefecture of Japan 900 miles away, each dated to around 13,000 years, there is evidence for the cultivation of crops like barley and wheat in the Near East, rice in Indonesia and China, maize in Central America and Peru, all between 10,000 and 11,000 years ago. The possibility that global warming, beginning to take place around 15,000 years ago, had an influence on these events surely needs further examination.[15] Taming of animals, for food and for work, followed: sheep and goats were being reared 9000 years ago; 2000 years later the ox-drawn plough made its appearance. By 5000 years ago crops were being irrigated in Babylonia, Egypt, the Indus valley and China. It was around this time that the wheel emerged throughout the Old World,[16] originally in Mesopotamia. First constructed of solid wood, the wheel was used largely on ox-drawn carts. A thousand years later chariots with spoked wheels, pulled by horses, were being employed for war-like purposes in Mesopotamia, China and Scandinavia. We have referred to the fact that agriculture and some of its technological offshoots arose all over the globe, in Europe and North America as well as in the areas that gave birth to the seven primary civilisations. Conversely, the culture of the Jomon in Japan, which produced thousands of clay artefacts, did not spawn agricultural practices: these were dormant until imported from China around 400 BC.

There are those who believe that symbols and motifs inscribed on some of the later cave paintings—those between 12,000 and

17,000 years old, as opposed to the ones that go back 30,000 years—represent a form of communication that is the precursor of the written word (Figure 9.1). Lines and dots at Altamira in Spain are said to refer to the male sexual organ, ovals and triangles to the female one.[17] Motifs inscribed on animal bones and other artefacts of this period have been interpreted in a similar way: a V and its upside down version for the vulva, a zigzag line for water, and so on. We should not be surprised by frequent reference to human genitalia: they are the most striking differences between unclothed men and women, and the act of procreation to produce new life has long had religious connotations. A particularly imaginative archaeologist, Marija Gimbutas, has associated such apparent references to the female organs with the great earth Goddess whose benign influence is said to have protected much of Europe at this time.[18]

But did not the earliest scripts, those found in the Sumerian city of Uruk, have their origin in accountancy, not folklore or myth? A strong proponent of this view is Denise Schmandt-Besserat.[19] She has studied over 10,000 small clay objects or 'tokens' that have been found throughout the Near East.[20] Many are up to 10,000 years old. They come in various shapes: spheres and egg-like ovals, cylinders and discs, cones and little pyramids. Schmandt-Besserat believes that each shape indicated a different commodity: a measure

Figure 9.1 Stone Age symbols. These marks were found, alongside drawings of animals, on the walls of caves in southern France and northern Spain, as well as on small portable objects. Reproduced from Allen Forbes and Thomas R. Crowder, 'The problem of Franco-Cantabrian abstract signs: agenda for a new approach', *World Archaeology* **10**(3): 350–366; 1979, by permission of The British Library Document Supply Centre, Boston Spa, Wetherby, West Yorkshire LS23 7BQ, UK.

of grain, a jar of oil, a unit of labour, a domestic animal, and so on. The number of tokens, some of which were perforated and strung together on a string, denoted the quantity of any one item under consideration. Recall that the Incas used knots on strings to indicate quantity (although they never went on to develop a script). So what is the link between the clay tokens and the emergence of written numerals? It is the finding that by around 5500 years ago, a second system of accountancy was developed. In this, the tokens were placed inside a larger clay tablet shaped like an envelope, which was then sealed off. A two-dimensional depiction of the kind of tablets that were contained in any one envelope—sphere or oval, cone or cylinder—was then inscribed on the outside of the envelope. Subsequently it occurred to the accountants of Uruk that there was no need to actually place the tokens inside the clay container at all. Why not simply denote the type of commodity on a clay tablet by the usual symbol and then add another mark to indicate the quantity? The symbols gradually changed, and others were added, but in essence the sequence of events postulated by Denise Schmandt-Besserat could well represent the origin of man's first script: the cuneiform of the Sumerians.[21]

The practice of medicine typifies technological innovation: trial and error is at its heart, not science.[22] The extent to which Stone Age man practised the art is very limited. Curing people of their ailments by one means or another was restricted to cultures such as those of Egypt and China. On the other hand, early man was ingesting molecules with psychoactive and analgesic properties, probably for pleasure as much as to reduce pain. There is evidence of chewing betel (*Piper betle*) in north-west Thailand around 7500–9000 years ago, while in southern Europe cultivation of the opium poppy (*Papaver somniferum*) had begun. Several millennia were to elapse before alcohol made its appearance: beer was first brewed in Egypt around 4000 BC, and was followed by the use of yeast to leaven bread only 2000 years later; it is at this time that we find reference to the consumption of wine.[23] The distillation of alcoholic beverages to produce spirits came later.[24] The practice of trepanation—removing a small piece of the skull—has been attributed to Stone Age man and, like the use of psychoactive plants, has continued among primitive tribes into modern times.

Exactly what the point was we do not know; one would have had to suffer a very severe headache indeed before allowing a colleague to scrape away at one's skull with no more than a pointed stone.

The legacy of China

Silk worms were being cultured to produce garments made of their exudate during the Shang dynasty more than 3000 years ago. The processing of pottery into fine porcelain ware soon followed. By the second century BC cast iron was being produced throughout China in quantities that would not be reached in Europe for nigh on 2000 years. During the ninth century, for example, China was producing 13,500 tons of iron a year; within 200 years the output had increased almost 10-fold. Swords and suits of armour increased the country's capacity for war, iron-tipped ploughs and mould boards (for turning the earth), sharpened scythes and hoes, boosted its agricultural output. At this time the Chinese were already manufacturing steel (a harder version of iron), by blowing air through a furnace in order to increase the temperature; not until Bessemer's invention of the blast furnace more than 800 years later would this technology be employed in Europe.

The Chinese use of herbal medicines and procedures like acupuncture is well known, but only now are western practitioners beginning to follow suit. By the time of the Tang dynasty (618–906), an amalgam of silver and tin was being employed to fill holes in teeth. Small doses of mercury were being administered against bacterial infections—a procedure that would not be used in the West, against syphilis and gonorrhea, for another 1000 years. 'Variolation' against smallpox[25] was being performed by the tenth century. Only 800 years later was it introduced into Europe by Lady Mary Wortley Montagu, who witnessed its efficacy in Constantinople between 1716 and 1718 and became sufficiently impressed to variolate her own son.[26] Marie Antoinette did likewise half a century later, though the Dauphin died anyway at the age of seven and a half.[27]

Accurate time-keeping is an important element in a sophisticated culture. The Chinese had developed a water-driven mechanical clock by the second century AD, and the elaborate clock made for the emperor Su Song in 1088 preceded similar devices in Europe by some 300 years. He used it largely for making astronomical predictions with greater accuracy than had been possible earlier: forecasting events was traditionally one of the roles played by the emperor of China. Perhaps because of such limited use, mechanical clocks seem then to have disappeared; they did not return until the sixteenth century, with the arrival of Jesuit missionaries.

Paper was also being made by the second century, partly in order to disseminate more effectively the sayings of Confucius and partly for use during the rigorous examinations that a scholar had to sit in order to enter the Chinese civil service. As seen in the last chapter, texts had been inscribed on bone and tortoise shell, then bronze and wood, 1000 years earlier during Shang times; in Egypt, historical events that had formerly been inscribed on the stone facings of the pyramids were being recorded on papyrus at this time.[28] An early form of library existed in a temple at Xi'an. Confucian texts carved on stone slabs were available for perusal by scholars: imprints of what they wished to copy could be transferred on to paper, rather like the procedures of 'brass-rubbing' or lithography. By the eighth century the technique had been modified to produce the world's first printed material and by the twelfth century books were in circulation. Printing was not introduced into Europe until the fifteenth century, when Johannes Gutenberg in Germany invented movable type and the printing press: the first book so produced was the Bible, in around 1455. In China, the dissemination of knowledge and the wisdom of Confucius were the driving forces behind the development of printing; in Europe it was religion.[29]

Salt is an important ingredient of any thriving economy, for without it food cannot be preserved during the winter months, when fresh supplies are unavailable. By the thirteenth century salt was being mined from a depth of 2000 feet in parts of China. The process was essentially that of raising an iron bit some 200 feet above the ground by means of a derrick and then dropping it sharply to create an ever-deepening well, from which the brine was pumped through bamboo pipes into a vat. Methane gas present below ground was then mixed with air and ignited in order to heat the brine and evaporate its content of water. Within 300 years these techniques were being used to drill for oil in China.

By the time of the Ming dynasty in the fourteenth century, water-driven spinning wheels were in use and bricks were being hardened at temperatures of 1100 °C by methods similar to those employed throughout the world today. If many European innovations are based on Chinese inventions, how did the technology seep westwards? Already in Roman times, galleons were bringing back Chinese silk in exchange for products made of iron and glass. From the time of the Tang dynasty (618–907) there was trade between Muslim communities in southern Chinese cities like Guangzhou and their Arab brothers in the Near East. During the thirteenth century the merchant and adventurer Marco Polo spent 2 years travelling throughout China in the service of the emperor Kublai Khan. On his return to Europe he described, to an admittedly sceptical audience,[30] the sophisticated life styles he had witnessed. Between 1405 and 1433 the Chinese admiral Zheng He made voyages of exploration, intent on initiating trading links, to southern India, Arabia and eastern Africa.[31] From these same regions information was brought to Europe by the Portuguese, once they had sailed around southern Africa, by Bartolomeu Dias in 1488 and Vasco da Gama (together with Bartolomeu Dias) in 1497. In any case, at this time the Chinese controlled Afghanistan and Persia, and its western border extended southward from the Black Sea to the Arabian peninsula, whence technology filtered back to Europe — to be used or to lie ignored for centuries. But the Silk Road brought not only goods and knowledge. In the fourteenth century it was the means by which the bubonic plague (*Yersinia pestis*) spread to Europe; over a third of the population died.

Islamic technology

As I stand on the balcony of the house situated in an Andalucian valley, in which I am writing at the moment, I see traces of terracing on every slope around me. There is hardly a metre of ground that was not actively and efficiently farmed during the time that the Arabs occupied this land between the beginning of the eighth century and the end of the fifteenth. Yet agriculture was not the only cornerstone of their economy: trade was as essential an ingredient. What they were exporting to the rest of the world—to India and China, sub-Saharan Africa and Europe—were products that depended for their manufacture on novel or improved technology: textiles and leather, sweetmeats and cereals, perfumes and medicaments. They improved the manufacture of glass and ceramics through the discovery of alkalis. They developed the tidal mill, the water wheel and the windmill. They produced naphtha, an inflammable fuel akin to kerosine. They introduced the use of animal intestines ('catgut'[32]) for stitching wounds and pioneered the manufacture of surgical instruments: scissors, syringes, probes and forceps. They used novel natural remedies against a variety of ailments and appreciated the fact that contagion lies at the heart of many diseases. They were among the first to bind paper into books, two centuries before the Chinese. And what did those books contain? Not just the religion of the Koran, but texts on mathematics and philosophy, chemistry and medicine. Some of these were to remain standard teaching material in the universities of Europe for centuries after the remnants of the Ottomans were driven from southern Spain. Words like 'algebra' and 'alkali'[33] have been retained to this day. As for mathematics, they incorporated the concept of zero, which had originated in India,[34] into the most innovative numerical system the world has ever seen. The abacus can truly be said to be the forerunner of every cash machine, nay of every computer, in use today.

There are those who disparage the contribution that Islamic culture made to the renaissance in Europe. Were the works of Greek and Roman scholars not preserved by monks scattered throughout Europe after the fall of Rome? To a certain extent, no doubt. But what was mainly kept alive by them was Christianity, which had been incorporated into Roman life already a century or so before the invasions of Vandals, Goths and Huns began. The input of the Islamic tradition was much more than the mere retention of Graeco-Roman values in medicine, philosophy and art. The Andalucian[35] city of Cordova alone produced two of the greatest philosophers of the time: Averroes or Ibn Rushd (1126–1198) and Maimonides (1135–1204), both thinkers in the Aristotelian tradition. As the preceding paragraph indicates, Arab culture was not merely conducive to innovation:[36] it actively promoted new technology. And this has become as much a part of modern life in Europe and beyond as has that of China. While the Arabs spawned no scientists, neither did the Chinese or any other culture, save that of Greece, prior to the sixteenth century.

Instruments of war

By the time that China was united under the Qin in 220 BC and the construction of its Great Wall—designed to keep out northern aggressors on horseback—had begun, its armies were fighting with the cross-bow and swords of steel. Such weaponry would not be seen in Europe for another 1300 years. The Chinese invented gunpowder,[37] but the supposition that they used this only in fireworks (reminiscent of the Mayans' use of the wheel merely as an appendage to toys) is incorrect. By the eleventh century gunpowder was being used to to fire cannon, to make small bombs and possibly make explosive arrows too, in an effort to keep out the invading horsemen of the north. The weaponry proved as ineffective as the Great Wall itself: by 1279 the aggressive Mongols had acquired the technology and Kublai Khan was able to complete the conquest of China. It is, however, true that the Chinese hit on the concept of the hot air balloon—heating air expands it so that it becomes lighter—and then employed it only in the form of small candle-lit lanterns that floated upwards at festivals. In the West, hot air balloons (pioneered by Mongolfier in 1783) would be used for military reconnaissance and, briefly, in the form of gas-filled zeppelins in World War I, for dropping bombs on the enemy. But battles are not won by hardware alone. Strategy is an equally important ingredient.

Sun Tzu was a general in the kingdom of Wu for some two decades from 512 BC onwards, during which time the army of Wu was able to defeat the forces of its old enemies, the Yueh and the Ch'u. Sun Tzu's tactics were so successful that he wrote them up as *The Art of War* in around 490 BC.[38] With the exception of Mao Zedong and the Soviet military, for whom it was prescribed reading, most commanders over the centuries have been unaware of his simple yet effective maxims, although often they intuitively employed similar tactics. By quoting from Sun Tzu, I am able to summarise the strategies of victorious generals over the past 2500 years:

> In peace prepare for war, in war prepare for peace ... The art of war is of vital importance to the State. It is a matter of life and death, a road either to safety or to ruin. Hence it is a subject of inquiry which can on no account be neglected ... The purpose of war is peace ... The supreme act of war is to subdue the enemy without fighting ... All warfare is based on deception. Hence when able to attack, we must seem unable; when using our forces we must seem inactive; when we are near, we must make the enemy believe we are far away; when far away, we must make him believe we are near ... Hold out baits to entice the enemy. Feign disorder, and crush him ... If he is secure at all points, be prepared for him. If he is in superior strength, evade him ... If your opponent is of choleric temper, seek to irritate him. Pretend to be weak, that he may grow arrogant ... If he is taking his ease, give him no rest. If his forces are united, separate them ... Attack him where he is unprepared, appear where you are not expected ...
>
> Now the general who wins a battle makes many calculations in his temple ere the battle is fought. The general who loses a battle makes but few calculations beforehand. Thus do many calculations lead to victory, and few calculations to defeat.[39] In the practical art of war, the best thing of all is to take the enemy's country whole and intact: to shatter and destroy it is not so good. So, too, it is better to capture an army entire than to destroy it, to capture a regiment, a detachment or a company entire than to destroy them. Hence to fight and conquer in all your battles is not supreme excellence; supreme excellence consists in breaking the enemy's resistance without fighting ...

and so on, and so on.

In his introduction to Sun Tzu's treatise in 1981, the American writer James Clavell went so far as to say 'I truly believe that if our military and political leaders in recent times had studied this work of genius, Vietnam could not have happened as it happened; we would not have lost the war in Korea ...; the Bay of Pigs could not have occurred; the hostage fiasco in Iran would not have come to pass; the British Empire would not have been dismembered; and, in all probability, World Wars I and II would have been avoided ...'. Well, you may, like me, find this a bit exaggerated, but Sun Tzu's words do not lack credibility.

Has technology affected the thirst of man to destroy his neighbours? No. As I have stressed before, the aggressive nature expressed by some, but not by others, is in their genes: the technological advances of the last 10,000 years have had little impact on human behaviour. What about the effect of technology on the means of warfare? To me there is little difference between being killed by a blow from a hand axe, an arrow, a spear, or a bullet; whether I die on the ground, in the sea, or in the air is of little consequence. What has changed is the extent to which the non-combatant population has become affected. As recently as Napoleonic times, men like Tolstoy's Pierre Bezukhov were able to witness the battle of Borodino from the side-lines, and during the battle of Waterloo the ball in nearby Brussels continued unabated. It was not new technology that killed the citizens of London and Coventry, Berlin and Dresden during World War II (or, for that matter, the peasants of Vietnam, Laos and Cambodia a few decades on). It was a change of strategy: to harrass the civilian population to such an extent that they beg their leaders to sue for peace. Where technology has had an impact on the instruments of war is in the development of weapons of mass destruction. It began 60 years ago. Using the energy released by nuclear decay was so innovative a process that 12 years earlier, Ernest Rutherford—the physicist who first split the atom—called such technology 'moonshine'. Not so Albert Einstein. In August of 1939 he wrote to President Roosevelt urging him to order the development of an atomic bomb without delay: Einstein was aware that German scientists might be pursuing the same goal. Roosevelt was persuaded and the Manhatten Project was initiated. In March of 1945 Einstein once more wrote to the

President, now urging him to abandon the project, as Germany was virtually defeated. This time Einstein's plea fell on deaf ears.[40]

Since the detonation of the first atomic bomb in 1945, nuclear energy has been developed for peaceful purposes as well as for war; indeed, it remains one of the major options for the world's supply of energy when oil and gas run out. Finding the means to spread pathogenic microbes over as large an area of the population as possible can have no beneficial application: the technology behind germ warfare is of destructive applicability alone. So far its uses have been limited. The Japanese employed it against China during World War II, and Saddam Hussein did so in Iraq's war against Iran in the 1980s.[41] But he was not the first to build up stocks of infectious microbes.

During World War II, the USA was carrying out research and development of anthrax spores and botulinum toxin for possible use against Germany. By 1944 it had installed 12 20,000-gallon fermentors at Vigo, Indiana, capable of producing more than a million 4-lb anthrax bombs a month; Britain alone had ordered an initial shipment of 500,000 bombs. In the event, none was used. In the subsequent period of the Cold War against the Soviet Union, anthrax was replaced by *Francisella tularensis*, another potentially fatal microbe when inhaled, and to it were added other incapacitating but less lethal bacteria, such as those reponsible for brucellosis and Q-fever, as well as Venezuelan equine encephalomyelitis virus; fungi that destroy wheat and rice were included for good measure. Again, these weapons were never deployed, for the simple reason that the Soviet Union was building up its own arsenal for germ warfare: not only the bacteria causing anthrax and tularaemia, but also microbes responsible for highly contagious diseases like plague and smallpox.[42] As with nuclear weapons, both sides realised that deterrence is preferable to engagement. Sun Tzu would surely have agreed.

Leonardo da Vinci

Technological innovations, unlike works of art or scientific theories, are not generally associated with any one person. Why then do I digress to focus on one individual, the man who came to be known as Leonardo da Vinci (1452–1519)? Some will no doubt be surprised to find his accomplishments enumerated in a chapter on technology. Was he not one of the greatest artists of the western world? Do not others consider him a scientist—'The First Scientist', in fact[43]—and therefore worthy of inclusion in a chapter devoted specifically to that topic? I agree with the first response, but tend to ally myself with Stephen Jay Gould[44] in disputing the second. Leonardo was not a scientist: he may have been a great experimentor, but he did not produce explanations for the phenomena around him.[45]

True, he conducted well-designed experiments on optics, but he did not interpret them with the insight of an Isaac Newton. Yes, he made shrewd observations like 'The moon is not luminous in itself. It does not shine without the Sun'; 'The moon acts like a spherical mirror'; but he was not the first to do so.[46] His comment that 'There is not to be seen in the Universe a body of greater magnitude and power than the Sun; its light illuminates all the celestial bodies distributed through the Universe' is wrong, and while the next statement, that 'the life forces descend from it' (i.e. the sun) 'because the heat which is in living animals comes from life forces and no other heat is there in the Universe'[47] is an amazingly perceptive statement—centuries before its time—he offers us no speculation of *how* this might be brought about.[48] Yet include his achievements in a book on quest I must, if for no other reason than to echo the words of the art historian Kenneth Clark, that he was 'the most relentlessly curious man in history'.[49]

Few before Leonardo had the courage—it was a proscribed activity—or the enthusiasm to dissect the human cadaver in such detail. By carefully exposing every organ and tissue—eye and brain, larynx and trachaea, heart and lungs, the systems of digestion and reproduction, the muscles, bones and nerves of face and hands, arms and legs—and then recording each assembly with almost three-dimensional accuracy through his superb drawings, Leonardo revealed features of anatomical structure that would not be surpassed until the invention of the electron microscope. He recognised that the heart is made essentially of muscles, similar to those that power limbs; he described arteries and veins and, although he could not see them, he predicted the existence of capillaries (the light microscope would not be developed for another 100 years). By comparing the arteries of an aged man, who had probably died of heart failure, with those of a recently deceased 2 year-old child, he concluded that the thickening of the arteries in the former case—to the point that the flow of blood was stopped—had been the cause of death. Moreover, he suggested that the gradual narrowing of arteries was due to the absorption of nourishments from the blood; 450 years would elapse before cholesterol-containing plaques were found to be the main cause of atherosclerosis and subsequent coronary failure. He recognised the function of the aortic valve—to push blood into the lungs by sequential opening and closing—by experiments with seeds of millet, again almost five centuries before the experiment was repeated by physiologists using advanced techniques. These accomplishments surely place him in a category occupied by experimentors like William Harvey two centuries on. On reflection, perhaps we should acknowledge Leonardo to have been a scientist of biology, if not of physics.

Leonardo's designs for military apparatus were again centuries ahead of his time: a parachute and a diving suit (the wearer would walk along the river bed and gouge holes in the underside of an attacker's boats), a tank and a helicopter (Figure 9.2). His inventions were never tested, nor would most of them have worked,[50] but that is beside the point. In designing them Leonardo foresaw materials of war that would come into everyday use once the requisite adjunct technology, such as the internal combustion engine, had been invented. He designed buildings and cities—to be divided into townships restricted to 30,000 people—with an eye on salubrious living. He would '... distribute the masses of humanity, who (now) live crowded together like herds of goats, filling the air with stench and spreading the seeds of plague and death'.[51] He planned plumbing and drainage for houses, parks and broad streets on two levels: pedestrians above and vehicles below. Automated washing machines would keep the environment clean (refuse and human excrement were still being dumped from houses straight on to the road).

And then there are his paintings. In one of his earliest, the one now known as the *Virgin of the Rocks*, his approach was so

Figure 9.2 Design for a helicopter sketched by Leonardo da Vinci. Reproduced courtesy of Sheila Terry/Science Photo Library, London.

innovative, especially in his depiction of the way light falls on different parts of the human face, that the Confraternity of the Immaculate Conception of the Virgin Mary, who commissioned it, took him to court: it was not what they had expected. *The Last Supper*, considered by many to be Leonardo's greatest painting,[52] fared no better: its patrons complained bitterly over the inordinate delay in its completion. The reason is that Leonardo spent time producing his own pigments and scouring the streets of Milan to find people with what he considered to be precisely the right visages to depict the participants of the occasion; these were then invited to sit for him while he completed the fresco. Even one of his last paintings, the *Mona Lisa* (*La Gioconda*), which is the only work signed and known to be by him alone and which reflects the years of practised draughtsmanship, is so revolutionary in style that is has beome the most controversial picture of the last 500 years. Artist and architect, experimentor and innovator, Leonardo encapsulates better than anyone the qualities that contribute to human quest. For good reason has he become known as 'the greatest genius the world has ever seen'.[53]

Technology and wealth

Technology, whether through better housing, food or medicine, improves the living conditions of the people and in so doing increases life expectancy. 10,000 years ago the population of the world was an estimated 6 million; 7000 years later it had risen to over 40 million:[54] the advent of agriculture throughout the world during this time must surely have been a contributing factor. Between 1750 and 1850, when the Industrial Revolution was reaching its peak, the increase in the population of western Europe began to overtake that of India and China: England's population grew three-fold (from 5.7 million to 16.5 million), whereas that of China did not quite double (from 215 million to 420 million).[55] Technology also creates wealth: partly by creating a surplus of food, that allows some members of the community to devote themselves to tasks other than food production (like inventing new technology, which makes it an autocatalytic process[56]), and partly through an increase in the population.[57] But devoting the fruits of technology to war diminishes wealth (through a reduction in the population and the wastage of materials). Only once political settlement between the warring parties has occurred is the situation stabilised and the accretion of wealth resumed. The economist Peter Jay compares this three-step process to a waltz motif, a waltz that underlies the gradual accumulation of wealth across the globe.[58] Let us pause to examine these points.

First, does an increase in the population really create wealth? On the basis that every family, on average, owns one pig—or its equivalent in currency—then a nation of 10 million families is 10 times as wealthy as a nation of 1 million. But if a large proportion of families actually owns nothing and, worse, needs to be supported by the better-off, then the difference between the wealth created by the rich and that consumed by the poor becomes the decisive factor. I cannot think of an instance where the wealth of a country actually declined because of its generosity to the poor (post-World War II Britain may have come close). The opposite situation — employing the poor to create wealth — is a more familiar one and the use of slavery is an obvious example. During the height of the Roman empire, half its people were slaves: Rome prospered. On the other hand, slaves do not contribute to the development of new technology, and Jay sees that as a contributing factor to the empire's eventual decline. So the relationship between wealth and the size of the population is not straightforward. Indeed, today the correlation may be the opposite: Switzerland, Singapore and Brunei are all small but wealthy countries (it has to be said as a result of other people's technology: the banking system, the use of containers to transport goods and the drilling for oil, respectively); Japan's population is a tenth that of China, but its *total* wealth is greater.[59]

Second, the extent to which a country recovers its wealth after a war depends on how much was squandered during the conflict, and how quickly the country can revert to growth during the period of stabilisation. All the countries involved in the Napoleonic wars eventually recovered, but then the nineteenth century was a particularly favourable one for the development of new technology in Europe. On the other hand, the money spent on weaponry by the USSR during the second half of the twentieth century — with virtually no shots fired — brought the Soviet Union to the brink of bankruptcy by the end of the Cold War. More than a decade on, it has barely begun to recover. Where my heart warms to Peter Jay is in the first of the four propositions with which he defines a country's economic success: '... given half a chance he [i.e. man] will seek to maintain and, if possible, to improve his material condition'.[60] Does this not underlie the gist of my argument regarding the quest for new technology?

Technology and wealth are related in a more direct way, if we include the substitution of money (metal, silver, gold) for barter as a technological innovation. The promissory note is a consequence of the use of coinage. It underlies the issue of paper money by banks, and was important for commerce when dealing with large sums. The Chinese were trading with paper money of a sort by the seventh century. Although banking houses had been established in

Italy by the thirteenth century, the banknote as we know it did not enter circulation until more recent times. Notes began to be issued in Amsterdam in 1609, in Stockholm in 1661, in the Massachusetts Bay Company in 1690, and in London in 1694.[61] Of course, private promissory notes or 'IOUs' had been in existence long before, but their use depended on how much the borrower could be trusted. The essence of the banking system is that trust can be taken for granted. The accounting system developed under the Ottoman empire and the 'double entry' form of book-keeping pioneered in Italy between the thirteenth and fourteenth century (that shows changes in assets as well as in expenditure and income) were key advances in the generation of that confidence. When I asked the English economist Sir Alan Walters a few years ago to what extent technology contributes to a nation's economic strength, his response was 'rather little'; 'look at Singapore and Hong Kong: both are wealthy, yet neither has any technology'. The main factors, in his view, are the rules of law and the degree of trust one can place in a country's banks and other commercial institutions.[62]

We end this chapter on a different note. Some technological innovations—and I am not referring to those used for war—result not in benefit but in disaster. The use of thalidomide to prevent 'morning sickness' in pregnant women and the fate of the Chernobyl nuclear power station are but two of the more glaring examples. Should the state intervene in man's search for new technology if it deems this to be counter-productive? The trouble is that governments often get it wrong (and in the case of Chernobyl were themselves responsible for the installation of the plant).[63] It is a subject to which I return in Part III, when considering the fruits of today's technology. My view is that inventors are by and large decent people. Most evil men do not choose to spend their time on the laborious journey of trial and error that underlies a new invention. Frankenstein was a creation in Mary Shelley's mind: few exist in the real world. So far as the invention itself is concerned, we should give the outcome the benefit of the doubt. Of course governments must curb the development of technologies that appear foolhardy or objectionable. But the downside of missing an invention like the treatment of sewage or the use of penicillin, which between them have saved millions of lives, surely outweighs any potential risk.

Notes

1. Such as chalcopyrites ($CuFeS_2$) in the case of copper, and cassiterite (SnO_2) in the case of tin.
2. Trying to follow the builders of Stonehenge 3000 years ago by making the first part of the journey from the Preseli Hills of Wales to Wiltshire by water, a team of young enthusiasts lost the rock altogether: it toppled over and sank as soon as it was placed in a boat.
3. Vaclav Smil, *Enriching the Earth: Fritz Haber, Carl Bosch, and the Transformation of World Food*, MIT Press, Boston, MA, 2001.
4. Bacteria that symbiotically colonise legumes and carry out a version of the Haber – Bosch process by means of the relevant enzymes.
5. A polymer is a large molecule made up of repeating units, and in that regard similar to proteins and nucleic acids. Plastics are polymers synthesised from precursors found predominantly in petrochemicals, natural gas or coal.
6. James McNeill Whistler was thrown out of West Point Academy for answering, in a chemistry examination, 'silicon is a gas'. The American Army may have lost a potential general, but the world gained a brilliant artist.
7. See Richard Rudgley, op. cit., pp 176–183.
8. 300,000 years ago.
9. 250,000 years ago.
10. Between 300,000 and 200,000 years ago.
11. Ochre has been used in modern times for various purposes. The Himba in Africa smear themselves with a mixture of ochre and grease as protection against sunburn and insect bites, the Gugadja of north-western Australia employed it to treat sores and burns, while the indigenous Andaman islanders smeared it over new-born babies as a kind of protection. See Richard Rudgley, op. cit., pp 176–183.
12. What Jared Diamond, op. cit., pp 27–48, calls 'the great leap forward'.
13. See Stephen Mithen, op. cit.
14. As pointed out in Chapter 8, the evolution of language and the growth of the brain in the region of the neocortex appear in any case to be related.
15. Global temperatures are said to have risen by as much as 7°C; see Steven J. Mithen, op. cit., p 219.
16. In the Americas, the wheel was no more than a novel artefact.
17. Richard Rudgley, op. cit., pp 72–85.
18. Marija Gimbutas, op. cit.
19. Richard Rudgley, op. cit., pp 48–57, and Denise Schmandt-Besserat, op. cit.
20. In Turkey, Iraq, Iran, Syria and Israel.

21. Others, like Steven Fischer, agree that writing began with accountancy symbols. He, however, goes one further and makes the startling proposition that all forms of writing are interdependent and spread from the Middle East to the entire world, including China and Central America. See Steven Roger Fischer, *A History of Writing*, op. cit. A glance at Figures 8.1, 8.2 and 9.1 makes one tend to agree with him. But I would extend the point made at the end of Chapter 8, that there are only so many ways to build a boat or fashion a drinking vessel, to include symbolic script.

22. At least not until very recent times, as described in Chapter 11.

23. The Old Testament (*Genesis* 9:20) mentions wine in relation to Noah.

24. 'Toddy' made from rice and molasses was being distilled to produce arrack in India and Ceylon by 800 BC.

25. Inhaling live pus from a victim in order to become immune to a subsequent infection.

26. Lady Mary was a truly innovative character, in many ways centuries before her time. She considered that marriages should be fixed for a period of 7 years, renewable at the end of each term by mutual consent. True, she was married to a rather dull man (and 'the whiff of scandal clung to her like an expensive eau de cologne'), but the result was surely the first recorded acknowledgment of the 'seven year itch'. Taken from John Adamson's review of Isobel Grundy, *Lady Mary Wortley Montagu: Comet of the Enlightenment*, Oxford, 1999, in the *Sunday Telegraph* of 2 May 1999.

27. But from tuberculosis, not smallpox.

28. Papyrus, from *Cyperus papyrus*, the 'paper plant', was being made into books and documents in Egypt by the ancient Egyptians, the Greeks and the Romans right up to the eighth century, when it was supplanted by paper introduced by the Arabs. In Europe, vellum (parchment) had already begun to replace papyrus during the third century.

29. Although William Caxton went on to print Malory's *Le Morte d'Arthur* and Chaucer's *Canterbury Tales* in England later that century.

30. Marco Polo, through his book *Divisament dou Monde* (Description of the World, later called 'Il Milione' for reasons that are obscure). Although raptuously received by some (as a fable as much as factual description), others—the poet Dante Aligheri among them—paid no attention to it.

31. An early version of the compass had been invented during the Han dynasty, 1000 years earlier.

32. From sheep, goats and other animals; whether these actually included cats is not known. The dried, twisted entrails were employed also as strings for archery bows and for musical instruments.

33. 'Al-djabr' and 'al-qaliy' (but only the prefix of alchemy is Arabic: the rest of the word is derived from the Greek $\chi\eta\mu\iota\alpha$ (cheemia) = transmutation).

34. Said to have been first used—as well as negative numbers—by the astronomer Brahmagupta in the seventh century.
35. The name refers to its occupation by the Vandals in the fourth century—'Vandalitia', 'al-Andalus' is the term used to describe the Umayyad dynasty in Spain (736–1031).
36. At this time the Koran was still being interpreted within the liberal values prescribed by Mohammed himself, not yet tainted by the fanaticism and dogma of some of its later adherents.
37. A mixture of saltpetre (potassium nitrate), charcoal and sulphur, known as 'black powder', is said to have been used by the Chinese as early as the ninth century, but others attribute its invention to the Arabs.
38. Sun Tzu, op. cit.
39. General Bernard Montgomery refused to engage Field Marshall Erwin Rommel at El Alamein in October of 1942 until he was sure that he had enough men and supplies according to his reckoning: from then onwards, because of adequate supplies, he rarely lost an action. Operation 'Market Garden'—the airborne assault on Arnhem to secure the bridges across the Rhine ahead of the main army—was a disaster, because insufficient time was spent in preparation.
40. See Lewis Wolpert, op. cit., pp 154–155.
41. He deployed chemical weapons as well.
42. See Matthew Meselson, *New York Review of Books*, **XLVIII** (20; 20 December): 38; 2001.
43. Michael White, op. cit.
44. Ibid., pp 290–291.
45. Except in regard to his comments about the thickening of arteries and his experiments on the function of the aortic valve, as described in subsequent paragraphs.
46. Ibid., pp 293–294; as long ago as the first century, the Chinese astronomer Zhang Heng, in an accurate description of a lunar eclipse, wrote '... since the moon reflects the sunshine, it will be eclipsed when it travels into the shadow cast by the earth': quoted by John Merson, op. cit., p 38.
47. Ibid., pp 294–295.
48. The transformation of one form of energy (light) into others (chemical energy and heat)—the science of thermodynamics—would not be expressed mathematically for several centuries.
49. Sherwin B. Nuland, op. cit., p 4.
50. No human being, for example, has sufficient energy to power the 'aerial screw' of his helicopter.
51. Ibid., p 51.
52. 'The keystone of European art', according to the late Kenneth (Lord) Clark.
53. Ibid., p 12.

54. Massimo Livi-Bacci, *A Concise History of World Population*, Blackwell, Oxford, 1997, p 31.
55. Peter Jay, op. cit., p 180.
56. See S. A. Kauffman, *The Origins of Order*, Oxford University Press, Oxford, 1993.
57. Peter Jay, op. cit., p 29.
58. Ibid., p 36.
59. And China is not known for its largesse to the poor (neither, for that matter, is Japan).
60. Ibid., p 309.
61. See Janet Gleeson, *The Moneymaker*, Bantam Press, London, 1999.
62. Personal communication, November 1999. But others, like Jeffrey Sachs, director of the Center for International Development at Harvard University, do view '... technological change [as] the main driver of economic growth': see *Nature* **407**: 276; 2000.
63. An energetically argued, although by now rather outdated, opinion on these matters is presented by Nigel Calder in *Technopolis: Social Control in the Uses of Science* [he means technology], MacGibbon & Kee, London, 1969.

CHAPTER TEN

Religion: belief and dogma

'Religion is the opium of the people'. Karl Marx's remark was not merely patronising; it was wrong. Opiates make you forget the world around you; religion is early man's search to understand it and to incorporate spiritual beliefs into his life. Perception of the world through religion may have been abandoned by the Greeks in favour of philosophy, but elsewhere religious doctrine continued to provide the only answers. Not until the seventeenth century did science begin to supply more satisfactory explanations. And if today millions of people throughout the world continue to practise religious principles through prayer, it is for calmness, not oblivion.

Early beliefs

The nature of the physical world in which he lived must have puzzled man from the earliest days. It probably does so for most conscious animals as well. Even the most educated within the ancient worlds of Sumeria, Egypt, India, China, Crete, central and southern America must have wondered about the origin of those twinkling dots they could see in the sky at night but not during the day. They realised that these celestial bodies move to a pattern and they were even able to predict precise changes in their positions. But what was their origin? Wonder must have been coupled with fright, not so much by the passage of day into night (although being in the dark frightens us still) or of summer into winter, but at every occurrence of lightning and thunder, earthquake and volcanic eruption, hurricane and flood. The unexpected is more fearsome than the repetitive. And then there is death, the most frightening event of all.[1] Fear, of course, is not a particularly human emotion: we share it with most animals. My dog Pedro used to shake and cower in the corner of the room at every peal of thunder (and my mother pulled the bedclothes over her face). It is as surprising as the simultaneous emergence of agriculture in communities separated by thousands of miles of ocean, that belief in some form of supernatural deity should have sprung up throughout the world, whether in sophisticated cultures or in the backwaters of sub-Saharan Africa, northern Europe or North America. If frightening phenomena are the work of gods in whom we believe, then we can more easily accept such events. Our search for an explanation is satisfied.

Some form of ritualistic worship can be traced back to Stone Age cave dwellers 30,000 years ago. The pictures on the walls and roofs of caves often display the outlines of animals they feared or hunted. The fact that they bothered to engage in such an activity, when they might have been out foraging for food or chiselling their tools, has led us to infer a magical or religious purpose. By depicting a leopard, they might somehow avoid being attacked by one; by drawing a deer, the chances of a successful kill were improved.[2] Portraying the human form—the female one in particular—would lead to a fertile outcome. But how could the creatures around them be aware that someone was copying their form, and why should that lead to the desired result? The idea was born that there existed in nature some force powerful enough to influence the activity of animals and humans; it is accepted in the minds of some to this very day. Such supernatural beings controlled everything: the rising of sun and moon, the movement of stars, the outbreak of thunder and lightning, the flow of water in rivers, the onset of rain and the growth of crops; and yes, the moment of death was in their hands also. By venerating and propitiating these spirits—for they could be as malign as a snake or a jaguar—a better life was assured. There is a similarity between primitive religions and the beliefs and practices of pagan tribes living outside the developed world in present times,[3] just as there is in the way that the technology of the latter resembles that of Stone Age man: both religion and technology have become frozen in time through isolation from the main streams of human quest. Far from disparaging either, they indicate to me the subtlety of human endeavour. Whether current or practised 5000 years ago, religious beliefs—like technology—represent a huge step forward in the development of the human mind over the past 100,000 years.

The Old World

The Sumerians worshipped several gods. The saga of Gilgemesh tells of his original indifference to their powers, and ends with his humble acceptance of their authority. On his journey through life he is beset by a huge flood, which he survives by building himself a boat. Was the melting of the Arctic ice sheet 7000 years ago, at the end of the last ice age, the source of this story? The level of the Mediterranean rose by as much as 20 metres in a relatively short time, and water surged across the Bosphorus, then a land bridge at the western end of the Black Sea, with the force of 200 Niagaras. Salt water flooded into the Black Sea, introducing oceanic fauna into its previously fresh waters for the first time. The shore line of the Black Sea rose by more than 100 metres in places. Whether this event was indeed passed on by word of mouth for 3000 years before it was written down, we do not know. But once written down, it probably then inspired the saga of Noah and his ark as recorded in Genesis 1000 years later.[4] Floods were occurring elsewhere—from the Caribbean to the Great Barrier Reef—at the end of the ice age, and are the likely sources of flood legends throughout Asia and other parts parts of the world.[5]

The afterlife did not feature in the religion of the Sumerians:

... man was fashioned of clay and created for one purpose only: to serve the gods by supplying them with food, drink and shelter, so that they might have full leisure for their divine activities. Man's life was beset with uncertainty and haunted by insecurity, since he did not know beforehand the destiny decreed him by the unpredictable gods. When he died, his emasculated spirit descended to the dark, dreary nether world where life was but a dismal and wretched reflection of its earthly counterpart ... the Sumerians accepted their dependent status just as they accepted the divine decision that death was man's lot and that only the gods were immortal'.[6]

Not so Egyptian beliefs. The spirit of man lived on after death, and in order to ensure a good outcome, it should be dispatched in as favourable a way as possible: preserved by mummification, with food and weapons, clothing and trinkets alongside; in the case of the king, the body was placed inside a sarcophagus within a pyramid built for him alone. The earliest ruler over the world of the dead was the god Osiris: it was before him that man had to explain away the shortcomings of his earthly life. If he was unable to do so, he would be condemned to carry out unpleasant tasks for all eternity. All was not lost, however: a small statuette placed in his grave might perform the drudgery in his place.[7] It is important to remember that the rituals and the gods to whom homage was accorded changed with time, as peoples of varied origin were assimilated into a realm as extensive and as enduring as that of Egypt. We should not be surprised: different groups worship the same gods in different ways. The Christian church diversified into half a dozen distinct denominations in parts of Europe within no more than a few hundred years after the Reformation: there was the original Roman Catholic version, the Lutheran Church in Germany, the Presbyterian Church—through Calvinism—in Switzerland, the Anglican Church—and later the Methodist one—in England, the Baptist sect in The Netherlands.

The worship of Ra, the sun god, began at Heliopolis (now Cairo), as the name suggests. However, it was not until the Vth dynasty (around 2500 BC) that a Ra priesthood was established: this made Ra as important a god as Osiris. His travels across the heavens were made in two huge boats, one in which to ascend at dawn and one to return in at dusk; they are depicted at the side of a temple built in his honour. Since the rising and setting of the sun is the most distinctive feature of daily life, it is not surprising that sun worship played as important a role in the religions of Central and South America as it did in Egypt. It would not have occurred to the

Egyptians that the the rays of the sun were crucial to the growth of their crops, since few days were without sunshine. Equally, the Nile was so central to their lives—the country never expanded into the deserts to the east or west of the great river—that they took its supply of water for granted. Thus, there was no god of rain, and we know only of a mere magician attached to the Roman army who is said to have invoked rainfall (through the moon god Tehuti).[8] In Europe today, prayers for rain by Christian clergy in times of drought arc not so rare an occurrence. Fertility, on the other hand, was sought through a number of animal gods: predominantly these were the bull (Apis was also the god of power), the cow and the ram. The Egyptian priesthood, of which women were a part, had considerable influence. They were responsible not only for conducting worship and maintaining morality, but for education of the people as well; the role of the priest as teacher would be continued within the Christian and Islamic traditions through to modern times. By the time that Rameses III came to power around 1200 BC, during the XXth dynasty, the rule of the land was virtually under the authority of priests: they had wealth and land (and paid no taxes). This was a change from earlier times: then, it had been the Pharaoh who was the supreme ruler and it was he, not the priesthood, who had a direct link to the gods.

To the inhabitants of the Indus valley, a safe journey into the after-world was not the focus of their religion. What they and their Hindu successors sought was a spiritual dimension to their daily lives: to be linked to the world's soul (the *atman*, which is Sanskrit for 'essence'), that was itself a part of the universal absolute (the *brahman* or ultimate holy power). Although men were divided by caste, their aspirations were the same—to rise above the physical dimension of the world in which they lived. The main precepts of the Hindu religion are *dharma* (truth) and *karma* (the structure of society) and together they constitute a code of behaviour. *Karma* is central to the caste system. Its concept embraces a continuity of cause and effect in the human spirit, and allows someone born into the lowest caste, or even outside it altogether (the 'untouchables' or *dalit*), to improve his status in the next life. Through *karma* the fate of one's soul on its journey to reincarnation in the form of another person is decided (animals undergo a similar process).[9] According to the Hindu religion, there is no need to fear death: immortality is assured.

Chinese beliefs followed a different path. The soul is made up of two parts: the *po*, which begins at conception, and the *hun*, which starts at birth. Together they see man through his earthly life, but at death the *hun* leaves the body. The *po* remains until the corpse has decayed, after which it joins the kingdom of the dead. This is a copy of life on earth, continued underground: the 7000 strong terracotta army entombed at Xi'an with the self-styled First August Emperor of Qin bears witness to this ideology. One of his successors during the Han dynasty was a less war-like ruler: he was buried with statues not just of soldiers, but of women and animals as well. But even the Qin emperor had been relatively benign: in earlier times actual people—part of the court, for example—had been buried alive to keep the ruler company in the after-life.

There is no social mobility after death: the *po* of a wealthy man remains rich, that of a pauper stays destitute. Gods do not appear much in Chinese devotional practices, although magicians or shamans do. In fact, religion is not an appropriate word for Chinese beliefs at all: somewhat akin to Hindu principles, the way that life is led is all-important. It should be along the lines laid down by the Great Principle, *hong fang*.

Hong fang embraces the Five Elements of water, fire, wood, metal and earth, that correspond to the Five Activities of gesture, speech, sight, hearing and thought. The way that the Five Activities are to be carried out so that they conform to the Five Elements was laid down by the ruler, according to Eight Methods of Government: these comprise the three occupations of agriculture, artisanship and sacrifices, their control by three Ministers (Public Works, Justice and other matters, like education and the economy), and two ways in which the ruling class interacts with the rest: peacefully or belligerently. The Eight Methods of Government operate according to the Five Regulators (the year, the month, the day, the constellation and the calendar). The royal power, that provides the link between humanity and what is Above and Around it, performs its role in one of Three Manifestations of Activity: with equity, severity or mildness. The criterion of successful application of these rules depends on the elements of rain, sun, heat, cold, wind and so forth: if they arrive within the appropriate season, governance has been good; if not, the ruler has governed badly. The outcome in the first instance are the Five Happinesses of longevity, wealth, health, love of virtue and a favourable demise; in the second, the Six Calamaties ensue: illness, suffering, poverty, misfortune, weakness, violent and premature death.[10]

Chinese beliefs began to change after the time of Confucius in the fifth century BC. The outcome of events continued to depend on the luck—or misfortune—of the emperor. It is for that reason that the practice of astronomy came under his control: the movements of the stars provided the basis for his divinations. Yet the rigidity of the rules by which life was to be enacted was crumbling. This did not represent a sudden shift of emphasis by the whole population. On the contrary, different strands of society followed independent paths. The Confucians averred that man is by nature good; the Legalists saw him as essentially evil. So many other points of view were put forward that the various arguments were dubbed the 'Hundred Schools of Thought'. But debate is healthier than mute acquiescence. It fosters an atmosphere conducive to new ideas and it is no coincidence that this period of Chinese history—the rule of the Eastern Zhou that ended in 221 BC—was also a time of invention and innovation, despite the turbulent wars that were being waged: multiplication tables and cast iron appeared. Other ideologies followed, of which Buddhism and Daoism (or Taoism) exerted the most influence. Indeed, together with Confucianism, they continue to be practised throughout China and much of eastern Asia today.

The religion of the Greeks, inherited from Crete by way of the Mycenians, focused heavily on gods: first the Titans, then the Olympians by whom the Titans were destroyed. Since much of our knowledge concerning Greek beliefs is derived from the writings of Homer, there is somewhat of a fusion between the acts of gods, mythical figures, and humans. While death did not obsess the Greeks as much as it had the Egyptians—they were more concerned with success in war and sport, equity in politics and law, excellence in art and scholarship—immortality was not beyond their comprehension.

One fate was eternal abode in the underworld (*hades*); alternatively, the spirit (*psyche*)—as opposed to the body (*soma*)—might survive. Yet the belief in divine rule of the world was beginning to crumble. The absence of a single ruler who was himself a quasi-god, like the Pharaoh in ancient Egypt, or who was inspired by divine advocacy, like the Emperor of China, may have played a part. By the end of the seventh century BC, there was one man for whom the deeds of gods were no longer a satisfactory explanation for the natural world. He was Thales of Miletus—the father of philosophy, and considered by some[11] to be the first scientist. True, divine mythology would continue to satisfy the masses, and would be avidly absorbed into the succeeding Roman culture, but the conduct of life was beginning to be subject not to the edicts of emperors or gods, but to common sense: humanism had arrived.

During the time of the Republic in the fifth century BC, Socrates and his disciple Plato laid the foundations of what is essentially moral philosophy. To Socrates, the virtuous life is based on knowledge: it is knowing about oneself, and in particular admitting what one does not know, that is fundamental. Plato incorporated these ideas into metaphysics and ethics, as well as into politics. Education, not birth or wealth, should determine who governs. In discussing this topic in Chapter 6, I compared inheritance with selection as a means of deciding on the next ruler. Rarely, however, does the people's choice fall on the most educated: pragmatism—anathema to the intellectual—has over the years proved a more valuable quality in a ruler than erudition. The most outstanding of Plato's pupils moved the argument from ideals back to the natural world: throughout the fourth century Aristotle used the rules of argument—proposition followed by deduction—in his attempt to explain physical phenomena without recourse to divine mediation. He concurred with the philosopher of the previous century, Empedocles, that the world is made up of four elements: earth, fire, air and water. Moreover, to Aristotle, each is either wet or dry, hot or cold. The fact that this echoes somewhat the five Chinese fundamentals of water, fire, wood, metal and earth should not be interpreted as implying some link between Greek and Chinese culture: they are as obvious to anyone thinking about these matters as the fact that some animals fly, others swim, some walk, others crawl. The point about Aristotelian philosophy is that it provided, for the first time, logical explanations for the world in which man finds himself: the movement of stars—indeed of all objects—the flight of birds, the development of the human body. His reasoning would dominate European and Arab thinkers for 2000 years. The fact that most of his basic assumptions were wrong was not appreciated until the advent of experimental science in the hands of men like Galileo and Newton, and their successors in the field of biology during the nineteenth and twentieth centuries.

The beliefs of the five cultures so far considered have been ingeniously summarised in the following way: the religion of the Sumerians was essentially theocentric (god-centred), that of the Egyptians, thanatocentric (death-centred), that of the Indians, psychocentric (soul-centred), that of the Chinese, cratocentric (rule-centred) and that of the Greeks, anthropocentric (man-centred).[12] What of the religions that emerged in central and southern America?

The Americas

The focus of worship among the peoples of meso-America was, like that of the Egyptians, the sun: the inhabitants of Teotihuacan, the Olmecs, the Toltecs, the Maya and the Aztecs all built elaborate temples from which to venerate the giver of light. The symbolic god of the night was generally the moon (an evil goddess in the case of the Maya). Both had to be appeased in order to ensure the diurnal variations of light and dark. So far as agriculture was concerned, a youthful corn god supplemented the god of the Sun. The Maya realised that water is as essential an element for a successful harvest as sunshine; their sophisticated method of irrigation is proof of that. The Sumerian, Egyptian, Indic and Sinic civilisations, each of which grew up along the banks of a great river that regularly flooded the crops planted along its banks, had no need of rain gods. The Maya, whether in the lowlands of Yucatan or the highlands of Guatemala, did. It is not surprising, therefore, that the Maya worshipped rain gods: in the Yucatan the Chac gods,[13] in the highlands the related Chicchans. The Chacs produced rain by pouring water out of gourds from the sky; they were also responsible for lightning, which they achieved by hurling down stone axes. Like other gods, they also existed as four entities, each associated with one of the four cardinal points. These had different colours: north was white, east was red, south was yellow and west was black; the centre, pertinently, was green.[14]

Like other gods, Chacs were appeased by different types of offering: everything from jade artifacts, through flowers and plant produce, to animals, birds, insects and fish. But the prize offering was undoubtedly a human. Blood was often first drawn from the victim, as well as from animals, and sometimes this sufficed. Otherwise the victim was next held, spread-eagled on the sacrificial stone, by his arms and legs, perhaps to indicate the four cardinal points, by priests called *Chacs*, before a knife was plunged into the body and the heart removed. The victim was generally a child, a captive ruler or a noble who was otherwise in good health (the gods would hardly be impressed by the sacrifice of an old man on the verge of death). Another god to be placated was Quetzalcoatl, who appears as a plumed serpent in the religious worship of the Toltec, Olmec, Maya and Aztec cultures. Apart from snakes, the other main predator of humans and their domesticated animals in meso-America would have been the jaguar, and we find several temples devoted to his appeasement. Worship by the descendants of the Maya who live in Central America today, and are nominally Roman Catholics, is infused with earlier beliefs in Mayan gods, in the same way that the Christian religion in Europe is interwoven with the pagan festivals that had been observed by northerners, as well as within the Roman Empire, in earlier times.

'The Indians of Peru were so idolatrous that they worshipped as Gods almost every kind of thing created'. So begins the description of Inca religion by the Jesuit scholar, Father Bernabe Cobo.[15] The centre of their veneration was the god of creation, Viracocha. Like the Sumerians, the Israelites and some of the peoples of south-east Asia, they believed themselves to be descended from those who had survived a great flood. Exactly where this occurred is not clear: the waters are said to have covered the entire country, from the highest peak to the ocean, and all but one man and one woman perished. The perpetrator of the flood, as well as its saviour, was Viracocha.

Second to him was the god of the sun. The Incas appear to have related the power of the sun to the growth of their crops, so it is not surprising that they, like the Mochica and the Chimu before them, built temples in every location to the giver of life. At the festival of Capac Raymi, held annually in the first month of the year, the priests would distribute cakes to the people, saying, 'What you been given is the food of the sun, and it will be present in your bodies as a witness ...;[16] (do I detect the good Father Cobo slipping unwittingly into the words of the Last Supper?). Naturally an eclipse of the sun was a bad omen and required the sacrifice of many children as appeasement. The third-ranking deity was the god of thunder. Because he brought with him lightning, he was greatly feared. But since he was responsible also for the nourishing impact of rain—as well as for the waters of the sea, whence the coastal people derived an important source of food—he was also highly revered. So, in times of drought—more human sacrifices. The Incas believed in immortality: the souls of those who had led unblemished lives would ascend to the heavens and turn into a star; this was the origin of all the shining flecks in the night sky. In order to help them on their way, their possessions, together with a supply of food and drink, would be placed in their graves, as had been the practice of the Egyptians. But those who failed to heed the strictures of the priests and teachers would be condemned to a nether world.

Contemporary faiths

If the events of the physical world around us, whether frightening or not, have been explained in terms of scientific principles with which none can argue, why is religion practised at all today? For what are we searching? Essentially for three things. First, for a code of values by which to live. It is easier for many to accept a moral way of life if it is part of their faith than if it is forced on them by government. To lead an upright life is one of the fundamental tenets of all faiths, from Hinduism and Buddhism, to Judaism, Christianity and the religion of Islam. Abiding by them makes sense: incest eventually leads to physical deformation and mental retardation, while rules associated with the Judaic and Islamic faiths, such as male circumcision and avoidance of pork and shellfish, constitute a hygenic benefit in the hot climate of the Near East. The second object of our search is spiritual comfort in our daily lives. For many, the religious experience provides just that: whether expressed through public worship in temple, synagogue, church or mosque, or through private prayer in the home.[17]

And the third? The question of immortality plagues us still. Modern man has not been able to rid himself of the fear that obsessed his ancestors. He finds it difficult to accept the scientific reality that at his death the molecules within his body, which have sustained every moment of his activity, every thought in his brain, simply start to decompose; that the consequences of death are no more than the rotting of meat. So every religion continues to address the problem of an afterlife. Whether it be reincarnation or continuation, a belief in the enduring existence of one's soul provides reassurance. Why do I dwell on this topic? Can it be that I am frightened of something to which I am seeking an answer?

Hinduism

The oldest religion practised today is Hinduism. It goes back 5000 years, to the time that the Indic civilization was growing in the valley of the Indus, and its essential precepts have therefore already been described. It has never been a state religion: current attempts by the strongly nationalistic and Hindu BJP (Bharatya Janata Party) to make it one have not as yet succeeded. But then of course India was not a united country until Chandragupta Maurya founded his empire at the end of the fourth century BC. Hinduism might have been adopted as the official religion at that time, were it not for the fact that its third and greatest leader, Ashoka, who consolidated the might of the empire during the third century BC, became disillusioned with war and formal religion, and turned to Buddhism instead. The Muslim invasions of the thirteenth century, however, marked the virtual demise of Buddhism in India. From that time to the present, the religion of Islam has been practised by some, Hindu beliefs by the majority, Buddhism by a few.

Hinduism is a much more tolerant religion than any of the Judaeo – Christian – Muslim trio: it lays down no hard and fast beliefs in the nature of God. Indeed, it does not stipulate a single God at all, but embraces polytheism and monotheism: Vishnu (the 'all pervador') and his consort Lakshmi (goddess of wealth and beauty) are worshipped alongside Brahma (the creator) and Shiva (the destroyer). As mentioned earlier, the religion is more concerned with man, his reincarnation and the nature of the universe. Being essentially free of dogma, the violent slaughter of Muslims that was exacerbated by the partition of India in 1948 is no part of the Hindu religion. I referred earlier to the central position of *dharma* in Hinduism. There are actually two types of *dharma* and they are in some conflict with each other—the *sanatana dharma* or absolute moral order and the *dharma* of caste and canon law. The tensions between the two form an integral part of the *Mahabharata*, which is India's 'great epic' and the fullest account of classical Hinduism. During the last century Mahatma Gandhi preached forcefully against the inequity of the caste system and the two *dharmas* (as well, of course, against British rule, and the ill-treatment of Muslims). The implications of his crusade were well understood: in January 1948 he was assassinated.

Today, over 800 million people—most of them living in India—follow one or other aspect of Hinduism.

Judaism, Christianity and Islam

To orthodox Jews, their religion began in 3760 BC, the day of creation, and the year from which the Jewish calendar is dated. The story of Genesis and the rest of the Old Testament is pretty familiar to most readers, so there is no need to repeat it here, except to point out that, like the teachings of Hinduism, it provides answers to the three questions outlined at the beginning of this section: a precisely defined ethical code, namely the Ten Commandments; a focus for worship, namely God (Yaweh); and the recognition of an after-life, namely heaven and hell (*Gehenna*)—although the latter is not very reassuring for the sinners of this world. The first five books of the Old Testament constitute the Pentateuch or Torah (teaching in Hebrew) that was revealed by God to Moses on Mount Sinai. It describes the origins of mankind, and of the Jewish people—'the chosen ones'—in particular. The creation of the world took God 6 days to accomplish (he rested on the 7th); since our solar system is around 6 billion years old, one has only to substitute a billion years for one day, and the story of Genesis is not so outlandish a guess at evolution; at least the sequence of events is more or less correct.

Judaic beliefs have much in common with those of the Sumerians. Abraham—the prophet acknowledged by Christians and Muslims as well as by Jews—is said to have been born in Ur. The first identifiable figure in the Old Testament is probably Moses in the thirteenth century BC, who may indeed have been the Hebrew prophet who led the Israelites out of bondage from Egypt. The first record of the actual practice of the Judaic religion is not evident much before 600 BC.

The number of those who consider themselves to be Jews is currently around 17 million, 40% of whom live in the USA and 20% in Israel.

Christianity accepts the Judaic Old Testament more or less intact as part of its religious heritage. Where it departs is in the belief that Jesus of Nazareth[18] is the Messiah (or Christ, meaning anointed one) of the Jewish scriptures. The teachings of Jesus, which form the basis of the New Testament, differed from those of his fellow Jews. He emphasised repentance, faith and love of one's neighbour—be he enemy or friend. He preached that the Kingdom of God would be for everyone, not just for Jews, but that it would not arrive until after his death. He opposed the power of the predominant religious party—that of the Pharisees—and exposed their abuse of it. It was largely through Paul of Tarsus, a Jew and a Pharisee himself who was originally in conflict with the followers of Jesus but whose heart changed on a mission to Damascus, that the Christian belief became a separate religion, practised predominately by non-Jews. The persecution of Christians by Roman overlords—far worse than their treatment of the Jews—came to an end under the emperor Constantine (who himself converted to the new faith) in 313 AD, and by 380 Christianity had become the state religion under Theodosius. From then on, the Church of Rome, with the Pope at its head, grew in power and influence.

Papal interests expanded: from the divine to the secular, from affairs of the Church to meddling in politics. By the end of the eleventh century Pope Urban II was encouraging warfare: the Crusades on behalf of Christendom had begun. The aim was to rid Palestine—the Holy Land—of Muslim domination. It was never permanently achieved. In 1099 the Crusadors did capture Jerusalem and installed the gastronomically named Godfrey of Buillon as King (having massacred all the inhabitants). But by 1187 they were out—defeated by Saladin, the Sultan of Egypt and Syria—and Palestine remained under Muslim rule until 1917, when British forces freed it from the Ottomans. As we saw in an earlier chapter, it was eventually returned to the Jews, with Jerusalem a divided city—as it is to this day—giving Judaism, Christianity and Islam equal right of worship. What the Crusades did accomplish was the generation of bad blood, much of it extracorporeally, between crusading warriors and innocent civilians: Muslims, Christians and Jews suffered in equal measure. None of this greatly affected the Papacy. It distanced itself from the events it had unleashed, and continued its sway over Christendom, which by now stretched across most of Europe. By the fourteenth century discontent with the Church of Rome was fomenting: its dogma and inflexibility were causing men in northern lands to seek an alternative form of Christianity. Protestantism began to emerge.

John Wycliffe, a lecturer at Oxford in the fourteenth century, criticized the Church on several counts: its wealth and influence (precisely the reasons for which Jesus had reprimanded the Pharisees), the infallabilty of the Pope, its stubborn refusal to contemplate the translation of the Bible into the vernacular. Wycliffe began this task, which William Tyndale completed with the New Testament in 1526 (he was subsequently burnt at the stake in Antwerp for his pains). Reformers were arising elsewhere. In Wittenberg, Martin Luther opposed particularly the sale of indulgences, by which the sins committed by repentant Christians, including the atrocities of the Crusaders, were expunged through good deeds that specifically did not exclude the payment of money to the Church of Rome. He publicly declared his 95 reasons for disapproval in 1517. Four years later, Luther was condemned for his insubordination and excommunicated; he retaliated by translating the Bible into German. I have dwelt on these events in order to show that for many, the Roman Catholic Church was not delivering the spiritual succour they were seeking. Yet its dogma continued.

In 1531 Henry VIII petitioned Pope Clement VII for a divorce from his first wife, Catherine of Aragon, in order to be able to marry Anne Boleyn. Catherine had borne him a daughter (Mary), but their son (Henry) had died when only a few weeks old, and Henry VIII wanted a male heir. When his appeal was refused, he declared himself Supreme Head of the Catholic Church in England (he remained a devout Catholic for most of his life[19]). Two years later Henry appointed Thomas Cranmer as Archbishop of Canterbury. He then persuaded Cranmer, first to pronounce his marriage to Catherine void and second to lawfully wed him to Anne. The ensuing excommunication by Pope Clement was ignored. In one stroke Henry had achieved his aim and in so doing established an offshoot of the Roman Church in England. The Church of Rome has not forgiven this act of defiance. As I write, the Congregation for the Doctrine of the Faith — the present title of the Holy Office of the Inquisition, that has sought out and punished heresy over the centuries — has issued a document[20] in which the Anglican Church and other Protestant denominations — indeed, all other non-Roman Catholic faiths — are dismissed as being 'imperfect' and suffering from 'defects'. On the other hand, it has relented its treatment of Galileo (whom it excommunicated for ignoring its edict not to teach the views of Copernicus, that the earth is not the centre of the universe): a mere 360 years after the event it has accepted reason over dogma ('A tragic mutual incomprehension has been interpreted as the reflection of a fundamental opposition between science and faith', as Pope John Paul II put it — not exactly pithily — to the Pontifical Academy of Sciences in 1992).

Lest I should be accused of bias in my description of matters within the Church of Rome, I hasten to add that dogma sits equally well on the shoulders of some Protestants. In many southern states of the USA, the creation of the world 6000 years ago, within 6 days, and of man, as described in Genesis, is taught to schoolchildren (in *science* class; religious instruction is banned from the school curriculum in the USA). New-fangled ideas about the world being 5 billion years old and the creatures on it—including man—having evolved gradually through selection of the fittest, are grudgingly taught only as a possible alternative. And this is a recent step forward: for many years following the Scopes trial of 1925, when a Tennessee schoolmaster was successfully prosecuted for teaching Darwin's theory, the schools in many southern States were forbidden to teach evolutionary theory at all. Every few steps in one direction are accompanied by some in another: in 1999 the State Board of Education in Kansas voted to remove the teaching of Darwin's theory of evolution from every one of its schools.

Creationism surfaced in England recently, when a school in Gateshead decided to teach it alongside evolution. Their reason was to give the pupils a flavour of competing theories for the emergence of man. But Darwin's theory of evolution is as firmly supported by scientific evidence as is the notion that the earth is round not flat, and that it moves in an orbit around the sun, not the other way round. To compare *The Origin of Species* with the book of Genesis seems to me almost as ludicrous as comparing the quest of Christopher Columbus with that of Hänsel and Gretel: one is reality, the other myth. If the teachers of Gateshead had wanted to illustrate rival theories of evolution, why did they not encourage their pupils to judge between evolution and adaptation, between Darwin and Lamarck? In any case, if one accepts that religions other than the Judaeo – Christian – Muslim trilogy are based on beliefs that have equal force in so far as their followers are concerned, then the notion that the whole world was created by one particular God—the Judaic one—becomes illogical. But when has religious belief not been the substitute for logic? Is that not its very strength?

So Christianity has more adherents today than any other religion: there are over a billion Roman Catholics and some 350 million Protestants (80 million of them Anglicans) spread throughout the world.

The Islamic faith shares many of its beliefs with those of Judaism and Christianity: its God (Allah), for one, is the same; Abraham (Ibrahim) is as much the father of Arabs as of Jews. The word 'islam' essentially means 'submission' (to Allah), and a 'muslim' is one who submits. The religion was founded by the Prophet

Muhammad (Mohammed) around 610 AD in Mecca in Arabia, the town of his birth. Muhammad started life in commerce, married to a wealthy widow. When he was 40, sleeping quietly one night on Mount Hira near Mecca, he was visited by the angel Gabriel. Through him he received his prophetic mission and the essentials of the Koran or Qur'an, which subsequently became the holy scripture of Islam. For the next 12 years or so Muhammad espoused the holy life in Mecca, and began to make converts to the new religion that was being revealed to him — through Gabriel — by God. But the pagan Meccans were unfavourably disposed towards Muhammad's teachings, and by 622 he and his followers were in some danger. They decided to make their way to Medina, where they found safety. This journey, the Hegira, is commemorated by the fact that the Islamic calender is dated from this time (1 AH = 622 AD = 4382 of the Jewish calendar).

During his lifetime Muhammad was more than just a religious leader: he was the head of the army, collected taxes and fulfilled all the roles of a secular ruler. This is an important distinction between Islam and Christianity: whereas Jesus said 'Render unto Caesar the things which are Caesar's and unto God the things which are God's', the distinction between church and state has no place in Islam: the two are one. It explains why the Muslim faith is the state religion in over 50 Islamic countries. Since there are no official religious leaders — only teachers — there is no conflict between the political head of an Islamic country and its spiritual leaders. Present-day Iran is exceptional in giving the Imams a status more equivalent to that of a Christian Bishop or Cardinal; so long as their views coincide with that of the Head of State, there is no problem. But there is another, more subtle, difference between the teachings of Islam and those of Christianity and Judaism — or, for that matter, any other religion. The Qur'an exhorts its followers 'to command good and forbid evil': not just to *avoid* evil, but to *forbid* it. It is for this reason that many Muslims today regard it as their spiritual duty to engage in such matters as the condemnation of the writer Salman Rushdie over his controversial novel, *The Satanic Verses*.

The Qur'an acknowledges the descent of Muhammad from Abraham, and its tenets echo many of the Ten Commandments revealed to Moses. The five duties of a devout Muslim are *Shahadah*,

Salah, Zakah, Sawm and *Hajj.*[21] *Shahadah*, the most important, is bearing witness to God: 'there is no god but God'. The words are spoken into the ears of the new-born, repeated daily (including in the muezzin's call to prayer), and are uttered by the dying. *Salah* prescribes the times of ritual prayer: at first light, just after midday, between three and five in the afternoon, at last light, and at some time during the hours of darkness. *Zakah* is the giving of alms to the poor. *Sawm* prescribes fasting during the month of Ramadan. *Hajj* (Hadj) is the pilgrimage to Mecca that every devout Muslim must try to undertake at least once in his lifetime. From Mecca he should then go to Medina, in memory of the Hegira made by the Prophet Muhammad in 622.

The Arab followers of Muhammad and their successors—the Seljuks and the Osmanli founders of the Ottoman Empire—forged an enlightened society that lasted 1000 years and stretched across three continents. That culture kept alive, and enriched, the Graeco-Roman heritage when the rest of Europe was in turmoil and decline. Why? Because the religion of Islam is not an exclusive one: Jews and Christians, like Muslims, are the children of Abraham. Moses and Jesus are recognised as prophets and messengers of God as much as Muhammad (they merely erred by distorting their original mission). Islamic society, as it expanded, gave Jews and Christians the option of converting to its faith; if they chose not to do so, they were not persecuted—in sharp contrast to Christian practice from the thirteenth century onwards. The philosopher, scholar and physician Maimonides, a Jew who decided not to convert, was a respected figure in twelfth century Cordoba and Cairo. Intolerance does not feature in the teachings of the Qur'an (any more than it does in those of the Bible). It was through respect for other religions that art and medicine, mathematics and astronomy, flourished in Islam while they lay dormant in Christendom.

Intolerance and progress are incompatible. The rigidity of the Catholic Church may not have prevented the creation of great works of art during the renaissance—the early themes in painting and music were after all largely religious—but it held back science, which was beginning to flourish in northern Europe. Today, intolerant fundamentalism is holding back progress in much of the world. Fundamentalists in the USA continue to oppose abortion, and within parts of the Islamic realm fundamentalism and militarism have merged.[22] If its nations—from Algeria to Iran, from Afghanistan to Sudan—wish to climb back up the ladder and give their people a better quality of life, one of the things they should do is to reintroduce religious tolerance. Only then will innovative construction by its people, not wanton destruction of its competitors, once more characterise the Islamic movement. At this moment countries like Turkey, Malaysia and Indonesia, who wish to modernise their countries economically and to revitalise their science and technology, rightly fear the consequences of an increase in fanatical dogma among their citizens. Fortunately, bigotry is espoused by only a minority of true believers.

The followers of Islam today number 1.2 billion. Over half of these live in just four countries,[23] Bangladesh, India, Indonesia and Pakistan. They therefore represent one of the largest single faiths in the world today (second only to Christians). Muslims are also, together with orthodox Jews and conscientious Roman Catholics, probably the most devout in the practice of their religion.

Buddhism, Confucianism and Daoism

The three doctrines now to be described, all of which originated in Asia, are not so much religions as philosophies: tenets by which to lead one's life. None contains the dogma that characterises Christianity and Islam, and each is therefore free of the malign influences that deliberate misinterpretation of the teachings of Jesus Christ and the Prophet Muhammad have had.

Siddhartha Gautama—later known as the Buddha (the word means 'enlightenment' in Sanskrit)—was an Indian prince living in what is now Nepal in around 563–480 BC. He renounced his kingdom and its pleasures—and for good measure his wife and child as well—and took up the ascetic way of life: an early-day Tolstoy, you might say. He taught men to focus more on themselves than on any god: the Hindu concept of *dharma* was central to his message. Neither he nor his followers recorded any of his exhortations; writing was not then part of Hindu life. Accordingly, Buddha is as much—if not more—of an elusive figure than Jesus. Indeed, it is surprising that his teachings survived at all: passed on merely by word of mouth over four centuries, and spreading slowly from the mountainous region of the north to the banks of the Ganges, across disparate lands that were a far cry from the unity of the Roman Empire, through which the words of Jesus rapidly diffused. Yet they endured. The earliest records were made in Pali—a north Indian dialect—and constitute what is known as the Pali Canon. This contains the Buddha's sermons (the *Sutta Pitaka*), the rules by which the monastic life is to be lived (the *Vinaya Pitaka*) and a number of philosophical and doctrinal evaluations (the *Abhidhamma Pitaka*). Just as Christianity never supplanted Judaism in Palestine but replaced paganism elsewhere, so Buddhism has not ousted Hinduism in India (although it was exercised there for over 1000 years), but instead spread northwards to Tibet, central Asia, China, Korea and Japan, and southwards to Sri Lanka and south-east Asia. In Japan it is practised in the form of the modified version known as Zen Buddhism (that itself evolved out of Daoism in China during the seventh century), alongside the main religion, Shinto, that has no known founder but has been followed for over 1000 years. As you travel throughout Asia today, you will see enormous statues of the Buddha, to which people flock to pay homage. Yet Gautama was no deity, nor even the Son of one. He would have abhored such personal veneration, as his teachings clearly showed.

What is particularly relevant to the theme of this book is the fact that Buddhists, like Hindus, do not draw the sharp dividing line between humans and animals that is characteristic of Judaeo–Christian theology. All creatures have a mind that allows them to have feelings like man; hence reincarnations between humans and animals do not pose a problem. Had Charles Darwin published *The Origin of Species* in Asia, he would not have engendered the hostility he received in Europe.

The spirit of Buddhism is encapsulated by the account of the Buddha's last days. He was sitting with his cousin and disciple, Ananda. Turning to him, he said: 'You may be thinking, Ananda: "The word of the Teacher is now a thing of the past; now we have no more Teacher". But that is not how you should see it. Let the Dhamma [=*dharma*] and the Discipline that I have taught you be your Teacher when I am gone'.[24] It is the simplicity of dhamma and its associated discipline that have sustained Buddhism for two and a half millennia: it is the reason that Buddhism now appeals to some 360 million adherents world-wide.

Kong Fuzi [K'ung Fu-tsu] or 'Kung the Master', better known as Confucius, was a Chinese government official who lived from 551 to 479 BC. Although an exact contemporary of Buddha, there is no evidence that the two men ever met: contact between India and China, separated as they are by the Himalaya mountain range, was virtually non-existent at that time. Growing up during a period of warring and conflict between the western and eastern Zhou, Confucius became convinced that a return to former, peaceful, values was required. In common with the views being expressed almost contemporaneously by Plato in Athens, Confucius held that power should be in the hands of the wise and virtuous: the fact that entry to the higher echelons of government was based on merit owes much to Confucian doctrine. In Europe, Platonic ideals were soon forgotten; in China, Confucian philosophy permeated society for over 2000 years.

The clarity and wisdom of the Master's message is so persuasive that his aphorisms have found their way to the lips of politicians throughout the world today. Yet Confucian ideology was associated with the rigid society of the imperial period, and its influence waned in China only after 1911. Indeed, it was blamed in part for the empire's decline at a time when European innovation and progress brought its nations prosperity and domination over the rest of the world. Under Mao Zhedong, Confucianism—like every other belief save that of Mao in himself—fared even worse. The sayings of Confucius were replaced by those of Chairman Mao. In common with the pronouncements of other tyrants who profess idiotic and evil policies, however, Mao's adages did not last. It is Master Kung's pithy maxims that are once more being heard in Beijing and Wuhan, in Shanghai and Guangzhou. The traditional Confucian values of filial piety and respect for one's teachers are again reinvigorating Chinese education, at a time when a lack of discipline and zest are undermining that in the West. Nevertheless, there are said to be only 6 million adherents of Confucianism.

Another influential sage emerged during the sixth century BC. He was Lao Tzu [Lao Tsu], also a state official, and his beliefs contrasted with those of Confucius in being more concerned with the natural world than with the social ethics of man: with the way (*dao*) of nature. The precepts of Daoism (Taoism) were refined by the Chinese philosopher Zhuangzi during the fourth century BC, and are set out in the book of 'the way and its power' (*Daodejing*). By contemplating the manifestations of nature, man achieves an inner calm. Followers of Lao Tzu and Zhuanzi incorporate the Chinese concepts of *ch'i* (the vital energy, that powers the universe through its many changes) and of *yin* and *yang* (the two opposite ways of looking at anything)—all of which predate Daoism and Confucianism—into its philosophy: *yang ch'i* flowed upward and created the heavens, *yin ch'i* moved downwards and formed the earth. *Yang ch'i* is pure and light, *yin ch'i* is turbid and heavy. Man must seek to be both *yin*, expressing receptive, feminine qualities, and *yang*, showing active, masculine characteristics, irrespective of gender. Sometimes a slight increase of one or the other may be called for, but in general one's life should reflect a careful balance between the two.[25]

Despite the difference in emphasis between Confucianism and Daoism, neither has replaced the other; the two philosophies are complementary and are followed side by side, in the way that Shintoism and Buddhism are practised simultaneously in Japan. Daoist teaching and its monasteries—like those of Buddhism in Tibet—were suppressed by Mao; his successors continue their repression. Nevertheless, pockets survive, and in places like Taiwan and elsewhere in Asia, Daoism flourishes.

Buddhism, Confucianism and Daoism each arose 2500 years ago; they are therefore younger than Hinduism and Judaism, but older than Christianity and Islam. Their endurance is evident from the fact that according to some, over half the world is said to subscribe to their tenets.[26] The continuity between man and nature that characterises them (and to a certain extent Hinduism, as well as other Asian beliefs like Jainism) contrasts sharply with the uniqueness of man as defined by Judaeo – Christian – Islamic precepts. The former seek a satisfactory outcome to their lives by following the tenets of their philosophy; the latter strive to fulfil their special relationship with God.

Conclusion

The manifestations of divine figures are not the only objects of people's beliefs. Astrology, fortune telling, extrasensory perception and other paranormal phenomena play to a large audience. While such pursuits provide a good example of human quest—to know the future, to locate perpetrators of criminal acts, to contact dead relatives[27]—there is little of significance that one can say about them except to note their popularity and to conclude that magic and shamanism live on.[28] Attempts to bring the occult within the realms of science[29] have not succeeded.

The dividing line between leading an upright life because of a belief in one of the religions practised today, and doing so for non-religious, philosophical reasons—the word humanism comes to mind once more—is a very fine one. Many, perhaps most, of those who class themselves as following one or other religion do little more than pay lip service to its doctrines. Yet the power of religious belief persists. I am reminded of an example that I mention only because the person concerned was a scientist. I was visiting the Taj Mahal. The day, I recall, was grey and overcast, which made the subtle contrast between the colour of the marble and that of the sky even more remarkable. The proportions and scale of the building—superb.[30] The motivation for its construction—touching.[31] But what sticks in my memory also, as we walked around this magnificent building, is a conversation I had with one of my fellow scientists. We had all come on a day's excursion laid on by the organisers of a conference that we were attending in Delhi. My colleague, a serious and cultured Indian microbiologist, pointed to the Yamuna river winding its way gracefully below the Taj Mahal: 'that water is so holy, you can fill a glass container with it, seal it, and no microbes will ever grow in the water. I know you don't believe it'—I was trying to combine scepticism with courtesy—'but it is true'. Religious belief is strong indeed.

Is the conflict between faith and science then irreconcilable? I do not believe so.[32] We should not assume that religious beliefs and scientific explanations cannot sit side by side. So long as religion is only a matter of faith, and its teachings are not taken to underlie phenomena for which a rational explanation exists, science and religion do not impinge on each other. Albert Einstein believed in God ('Religion without science is blind. Science without religion is lame'), and so did Galileo and Newton. But this does mean adapting religious beliefs somewhat. Buddhism, Confucianism and Daoism do just that. Now some Christians of the Protestant faith, too, are beginning to accept the idea that God is largely in the mind of the believer[33] (put there, presumably, through upbringing). The concept is as satisfying to some as an altruistic act is to the non-believer. It also overcomes the problem of different Gods being responsible for the same act of creation.

What else can we conclude from this short account of the spiritual nature of man's quest? That it is as fundamental a part of his behaviour as his search for novel technology, for artistic expression, for scientific explanations. A feature that is common to most of the religions of the seven primary civilisations and their successors, as well as to the beliefs of primitive communities elsewhere, is burial of the dead. Other primates simply push their departed aside, although they are as capable of expressing sorrow as a human.[34] What lies behind man's interment of corpses? A fear of contagion may be one reason, and the Hindu solution of substituting cremation for burial is a sensible one. Yet burying a body under the earth, as one does with excrement, is one thing; commemorating the departed in a simple coffin or in a sarcophagus within the pyramids of Sumeria and Egypt, the tombs of the Chinese emperors, the mosques of Islamic rulers or the pantheons of Christianity, is another. I have pointed to man's fear of death as a reason for his worship of the deceased. The Danish psychologist Arne Petersen goes one further and suggests that man's veneration of the dead is related to the consciousness of his being. It is self-awareness, which is derived through symbolism in language, that leads to man's views about life and death.[35] Religious belief, in short, is a consequence of the development of speech. Add manual dexterity and neuronal capacity, and you have an explanation for the physical expression of man's faith in the unknown.

Notes

1. Among those who considered man's mortality to be the root of religious belief was Sigmund Freud; quoted by Stephen Jay Gould, 'More things in Heaven and Earth', in Hilary and Steven Rose, op. cit. pp. 85 – 105.
2. According to David Lewis-Williams (op. cit.), depicting animals was not so much an act of appeasement as of demonstrating man's superiority.
3. See e.g. Bruce Lincoln, op. cit.
4. *Secrets of the Dead: the Quest for Noah's Flood.* Shown on UK television (Channel 4), 16 March 2002.
5. Stephen Oppenheimer, op. cit., p 38 et seq.
6. From S. N. Kramer's *The Sumerians,* quoted by Jaroslav Krejci, op. cit., p 11.
7. Jaroslav Krejci, op. cit., p 16.
8. Sir Flinders Petrie, op. cit., p 203.
9. The immortality of the soul — the endurance of life — was presciently illustrated by the early Christian monk, the Venerable Bede: 'Such ... seems to me the present life of men on earth ... as if when on a winter's night you sit feasting ... a single sparrow should fly swiftly into the hall, and coming in at one door, instantly fly out through another. In that time in which it is indoors it is indeed not touched by the fury of the winter, but yet, this smallest space of calmness being passed almost in a flash, from winter going into winter again, it is lost to your eyes. Somewhat like this appears the life of man; but of what follows or what went before, we are utterly ignorant' (from Bede's *Ecclesiastical History of the English People,* Book 2, Chapter 13, translated from the original Latin by B. Colgrave, 1969). This description of our ephemeral existence seems to fit rather well into the framework of Darwinian evolution.
10. From H. Maspero's *China in Antiquity,* quoted by Jaroslav Krejci, op. cit., pp 24 – 25.
11. Lewis Wolpert, op. cit., pp 35 – 55.
12. Jaroslav Krejci, op. cit., pp 8 – 29.
13. Visitors to Mexico may wonder what the reclining male figures called Chac Mol or Mool have to do with the god of rain. They are found throughout the territory of the Maya in the Yucatan, as well as at Teotihuacan, with whose peoples the Maya appear to have had contact. One of the best preserved was discovered at the Temple of the Warriors in Chichen Itza by an American explorer named Augustus Le Plongeon in 1875, and may now be seen in the Minneapolis Institute of Art. Although the statue is clearly human

and has none of the features associated with the rain god Chac, Le Plongeon somewhat arbitrarily named it Chac Mool, and the name has stuck.

14. The Aztecs subsequently switched two of the colours: north became black and west became white, but east and south remained red and yellow. At the opposite end of the world, the Chinese too associated the points of the compass with colours: north and west, black and white—as with the Aztecs—east green and south red.

15. Bernabe Cobo, op. cit., p 5.

16. Ibid., op. cit., p 133.

17. If in today's busy world you cannot find time to pray yourself, you can always ask someone else to do so on your behalf: the Salesian Sisters of St John in New Jersey are now offering this service, and will pray for the speedy recovery of your sick relative, for God to grant you a child, for whatever you feel requires a little divine help. Donations start at $100 upwards. You may say that delegated prayer defeats the object of the exercise, but it is amazing what can be achieved with faith on the part of both the participants. Proxy fasting during Lent is surely on the way. Of course, praying for others is the very cornerstone of Judaeo – Christian – Islamic worship, but the assumption is that the recipient of the prayers joins in. Buying your way out of this necessity surely savours of some of the practices objected to by Luther half a millennium ago.

18. Jesus probably lived from 6 BC to 30 AD: the world-wide celebrations of the year 2000 appear to have been 6 years out of date.

19. The title 'Defender of the Faith', conferred on him by Clement VII in appreciation of Henry's condemnation of Martin Luther's heretical views, is still used by British monarchs, despite its original reference to the Catholic faith. The current heir to the throne is said to consider 'Defender of Faiths' as more appropriate: it would embrace not only the Roman Catholic and Anglican faiths, but those of Jews, Muslims, Hindus and others as well.

20. Declaration Dominus Jesus.

21. For a fuller description see Caesar E. Farah, The Fundamentals of Islam: Obligations, op. cit., pp 123 – 146.

22. William Dalrymple considers the fundamentalist sect of Wahhabi Islam, that was 'promoted by Saudi Arabia ever since Ibn Saud conquered the Hejaz in the 1930s', to be 'the most severe and puritanical incarnation of a religion that historically has been remarkable for its tolerance of religious minorities (suicide is forbidden in traditional Islamic teaching)'. From his review of Malise Ruthven's A Fury for God: the Islamic Attack on America, (Granta, 2002): Sunday Times, 30 June 2002.

23. None, as it happens, populated by Arabs, who account for only one-sixth of today's Muslims.

24. Quoted in Karen Armstrong, op. cit., pp 170–171.
25. For a summary of the *yin – yang* polarity in relation to Daoism, see Paul Wildish, op. cit., pp 11–14.
26. This surprising figure, that includes 3 million Shinto worshippers, is given by C. Scott Littleton (op. cit., p 6). It sits uneasily with the numbers given in the text for the followers of Buddha and Confucius. The discrepancy, no doubt, reflects the difference between those Chinese who are genuine Confucians, and those who merely subscribe to certain aspects of Confucius' philosophy. If the estimate is true, Buddhists, Confucianists and Daoists would surpass Christians and Muslims put together.
27. Today's occult bill of fare, that includes e-mails and tape recordings, is well described by one woman's search to make contact with her dead sister: Justine Picardie, *If the Spirit Moves You*, Macmillan, London, 2001.
28. Nicholas Humphrey, in an article, 'Behold the Man: human nature and supernatural belief', op. cit., pp 206–231, goes so far as to compare the miracles of Christ with the spoon bending of Uri Geller.
29. A recent endeavour to merge religion, creativity and science and to explain homeopathy, ESP and other paranormal phenomena through the concept of Zero Point Field (Lynne McTaggart, *The Field: the Quest for the Secret Force of the Universe*. Harper Collins, London, 2001), fails to convince.
30. It took 20,000 men no less than 20 years to erect it.
31. It was built by the Emperor Shah Jahan as a shrine in memory of his wife Mumtaz Mahal, who died in childbirth (it was her 14th) in 1631.
32. Neither do recent writers, such as: Michael Ruse, *Can a Darwinian be a Christian? The Relationship between Science and Religion*, Cambridge University Press, Cambridge, 2000; and Arthur Peacocke, *Paths from Science Towards God: the End of All Our Exploring*, Oneworld, Oxford, 2001.
33. As Christ said, 'The kingdom of God is within you' (St Luke, Chapter 17, Verse 21; although this has also been interpreted as meaning 'amongst you'). The view of writers like David Lewis-Williams (op. cit.), that religious experience is no more than hallucination and that it has its roots in the shamanism of Stone Age man, sits fairly easily with the idea that religion (and fear of death) are largely a consequence of man's consciousness of himself.
34. See Jane Goodall, op. cit.
35. See Arne Friemuth Petersen, 'Biopsychological aspects of individuation —on the origin of and interplay between biological individuality, personality and self', *Psychol Yearbook* **1**: 45–62; 1994, and personal communication.

CHAPTER ELEVEN

Science: explanation and experimentation

A brief summary of what science is all about may be appropriate. Many of the readers of this book will probably not be scientists. I assume, and indeed hope, that this is so. First, because the number of those not versed in science greatly exceeds those who have studied some aspect of the discipline at college or university (the aspiration of a wide readership being shared with my publisher). Second, because I would like to give the general public, that includes politicians and bureaucrats, an opportunity to read an impartial account—as detached as I can make it—of current technologies dealing with genetically modified organisms in Part III. Third, because my scientific colleagues will be quick to jump on the assumptions and hypotheses that I have been emboldened to make and tear them to shreds. Is not competitiveness, the cousin of ambition, a very human quality? Fourth, because I am attracted to the views of Terence Kealey,[1] who dared to suggest that technology sometimes spawns science, not the other way round, and that occasionally the less a government spends on basic science, the better: needless to say, his scientific colleagues have given him short shrift.

If science means anything—and it actually means knowledge—then surely the first men to light a fire were scientists. But I have defined knowledge gained through trial and error as technology. It is knowledge gained through reasoning that is science.[2] Observation and experimentation are not enough. Mapping the positions of stars in the sky is no more science than mapping the coastline of a country, or mapping the human genome. It is knowing *why* stars appear to move (they are actually static relative to the earth), or *why* a coastline has a particular shape (through erosion and changing levels of the sea), or *what* the sequences of A, C, G and T in DNA specify (different proteins and the control of their functions), that is scientific knowledge. We can all predict— without knowing the underlying cause—that if the sun sets at a particular point on the horizon around 8 p.m. today, it will do so in a slightly different place, at a slightly different time, tomorrow (unless we are on the equator, when little changes). Yet the calculations of early explorers of the sky are so accurate that they deserve mention.

In Egypt, the builders of the pyramids of Giza 4500 years ago had access to extremely accurate astronomical detail (all without telescopes, of course). Two of the sides of all three pyramids point pretty accurately to the north. On the supposition that this was the intention of the pyramid builders, how did they achieve such an alignment? The magnetic compass was unknown to the ancient Egyptians, and the pole star (that in today's northern hemisphere always lies due north) was not at that time in their night sky. They might have used the sun (to establish due south), but another stellar method has recently been suggested. The architects may have aligned the pyramids by extending a line between two bright stars— one in the Little Dipper (Ursa Minor) and one in the Big Dipper (Ursa Major)—to the ground; that line would invariably have pointed north. I say 'pretty accurately' because the orientation of the sides of the pyramids are out by a few arc minutes,[3] the error being slightly different for each pyramid. Egyptologist Kate Spence, however, believes they *were* accurate at the time the pyramids were actually built, each for a different ruler. She has calculated the amount by which the line joining the two stars shifts very slightly over the years, and on the assumption that each was precise at the time of construction, has been able to identify that date. As a result she has produced a chronology of the reigns during which the pyramids were built that is accurate to within ±5 years (compared with previous estimates that were accurate to within ±100 years).[4]

Chinese astronomy, although a mere 2000 years old, is equally impressive. Astronomers whose task it was to record the positions of all the stars on a daily basis, used this information to predict the pattern of the night sky on any one day, including the appearance of more than 40 comets. That described by Halley at the end of the seventeenth century had been identified in China two centuries earlier. The Chinese records are so precise that modern astrophysicists use the information to confirm the age of specific stars. By the thirteenth century the length of the year had been calculated to four decimal places (365.2425 days).[5]

In Greece, Ptolemy was predicting eclipses of the sun and moon, and correctly describing the motion of the planets in terms of orbits, by the middle of the second century AD (he thought them circular; it was Johannes Kepler in the early years of the seventeenth century who realised they were elliptical and formulated his second law of planetary motion to take this into account).

The ways of science

Exploration—by foot or by boat, by hand or by eye—is very much part of the human endeavour. Exploration also underlies the progression of science: in this case the quest is for knowledge. An attempt to understand how the world works drove man to religious beliefs. But as we have just seen, religion provides only symbolic interpretations. Science alone can yield a rational explanation. We should, however, note Niels Bohr's comment that physics concerns not what nature is, but rather what we can say about it[6]—a view not so different from Isaac Newton's three centuries earlier. Curiosity may be an essential attribute, but on its own does not make a scientist. To grapple with a problem that has eluded all who have come before, to explain a part of the world in a novel way with clarity and logic, requires not merely a great deal of thought and experimentation, but also a flash of insight, a moment of creativity. It is in that sense that the search for inspiration is common to scientists and artists.[7] New concepts in science, as in mathematics or philosophy, depend on thoughts that no one has had before. The postulate that the earth is not the centre of the universe, that all bodies attract one another, that the heart pushes blood around the body in a closed circulation, that many diseases are caused by contagious microbes, that life on earth evolved through a process of gradual change, that time is the fourth dimension to space, these are ideas as original as the plays of Shakespeare, the paintings of Vermeer, the music of Mozart, the writings of Voltaire. The only difference is that if Shakespeare, Vermeer, Mozart or Voltaire had not lived, *Hamlet*, *The Girl with the Pearl Earring*, the 'Jupiter' symphony and *Candide* would not have been produced. But had Copernicus,[8] Newton, Harvey, Koch, Darwin or Einstein not been born, someone else would eventually have come up with their discoveries.[9] We know that during the time — or shortly thereafter — that Newton was working out the basis of the calculus in England, Leibnitz was formulating differential equations in Germany (originally unbeknown to each other). While Florey and Chain were isolating penicillin and determining its structure in Oxford, scientists in Holland were doing the same: their work never reached fruition because in 1940 The Netherlands were attacked and the country was overrun by German troops.[10]

Science, unlike art, is not subject to regional influences and suffers little from the passage of time. There is no 'western' or 'eastern' science, no ancient or modern science, in the way that art can be Chinese or Egyptian, primitive or classical, depictive or abstract. The explanations a scientist comes up with should have universal validity. I deliberately avoid the word 'truth'; truth — and falsehood — are concepts developed by mathematicians and philosophers: scientists use them at their peril. Scientific explanations stand up to the test of time and place. That the orbits of planets are due to gravitational pulls, that thunder and lightning result from an electric discharge, have as much validity today as they did in the days of Newton or Benjamin Franklin (he invented the lightning conductor). The explanations are as true in Kraków and Cambridge as they are in Kobe and Calcutta. How can we be sure? Because all scientific theories can in principle be tested. Some at once, others when the requisite technology is to hand, others when a chance event makes testing possible. An illustration of the first is Galileo's hypothesis that the speed with which objects fall to the ground is independent of their weight: he went and did the experiment. An example of the second is Darwin's view of evolution: 100 years were to pass before molecular analysis was able to confirm his thesis. An instance of the third is Einstein's general theory of relativity: an opportune eclipse of the sun provided the proof for which he was waiting.

Testing predictions, repeating again and again the experiments on which explanations are based, are what give scientific theories credibility. Even more convincing is the absence of negative data. To have faith in a hypothesis, you must be able to show that all attempts to falsify it fail.[11] I have implied that the validity of scientific explanations does not change with time. I must now admit that this is only partially so. As the techniques for measuring natural phenomena are refined, so the results of yesterday seem a little blurred today. The motion of the planets around the sun *is* explained pretty well by the concept of gravity, but not *entirely.* By allowing for the fact that space is 'bent', a more accurate answer is obtained. The effect on earth is very slight (over the universe, of course, it is enormous) and could not have been measured by Newton, even though he suspected it to be the case. His explanation for the motion of objects is essentially correct; it is only the fine detail that requires adjusting. We shall meet some more instances of the need to refine a particular hypothesis as new data emerge, in discussing modern biology. An example of a hypothesis that is just wrong is the Aristotelian proposal that all matter is made of four elements, namely earth, fire, air and water; another is the late seventeenth century supposition that when metals are heated, they lose a gas termed 'phlogiston'. Chemistry during the eighteenth and nineteenth century showed both propositions to be false: the elements that constitute matter are hydrogen, carbon, sulphur, silicon and so on; when metals are heated they *gain* a gas, namely oxygen (to become oxides).

The emergence of language, the development of technology,[12] the evolution of religion, the formulation of laws—these are all gradual processes. They underlie the growth of societies through the quest of groups of people over long periods of time. Science, like more recent technology, is different: it progresses in leaps and bounds, and each step forward can be identified with a particular individual.[13] It is for that reason that the next section will focus on specific scientists, each of whom significantly advanced our knowledge of the world.

Scientists

The earliest thinkers who have been accorded the status of scientist were the ancient Greeks. Thales of Miletus in Ionia (in today's Turkey), who lived from ca. 624 to ca. 545 BC, was the first. Apart from his mathematics (he introduced geometry from Egypt to Greece) and his astronomical knowledge (he predicted the solar eclipse of 28 May 585 BC[14]), Thales also proposed a theory of matter. This he based on water: it is essential for the growth of plants, and everything gives off water when heated (because, as we now know, all biological material is largely water); moreover, water is a substance that exists in all three forms of matter: solid, liquid, vapour. A century later, Anaximenes[15] proposed that air, not water, is the fundamental material. During the fifth century BC, Empedocles of Sicily postulated matter to be made up of the four basic elements—earth, air, fire and water. A century on, Aristotle embraced this hypothesis; he was also the first to develop a coherent theory for the study of mechanics. Although none of these premises on the fundamental nature of matter proved to be correct,[16] each was at least based on logical argument, not myth. And then there were the great mathematicians: Pythagoras (he also realised that the earth is spherical, not flat), Hippocrates of Chios,[17] Eudoxus of Cnios, and Euclid. But the man who outshone them all, the first scientist whose theories have withstood the test of time, was Archimedes.

Archimedes

Archimedes lived in the Hellenic world of Syracuse and Alexandria, from around 287 to 212 BC. He was trained as a mathematician[18] and he used mathematics to lay the foundations of physics. It is to Archimedes that we owe the simple relationship between the distance at which force applied to a lever causes it to move, thus raising an object at the other end ('Give me a fulcrum and I will move the world'). This fundamental principle underlies much of mechanics, from a simple balance and the see-saw of children's playgrounds to the most sophisticated levers used in engineering. Archimedes was a practical man as well as a thinker. Like Leonardo da Vinci, he devised engines of war—to keep the Roman invadors out of Syracuse—and he is also credited with the invention of the screw for raising water from a lower to a higher level.

Few scientific discoveries result from a commission. Technological innovations, yes; voyages of discovery, certainly; artistic creations, all the time. It is therefore remarkable that one of the most fundamental break-throughs in physics was made in response to a commission. A golden crown had recently been delivered to King Hieron of Syracuse. The king suspected that he was being cheated, and that the maker had mixed silver in with the gold. Archimedes was told to find out if this was so. The scientist was aware that gold is heavier than silver, and that the weight of a substance is related to its volume.[19] If the object Archimedes was being asked to assess were a cube or a sphere, for which he could easily calculate the volume, there would be no difficulty. But how to measure the volume of an article like a crown? Most of us ponder over our problems when we are still: lying in bed, sitting on the lavatory, gazing out of a window, soaking in a warm bath.[20] Archimedes was bathing himself. As he stood to get out of the tub, or perhaps as he was lowering himself in, the significance of the fact that the water level changed hit him. The extent by which this altered, must be equal to the volume of his body. He had discovered how to measure the volume of objects that are not of geometrical shape: simply by measuring the amount of water they displace. Knowing the weight of the king's crown and now also its volume, it was merely a matter of dividing one by the other to obtain its density. The king's suspicion was justified: his crown was not pure gold.

Galileo

Galileo Galilei (1564–1642) (Plate 6) was, like Leonardo da Vinci, an innovator: he designed better telescopes than anyone before.

But unlike Leonardo, he did not merely observe and record. He designed experiments in order to support or refute a particular theory. As an experimentor who drew precise conclusions from his results, he resembled Archimedes and Newton. Darwin's experiments, we may note, were done for him by nature: he merely (merely!) had to deduce the meaning that lay behind them. So, for that matter, were Einstein's: in his case a couple of measurements made by others were all that was necessary to verify his theory.

Until Galileo's time, no one doubted the view of Aristotle, that the heavier a body, the faster it falls to the ground. Galileo decided to do the experiment. It was simple enough, and we are all familiar with the result: he took two stones, one weighing ten times as much as the other, and climbed the tower of Pisa. At the top he dropped both together: they hit the ground simultaneously. Had Aristotle been right, the lighter would have taken 10 times as long to fall to the ground. It is not often that so simple an experiment shatters our previously held view of the world. Galileo did not leave it there. He went on to devise an entirely logical argument to show that Aristotle's proposition could in any case not be correct, as it led to an obvious inconsistency.[21]

Galileo's telescopes allowed him to observe sunspots and to discover the moons of Jupiter. It was the realisation that the satellites of Jupiter moved round *it* and not round the earth, together with more accurate data about the orbit of Venus, that convinced him that the proposal of the Polish astronomer Nicolaus Copernicus was correct: the earth (and other planets) did move round the sun, not the other way round. This assertion, that the earth is not the centre of the known universe, was an indisputable heresy to the Church of Rome. Galileo realised this, but decided to follow Giordano Bruno (a priest later branded a heretic) in asserting that the Bible should be followed for its moral teaching, not as a source of astronomical knowledge: why did God give man a mind, if He did not intend him to use it? So Galileo did not refrain from publishing his views. What scientist can forbear to put on record the implication of his exciting result? Sometimes they have no choice. Soviet biologists had to restrain themselves, on pain of prosecution, exile and death, from pointing out that Lysenko's views on the inheritance of characteristics acquired through adaptation were rubbish: Trofim Lysenko was Comrade Stalin's friend and protégé. The Office of the Inquisition was more lenient on this occasion than the Office of the Public Prosecutor in Moscow. It merely excommunicated Galileo. His trial in 1633 was not so much a matter of religion versus science, but of personal animosity towards him: the actual grounds of his prosecution were that he had ignored an earlier edict specifically forbidding him to discuss Copernicus' views in any way—irrespective of whether he supported or opposed them. Copernicus himself suffered no such censure: luckily for him, the religious atmosphere in Poland during the sixteenth century was relatively liberal. Dare I point out that this coincided with the advent of Protestanism in northern Europe?

Newton

To move from Galileo to Newton is a seamless progression: Isaac Newton was born in the year that Galileo died. Like Archimedes before him, Newton was first and foremost a self-taught mathematician: by the age of 27 he had been appointed to the Lucasian Professorship of Mathematics at Cambridge, the university he had entered as a student 9 years earlier. What tuition he received there was centred on philosophy: Aristotelian logic and ethics (most of which he had acquired before his arrival, so that his knowledge of logic outstripped that of his tutor). Much of Newton's greatest work, however, was not done within the walls of academia, but at his home, Woolsthorpe Manor, near Grantham in Lincolnshire. By the time he achieved Bachelor of Arts, 4 years after entering Cambridge, the university was closed: plague had once more arrived in England. The latter part of 1665 and all of 1666 was spent by the young Newton at home, in solitary study. It proved to be the most productive period of his life.

First, he continued with his search for a solution to the binomial theorem, $(a + b)^n$. This led him to the concept of infinite series in mathematics, and from there to formulating the principles of the calculus: expressing in algebraic terms (which he called 'fluxions'[22]) the relationship between a point in space and its movement with time. This achievement alone would have marked him out as one of the most creative mathematicians of all time. But his inquisitiveness did not rest there. Like Leonardo da Vinci, he was drawn to the properties of light. He felt there was something wrong with the accepted notions of colours that were being pioneered by men like René Descartes in France and Robert Hooke in England. The latter had just published his *Micrographia*, in which he asserted that colours arose through an admixture of 'darkness' to the fundamental pulse of white light: a little darkness produces red light, successively more darkness yields the other colours of the rainbow, through to blue. Newton had his doubts and chose to conduct an experiment. He bought himself a glass prism, probably at a country fair, and began to polish the sides. He fixed up his room so that a shaft of sunlight falling on one side of the prism would be reflected through another side on to a wall: the colours of the rainbow—red to blue—appeared. He then took a second prism through which the individual colours were reflected back. The result was white light. In other words, white light is a composite of colours, not the other way round.

Fifty years later Newton pithily summed up these achievements: 'In the beginning of the year 1665 [he was just 23 years old] I found the method of approximating series and the rule for reducing ... any binomial into such a series. The same year in May I found the method of tangents ... and in November had the direct method of fluxions and the next year in January had the theory of colours (Plate 7) and in May following I had entrance into the inverse method[23] of fluxions'.[24] Like Charles Darwin almost 2 centuries later, Newton was a loner who did not publish his hypotheses at the time they crystallised in his mind. Just as it was Alfred Wallace's conclusion regarding natural selection that drove Darwin to complete *The Origin of Species*, so Leibnitz's publication of the differential calculus probably contributed—as well as the inducements of Edmund Halley—to Newton's decision to set down the fruits of his discoveries in the *Principia* (Plate 7), not published until 1686. By that time Newton had answered another of the 'Quaestiones' that he had set himself (being a fluent Latin speaker since his boyhood, he wrote all his scientific papers in Latin). The issue was fundamental: why do the planets move around the sun in elliptical orbits? Indeed, why do they move at all? The story is that while he sat in his garden at Woolsthorpe, he noticed an apple falling off a tree, which sparked off the concept of gravity. Unlike Archimedes' sudden inspiration in his bath, however, it is probable that Newton had been mulling over the whole matter of motion for a considerable period of time. In this, as in optics, he was much influenced by the ideas of Descartes.

Newton's Laws of Motion, that *Every body continues in its state of rest, or of uniform motion ... unless it is compelled to change that state by forces impressed on it*, that *Change in motion is proportional to the motive force impressed ...* and that *To every action there is an equal and opposite reaction*,[25] are the basis for his thoughts about gravity. They are also the foundations of modern physics, that have not changed to this day. The link between a falling apple, gravity and the movement of the heavenly bodies originates from reminiscences about Newton by some of his contemporaries. One of these was John Conduitt, the husband of Isaac's niece Catherine. Conduitt wrote that '... whilst he was musing in a garden it came into his thought that the power of gravity (which brought an apple from the tree to the ground) was not limited to a certain distance from the earth but that this power must extend much farther than was usually thought. Why not as high as the moon he said to himself ...'.[26] In other words, the reason that gravity does not cause the moon to collapse into the earth (or the earth into the sun, for that matter), is that each of the smaller bodies itself exerts a slight attraction on the larger one.

By 1684 the question in the minds of the most eminent Fellows of the Royal Society — Edmund Halley, Robert Hooke and Christopher Wren in particular — was this: if bodies attract one another by a force that is inversely proportional to the distance between them, can the orbits of the planets around the sun be predicted? Halley travelled to Cambridge to consult Newton. As the mathematician Abraham de Moivre, another of Newton's contemporaries, described it, 'Dr Halley ... asked him what he thought the Curve would be that would be described by the Planets, supposing the force of attraction toward the Sun to be reciprocal to the square of their distance from it. Newton replied immediately that it would be an Ellipsis, the Doctor struck with joy & amazement asked him how he knew it, why, saith he, I have calculated it ...'.[27] Thus were the observations of Copernicus and Galileo, of Tycho Brahe and Johannes Kepler, finally put on a firm mathematical basis.

Isaac Newton's accomplishments epitomise—as none before or since—the essential ingredients of scientific enquiry: exploration and explanation. For 85 years his roving mind spanned mathematics and mechanics, optics and astronomy (he also dabbled in alchemy). As the inscription on his tomb puts it, 'Let Mortals rejoice That there has existed such and so great an Ornament to the Human Race'.[28]

Einstein

Albert Einstein (1879–1955) (Plate 8) was a rather mediocre student who dropped out of school at the age of 15. He failed at his first attempt to enter university, and did not manage to secure an academic post on account of his apparent laziness. He obtained employment instead as a junior clerk in the Patent Office in Bern. With time on his hands,[29] he found himself thinking about the fundamental laws of physics. In 1905—he was just 26 years old—he published his theory of special relativity, which has proved to be as influential as Isaac Newton's theory of universal gravitation. What Einstein in essence achieved was to show mathematically that time is a relative concept, a point that had been noted already by Galileo 300 years earlier. Part of the theory was that energy (E) and mass (m) are related by the equation $E = mc^2$, where c is the velocity of light.[30] But something about light was not right. Newton himself had suggested that light is bent as it passes an object of large mass like a planet or star, due to the gravitational pull of the larger object on the much smaller corpuscles of light. Since Newton's time, however, physicists had shown that light has no mass and therefore cannot be deflected by a gravitational pull: light travels in straight lines, according to Einstein's contemporaries. Einstein, in contrast, felt that Newton had been right—if for the wrong reason—and that light does bend as it passes a much larger object. On thinking about it, does not the equation $E = mc^2$ allow one to consider Newtonian interactions between objects in terms of energy—which light certainly possesses—rather than of mass? This is the core of Einstein's general theory of relativity, which he presented to the Prussian Academy of Sciences in 1915. Its proof took longer.

Several years passed, largely because communication between Germany and other countries had been disrupted by World War I. Then an English scientist, Arthur Eddington, became aware of the gist of the general theory of relativity. He, like Einstein, realised that there was a simple test to prove it one way or the other. This was to determine whether light from a distant star is indeed bent as it passes near the sun; in other words to compare the apparent position (X) of a distant star when the sun is between it and an observer on earth, and to compare this with the position of the star (Y) from the same location when the sun is behind the earth (Figure 11.1). If light is bent, X is displaced slightly from Y; if it is not, X and Y are the same. But there is a problem. The brightness of the sun under condition X prevents one from seeing any stars at all. On the other hand, if one were to make the measurement of X during a total eclipse of the sun (when the moon is between the sun and the earth, and darkness temporarily falls on earth), it should be possible to see a distant star sufficiently well to measure the position of X. Eddington decided to conduct the experiment at the next opportunity. On 29 May 1919, a total eclipse of the sun enabled observers at two locations to make the necessary observations. One site was in Principe off the coast of West Africa, the other was in Sobral in northern Brazil. The watchers in Africa had difficulty in seeing any stars because of cloud, but nevertheless came up with a value of 1.61 ± 0.4 arc seconds[31] ($\pm$ standard error) as the difference between X and Y. The second group, in Brazil, had better weather and came up with a figure of 1.98 ± 0.16; Einstein had predicted a value of 1.74: the theory of general relativity was confirmed. Naturally at every subsequent total eclipse of the sun, scientists tried to sharpen up the results of the 1919 observations to see if they got any closer to 1.74, and with less of a standard error. In 1922 an opportunity to do so from Australia occurred. Einstein was in the middle of his favourite lecture on relativity in Berlin (which my mother attended), when he casually said to his audience, 'And now you will have to excuse me for a moment while I go to the telephone to await a call from Australia'. A few minutes later he was back with a smile on his

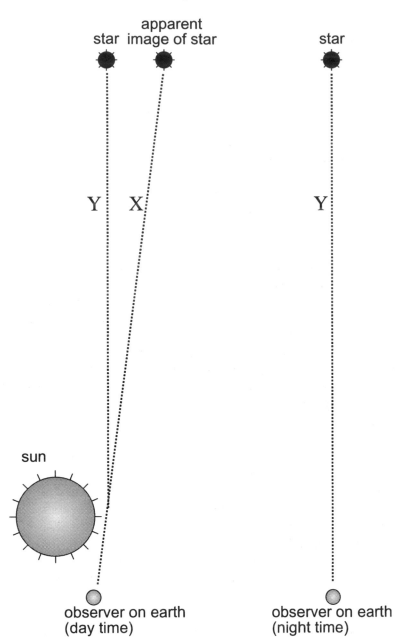

Figure 11.1 The bending of light. Adapted from Peter Coles, op. cit., p 43. See text for details.

face: 'the predictions of the theory have just been confirmed yet again'.

The reader will note that I have not included four outstanding biologists in this dicussion of scientists: William Harvey, Charles Darwin, James Watson and Francis Crick. The reason is simple. The findings of Harvey were related in an earlier book of mine;[32] Darwin's thesis, and the illuminating experiments of Watson and Crick, were described in Chapter 2.

The foundations of medicine

Curiosity about our bodies and our surroundings is as old as man himself, which is why medicine and astronomy are among the earliest-taught disciplines. The practice of medicine—healing—is rightly called an art (in the sense of skill); it is also a technology that goes back over 4000 years. When were rational explanations for the way our bodies work first advanced? When did medicine become a science? Well, strictly speaking, medicine is not a science: it is the knowledge on which it is based, that of anatomy and physiology, biochemistry and microbiology, embryology and psychology, immunology and oncology, that constitutes science. And until each of those disciplines offered rational explanations for the way things worked, they were not science either. Identifying and naming different bones and muscles, blood vessels and nerves, does not constitute science any more than the recording of different plants and trees, animals and stars. It is knowing *why* bones have strength, *how* muscles contract, *what* substances are delivered through blood vessels, *how* nerves pass impulses, that is science. Noting that the liver is made up of four lobes, that kidneys, adrenals and lungs come in pairs, does not explain their function. Physiology as a science can be said to have begun only in the second half of the seventeenth century, when Robert Boyle ('father of chemistry and son of the Earl of Cork') showed that animals deprived of oxygen die, and William Harvey demonstrated how the heart is able to pump blood around the body without loss. Biochemistry—the description of life in chemical terms—did not begin until well into the twentieth century, when the structure and function of molecules like carbohydrate and fat, protein and nucleic acid, was worked out.

The existence of microbes was discovered by van Leeuwenhoek in the seventeenth century: he presciently called them 'animalcules'. The significance of microbes to medicine was clarified 200 years later by scientists like Robert Koch in Germany and Louis Pasteur in France. They showed that diseases like anthrax, cholera, rabies and tuberculosis result from infection by some kind of pathogenic agent; in the case of anthrax, cholera and tuberculosis, these were identified as bacilli (bacteria). Of equal, if not greater, importance was Pasteur's finding that vaccination with a small dose of heat-treated agent afforded protection against a subsequent infection. The success of variolation,[33] employed for centuries earlier by the Chinese and then by the Turks against smallpox, and placed on a scientific footing by Edward Jenner at the end of the eighteenth century,[34] was clearly the result of some general response within the body. Protection against infectious diseases by vaccination revolutionised the practice of medicine and has kept scientists busy in searching for novel vaccines to this day.[35]

During the last years of the nineteenth century, a Scottish officer of the Indian Medical Service[36] was investigating the disease that continues to kill more children today (through cerebral malfunction) than any other: malaria.[37] It was realised that malaria is transmitted through the bite of an insect, in the way that rabies is passed to man through the bite of a dog (and cholera through ingestion of toxic bacilli, anthrax and tuberculosis through their inhalation). But how exactly does the bite of a mosquito cause the affliction? Is it through the introduction into the circulation of some toxic molecules, like those delivered by the sting of a bee or the bite of a snake? Surgeon-captain Ronald Ross, stationed in Secunderabad, thought not. He felt that some kind of organism was involved. Persuaded by his mentor, Dr Patrick Manson,[38] to equip himself with a microscope, Ross began to scan blood samples from malarial patients. In order to increase his chances, he worked in a highly malarious area, dosing himself with large amounts of quinine daily. Like others before him, he found foreign bodies in the red cells of sufferers of the disease. Now he needed to show that the parasites were transferred to mosquitos feeding on infected humans. He caught hundreds of insects and released them one by one on to consenting patients lying under a net. He then removed the stomach of any mosquito that had clearly had a meal of human blood, and searched for parasites with the aid of his microscope. Failure upon failure. Unknown to him, few mosquitos are vectors of the human disease. Most of the insects he was using were *Culex* or *Aedes*, not the deadly *Anopheles*. But he persevered.

On 20 August 1897 Ross's search was rewarded: he found a spherical body (an oocyst) in the stomach wall of an anopheline mosquito that had earlier bitten a patient (who was being compensated with one anna per mosquito successfully recovered: Husein Khan made 10 annas that day). But how to show that the parasites in the oocyst would then complete their life cycle and be passed on through a subsequent bite? Experiments with uninfected human subjects were not on the cards. Ross, however, knew that birds are also targets for malaria. So a year later, now working in a Calcutta laboratory, he started examining culex mosquitos known to bite birds. Not only did he find oocysts in the stomach of these vectors, he saw that when an oocyst burst, it released masses of stringy parasites: these he could then trace through to the salivary glands of the insect. The fact that culex mosquitos do not infect humans seemed irrelevant. In this, Ross was behaving as a true scientist. Most of the experiments on which modern medicine is based were carried out with organisms other than humans: William Harvey demonstrated the circulation of the blood in snakes, the biochemists of the twentieth century elucidated metabolic pathways and the central position of ATP with rat liver and pigeon muscle, the way that nervous impulses are transmitted was shown with the organs of squid. Ross's contribution was swiftly recognised by the Swedish Academy and he received a Nobel Prize in 1902 (the second year of these awards[39]).

Although the composition and life cycle in humans of bacteria (tuberculosis, anthrax), viruses (smallpox and rabies) and protozoa (malaria) were not elucidated until much later, the contributions of Jenner, Koch, Pasteur and Ross were clear examples of scientific insight. When in 1910 the American scientist Peyton Rous showed that a virus was able to transmit cancer to chickens, the study of microbiology as a science integral to medicine was truly born.[40]

Psychology and psychiatry did not became a science until the twentieth century. Only within the last decade or so have certain kinds of mood and behaviour been ascribed to the action of particular molecules. Such molecules, called neurotransmitters, are released at one end of a neuron, and act at the beginning of another. Gradually, rational explanations for our behaviour are emerging. The technology of designing molecules that boost or depress the action of specific neurotransmitters has burgeoned to the extent that its fruits—Valium and Prozac, for example—are today some of the most frequently prescribed medicines: neuropharmacology has become a highly lucrative branch of the biotechnology and pharmaceutical industry, generating billions of dollars in profits.

Oncology, the study of cancer, did not become a science until late in the twentieth century. The earlier discovery of chicken sarcoma virus[41] by Peyton Rous heralded a half century of claims and counter-claims. Viruses are not the cause of human cancer. Sarcomas are rather rare: the most common forms of cancer are carcinomas—cancers of epithelial origin like breast and lung, bowel and colon, uterus and prostate—and there is no link between these diseases and viruses. Some cancers run in families, so a genetic origin seems the most likely. No, viruses do cause cancer—look at Burkitt's lymphoma,[42] a disease related to infectious mononucleosis that is caused by the Epstein–Barr virus. No, this is again an exception. And so on. Few serious scientists championed one hypothesis or the other with vigour: there was simply not enough compelling evidence either way. Then, during the 1980s and 1990s, things began to move. By this time it had become apparent that, just as with other common ailments like heart disease and diabetes— another affliction linked to viruses on and off—cancers are due to a combination of inherited and environmental causes. The hereditable element includes genes like BRCA1 and BRCA2, the possession of which correlates significantly with an increased susceptibility to breast cancer. Environmental factors encompass diet, infectious agents like viruses,[43] and pollution. The latter is responsible for lung cancer from tobacco smoke and leukaemia from radioactive fall-out.

A considerable advance was that, finally, studies on the proliferation of cancer cells in the laboratory could be directly linked to analysis of human cancers in the clinic. So far, a minimum of three steps, resulting from the malfunctioning of particular proteins, have been recognised as leading to cancer (it had long been suspected that cancer is a multifactorial disease). Some proteins, like the products of the BRCA1 and BRCA2 genes, are inherited; others arise as a result of a genetic mutation caused by one of the environmental factors referred to above. Faulty proteins at two of the steps cause cells to overcome the controls that normally limit their proliferation.[44] The third step involves proteins concerned in the setting up of a blood supply to a growing mass of tumour tissue: without nutrients, cancers cannot enlarge. Altered forms of the genes underlying each step can be detected in cancer patients by an innovation known as DNA chip technology. Recognising which genes are responsible for the development of a particular form of cancer gives scientists a chance to redress the situation.[45] Oncology, in common with microbiology and its offspring immunology, as well as with neuropharmacology, has become a science through elucidation of the underlying molecular changes.

Scientific discoveries sometimes move diseases from one branch of medicine to another. Most disorders, as we have seen, are due to a subtle interplay between genes and the environment. A few years ago, a quite unexpected role of microbial infection in the development of gastric ulcers came to light. Stress had always been considered to be the main factor leading to ulcers: worry over one's job, concern over money, grief over the death or illness of a loved one. The difference between worriers and those able to take misfortune in their stride is partly genetic. What was shown is that a bacterial infection is as decisive a cause of ulcers as stress. The offending organism has been identified: it is a microbe called *Helicobacter pylori* that lives particularly happily in the acid environment of the stomach. I mention this finding, which is of wide importance because an ulcer can develop into cancer, to illustrate that advances in medical research often reveal unsuspected links, and emphasize again the rewards that studies of microbial infections bring.

The same is true of treatments. A drug developed against one disease proves to be effective against a completely unrelated illness. Idoxuridine was synthesised as a potential anti-cancer drug: it proved more useful against eye infections caused by herpes viruses. Quinacrine is an anti-malarial based on quinine (the natural compound found in the bark of the cinchona tree): it is being used to relieve some of the symptoms of Creutzfeldt – Jakob disease (CJD),[46] which has been linked to eating meat infected with BSE.

Molecular biology

I now return to instances of a valid hypothesis having to be amended in the light of new experimental results. To appreciate what follows, we need to revert to molecules.

As the relationship between DNA and proteins was being worked out, it became clear that the code by which the information in DNA is used to synthesise a protein[47] is not read off *directly* from DNA, but via RNA. RNA resembles DNA in most of its features,[48] except that it is much shorter: it is roughly the length of a protein, which is also the length of a gene.[49] The mechanism by which a stretch of DNA is copied into RNA is essentially the same as that by which DNA is duplicated.[50] Molecular biologists of the 1960s therefore defined the central proposition of their science as 'DNA makes DNA, and DNA also makes RNA that makes proteins'. Actually, they called the proposition the 'dogma' of molecular biology, but I will shun that word for the same reason that I avoided the word 'true' earlier on. 'Dogma' and 'truth' imply religious conviction, which is not what science is about.

No experiment carried out since then has shown that DNA does *not* make DNA, or that DNA does *not* make RNA, or that RNA does *not* make proteins. The proposition is as valid today as it was 40 years ago. But the fact that the genes of many viruses—like measles and mumps, rabies and polio—are RNA, not DNA, meant that virologists needed to insert a corollary to the central proposition. Since RNA viruses are as capable of reproducing themselves—

within an appropriate plant or animal host—there therefore needs to be added the clause 'RNA makes RNA'. Nevertheless, the underlying assumption of the central proposition, that information between the three main players—DNA, RNA and protein—is passed only in the direction from DNA to RNA, and from RNA to protein, appeared to hold.

Then something happened. As scientists studied the behaviour of viruses in greater detail—a quest driven by the possibility that viruses cause cancer—it bcame clear that, in the case of certain RNA viruses,[51] RNA *does* make DNA, as well as making more RNA and proteins (it is by making DNA from RNA that such viruses can cause cancer). The validity of the proposition that information travels from DNA to RNA to protein holds, but it now needs refinement: 'DNA makes DNA, and DNA also makes RNA that makes proteins; in addition RNA makes RNA and and can also make DNA'. So far no experiment has contradicted the assumption that the flow of information between RNA and protein is in one direction only. Such adaptations—more precise restatements of propositions—happen all the time in biology.

'Enzymes are proteins' is a proposition that goes back well over half a century. An enzyme, you will recall, is a biological catalyst: a molecule that speeds up reactions between other molecules. The digestion of food, the contraction of muscle, the synthesis of DNA, RNA, protein, fat and carbohydrate in the body, all are catalysed by enzymes. Instead of taking years, the reactions happen within seconds; without enzymes, life on earth as we know it could not proceed. Around 3.5 billion years ago, when living organisms first appeared on earth, it probably *did* take years for reactions between molecules to occur. Then a class of proteins that has catalytic activity evolved, and things speeded up. What has now emerged is that some types of RNA *also* have catalytic activity:[52] they speed up the reactions by which parts of their own molecule are split off. All the enzymes that had previously been described, about which it was said 'enzymes are proteins', are indeed all proteins. But the statement should now be refined as 'enzymes are proteins; RNA can also act catalytically'.

Until a decade or so ago, the proposition that all infectious agents—be they protozoa, moulds, bacteria or viruses—contain

DNA or RNA, was accepted as valid. Protozoa, moulds and bacteria, being cellular, of course contain both DNA and RNA. What occurred next was that a certain class of protein, called a prion, was shown to be infective on its own. Prions are the agents responsible for transmitting BSE ('mad cow disease') and Creutzfeldt – Jakob disease (CJD).[53] So the proposition needs refinement. As new knowledge emerges, explanations have to be modified, and they become more — or less — inclusive. That is precisely why science, a discipline based on experiment, cannot propose 'truths' in the way that mathematics or philosophy can. Being an experimental discipline, it is inevitable that its practitioners will seek ever sharper lenses through which to examine nature. The sharper the lens, the more detail will emerge. And as more new detail emerges, so propositions will require modification. That is the way of scientific progress: a search for explanations of the world in ever greater detail.

Finale

If the scientific process has been going on for hundreds of years, what is there left to explore or to explain? Scientists continue to be drawn to the largest and the smallest entities in the universe: astrophysicists to the furthest stars, particle physicists to sub-atomic particles. The difference in scale between the two could not be greater. The *nearest* star (Proxima Centauri) to our sun is 4.2 light years away;[54] the *nearest* galaxy (Andromeda) to that of our own (the Milky Way) is 1.5 million light years away. On the other hand, the constituents of the elementary particles — mesons and quarks — that make up atoms are a minute fraction of the size of the smallest molecule.[55] Astrophysicists and particle physicists, however, have a similar aim: each is searching to explain an event of no less a significance than the origin of the universe itself.

The expense of conducting such research is not trivial. A recent space probe, that measures microwave radiation instead of light, cost $150 million. That was relatively cheap. A space telescope that will record infrared radiation, planned for a launch in 2010, will

cost an estimated $2.8 billion.[56] A conventional optic European
Extremely Large Telescope now being designed—its mirror might
be 60 metres across—will cost $1 billion to construct and the
annual running expenses will exceed the entire European budget
for astronomy.[57] Telescopes like these will explore the birth of stars
and planets and will explore the very edges of the universe. As a
result we will learn more about events shortly after the Big Bang
('shortly' meaning approximately 500,000 years). They will also
reveal whether the universe is indeed expanding and, if so, at what
rate.

The goal of exploring the interactions of sub-atomic particles is
to learn what happened within a million millionth[58] of a second
after the Big Bang. A Superconducting Super Collider (SSC),
designed to accelerate electrically charged particles like electrons,
protons and their anti-matter equivalents, and then to observe the
consequences when they collide,[59] was initially estimated to cost
$4.4 billion; within a few years, the cost had doubled. Construction
on digging a circular pit some 54 miles in circumference had begun
south of Dallas, Texas, when the project was abandoned in 1993 as
being too expensive ($2 billion had already been spent). Now it is
back on track.[60] A similar instrument, the Large Hadron Collider, is
being planned by a European consortium.

Are these costs, borne ultimately by the tax-payers of the world,
worthwhile? Is knowing that the universe is shaped like a deflated
football (the US version; elsewhere, the rugby sort) going to enrich
our lives?[61] Will the realisation that for every particle that has
gravity there is an anti-particle, help to cure cancer? The answer
to the first two questions, I believe, is yes; to the third, perhaps. It is
impossible to predict what parts of scientific knowledge may one
day lead to new discoveries, to novel technology. In any case, many
subscribe to the proposition that 'science spawns technology,
technology creates wealth, and part of that wealth can then be
used to support more science'. But as I indicated in Chapter 9 and
at the beginning of this,[1] that argument is too simplistic, especially
when the sums spent on science begin to exceed the possible
rewards.

Once we have explored the limits of the universe on the one hand,
and of the fundamental composition of matter on the other, will we

have discovered everything there is to know? There are those who believe that further discoveries are mere detail, and that the world around us will shortly be explicable in terms of fundamental physics alone.[62] Others disagree.[63] I side with the second view. A mere decade ago a totally unforeseen infectious molecule—the prion—was discovered. How do we know what other pathogenic agents may not be lurking on this earth? The fundamentals of molecular biology are less than 50 years old. We do not understand the basis of thought and memory, love and hate; we are ignorant of the nature of dreams and the mechanism of creativity; the molecular details of curiosity elude us still: just how are impulses between the 10^{14} neural connections in our brain integrated? Are we really so arrogant as to dismiss such knowledge as trivial?

Notes

1. Terence Kealey, op. cit.; and Terence Kealey and Aram Rudenski, 'Endogenous growth theory for natural scientists', *Nature Med.* **4**: 995–999; 1998.
2. For an excellent account of what science is, and especially of what it is *not*, I cannot do better than recommend Lewis Wolpert's *The Unnatural Nature of Science*, op. cit.
3. An arc minute is one-sixtieth of a degree.
4. Kate Spence, 'Ancient Egyptian chronology and the astronomical orientation of the pyramids', *Nature* **408**: 320–324; 2000.
5. See John Merson, op. cit., pp 37, 38.
6. See Philip Morrison, *Nature* **413**: 461; 2001.
7. The neurologist Semir Zeki (op. cit.) believes that artists activate, to a greater extent than others, specific areas of the brain—visual cortex, fusiform gyrus, frontal lobe and hippocampus—in order to focus on such aspects as colour and form (especially if they record their scenes from memory within the studio). Perhaps scientists utilise the same pathways when they synthesise a novel hypothesis that is based on many disparate, and long ago, observations.
8. We should note that Leonardo da Vinci preceded Copernicus by 100 years in his assertion that 'the sun does not move' (quoted by Sherwin B. Nuland, op. cit., p 103), and that Aristarchus of Samos had proposed a heliocentric universe in the first half of the third century BC.

9. A point emphasised by Nicholas Humphrey, op. cit., pp 162–164.

10. Personal communication from Dr Fred Brown, Department of Agriculture, Plum Island Animal Disease Center, PO Box 848, Greenport, NY 11944, USA.

11. An important criterion promoted by Karl Popper. See his *The Logic of Scientific Discovery*, Basic Books, New York, 1959, p 40 (which first appeared as *Logik der Forschung* in 1934).

12. At least in neolithic times.

13. Of course the fact that we are now speaking of events within the last 1000 years or so is another reason why it is possible to recognise specific players.

14. See Sir Thomas Heath, op. cit., p 8.

15. Not to be confused with Anaximander: both were from Miletus.

16. It was Democritus (c. 460–370 BC) who came the closest, by proposing a theory of matter based on atomic particles. And Parmenides, around the same time, espoused the equally correct notion that matter is essentially indestructible.

17. Not to be confused with Hippocrates of Cos, the 'Father of Medicine'.

18. He calculated π, the ratio of the circumference of a circle to its diameter, to be between $3 + 1/7$ and $3 + 10/71$, a pretty good approximation.

19. Weight (more correctly, mass) = volume × density (i.e. specific gravity).

20. Charles Darwin thought about the evolution of species on his daily walks around Down House, but the path was sandy and he was unlikely to trip; US President Gerald Ford, it was said maliciously, was incapable even of chewing gum while he walked.

21. See Lewis Wolpert, op. cit., pp 44–45.

22. The notation in terms of derivatives, $d(x)/d(t)$—we owe to Gottfried Leibnitz, who developed the concept of the calculus in Germany, independently of Newton. Although Leibnitz visited London in 1673, Newton did not meet him. Their only contact was through correspondence (largely acrimonious).

23. Meaning the integral, as opposed to the differential, calculus.

24. Quoted in David Berlinski, op. cit., pp 60–61.

25. As set out by David Berlinski, op. cit., pp 98–103.

26. Quoted by Richard Westfall, op. cit., p 154.

27. Quoted by David Berlinski, op. cit., p 91.

28. Richard Westfall, op. cit., p 874.

29. As Einstein later wrote to the physicist James Franck: 'I sometimes ask myself how it came about that I was the one to develop the theory of relativity. The reason, I think, is that a normal adult never stops to think about problems of space and time. These are things which he has thought of as a child. But my intellectual development was retarded, as a result of which I began to wonder about space and

time only when I had already grown up'. From Walter Gratzer, *Eurekas and Euphorias. The Oxford Book of Scientific Anecdotes*, Oxford University Press, Oxford, 2002, p 2.

30. The reader who would like Einstein's theories, and those of his predecessors, explained in simple language could do worse than read Gary F. Moring, op. cit. Do not be put off by the title; the chances are that you will learn more from reading Moring than from trying to get to grips with Stephen Hawking.

31. An arc second is one-sixtieth of an arc minute (see Note 3 above).

32. Charles Pasternak, op. cit., pp 4–5.

33. Inhaling the pus from the wound of an infected patient, or—as Jenner showed—from an infected cow.

34. The word 'vaccination' was introduced by Pasteur to honour Jenner, since Jenner had used cowpox (*vacca* = cow).

35. Despite the use of the BCG (bacille Calmette-Guérin) vaccine for decades, a really effective vaccine against tuberculosis eludes us still (as do vaccines against such devastating infections as HIV and malaria).

36. See Nye and Gibson, op. cit.

37. Currently some 2.7 million people (out of 500 million infected) die every year: most are children. For adults, the disease is second only to HIV/AIDS. Most infected people are in Africa, and the cost to that continent has been estimated by the UN at $12 billion per year.

38. Manson had earlier discovered filarial worms—which give rise to elephantiasis—in the stomachs of mosquitos.

39. But Italian scientists working on malaria were not pleased. The disease was as much in their province as in Ross's. The very name 'mal air' was coined in Italy, where malaria had been a major killer during Roman times (the disease was originally thought to be spread—as was cholera—through foul air). More to the point, the Italian team had demonstrated the life cycle of the malarial parasite within the *Anopheles gambiae* mosquito that infects humans (*A. gambiae* has turned out to be the only one out of some 422 species of *Anopheles* that nurtures the *Plasmodium* parasite, and solely in pregnant females at that) a mere year after Ross announced his breakthrough with culex mosquitos feeding on birds. In his acceptance speech at the Nobel ceremony, Ross acknowledged the contributions of Drs Bignami, Bastianelli and Celli, but was silent in regard to his main competitor, Giovanni Grassi (who had himself been nominated).

40. Elucidating the complete genome of infectious microbes is helping to provide better therapies and vaccines. The sequencing of the *Plasmodium falciparum* genome (Declan Butler, 'What difference does a genome make?' *Nature* **419**: 426–430 and '*Plasmodium* genomics', *Nature* **419**: 489–542; 2002), and of its *Anopheles gambiae* vector

(Robert A. Holt *et al.*, 'The genome sequence of the malaria mosquito *Anopheles gambiae*', *Science* **298**: 129–149, 2002) are a major step forward in this regard.

41. A sarcoma is a cancer of connective tissue, such as muscle.

42. Lymphomas and leukaemias are cancers of the white blood cells.

43. Hepatitis B, and to a lesser extent hepatitis C, is a major cause of liver cancer. A huge vaccination programme against hepatitis B, begun a few years ago in China and south-east Asia, where the incidence of hepatitis B is especially high, has proved so efficacious that it has been expanded to the rest of the world. The World Health Organisation (WHO) has hailed this attempt to eradicate hepatitis B-induced cancer of the liver as the second largest cancer prevention programme (after smoking cessation). The story is well told by Baruch Blumberg (op. cit.), the discoverer of hepatitis B virus.

44. Through pre-programmed cell death, a mechanism known as apoptosis.

45. Molecular forecasting and cancer therapy: see Carlos Caldas and Samuel A. J. Aparicio, 'The molecular outlook', *Nature* **415**: 484–485; 2002: and Alison Abbott, 'On the offensive', *Nature* **416**: 470–474; 2002.

46. *Nature* **413**: 341; 2001.

47. For details, see Chapter 2.

48. Except that instead of the T of thymine in DNA, RNA has U (uracil), and instead of deoxyribose, it has ribose (see Figure 2.1).

49. The reason DNA is so much longer is because each molecule specifies not one but thousands of genes.

50. Pairing between a C (or G) on DNA and a G (or C) that becomes inserted into the growing RNA chain, and pairing between an A (or T) on DNA and a U (or A) that becomes inserted into the growing RNA chain. When DNA is duplicated, C (or G) likewise pairs with G (or C), but A (or T) pairs with T (or A). See Chapter 2 for details.

51. HIV (human immune deficiency virus) is an example.

52. Thomas R. Cech and Brenda L. Bass, 'Biological catalysis by RNA', *Annu. Rev. Biochem.* **55**: 599–629; 1986.

53. Fred E. Cohen and Stanley B. Prusiner, 'Pathological conformations of prion proteins', *Annu. Rev. Biochem.* **67**: 793–819; 1998.

54. 1 light year is the distance travelled by light in 1 year, namely 6×10^{12} miles (the speed of light being 3×10^8 metres (or 2×10^5 miles) per second).

55. Mesons and quarks make up neutrons and protons (that together with electrons constitute an atom). Mesons and quarks are too unstable for their size to be assessed; the smallest particle that is stable is an electron: its weight is 9×10^{-30} (9 million million million million millionths) of a gram.

56. See *Nature* **419**: 235–236; 2002.

57. See *Nature* **420**: 598; 2002.

58. 10^{-12}.

59. The aim of the SSC is to discover the Higgs particle: of all the fundamental forms of matter postulated to exist, this is the only one that has eluded detection so far. If the Higgs particle turns out to be too heavy to be revealed by the SSC, then 'something else equally interesting will turn up' (Steven Weinberg, op. cit., pp 7–25). Thus do scientists justify spending tax-payers' money.

60. See *Nature* **415**: 459; 2002.

61. When a lady asked Benjamin Franklin, 'What is the use of electricity?', he replied, 'Madam, what is the use of a new-born child?' A similar riposte has been attributed to Michael Faraday: see Walter Gratzer, *Eurekas and Euphorias. The Oxford Book of Scientific Anecdotes*, Oxford University Press, Oxford, 2002, p 31.

62. Such as Stephen Hawking, *A Brief History of Time*, Bantam Books, London, 1998. Steven Weinberg muses on this topic in *Dreams of a Final Theory*, Vintage Books, 1993 and Random House, New York, 1994) and comes to the conclusion that if such a theory will indeed emerge, it is probably many years away (and is likely to be based on quantum mechanics, which holds up best to the challenges of new discoveries).

63. Among them is David Deutsch, himself a physicist; see his *The Fabric of Reality*, Allen Lane/Penguin, London, 1997. Another is John Maddox (also a physicist by training), op. cit. (a good account of what has been, and what remains to be, discovered in physics and biology).

PART III

Controversy:
current quest

CHAPTER TWELVE

Tinkering with genes 1:
GM foods

*I*n no area of biological science is today's quest for new technology greater than in that involving the modification of genes: the genes of plants and animals, the genes of our own species itself. The consequences of that search — the production of genetically modified (GM) food and people — has created so much controversy that it would have been remiss of me to have passed it by. I have therefore added a third part to my story to reflect these themes.

The possibility that genes can be isolated and introduced into foreign organisms — a human gene into a pig, a bacterial gene into a cotton plant — came about as a result of a quite different search: the search for a cure for cancer. During the 1960s and 1970s, the idea that cancers may be caused by viruses was revived. As we saw in the last chapter, it had been shown more than half a century earlier that a certain type of chicken cancer is caused by a virus, but the observation had lain forgotten: not until 1966 did its discoverer, the American scientist Peyton Rous, receive the recognition he deserved through the award of a Nobel prize. As these prizes are given only to living persons capable of collecting them in person, it was lucky that Peyton Rous was a fit man, able to wait until his 87th year for the trip to Stockholm.

In the early 1970s the US President Richard Nixon decided that he could make some political capital out of a generous increase in the budget of the National Cancer Institute, one of the National Institutes of Health near Washington, the largest medical research centre in the world: the money would go towards funding research aimed at establishing a viral cause of cancer. The outcome was rather different. As mentioned, few cancers proved to be directly caused by a viral infection. On the other hand, the fundamental mechanisms by which viruses grow inside the cells of their host, and occasionally become integrated into one of its chromosomes, were revealed. It was knowing how this transfer of genes, from a virus into the DNA of an animal, is accomplished that has opened up the prospect for developing the technology required to introduce genes from one species into another. But there is a problem.

Science, as we enter the new millennium, is receiving a bad press. The quest for knowledge is turning sour on us. In Europe, protesters against GM foods are destroying trial crops; our environment, they say, is in danger and our lives are at risk. The possibility of cloning people is fertile ground for journalists. Advances in the physical sciences do not exercise the public so much these days. The nuclear debate of the 1960s has largely died down, and the fact that the number of telecommunication satellites in orbit is making it difficult for astrophysicists to learn about galaxies beyond our own solar system, or that every satellite launched into the atmosphere creates a small hole in it, worries no one. Are our concerns over the new biomedical technology justified? Everyone is entitled to his or her opinion, especially if based on genuinely held religious beliefs. But if the views depend on a misunderstanding of the facts, the remedy is surely to explain the underlying principles better, in simple language that is understood by all. Yes, the media do a splendid job; but their stories are often slanted and biased in a particular direction. An English newspaper (the *Sunday Times*) for several years promoted the view—against all scientific evidence—that AIDS results directly from drug abuse and that infection by the human immune deficiency virus (HIV) is not the major cause. A similar opinion has resurfaced with regard to AIDS in southern Africa, and has led to the loss of thousands of lives. The trouble with such reports is that they reach a much wider audience than do critically-written articles by scientists. We have got to do a better job of explaining the intricacies of science to the public. In the two chapters that constitute Part III I will try to steer an unbiased course with reference to GM foods and GM people. One of the most misunderstood aspects of the new technology, that surfaces every time the use of genetically modified organisms is mentioned, is the nature of risk.

Risk

Risk is about chance, and chance is governed by statistics. Suppose your birthday is in January. The chance of someone you have just met also having their birthday in January is 1 in 12, as there are 12 months to the year. If your birthday is on 27 January (as was that of Mozart), the chance of your new friend having his/her birthday on the same day is approximately 1 in $12 \times 30 = 1$ in 360, as there are approximately 30 days per month.[1] If you think that the age of your acquaintance is within 10 years of your own, the chance of his/her birthday being on the same day of the same month of the same year as yours is 1 in $12 \times 30 \times 10 = 1$ in 3600. If you happen to know that you were born at 5 o'clock in the morning, the chance of your friend being been born at the same hour on the same day of the same month of the same year as yourself is 1 in $12 \times 30 \times 10 \times 24 = 1$ in 86,400. In other words, the more precisely you define your birthday, the less the chance of meeting someone of exactly your age. The numbers just calculated do not mean that you have to meet 86,400 people before you find someone born at the same time on the same day of the same month of the same year as yourself. The first person you meet may have precisely those coordinates. But the chances against it happening are 86,400 to 1. The chance against you winning the UK lottery (six numbers each between 1 and 50, with a 'bonus' number) is approximately 14 million to 1. Chance is the opposite of certainty and it is the same with risk. Calculating the risk of something happening does not mean that it *will* happen; it merely expresses the chance that it *may* happen.[2]

The risk of anyone dying is 1, but the risk of dying at a particular age obviously depends on that age: at 16 it is 1 in 2000; at 100 it is 1 in 2. The risk of dying from a particular disease also varies greatly. For any form of cancer, the risk is roughly 1 in 4 (males) or 1 in 5 (females). Cancer of the lung comprises approximately 1 in 4 of all types of cancer in males and approximately 1 in 6 of all types of cancer in females; the risk of dying from lung cancer is therefore 1 in $4 \times 4 = 1$ in 16 (actually 1 in 14) for males and 1 in $5 \times 6 = 1$ in 30 (actually 1 in 25) for females. That is the average; for smokers the risk is much higher: around 1 in 8, depending on the amount smoked and the sex of the individual. Smokers please note that the risk of dying from heart disease is even higher than that of dying of cancer of the lung. Age, too, plays a role in cancer. The risk of a woman developing breast cancer—from which under half currently die—is 1 in 11 by the time she is 85 years old; around age 40 it is 1 in 220, and between 20 and 30 years of age it is 1 in 2165. Consider vaccination against bacterial meningitis.[3] The risk of an unvaccinated child developing bacterial meningitis is around 1 in 1000. If vaccinated it is 1 in 100,000. The risk that the vaccine alone will cause meningitis is less than 1 in 10,000,000: no cases have been reported with the vaccine against meningitis C, despite the fact that 14 million children have been vaccinated with it in the UK. As a result of the vaccination programme, the offending microbe is gradually being wiped out and the number of new cases is on the decline. It is true that out of those 14 million there have been 16,000[4] adverse reactions, such as dizzy spells and headaches, but this is normal for any treatment; there have also been 11 deaths:[5] none was due to meningitis C contracted as a result of the vaccine.[6] Is the decision whether to vaccinate your child really so difficult?

Now let me turn to the risk of dying from the new variant form of Creutzfeldt – Jakob disease (vCJD) that is said to be caused by eating meat from cattle infected with bovine spongioform encephalitis (BSE, or 'mad cow' disease). During the 1980s serious outbreaks of BSE occurred on English farms. The most likely cause for the spread of the disease was the practice of feeding cattle on offal such as brain, prepared from other cattle or from sheep. The first death from vCJD occurred in 1995; during the following 5 years, 70 more people fell victim to this devastating disease. In other words, just over an average of 10 per year, out of a population of some 59 million. The chance of dying from vCJD is therefore currently approximately the same as being struck by lightning: around 1 in 10 million. This is infinitesimal compared to the risk of dying in an automobile accident, which is roughly 1 in 8000. But we must not underestimate the future danger: the incubation time for vCJD is very long and the disease develops only several years after BSE-infected meat has been consumed. The numbers of vCJD victims is rising all the time and within a few years is anticipated to reach one death per day or even higher, even though the sale of meat that might have been infected with BSE was halted several years ago. Of course we should not disregard low-risk causes. CJD is a particularly agonising and invariably fatal disease. If it can be avoided, it is the duty of scientists to tell us how to do so. But anyone who gives up eating beef because of a fear of contracting vCJD should understand what kind of risk underlies their decision. Because all BSE-infected herds in the UK have been slaughtered—some 2.5 million heads of cattle by 1998—the incidence of BSE is now no higher in the UK than it is in other parts of Europe, so that eating a beefburger in London carries no more risk than eating one in Frankfurt. But the overall cost to the British tax-payer of his government's failure to act quickly has not been trivial: around £3 billion to date. While it is always easier to pronounce on matters with hindsight than with foresight, is it really so difficult to grasp that eating the meat of seriously ill animals, teetering around the farmyard to the point of collapse, might not be such a good thing?

Risk is perceived differently by different cultures. Take the contraceptive drug Depo-provera. It is effective in women with a single intramuscular injection every 3 months. Because it carries a significant risk of bleeding and other side effects, it is no longer used much in the developed world. Not so in sub-Saharan Africa. There women are prepared to face the possibility of complications arising from the use of Depo-provera because the risk is less than that of the husband finding birth control pills or an intrauterine device. Husbands throw these away and subject their women folk to yet another pregnancy in order to produce a child that neither of the parents has the wherewithal to feed: it is easier to hide the pinpricks of an injection and risk the consequences. A colleague recently passed through a village in The Gambia, in West Africa. She was dismayed to see a bright new car winding its way through the filthy streets, advertising a well-known brand of cigarette. The promoters were also giving away free cigarettes. Not only that, but each packet of cigarettes contained a coupon that gave you a chance of winning the car. This in a village that lacked every amenity from clean drinking water upwards. My colleague spoke to a group of villagers: did they not realise that smoking gives you cancer? Yes, they were aware of the dangers, but felt that cancer of the lung is a disease of older people, and that they were more likely to die of malaria or dysentery by the time they were 50. For them, smoking cigarettes was one of the few pleasures that they had in life.[7] To them, dying of cancer was a luxury. It was a risk worth taking.

The point I am making is that everything we do carries with it a certain amount of risk: the food we eat, the water we drink, the air we breathe. Crossing the road can be a risky business. Sitting under a palm tree in the tropics has its hazards.[8] Do you stop swimming in the sea because you may develop stomach cramps and drown? Do you stop using aeroplanes because of the risk of being killed in an air disaster? Flying is far less risky than driving an automobile. In the UK during 1999, there were 11 deaths from air accidents, 33 from rail accidents and 3423 from road accidents; 50 billion kilometers were travelled per death in the air, 2 billion kilometers per death in a train and 0.3 billion kilometers per death in a car. Of course the chance of being killed in the air depends on your choice of airline: with the best of the established airlines of Europe and North America, the risk of merely being involved — not necessarily killed — in an air accident is less than one in a million;[9] with certain of the companies now operating in the former Soviet Union, that chance increases 3000-fold. Worrying about such things carries its own risk because worry leads to stress, and stress is a contributing factor to common diseases like cancer or a heart attack. I have cited travel as an example of an activity with a significant risk. Has man's quest for faster travel resulted in modes that are increasingly risky? The answer is no, once the number of people who participate in it is taken into account. The most common means of intracontinental travel in Europe today is by train or automobile; prior to that it was by stage coach, travelling at much slower speeds. Yet cars and trains are safer than overloaded horse-drawn vehicles rattling along badly-surfaced roads. The ocean liner is safer than the sailing ships of yesterday, and a jumbo jet is safer than a zeppelin. So far as public transport is concerned, man's quest for safety has kept pace with his search for greater speed. And so, I believe, it is with food.

The need for novel foods

The successful search for improvements in health care and sanitation over the past few hundred years has led to a decline in infant mortality and an increase in life span. As a result, the population of the world is growing at a faster rate than ever before: during the last 50 years alone it more than doubled—from 2.5 billion to 6 billion people—and over the next 50 years it is estimated to rise by a further 3 billion people. Most of the expansion is taking place in the poorest countries of the world, in Asia, Africa and Latin America,[10] despite high rates of infant mortality in those very areas. If new agricultural methods are not developed, these countries will be able to feed their inhabitants even less well than they do today: over 800 million people[11] have a deficit of more than 300 calories—equivalent to one bowl of rice— per day; 40,000 people, half of them children, are dying from malnutrition daily. Water and suitable land are the major factors that limit food production in the Third World, with loss from spoilage and low efficiency contributing to the dilemma. The search for novel forms of food that increase the yield has to be stepped up unless we are prepared to consign one-sixth of the world's population to episodes of mass starvation. Fortunately the techniques for modifying the genomes of plants and animals, which have now been worked out, are ready to be exploited. Surely the development of genetically modified crops like wheat and maize, oilseed rape (canola) and cotton, sugar beet and potato should be encouraged—particularly for use in the poorest countries of the world—or at the very least evaluated, not prevented?

The argument that globally there is enough food for the present, is flawed. It is unrealistic to expect the countries of North America and Europe, capable of producing a surplus of grain and other foods, to routinely give it away to the under-producers; that they do so in times of crisis is laudable. For their self esteem alone, some of the countries we have mentioned should be helped to increase their agricultural output. At present, the production of crops in much of the African continent is the lowest in the world. The yield from maize, for example, is 1.7 tonnes per hectare; the global average is 4. The yield from the production of sweet potato, which is the staple diet for many Africans, is 6 tonnes per hectare; the global average is 14 tonnes (and in China it is 18 tonnes). What is the reason for such low yields? Partly, of course, it is the weather— long periods of drought—but over 50% of crops are also lost annually because of overgrowth by weeds and attack by viruses, moulds and insect pests. As a result, Africa needs to import more than 25% of its grain.[12] In Russia almost half the potato harvest is lost because of destruction by the Colorado beetle and by fungal blight; a shortage of potatoes has become particularly serious over the last decade, because *perestroika* and *glasnost*, that gave everyone in the former Soviet Union democratic freedom, resulted in the mass of the population being considerably worse off economically and forced to rely on cheap staple foods like potatoes. Russians may be happy to accept genetically modified products, but other nations are less compliant. Despite the shortfalls within their region, a group of African countries, led by Ethiopia, has taken on the grain-exporting countries, led by the USA, in a legal battle over the African countries' right to ban the import of GM food if they do not consider it safe: there is no question that the choice is theirs, but one wishes that it were based on scientific evidence, not political whim.

What of the countries that produce enough for their own use? India may claim to be self-sufficient today—despite the fact that 30% of its population is living on the bread-line—but its current agricultural output will not be able to sustain the projected increase of its inhabitants, from a population of 1 billion today to one of 1.5 billion within 30 years. Indira Gandhi tried valiantly to promote birth control several decades ago, by measures such as giving away a free dhoti to every man who agreed to have a vasectomy; her attempts were unsuccessful, and the position has not changed much since then. It is difficult to persuade people to alter their life style if they are unused to the quest for novelty that typifies life in the western world. Birth control is working better in China only because procreation of a second child is proscribed.

Although India ranks first or second in the world in terms of its production of rice, wheat, milk, sugar, tea, peanuts, fruits and vegetables, its yields are 20–40% below world average. That for rice, for instance, is 1.9 tonnes per hectare; the global figure is 3.7, and that of China is nearly 6.0.[13] The yield from groundnuts (also called peanuts or monkeynuts) is 900 kg per hectare; the global figure is 1500 kg per hectare, and that of the USA is 3000 kg per hectare. Many of these discrepancies are due as much to climatic problems as to differences in agricultural efficiency, but that merely makes the search for novel seeds, that resist drought for example, more pressing. Another of India's difficulties—like that of the Soviet Union's heirs—is wastage and decay of its products: 25–30% of fruit and vegetables are lost before they ever reach market. If genetic modifications could increase yield and decrease spoilage, would their exploitation not be a worthwhile goal? Such improvements in agronomy *are* now possible and it is surely inappropriate for uninformed polemicists to persuade the public at large to ignore the scientists' achievements.

Risks to health of eating GM foods

Doubts have been raised about the safety of genetically modified plants. Yet improving the quality of crops by bioengineering— resistance to frost or drought, to spoilage or disease, to insects or weeds—is not so different from the cross-breeding of plants and livestock that man has been practising for 10,000 years. The philosophy is the same. The difference is merely this: the technique of producing GM foods and animals depends on introducing specific genes, whose function we understand, into an organism. The technology of cross-breeding jumbles up genes without any knowledge of the outcome. Breeding new generations of animals or plants takes many years; introducing a gene into the seed of an animal or plant takes less than an hour. My view is that altering the genes of plants by one means or another is less damaging to health than eating food that has been grown in fields sprayed with pesticides.

If introducing genes into an organism is simply a more efficient way of altering its genetic make-up than traditional cross-breeding, what is all the fuss about? Well, for a start, critics say that there is a risk that the modified crop, whether it comes to your table as a slice of bread, a baked potato, tomato paste or a bowl of rice, will make you ill. Why should it? If the gene that has been introduced is that of wheat, potato, tomato or rice, there is no more risk of falling ill than there is of eating unmodified bread, potato, tomato or rice. If a foreign gene, like that of a microbe, has been introduced, the risk is greater but is still very small. Why? Because the gene is a bit of DNA and its product is a protein. DNA and protein are present in all food and are broken down to innocuous products—nucleosides in the case of DNA and amino acids in the case of protein—before being absorbed into the blood stream. The nucleosides and amino acids of microbes—and of plants for that matter—are exactly the same as those of man and all other animals. What makes one molecule of DNA or protein different from another is merely the sequence in which nucleosides are arranged in DNA, and the sequence in which amino acids are arranged in protein. It is true that occasionally a protein that is foreign to our system, like one derived from a plant or microbe, makes us ill through an immune response before it is fully degraded within the gastrointestinal tract. Allergic reactions of this kind, to proteins contained in foods like peanuts, chocolate or products made from wheat, are well documented; they occur in some people more than in others. So far, however, allergic responses to a protein made by a gene that has been deliberately introduced into a plant appear not to have been recorded. The mechanism of invoking an immune response through a protein in the gut, incidentally, is how the oral vaccines—like that for polio—work. Unfortunately, most other vaccines consist of proteins that do not function in this way and therefore need to be administered by scratching the skin or by injection into the blood stream in order to be effective; would that it were otherwise.

What are not degraded in the gut are intact, infectious microbes, because they have a protective layer of special molecules covering them. It is such microbes, bacteria like *Escherichia coli* and *Salmonella typhimurium*, that give rise to food poisoning. Others, like *Vibrio cholerae* and *Corynebacterium diphtheriae*, lead to worse diseases. In each case it is the intact microbe, not one of its proteins or its DNA, that needs to be ingested to cause the disease. The risk of falling ill from eating genetically modified food is far less than that of eating food that has begun to go off because of microbial contamination. Indeed, the very point of one type of genetically modified tomato is to prolong its shelf-life—the time before it starts to spoil. Remember that most food, however fresh, already has some bacteria in it. It is merely the rate at which they start to multiply that determines the 'sell by' date. So is GM food safe to eat? As safe, to my mind, as any other food. The production of GM foods has risen from 1.6 million hectares under cultivation worldwide a few years ago to 40 million by the turn of the century. During that time they have been eaten daily throughout Canada, USA, Mexico, China and Australia, without any adverse effects reported so far. For my part, I am ready to join them and eat any genetically modified food of the type we have been discussing that you care to put on my plate.

On the contrary, eating certain GM foods may be beneficial to health. Three examples will suffice. A compound called beta-carotene, that is present in carrots and other vegetables, helps to prevent blindness because it is converted in the body to vitamin A, a molecule that plays an important role in the visual process. Beta-carotene is also reported to boost the immune system and to counter heart disease and cancer. Tomatoes, which are one of the most widely eaten vegetables throughout the world, contain relatively low amounts of beta-carotene. By genetic manipulation it is possible to increase the content of beta-carotene threefold. Such tomatoes, once they become commercially available, will represent a genuine 'health food'. Instead of boosting beta-carotene, why not introduce vitamin A itself into common foods? At present we derive our vitamin A largely through eating expensive fish products such as cod liver oil. Since rice is the staple food of almost half the population of the world, it is the obvious target. Modifying rice to produce vitamin A would be particularly appropriate because blindness is high in parts of Asia where rice is grown and eaten: a quarter of a million children in south-east Asia become blind due to vitamin A deficiency. A report that scientists have managed to engineer rice so that it contains pro-vitamin A, a molecule readily converted to vitamin A in the body, is therefore encouraging. In terms of cost-effectiveness, however, it is hard to beat a microbe called *Spirulina* that grows in ponds in the tropics: the organism costs virtually nothing to cultivate, and a few grams of it in dried form gives a seriously malnourished child all the vitamin A—as well as iron, iodine, vitamin B_{12} and other micronutrients—that it needs to make a full recovery. My third example concerns coeliac disease, a disorder of the gastrointestinal tract that afflicts as many as 1 in 300 people in the developed world (the figures for developing countries are not known). The disease results from eating a protein called gluten that is present in foods derived from barley, wheat and rye (but not from rice or maize). In people sensitive to gluten, the protein elicits an immune (allergic) response, that leads to the destruction of intestinal cells. The reaction to gluten can be dramatic: a single communion wafer eaten every week is sufficient to cause vomiting and diarrhoea in children with coeliac disorder. One way to overcome the problem is to remove the gluten from common foods (and communion wafers). This is laborious and expensive. Altering cereal plants by genetic manipulation so that they contain the non-toxic protein of maize instead of the toxic gluten of wheat would be of obvious advantage to a large sector of the population. Such trials are now under way.

Risks to the environment from growing GM foods

The environmental argument against propagating GM food goes something like this. The novel technology is 'unnatural' and for that reason alone should be curtailed; it is organic methods of farming that should be encouraged. Note that the word 'organic' originally denoted the absence of inorganic contaminants like nitrates, and avoiding inorganic fertilizers such as ammonium phosphate. Use of the word has now been extended to exclude any manufactured product, like a synthetic weed-killer or pesticide, irrespective of the fact that such agents are organic, not inorganic, molecules. More importantly, there is a wide discrepancy in the definition of what constitutes organic foods. In Mexico, crops can be fertilised with human sewage and be called organic; elsewhere they cannot. In the UK, pigs can be given antibiotics and be termed organic, but chickens cannot. And so on. Despite such inconsistencies, there is nothing wrong with the overall aim of trying to feed the world on organically grown crops. The only problem is that it won't work: the yields are lower and the costs are higher.[14] Organic farming is a luxury of the affluent classes of western Europe (3 million hectares under cultivation), Australia (1.7 million hectares) and the USA (1 million hectares); a return to its use—all farming was of course originally organic—on a global scale could succeed only if the world population were in sharp decline. Instead, it continues to rise (although not, perhaps, as fast as once thought). Even the proponents of organic farming have their doubts. Listen to a typical supporter: 'Last year I resigned from Greenpeace because I was irritated by its dogmatic insistence that all things GM are bad and all things organic are good ... I recently bought some very expensive sticks of organic celery only to throw most of (them) away because (they) were infested with, and half-eaten by, caterpillars. I could hardly take it back and say they should have used more pesticides, could I?'. In any case, plants contain 'natural' pesticides—molecules that defend them against predators—that are present in food whether it is grown organically or not; half of those molecules tested for possible carcinogenicity proved positive. Again, over half of the ingredients of roasted coffee that have been tested have potential cancer-inducing properties. Generally, of course, the concentration of these molecules in the food that we eat is too low to pose a problem, but the risk is there.

So far as the environment is concerned, the cultivation of, for example, glyphosate-resistant or *Bacillus thuringiensis* (Bt)-toxin-containing crops (shortly to be described), directly benefits it. Anyway, do we not use the fruits of biotechnology in house and garden all the time without serious consequences? If you own a vegetable plot, are you sure that you have never resorted to any preparations to eradicate the slugs that feed on your lettuce and cabbages? If you own a pet, have you never used Frontline (fipronil) or Advantage (imidacloprid) to destroy the fleas on your cat, or Interceptor (milbemycin oxime) to eliminate the worms from your dog? Would you not employ similar remedies on yourself, if you found yourself infested with fleas or worms? Are you certain you have never used a fly spray in hot weather, or—if you happen to live in one of the southern states of the USA—hexaflumoron or permethrin powder against the termites that would otherwise destroy the foundations of your house? Yes, but these are all short-term measures, the critics respond. They do not permanently alter the environment. But has not man been doing precisely that since he started chopping down trees, cultivating domestic animals and tilling the fields from the holocene era onwards? Do you honestly believe that the environment then looked *remotely* like it does today? I appreciate that the wilful destruction of swathes of natural rain forest is to be deplored. It leads not just to the loss of valuable species of plant and animal, but to an increase in the level of carbon dioxide in the atmosphere, by preventing its absorption by leaves, and therefore contributes to global warming through the 'greenhouse' effect. Because carbon dioxide is being continuously released into the atmosphere as a result of man's activities,[15] a loss in its reabsorption through cutting down trees causes significant temperature change. For example, in the Amazon basin alone, the rate at which the rainforest is being reduced is alarming. In just one year (1996) around 18,000 square kilometres were lost, to which must be added between 10,000 and 15,000 square kilometres of foliage destroyed as a result of logging within the forest itself. Such tampering with the environment, however, is not the same as replacing a field of poorly growing corn with one of a faster-growing variety.

Recently there was an outcry in Europe in regard to rape (the seed, on this occasion, not the act). No one who travels across Europe or North America can fail to notice bright yellow fields in early summer: this is oil-seed rape or canola, a relative of mustard. Oil seed rape has gradually been replacing cereal crops in the northern hemisphere, ever since the price of grain started to fall due to overproduction. Rape seed is rich in oils, which are used in animal feeds and in the manufacture of margarine, cooking oils and other products. When it was discovered that much of the 'GM-free' rape seed that had been sown in parts of Europe actually contained some 1% of genetically modified seeds,[16] the protesters were up in arms. They ranted about possible dangers to the environment and began to destroy the fields. They did not need to do so. In order to appease them, the governments of the UK and other European Union countries themselves ordered the eradication of the crops — 12,000 acres in the UK alone — and paid the farmers compensation. The fear of losing votes outweighed the inconvenience and difficulty of persuasion; it is, after all, only tax-payers' money that pays for the weakness of Ministers. Yet there was no shred of evidence that GM rape constitutes an environmental threat. What was the nature of the 1% content of genetically modified seed? It contained a gene that makes the plant — be it rape or maize or soya — resistant to a herbicide called glyphosate. In other words, the genetic modification merely *protects* the plants being cultivated against inhibition of their growth by glyphosate. Glyphosate is a safe, cheap and effective weed-killer, but it is non-selective and kills all growing plants. Its use in farming is therefore limited, unless resistant organisms can be developed: GM technology has achieved precisely that. Such GM crops pose no more threat to animals or humans than glyphosate itself: because animal metabolism differs from that of plants in regard to the reactions that are inhibited by glyphosate, animals and humans are affected neither by the compound nor by the products of resistance genes.

And what if the resistance gene were somehow transferred to other crops? It would surely be a bonus, making them likewise resilient to being sprayed by herbicide. It is true that there is a possibility that GM 'superweeds', themselves insensitive to glyphosate, might arise, but the danger is no greater than that of weeds becoming resistant to any other herbicide in use today. Nevertheless, the unwitting generation of superweeds is rightly being carefully monitored.[17] The risk of changing the environment through the use of GM crops is the same as that caused by conventional breeding methods. If we move for a moment from hypothesis about GM technology to fact, the situation is clear. GM seeds were introduced into farming more than 10 years ago. Over 24,000 field trials have been conducted in the USA alone. Throughout this time, there has not been a single substantiated case of damage to the environment (or to health, for that matter). To me, the arguments against introducing genes that confer herbicide resistance, drought resistance, frost resistance and that lead to increased yields are not compelling to say the least.

The controversy continues. Ten years is a relatively short time for testing new technology. Genetic modification may have unforeseen long-term consequences that are beyond our control. Look at what happened with BSE in England; have you forgotten the thalidomide disaster? Such reminders have emotional appeal, but lack logic. The BSE disaster occurred because farmers ignored age-old customs and fed live-stock on their own carcasses: they should have known that cannibalism does not make good animal husbandry. The government should have stamped out the process as soon as it became aware of it. Where the BSE fiasco shares a similarity to the GM debate is in the suspicion people have of tests carried out in a different country. The French and Germans refused to accept the British tests that showed their beef to be finally safe to eat (the economic advantages of banning the import of their competitor's product may not entirely have escaped their reasoning). Now the antagonists of GM foods in Europe are ignoring countless tests carried out in the USA.

The thalidomide catastrophe occurred because insufficient animal experiments had been carried out before the drug— developed to prevent morning sickness in pregnant women—was introduced. The aim of 'animal liberation' movements in Europe and North America—to prevent animals being used to test the safety of new drugs—makes it possible that such a situation could occur again. Despite the devastating effects of thalidomide on foetal development, the drug is actually back in medical practice as a useful adjunct to prevent nausea in cancer patients receiving strong chemotherapy or radiotherapy, and it is being evaluated as an anti-cancer drug in its own right. As we saw in the previous chapter, searching for a medicament against one affliction often turns out to provide a useful therapeutic measure against another. Provided cancer patients receiving thalidomide do not go on to have children—which they are rarely likely to do—there is little reason not to use the drug.

Neither the BSE crisis nor the thalidomide tragedy involved the genes of animals or plants suddenly leaving their host and invading other organisms, which is a scenario envisaged by the opponents of GM technology. It is true that *infectious agents* do precisely this, as they did in the BSE crisis, but it happens all the time; that, after all, is how microbes propagate—searching for new hosts to invade. But infections are not known to cross the border between the plant and animal kingdoms. In any case, the genes that are being introduced into plants and animals are not infective agents like prions (the infective agent in BSE) or viruses. Although the genes *are* sometimes derived from bacteria—the glyphosate resistance gene is such a one and another will be described shortly—genes on their own are rarely infectious. Scientists know only too well how infectious agents like viruses can break out from an organism and spread among populations. The genes introduced into seeds are carefully screened to ensure that they do not contain any viral DNA that might allow them to do this, although I admit that this aspect of GM technology is the least well established scientifically. On the other hand, there is little reason to suppose that a gene deliberately introduced into a plant will be transmitted into another plant, any more than one of the genes the plant already possesses. Of course some wind-borne GM seeds are as likely to settle and grow in an adjacent field as non-GM seeds. If you are a farmer (and not a protestor who has overnight acquired the knowledge of agriculture, animal husbandry, biochemistry, microbiology, pharmacology and genetics), would you actually mind if your crop suddenly became more prolific, more resistant to drought or frost, less susceptible to damage by herbicides or insects? All without any cost to yourself?[18]

Another shift of argument. How about the effect of GM crops on other wildlife, like birds and insects? Did not the spraying of crops with DDT in the 1950s have disastrous consequences? Quite so, but that is precisely one of the reasons why GM technology is to be preferred. It is selective, and does not therefore suffer from the drawbacks of treatments that are indiscriminate, like DDT. A field of genetically modified maize is, at worst, unlikely to affect the environment any more than one that is sprayed with chemicals from an aeroplane. At best, it will have considerably less impact. A bee that feasts on the flower of a tomato plant engineered so that its fruit stays fresh longer, is unlikely to wreak much havoc among other tomato plants, and none among other bees or among the eventual consumer of its honey. However, it is true to say that it may transmit pollen that is resistant to herbicide to a weed, which then creates a problem. Of course, this can happen whether the pollen is from a GM plant or not, but it does place a limitation on the types of crop that may safely be genetically modified. As for the birds that suddenly find themselves deprived of their favourite meal, it is unlikely to have as much impact as the cutting down of hedges and woodland—by the non-genetic means of saw and tractor—has had; 13 species of bird living exclusively on farmland, such as the skylark, declined by an average of 30% between 1968 and 1995 in the UK. Yet through the use of GM crops, skylarks, as well as lapwings and finches, are actually reappearing in Britain.[19] The strawberry guava, a small edible and entirely 'organic' fruit introduced into Hawaii from its native Brazil recently, has destroyed plant life to such an extent that strawberry guavas are now considered the worst pest on the islands. The environment is being changed all the time, but we do little about it. In the UK, a larger percentage of its natural woodland has been lost— to farming and housing developments—than in Brazil. Older generations may regret the appearance of pylons on the sky line, but the young do not even notice them. You and I may prefer the sound of church bells to the noise of a 747 of an evening, but our children are probably indifferent to either. My point is simple. You cannot freeze the environment at any particular moment of time. You cannot prevent man from modifying it: you cannot halt his quest for change.

Resistance to antibiotics

Where I have reservations is in regard to eating food that may contain antibiotics. As mentioned in an earlier chapter, these are molecules that stop bacteria from multiplying. Most of the antibiotics that have been discovered to date are naturally-occurring products secreted by various types of mould: penicillin, streptomycin, tetracycline, cephalosporin are examples. Chemically synthesised derivatives have been introduced to try to overcome the problem of bacterial resistance. This dilemma arises because within a colony of multiplying bacteria there are always a few that are not killed by an antibiotic. Such resistant mutants are insensitive to the antibiotic because they are able to degrade or to eliminate it. Their infectivity, however, is unimpaired. If someone suffering from a bacterial infection is given an antibiotic, the chances are that all the sensitive bacteria are killed before the very small number of resistant ones are able to multiply sufficiently to cause an infection (eventually most are destroyed by the body's immune system). But if this does not happen, the resistant ones rapidly outgrow the sensitive ones and establish a colony of infectious, antibiotic-resistant bacteria. The process is similar to that which underlies the evolution of animal species: those able to breed the fastest gradually replace the others. Of course, the person who now has an infection caused by bacteria that are resistant to the antibiotic that was used, can be treated with a different class of antibiotic, to which the bacteria are sensitive. The same thing may then happen again, and so the process goes on. The trouble is that there is only a limited number of different classes of antibiotic available — no more than half a dozen at this moment — after which there is no way of eradicating the infection. The problem is compounded by the fact that bacteria can acquire resistance against several different antibiotics at once, a situation referred to as multiple-drug resistance. Since antibiotics are the only effective drugs currently available against potentially fatal diseases like bacterial pneumonia or sepsis, their use needs to be limited and very carefully controlled. Yet the number of infections caused by antibiotic-resistant bacteria is rising rapidly[20] and causing major health problems. Although these dangers have been apparent to microbiologists all along, they have gone largely unheeded by physicians. With infections of viral origin, incidentally, the problem is different: viruses are indifferent to the presence of antibiotics, so a search for new drugs that stop their multiplication is being vigorously pursued.

The practice of feeding livestock with antibiotics to prevent infections is therefore undesirable. Despite warnings at the very dawn of antibiotic discovery 50 years ago,[21] in recent years 25 million pounds — more than 10 million kilos — of antibiotics were being fed annually to cattle, pigs and poultry in the USA alone.

The danger is twofold. First, resistant strains may arise that will eventually kill the cattle, should they succumb to an infection. Second, when meat from antibiotic-containing cattle is eaten, there is a risk that some of the antibiotic will pass into one's system. The risk is not great, because antibiotics are generally destroyed by heating and will therefore be inactivated by the cooking process. Also, the amount present in those parts of the animal that are eaten are likely to be low. But antibiotics, unlike proteins, are not degraded in the gut, which is why they are effective orally. Because they are much smaller molecules—the size of cholesterol, for example—they are then readily absorbed. There is therefore a chance that some of the antibiotic fed to cattle may be ingested intact with our food. Once inside the body, there is danger that the antibiotic will encourage antibiotic-resistant bacteria to proliferate even before an infected person is treated with antibiotic.

Reading some newspaper articles, the public may be scared into thinking that eating antibiotic-containing food will make *them* resistant to subsequent treatment by an antibiotic. This is quite wrong. It is bacteria that become resistant, not people or animals. On the contrary, the reason why antibiotics are such effective medicaments is that they have no effect on man or beast: it is the microbes within us that antibiotics destroy.

To return to the danger of ingesting antibiotics unnecessarily. We harbour in our body—in the gut and on our skin—a pool of potentially pathogenic bacteria.[22] Normally the balance between antibiotic-sensitive and antibiotic-resistant strains is kept in check. Should we be exposed to antibiotics for any length of time, however, the selective pressure will favour the emergence of resistant strains.[23] The situation would be worse in regard to crops that may have the gene for an antibiotic (isolated from the relevant mould) inserted, for in this case, the antibiotic would be present in a vegetable or fruit at such a high concentration that it would most certainly be absorbed in an effective dose. That, after all, would be the aim of the genetic modification: to eat the antibiotic in the form of a tomato instead of a tablet. I am not aware that such 'designer' crops have yet been produced; their development should not be contemplated.

On the other hand, scientists are also searching for ways to engineer the genes for vaccines[24]—including an anti-fertility one that could potentially provide a new method of birth control— into plants. If they are of the type like polio vaccine that is able to initiate an immune response when taken orally, that is fine; if not, there is little point, as the vaccine will be inactivated when the plant is eaten. Several plant vaccines do appear to work through the oral route: having been tested in animals, clinical trials for human consumption are now under way. It may, however, still be preferable to take the vaccine as and when required, not at random every time a bowl of rice is eaten (although the latter may eventually be cheaper and therefore of benefit to Third World countries). Swallowing a few drops of polio vaccine is the least burdensome medication I can think of. And if we *are* contemplating the use of genetically-engineered vaccines, it is better to administer them directly to ourselves. Injecting into humans a bit of DNA coding for a microbial protein that on its own is incapable of initiating an infection, but that provides immune protection against the relevant disease, for example, is a medical advance that is well worth pursuing. Currently such 'DNA vaccines', against infections that include malaria, are being developed.

In the spring of 2001 a severe outbreak of foot and mouth disease in England meant that over a million pigs, sheep and cattle had to be destroyed, with disastrous consequences for the survival of the farming industry. Genetically engineering cattle to produce their own vaccines against afflictions like foot and mouth disease by *in vitro* fertilisation techniques[25] is another technology that may be of real economic benefit. For reasons already mentioned, eating meat from such modified cattle is unlikely either to harm or to benefit anyone. The same is true of boosting the secretion of growth hormone through genetic manipulation to make farm animals bigger. The outcome is the same as selecting large-growing animals by cross-breeding, or fattening them up with excessive calories. The consumer is unlikely to be affected because the hormone is a protein that is broken down in the gut after small quantities have been inadvertently eaten.[26] Increasing the hormone level in animals or humans is a well-established practice (but one of the reasons why consumers of hormone-fed animals have turned to 'organically' reared ones instead). Diabetics have been taking the hormone insulin (isolated from pigs, please note) for half a century and it has saved lives, not destroyed them. Menopausal women derive much comfort from an alteration of their hormone levels through hormone replacement therapy (HRT).

Foreign genes

Critics of genetically modified crops will point to the fact that one of the most common genes that is currently being introduced into plants is a foreign one, the bacterial *Bt* gene.[27] *Bt* stands for *Bacillus thuringiensis*, a microbe that produces a toxin which kills caterpillars and other forms of insect (Figure 12.1). The result is that farmers need to employ much less pesticide than would otherwise be necessary: *Bt* cotton is said to reduce pesticide use by

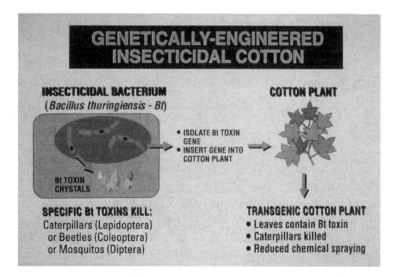

Figure 12.1 BT toxin technology. Reproduced from *Regulatory Toxicology and Pharmacology*, vol 32, F. S. Betz, B. G. Hammond and R. L. Fuchs. 'Safety and advantages of *Bacillus thuringiensis*-protected plants to control insect pests', pp 156–173, copyright 2000, with permission from Elsevier Science.

up to 60%,[28] while at the same time increasing yields up to 8%. How does the toxin do this? By making holes in the stomach lining of any caterpillar unfortunate enough to have swallowed the toxic molecule. The action of the toxin—a protein—is not so different from the action of other pore-forming proteins: the toxins secreted by *Staphylococcus aureus, Streptococcus pneumoniae* or *Clostridium perfringens* that are the cause of bacterial sepsis, pneumonia or gangrene. Knowing that, the critics will argue, only makes things worse, but admitting it shows my sense of impartiality. However, cotton or maize do not develop sepsis, nor are they susceptible to the Bt toxin, any more than man succumbs to potato blight or to tobacco mosaic virus. It is the caterpillars that feed on crops and destroy them that are eliminated by the toxin. This is no worse, but admittedly no better, than spraying crops with pesticide. The early trials with Bt toxin were in fact just that: crops were sprayed with dried bacilli.[29] The result was so successful in terms of protecting the crop that the far less damaging approach of genetically modifying plants to produce the toxin molecule themselves was developed. The toxin, unlike the bacillus from which it is derived, is completely non-infectious and cannot spread from one organism to another.

Nevertheless, a problem does exist. It is this. In any population of insect that feeds on Bt toxin containing crops, be it bollworm moths enjoying a meal of GM cotton or a caterpillar nibbling at GM maize, there is a possibility that some Bt toxin-resistant organisms are present. These will eventually outgrow the sensitive strains, and may then pass resistance to other insects of the same species through normal interbreeding. We saw earlier how antibiotic-resistant strains of bacteria begin to replace sensitive strains in the presence of the antibiotic, and the same is true of insects. It happened with insect resistance to DDT and it will happen with GM crops. It is a universal phenomenon that occurs even with human cells: one of the problems with cancer chemotherapy is the emergence of drug-resistant cells that outgrow the sensitive ones in the presence of the drug being administered. Special strategies have been devised by clinicians to cope with the dilemma, and agriculturists and ecologists need to address the same problem in regard to GM crops. It does not mean that their use should be abandoned: chemotherapy of cancer was not halted by the recognition of resistance; it was modified (no pun intended).

An alternative way to protect crops against the insects that feed on them is to eliminate the pests directly. This was tried several decades ago with DDT and resulted eventually in the emergence of DDT-resistant insects. But what if a lethal gene were introduced into the germ cells of insects so that the 'self-destruct' gene is passed to progeny during mating? It would be more difficult for the insects to become resistant in this case and an entire colony might be wiped out before it happens. In that case it could lead to the deliberate extinction of a species, which conservationists would surely find distasteful. The proponents of such a project would have to convince the objectors that losing a species is a price worth paying in order to prevent the destruction of an important crop. A target pest is the bollworm that feeds on cotton crops, and the gene to be introduced is a bacterial one that codes for an enzyme (RNAse) that destroys RNA, and hence the ability of cells to make proteins. Before this strategy is put into effect, trials will be conducted to see how rapidly the gene would spread among bollworm moths.[30] Such technology can also, of course, be applied to other pests, as well as to insects in general, to check on how rapidly foreign genes are spread among a population in the wild.

The argument shifts yet again. Genetically-modified crops are being developed to have another gene incorporated in them: a so-called 'terminator' gene, that renders them infertile, rather like seedless grapes or oranges that cannot be used to propagate new vines. In the same way, the seeds grown from crops that contain a terminator gene cannot be used for a second generation. But farmers, especially in poorer countries, often use some of their harvest for next year's sowing. In India farmers keep up to 80% of the best grain for sowing in the following year. With seeds containing a terminator gene the farmer will have to buy fresh seed all over again each successive year.[31] Inserting terminator genes therefore seems not to be good practice in so far as the interests of the developing world are concerned. The sponsors of such technology — the chief of which is the Missouri-based giant Monsanto — are aware of this: they realise that there is no point in modifying seeds with the terminator gene if farmers do not buy such grain. It is, however, a hard pill for Monsanto to swallow, seeing that it paid $1.2 billion to acquire Delta and Pine, the US seed company that owns the terminator gene patent. But Monsanto has indicated its intention not to manufacture products that contain a terminator gene.[32] In any case, we should not be too hard on Monsanto. It is after all a commercial organisation, with primary allegiance to its shareholders, who invest huge sums of money in research that governments cannot afford to foster. Let us also not forget that the aim of GM crops like *Bt* cotton is to reduce the need for pesticides: who are one of the main manufacturers of such pesticides? Monsanto. So investing in GM technology hits one of their own products. They can hardly be accused of being driven solely by greed in this case.

Viruses cause as much damage to plants as they do to animals and people. The first virus ever isolated was in fact a plant one: tobacco mosaic virus. The tobacco plant has no nutritional benefit—the opposite is true—but sugar beet, oilseed rape and potatoes do. If such crops could be 'vaccinated' against viruses that infect them[33] it would be of great economic benefit. The technology of DNA vaccines provides the answer. Certain genes from the viruses (they are all DNA viruses) are introduced into the susceptible host. This does not cause an infection, but now makes the plant resistant to attack by the relevant virus. A great deal of research has been carried out in order to test whether the procedure could lead to the generation of more virulent strains of virus, that might invade a greater range of hosts. So far the results have been encouraging, and the worst-case scenarios that have been envisaged are unlikely to occur. An important point to bear in mind is that introducing viral genes into plants poses no danger to human or animal health: plant viruses appear not to infect the animal kingdom (and animal viruses do not infect plants).

Conclusion

I began this chapter with a discussion of risk. Of course there is a risk that someone, somewhere, will fall ill after eating GM foods.

Indeed, we know they will. But there is no reason to suppose that the chance is any greater than that of falling ill from eating non-GM modified foods. Scientists employed by the UK Ministry of Agriculture, Fisheries and Food recently analysed 567 samples of ordinary, non-GM, cereal-based foods like flour: over 20% contained mites. Of course there are risks that introducing a gene directly into a plant, instead of altering genes by breeding, leads to quite unpredictable consequences. Scientists have tried to imagine what these might be, but have failed to come up with credible suggestions. They have also been monitoring the situation for a decade and have found no evidence of untoward effects. The opponents of GM foods are able to dream up scenarios of impending doom, but only because they are unfettered by scientific knowledge. The plea that all planting of GM seeds should be stopped, while at the same time asking for more trials to be carried out, lacks logic: how can you test the methodology if you forbid its implementation? Tests within the laboratory have long ago been shown to be without significant risk; if further tests are sought, they must be carried out by farmers. I promised at the start of this chapter to steer an unbiased course in assessing GM foods. Having considered both sides of the argument, I cannot but conclude that the risk to the consumers of GM products, and the risk to the environment of cultivating GM crops, are both low. If you don't believe me, search for more information: read Alan McHughen's *A Consumer's Guide to GM Food; from Green Genes to Red Herrings*[34] and other impartial accounts.[35]

Notes

1. To be exact, we would have to take into account the actual number of days per month—28 or 30 or 31—and then adjust for February having 29 days every 4 years.
2. A good introduction to risk was prepared by the British Medical Association (op. cit.) a few years ago. A more recent account is that by Gerd Gigerenzer, op. cit.
3. A disease in which the meninges—membranes in the brain that form a barrier between blood and spinal fluid—become infected: infection

by bacteria is more life-threatening than that by viruses. I am grateful to Professor Richard Moxon of Oxford University for the figures quoted here.

4. That is, approximately 1 in 1000.
5. Less than 1 in 1,000,000.
6. Two were from meningitis B, the others from totally unrelated causes.
7. As it is to many others: 5.6 billion cigarettes are still being smoked every year (see *The Stateman's Yearbook 2003*, Barry Turner (ed.), Palgrave Macmillan, Basingstoke, 2002).
8. 150 people a year are killed by falling coconuts. See Peter Barss, *J. Trauma* **21** (11): 1985.
9. Calculated according to number of flights, not distance travelled.
10. 25% of the world's population lives in poverty.
11. Living in Asia (Afghanistan and Bangladesh), Africa (Burundi, the Congo, Eritrea, Ethiopia, Liberia, Mozambique, Niger, Sierra Leone, Somalia, Zambia and Zimbabwe) and in the Caribbean (Haiti).
12. See Florence Wambugu, 'Why Africa needs agricultural biotech', *Nature* **400**: 15–16; 1999.
13. However, even with maximal yields, the global production of rice— the most important staple crop—will be insufficient to meet demand by the end of the century if current trends of population growth persist. An obvious solution, now that the entire complement of rice genes is being unravelled, is to engineer varieties that have a higher efficiency of photosynthesis. See Christopher Surridge, 'The rice squad', *Nature* **416**: 576–578; 2002.
14. It has been estimated that 2 billion people would die if the world returned solely to organic farming. See John Emsley's review of Vaclav Smil's book, *Enriching the Earth: Fritz Haber, Carl Bosch, and the Transformation of World Food*, in *Nature* **410**: 633–634; 2001.
15. Estimated at 2–4 million billion (10^{15}) tonnes per year.
16. It subsequently emerged that stocks of maize and soya were similarly contaminated with GM seeds.
17. But the agrotech business does itself no favours by blocking attempts to test some of its products: see 'Superweed study falters as seed firms deny access to transgenes', *Nature* **419**: 655; 2002.
18. The problem is the reverse: the holders of GM patents mind that farmers filch their seeds and sell them on cheaply. See K. S. Jayaraman, *Nature* **413**: 555; 2001.
19. Because in a field of glyphosate-resistant sugar beet, for example, a more abundant growth of weeds can be tolerated. The seeds of the weeds provide a desirable source of food for birds. See *The Times* of 26 December 2002.
20. The number of *Streptococcus pneumoniae* infections that are resistant to penicillin, for example, rose more than 30-fold over just 7 years in the USA: from 0.2% in 1987 to 6.6% in 1994.

21. 'Bacteriologists ... examined intestines of turkeys grown on a diet supplemented with streptomycin and found that it took only three days for a bacterial population completely resistant to the drug to appear ...': *Sci. Am.* **286** (January): 10; 2002 ('50 years ago').

22. The total number of microbes on us actually exceeds the number of cells—100 trillion—in our bodies.

23. That is why the prescription of antibiotics should be limited to severe bacterial infections: they should never be taken for a viral infection. It is also important that the patient completes the dose regime so that pockets of pathogenic bacteria do not survive.

24. William H. R. Langridge, 'Edible vaccines', *Sci. Am.* **283** (September): 48–53; 2000.

25. See Chapter 13.

26. I am not aware that eating growth hormone—as opposed to being injected with it—has any effect on our metabolism. Were it to do so, then consuming growth hormone-enriched meat would *not* be a good idea.

27. The glyphosate resistance gene that was discussed earlier is also a bacterial one, although the use of a similar gene derived from plants is being developed—not to overcome any possible health or environmental problems, but to evade patent protection of the bacterial gene.

28. 3 million litres of insecticide on crops of cotton and corn avoided.

29. The resulting products have rightly been deemed 'organic'; indeed, the preparation known as Thuricide is one of the few insecticides approved of by the organic movement.

30. In order to do this, a harmless gene derived from a jellyfish, that makes cells glow green when it is expressed, will be introduced into bollworm moth larvae instead of the intended lethal gene. By following the appearance of fluorescent moths, the spread of the gene among the population of bollworm moths can be assessed.

31. See John Vidal, 'The seeds of wrath', in *Guardian Weekend* of 19 June 1999.

32. And having kept their word, now find that scientists are asking for a return to terminator gene technology: the rationale for its use is to halt any unwarranted spread of GM crops into neighbouring areas; see 'The terminator's back', in *Sci. Am.* **287** (September): 16; 2002.

33. Beet mild yellowing virus, beet western yellow virus and potato leaf roll virus are examples.

34. Alan McHughen, op. cit.; sold as *Pandora's Picnic Basket* in the USA.

35. Click on to the website of the Animal and Plant Health Inspection Service of the US Federal Department of Agriculture, **http://www.aphis.usda.gov**

CHAPTER THIRTEEN

Tinkering with genes 2: The people

The technology of sequencing DNA—pinpointing the exact position of every A, C, G or T base along its length—has recently been applied to all 23 human chromosomes. Since there are 3 billion bases, the task is not inconsiderable. An international project, funded by governments and private charities, called the Human Genome Project (HGP) was set up to complete this undertaking. Its aim was nothing less than to produce a print-out of the precise sequence of every gene—plus the sequence of the 10 times longer stretches of DNA that separate them—in the human body. You may wonder how chemical analysis of DNA is able to distinguish between genetic and non-genetic regions. The answer is that it cannot.[1] The project was due to be completed by 2005. In the event, the venture was just about finished 5 years earlier. Why? Because an innovative and entrepreneurial American scientist called Craig Venter entered the field. Venter had devised a much quicker method of fitting together the many DNA sequences that were being generated by the sequencing machines. It has to be appreciated that the DNA of any one chromosome is far too large a molecule to allow one simply to start sequencing at one end and continue through to the other end. The molecule has first to be split up into thousands of shorter stretches—many of them overlapping—that can then be sequenced and arranged in order. Venter, who had set up a commercial company to raise the necessary funds, was able to do this more rapidly than the HGP scientists. Competition is healthy, and two groups searching for the same goal are likely to achieve it quicker. Once there, the two sets of data can be compared: agreement between them validates the results. There is only one snag. The HGP teams had always assumed that their findings would be published in the scientific literature and therefore freely available to all. Venter and his company, the appropriately named Celera ('speedy'), needed to recover their costs. To do this, his results would have to be patented. There was considerable dispute between the two sides (other commercial companies had entered the fray), but in the end a compromise of sorts was reached. The important point for us is that in principle the composition of every protein in our body is now known. There are two reservations. First, knowing the sequence of a protein tells us nothing about its function. Learning what all the proteins in our body actually do ('proteomics') is the next task, and is likely to take at least as long as identifying them in the first place. Second, the proteins that have been sequenced through their genes are not yours or mine. As I have mentioned earlier, some proteins—like insulin—are the same in all humans. But most proteins—especially those that underlie human individuality—differ very slightly from person to person. The teams sequenced the genes of *a* human being (actually several), which has given us a good idea of the general composition of the proteins in our body. If we want to know precisely which of *our* proteins might be faulty or even missing entirely, and therefore predispose us to some disease, we need to have our own genes sequenced. The achievements of HGP and Venter, by identifying the place along the chromosomes where the gene for any one protein is located, have made this a relatively straightforward task. Soon it will be as easy to have your genes analysed as your cholesterol content measured.

Gene therapy

The recogniton that some of the most debilitating diseases are due to a single faulty gene means that therapy by administration of a healthy counterpart of that gene (or knocking out the bad gene if it is dominant[2]) is in theory possible. Such diseases include hypertriglyceridaemia (too much fat in our blood stream), hypercholesterolaemia (too much cholesterol), cystic fibrosis (malfunctioning of lungs and pancreas), the haemoglobinopathies (disorders of the blood due to faulty haemoglobin) and many others. All are fairly rare. The most common, hypercholesterolaemia, occurs in 2 out of every 1000 live births; cystic fibrosis has a frequency of 0.5 (or less in certain populations) in 1000 live births. Where relatively simple treatments exist, such as cutting back on cholesterol and other fats, this is the obvious course to follow. But dietary control alone is often insufficient. It is not even an option in the case of cystic fibrosis, where sufferers face a difficult life style and in most cases an early death. The gene that is responsible has been identified and the protein for which it codes shown to be faulty in a recessive manner; that is to say, it does not interfere if the normal, 'healthy' version of the protein is present alongside it in a cell.[2]

The healthy counterpart of the gene responsible for cystic fibrosis has been isolated and is ready to be introduced into those suffering from the disease. The reader might rightly wonder, why bother with the gene; why not inject the healthy protein directly, as has been done for insulin in the case of diabetes for half a century? The reason is that proteins are constantly being degraded in the cells of the body, whereas DNA is relatively stable and, more to the point, DNA replicates itself and therefore continues to produce the relevant protein. In the case of diabetes, insulin does not need to enter cells. It works from the outside, within the blood stream, where it is not degraded so rapidly. However, as every insulin-dependent[3] diabetic knows, an injection of insulin once a day or more, for life, is a major burden. Insulin-dependent diabetics, like sufferers from cystic fibrosis, would be happy if a single, or even an occasional, administration of the gene would work, but there are difficulties. In the case of diabetes the gene for insulin—in contrast to insulin itself—would require injection into a small and specific group of cells called 'islets' within the pancreas, that is responsible for the synthesis and secretion of insulin. Such a procedure is currently not available. On the other hand, transplanting islet cells from a recently deceased but otherwise healthy person, such as a road accident victim, in the way that organs like heart and kidney are transplanted, does work. The islets do not need to be placed into the pancreas: transplantation to the liver (which is more accessible) works equally well, since the only function that islet cells perform is to monitor blood glucose and to secrete insulin whenever the glucose concentration rises. Of course, patients need to be treated with immunosuppressive drugs, as in any other transplantation procedure.

The problems associated with the targeting of specific genes is a general one. They pertain, for example, to sufferers from cystic fibrosis, but since there is no alternative, direct administration of DNA containing the missing gene is now being tested. Malfunctioning of the lungs is more serious than a poorly working pancreas: most sufferers with cystic fibrosis die of a lung infection because of accumulated mucus, rather than of pancreatic failure. Various preparations have therefore been designed as inhalants so that the necessary gene can reach the lungs directly. The results of such clinical trials have so far not been very encouraging, due to the fact that the technology for introducing the gene into a large number of cells simultaneously is not easy; nor has it been possible to incorporate the gene into the relevant chromosome so that its replication is assured. Treatment therefore requires repeated administration of the gene. Nevertheless, these are technical problems which further research and development should be able to solve. Patients with the disease may take heart from the knowledge that a curtailment of their misery is round the corner, and a possible cure not too far ahead.

I have described gene therapy for cystic fibrosis in some detail because the approach is in principle applicable to other single-gene disorders. Clinical trials involving gene therapy for the disease known as adenosine deaminase deficiency, in which patients suffer from severe immunodeficiency, for example, were initiated already a decade ago. Muscular dystrophy and hypercholesterolaemia are among future targets. Most of the common diseases that afflict us, however, are the result of the absence or mutation not of a single gene, but of the malfunctioning of several genes simultaneously, coupled to strong environmental influences like infectious episodes or an inappropriate diet. Even if the hereditary component is slight, though, this does not mean that gene therapy cannot help to alleviate the problem. Such diseases are obviously trickier to deal with than single-gene disorders, but they are still well within the goal of today's scientific explorers. Cardiovascular disease, arthritis, even cancer and leukaemias, are potential candidates. To me, there is little moral objection to this type of genetic replacement therapy. The fact that as yet it does not work too well because it is still in its infancy is surely beside the point. Would you deny sufferers hope by banning the technology?

Opponents of gene therapy are on firmer ground if genes unrelated to a serious disease are introduced. Administration of the gene for growth hormone to a child who lacks it and is fated to develop into a midget is one thing, but administration of an extra dose of the gene to one's son because one would like him to be taller than the other boys at school, is another.[4] Tinkering with genes so that your offspring may be blue-eyed or blond, competitive or docile, are still in the future but such issues will undoubtedly surface over the next decades. Already now the injection of genes not into organs like lung or liver, pancreas or kidney, heart or brain, where they alleviate the suffering of an individual without affecting his or her progeny, but into the germ cells, whence they are then passed on from generation to generation, is in principle achievable. It is being seriously advocated to prevent (in the long term to eliminate) lethal diseases. A first target would be muscular dystrophy, which affects predominantly males, by injection of the relevant gene into the testes. The time of 'designer babies' is not so far away. Indeed, the technique of *in vitro* fertilisation (that will be described in a moment), combined with gene therapy, makes this possible in a fairly straightforward way. Should it be condoned for producing offspring who would otherwise be condemned to a lethal disease? Would it be such a bad thing if a faulty gene were to disappear from the population? These are indeed matters for public debate. In the case of animals, introduction of genes into the germline is already happening for breeding purposes and, as discussed below under xenotransplantation, for generating human proteins in animals.

In vitro fertilisation

What about test tube babies and human clones? Fundamental to these technologies is the realisation that conception does not need to involve sexual congress. The semen from male ejaculate can be collected and introduced artificially into the vagina of an ovulating female: the eventual offspring is normal in every way. Artificial insemination has been used to breed horses, sheep and cattle for centuries. There is only one proviso: the seminal fluid has to be freshly obtained, or immediately frozen. The reason is as follows. Sperm needs to travel a considerable distance up the uterine tract to encounter a recently released egg, and is dependent on its flagellum to provide the necessary motion. Aged sperm that generates insufficient energy[5] to drive its flagellar motor is no more able to travel through the fluid of the uterine tract than a tired gondolier is capable of propelling his craft up the waters of the Grand Canal. If sperm—or any other cell for that matter—is carefully frozen and stored in liquid nitrogen,[6] its metabolism is halted but not destroyed. Cells can be stored in this manner for years. On thawing, their ability to generate ATP through the oxidation of nutrients is restored and, in the case of sperm, motility is re-established. Human artificial insemination has been practised for a surprisingly long time. John Hunter, the innovative eighteenth century surgeon at St George's Hospital in London, is recorded as using a syringe in order to impregnate a woman with the sperm of her husband, who suffered from the congenital anomaly known as hypospadia. In this ailment the urethra does not terminate at the end of the penis, making it impossible to release sperm directly into the vagina. Following John Hunter's intervention, a healthy baby was subsequently born to the grateful couple. Hunter died shortly thereafter, on 16 October 1793, the day on which Marie Antoinette went to the guillotine in Paris; she and her hapless husband Louis XVI might well have benefited from John Hunter's assistance 23 years earlier.[7]

There are other reasons for the failure to have children. If a man produces rather few sperm in his ejaculate, there may be insufficient for even a single one to reach the uterus: of the many millions of sperm in a typical ejaculate, most never make it to their final destination, for loss of motility sets in very quickly. In some cases, sperm lack sufficient motility in the first place. On the woman's part, a blocked Fallopian tube[8] is a fairly common cause of infertility. It is to surmount such problems that *in vitro* fertilisation (IVF) was developed.

The technique of IVF is, in principle, straightforward. A number of eggs are surgically removed from a woman at the time of ovulation and mixed with the sperm of her partner in a dish made of glass (whence the Latin *in vitro*) or plastic, under strictly sterile conditions. Once sperm have fertilised the eggs, development is allowed to proceed for a few cell divisions. Some of the resulting embryos are then implanted directly into the womb of the female donor. What is difficult is to ensure that the fertilised egg is not damaged in any way, and that the implanted embryo proceeds to term. Currently, the number that do so is barely 15%, which is why more than one embryo is implanted. If too many are implanted and all develop successfully, then twins, triplets, quadruplets and more are likely to result, which is not always a desired outcome. Generally, therefore, only two, sometimes three, embryos are implanted. Screening the embryos for potential defects before implantation and discarding doubtful ones would improve the success rate and reduce the number that need to be implanted. The procedure of IVF followed by genetic screening is likely to be taken in the future by women who repeatedly fail to become pregnant. Technical problems when IVF was begun in Britain over 20 years ago were compounded by the outcry from the public against tampering with nature in this way. The profession first opposed IVF on the grounds that it would not work; when the initial experiments with rabbits proved successful, they joined the public in condemning it on moral grounds. Two men had the courage of their convictions, that to enable infertile couples to have a child is not morally reprehensible, and persevered. Robert Edwards, a physiologist who had pioneered the rabbit experiments, and Patrick Steptoe, an obstetrician, in late 1977 implanted an embryo produced by IVF into the womb of a woman unable to conceive normally. On 25 July 1978, the first test tube baby, Louise Jay Brown, was born normal and healthy, as she is to this day. Since then, IVF has become almost commonplace in countries like Australia, Belgium, Egypt, France, Malaysia, The Netherlands, Pakistan, Thailand, Turkey, UK, USA and Venezuela. By 1995, 150,000 babies worldwide had been born using the technique of IVF, and the number is estimated to reach 500,000 in the USA alone by 2005. [By a strange coincidence, just as I am writing these words, two flies are mating at my work table (we are in the middle of a hot Andalucian summer). Unlike the writhing of our own species, the flies are locked together, completely still for almost an hour. What they do not realise is that the bed on which they have chosen to plight their troth is the outside of my can of fly spray].

The figures quoted above include the situation in which an embryo is implanted not into the womb of the donor mother, but into a surrogate mother, who then bears the developing foetus to maturity. The offspring in this case will have the genes of the maternal and paternal donors, but the expression of some of those genes will have been influenced by the environment inside the recipient mother's womb. Medical reasons for surrogacy might be the donor's lack of a proper womb, or the fact that she is suffering from a severe illness—sometimes even a terminal one like cancer. The ability to store sperm *or* eggs also means that conception, generally through a surrogate, can be delayed well beyond the menopause, during which time a woman can continue to hold down a full-time job. IVF is likely also to become more commonplace in situations where there is a risk of inheriting potentially lethal or debilitating genes. Currently there are two techniques for prenatal diagnosis: chorionic villus sampling, by which a few cells from the growing placenta are removed, is carried out during the first trimester;[9] amniocentesis, in which foetal cells from the amniotic fluid are sampled, is normally performed during the second trimester. In each case, genetic analysis of the cells is able to predict conditions like Down's syndrome, autism or spina bifida, or potential disorders such as muscular dystrophy, cystic fibrosis, or even cancer of the breast later on in life.

Diagnosis can be followed by an abortion if called for. Sometimes this is not even necessary, because certain crippling diseases can be checked if treatment is commenced early enough. As yet, however, this is generally not the case, and the pregnancy is terminated. Where the paternity of a foetus is in doubt, this can also now be checked by prenatal diagnosis, and the appropriate action taken. Of course, in those countries[10] where religious dogma triumphs over parental choice and abortion is limited or proscribed, this is not an option. 'Pro-lifers' please note that the number of abortions performed in countries where it is banned greatly exceeds that in countries where it is legal.[11] Genetic analysis of an embryo generated by IVF means that an embryo that is likely to develop into a severely debilitated child is simply not implanted. The technique, known as Pre-implantation Genetic Diagnosis (PGD), is not necessarily harmful. With skill and proper training, it is possible to remove 1 or 2 cells from an embryo at the 8-cell stage, without prejudicing the ability of the remaining cell mass to develop into a normal embryo. Genetic analysis based on material obtained from only one or two cells may be exacting, but is feasible, especially as the technology to do this is continuously being improved. For many people who know that they carry potentially lethal genes, the decision to use IVF and not to emplant the embryo if the diagnosis is bad is a less traumatic one than to terminate a pregnancy. And who knows, religious organisations may eventually come around to the same view.

Cloning

A few years ago Dolly the sheep—and the following year Cumulina the mouse—gained international notoriety: each had arisen by 'cloning'. The technique goes roughly as follows. Cells are isolated from the tissue of an adult animal: it does not matter too much from what part of the animal the cell is taken, whether from a piece of intestine or liver, neither does it matter whether it is from a male or a female. The cells are then propagated outside the body in a dish, dividing time and again, until a colony of identical cells is produced. One of those cells is then taken and its nucleus, the repository of the genetic material, is drawn into a narrow glass pipette (essentially just a narrow tube). The nucleus is then injected into an egg that has been shed by a female and placed in a dish, similar to IVF technology. The difference is that in this case the egg has first had *its* nucleus removed and discarded. Unlike a normal, fertilised egg that contains one set of paternal genes from the sperm and one set of maternal genes from the egg, the enucleated egg into which the nucleus of the adult cell has been injected contains both the paternal and maternal genes of the donor nucleus, and none of the genes from the egg. The egg is activated[12] and allowed to develop into an embryo. This is then implanted into a suitable female recipient (either the original donor of the egg, or another one), just as in human IVF. When the young—the term 'offspring' no longer seems appropriate—is eventually born, it is in essence a clone, an exact replica, of the animal from which the nucleus was taken: if taken from a male, it will be a male, if taken from a female, it will be a female.

Well, not quite an exact replica, for two reasons. First, the enucleated egg does contribute some genes to the offspring, because certain genes are present in the cytoplasm of the cell outside the nucleus, in the subcellular structures called mitochondria, of which there are some 100,000 in a mammalian egg. Mitochondrial genes code largely for proteins concerned with energy metabolism. As seen in an earlier chapter, they are always passed on through the female line, because sperm does not contribute any mitochondrial genes when it fertilises an egg.[13] The second reason why a cloned animal is not an exact replica of its donor, is that the maternal environment in which the embryo develops affects the expression of certain of its genes. The reason why the public press, and it has to be said the scientific papers that described the cloning of Dolly and Cumulina, did not mention these facts is that neither mitochondrial genes nor the environment within the womb appeared to affect their external features: the offspring *looked* like exact replicas of their donors. More recently, a kitten has been cloned from a donor cat. In this instance the pigmentation pattern of its coat—it was a black and white tabby—resembled that of the donor almost completely, yet not quite. Since the surrogate mother's pigmentation was completely different (ruling out an influence of mitochondrial genes), it appears that the development of pigmentation is in part affected by the environment in which an embryo develops.[14] The same will be true of qualities like intelligence and a predisposition to diseases like diabetes, heart attack or stroke, that are known to be influenced by non-genetic factors within the womb. Where a surrogate mother's mitochondrial genes might play a part is in situations where she has one of the rare disorders associated with mitochondrial gene dysfunction.

I should point out another fact. The whole procedure of generating a complete organism from the nucleus of one of its differentiated cells, such as intestinal epithelium, depends on the fact that all the genes in most cells are an exact replica of the genes in the fertilised egg. We know that DNA—the entire genome—is reproduced faithfully at each cell division. This means that cell specialisation—the development of liver and heart, brain and intestine, muscle and kidney—is due not to a change in the genetic content of the cells that constitute those organs, but to a change in their expression. In other words, the nucleus of differentiated cells has totipotency. This important scientific fact was shown over 30 years ago by an English scientist called John Gurdon, then working in Oxford. He refined earlier attempts along these lines by two American scientists, Robert Briggs and Thomas King, and was able to generate a freely swimming tadpole from the nucleus of an intestinal cell taken from an adult frog.[15] That was a scientific discovery worthy of a Nobel Prize (for which the world is still waiting). Cloning Dolly and Cumulina were very skilful technological advances that adapted to mammals a technique previously shown to work with amphibia.

What is the likelihood that in the future we shall be able to clone near-replicas of ourselves? The technology already largely exists, so the debate is not about scientific feasibility but about public acceptability of the result. At present attitudes are against allowing human clones to be produced. But opinions change. Not so long ago, suicide was a crime in countries that now accept it; religious leaders still condemn it.[16] Euthanasia is illegal in most countries; The Netherlands are a notable exception. I have already discussed how attitudes towards abortion differ: in the USA today the moral issue has become a political one. Some hundred years ago men were hanged for petty theft; today the death penalty for murderers no longer exists in most countries. Who is to say what the attitude of different societies towards human cloning will be in 10, or in 100, years? The appropriately named Dr Richard Seed, who is an American physicist, has launched a campaign to clone a human being, despite opposition.[17] What I shall repeat is that scientific advances are unstoppable: man's thirst for knowledge and novelty cannot be quenched. In any case, the potential technologies arising out of scientific discoveries are often not apparent for many years, and then may lead to benefit as much as to harm. Does cloning—not of people—provide any benefits?

Indeed it does. The following is an example, although it is not 'cloning' in the sense that whole organisms are reproduced. Cells taken from an adult, or a child for that matter, can now be propagated to produce a mass of identical cells; getting differentiated cells to do this had been a stumbling block in the past, but the techniques for achieving it have now been worked out. It is therefore possible to take skin cells, for example, and grow out a sheet of skin tissue. This is likely to be of immense advantage to people suffering from major burns. At present, grafting whole pieces of skin from one part of the body to the affected areas is the only solution. Taking merely a few cells would be an obvious boon. Of course, the patient will have to wait for the cells to grow into large enough pieces to be of use, so ways of speeding up cell division are being investigated. In principle, one could freeze skin cells taken from a healthy individual for their subsequent use in an emergency: for men, the foreskin is the easiest source and provides not just a few cells, but billions in one go; from a single piece of foreskin an amount of skin tissue equivalent in size to the area of a football field can be generated in a relatively short time. Replacement of other organs and tissues is more difficult but promises even more substantial rewards: liver cells for someone suffering from hepatitis, heart cells for someone with heart failure, kidney cells for nephritis, pancreas cells for diabetes, breast cells for a patient who has had to undergo a mastectomy because of a malignant tumour, lung cells for tuberculosis—the list is endless. In each case the newly supplied cells are not rejected because they are taken from the same person: there is complete immunological tolerance. There can be few moral objections to the procedure because one is merely multiplying differentiated cells: the germ cells are not involved. There is only one problem. The feasibility of the technique is still largely theoretical at the present time. The alternative, which is being actively pursued, is to start with IVF. Currently some 10 or so eggs are normally taken from a donor undergoing IVF treatment, from which perhaps two are fertilised and implanted. The remainder may be frozen for fertilisation and implantation at a later date, or they may be used for 'therapeutic cloning'. In this instance the donor egg is first enucleated. The nucleus of a cell taken from the person for whom 'spare parts' are to be grown—male or female—is then injected into the enucleated egg. The egg is activated and the resulting embryo allowed to develop for 5–6 days into a blastocyst, which is essentially a ball of undifferentiated cells. As no nervous system has yet developed,[18] the embryo may be said to be not yet 'alive', or at least not to feel pain. If a clump of cells is removed from the centre of a blastocyst and cultured on a dish, one obtains what are known as embryonic stem cells[19] (Figure 13.1). These have the capacity to undergo differentiation into various cell types like liver, skin, muscle or heart. They can also be frozen and stored for subsequent differentiation into these cell types. In other words, individuals— female or male—will be able to have recourse to the cells of any of their organs for replacement therapy, should the need arise. Immune tolerance is guaranteed.[20] With suitable immuno-suppressive drugs, of course, the recipient of embryonic stem cells does not even need to be the donor of the original adult nucleus. Therapeutic cloning is still very much in its infancy,[21] and in the first instance is likely to be used to generate cells for the repair of damaged tissue, rather than to produce entire organs. In the distant future it should be possible to transplant even nerve cells, generated in the same way, into the brain. At present the technique is restricted to the use of such cells taken from an aborted foetus: foetal cells are accepted by an unrelated individual better than adult cells, but the problem of immune rejection is not entirely overcome. The time for sufferers of Parkinson's disease, Alzheimer's disease and other neurological disorders, may indeed be at hand.

In the previous chapter, the possibilities of altering crops by introducing novel genes into their seeds were outlined. It is equally

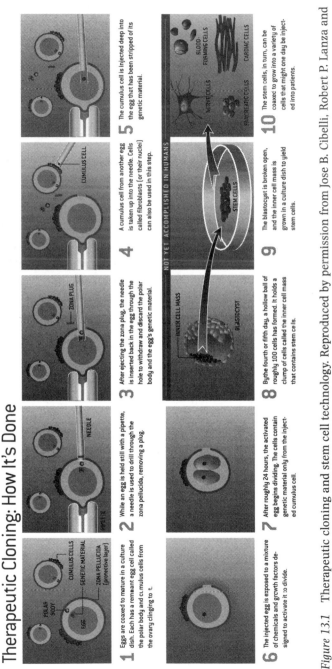

Therapeutic Cloning: How It's Done

1 Eggs are coaxed to mature in a culture dish. Each has a remnant egg cell called the polar body and cumulus cells from the ovary clinging to it.

POLAR BODY
EGG
CUMULUS CELLS
GENETIC MATERIAL
ZONA PELLUCIDA (protective layer)

2 While an egg is held still with a pipette, a needle is used to drill through the zona pellucida, removing a plug.

NEEDLE
PIPETTE

3 After ejecting the zona plug, the needle is inserted back in the egg through the hole to withdraw and discard the polar body and the **egg's** genetic material.

ZONA PLUG

4 A cumulus cell from another egg is taken up into the needle. Cells called fibroblasts (or their nuclei) can also be used in this step.

CUMULUS CELL

5 The cumulus cell is injected deep into the egg that has been stripped of its genetic material.

6 The injected egg is exposed to a mixture of chemicals and growth factors designed to activate it to divide.

7 After roughly 24 hours, the activated egg begins dividing. The cells contain genetic material only from the injected cumulus cell.

8 By the fourth or fifth day, a hollow ball of roughly 100 cells has formed. It holds a clump of cells called the inner cell mass that contains stem cells.

INNER CELL MASS
BLASTOCYST

9 The blastocyst is broken open, and the inner cell mass is grown in a culture dish to yield stem cells.

STEM CELLS

NOT YET ACCOMPLISHED IN HUMANS

10 The stem cells, in turn, can be coaxed to grow into a variety of cells that might one day be injected into patients.

NERVE CELLS
PANCREATIC CELLS
BLOOD-FORMING CELLS
CARDIAC CELLS

Figure 13.1 Therapeutic cloning and stem cell technology. Reproduced by permission from Jose B. Cibelli, Robert P. Lanza and Michael D. West, 'The first human cloned embryo', *Sci. Am.* **286** (January): 42–49; 2002.

feasible to introduce genes into the embryos of animals and humans, using the techniques of IVF and cloning. Sometimes it is not the gene that codes for a particular protein itself, but rather the bit of DNA that controls the switching on and off of that gene that is transferred. Remember that much of the DNA in our chromosomes does not code for specific proteins, but serves to boost or minimise their content in cells by regulating the *expression* of the relevant gene. In the case of animal husbandry, for example, the amount of growth hormone circulating in the blood stream can be manipulated in this way, and larger than normal animals produced. More important is likely to be the production of disease-resistant animals. This would enable farmers in western countries to cut back on feeding antibiotics to cattle (an undesirable practice, as explained in Chapter 12) and would help farmers in poorer, tropical parts of the world to breed animals resistant to blood parasites like *Trypanosoma brucei*[22] and to viruses like foot-and-mouth disease. An adaptation of the technology, by which human—not animal—genes are introduced into a farm animal, will be discussed shortly.

Xenotransplantation

Transplanting organs like kidney, heart, liver or lung obtained from cadavers has given terminally ill patients a new lease of life over the past decades. Two problems are associated with the procedure. The first is the rejection of foreign grafts by the immune system. Even tissues matched immunologically as closely as possible between donor and recipient tend to be rejected. The administration of immunosuppressive drugs, such as cyclosporin, has partly overcome the problem and enabled patients with a transplanted kidney, liver or heart to survive for more than 20 years in the best situations. But infection poses a major problem to immunosuppressed patients because the immune system, which normally acts to prevent infections, is effectively damped down. The second difficulty is a shortage of suitable organs. More than 150,000 patients worldwide are currently waiting for an organ transplant and the demand is growing at 15% per year. Only a third of these will actually be lucky enough to receive a transplant before it is too late. What can be done to remedy the situation? One solution will be to grow a person's own organ replacement through 'therapeutic cloning'. Another approach is to use the organs of an animal, such as a pig, that are of a size similar to those of humans. This is what xenotransplantation[23] is all about.

Transplants of pig liver have been carried out for some years, and seem fairly effective in liver failure. The fact that the pig organ becomes rejected after about a year generally does not matter, because the liver has the potential to regenerate itself. In other words it is sufficient to supply an alternative source of liver cells for only a limited time, during which the remnants of healthy liver cells are slowly regenerating. Once this has occurred, the need for the transplant is eliminated, and rejection is then actually beneficial. A recent advance is not to transplant the intact liver at all. Pig liver cells can be isolated and placed inside a glass column through which the blood from the patient is perfused. The pig cells carry out all the necessary metabolic changes, such as turning the alkaline ammonia of the blood into neutral urea and detoxifying other noxious molecules, without the need for any immunosuppressive therapy. Unfortunately, regeneration of other organs does not occur like that of liver, and a transplant of kidney, heart, pancreatic tissue or other organ needs to remain in place indefinitely. Recently the scientists who created Dolly the sheep by cloning have turned their attention to pigs. They have produced cloned piglets that have had the gene responsible for immune rejection by a foreign host removed[24] and therefore provide a useful source of organs for transplants. This seems a potentially valuable approach to overcome both of the problems associated with human transplants: rejection and a shortage of organs. However, there is a downside to the use of animal organs. The transplanted tissue could be harbouring a virus that may be innocuous to pigs but not to humans. It is very difficult to check for this possibility, especially in the case of retroviruses like HIV and certain leukaemia-producing viruses.[25] Of course, we all carry viral sequences that have become inadvertently inserted during our own lifetime or that of our ancestors in our chromosomes. So is the threat of yet another sequence from a pig really so dangerous?

In principle no, especially when you are suffering from a life-threatening disease. But scientists are wise to caution against the indiscriminate use of xenotransplantation in this regard. Recall, they say, what happened (most likely) when a monkey retrovirus accidentally found itself in a human host: it led to the appearance of HIV, which is now at epidemic levels in Africa and responsible for well over a million deaths a year from the ensuing disease of AIDS.

Xenotransplantation carried out in conjunction with cloning and IVF has another potential use: the preservation of animal species about to become extinct.[26] A cloned cell from a member of an endangered species is introduced into an enucleated egg from a different, non-endangered, species. The egg is activated and allowed to develop into an early embryo, which is then implanted into the donor of the egg. Provided the cloned cell has been genetically engineered so as to prevent immune rejection by the recipient animal, similar to the immune modification mentioned above for pig-human transplants, a healthy animal should be born. The first candidate for this technique is a gaur, an ox-like animal living in parts of India and south east Asia that is threatened with extinction. An ordinary Iowa cow was selected as surrogate mother. A seemingly healthy offspring was indeed born, but unfortunately died 48 hours later from a bacterial infection.[27] The next animal on the list is the giant panda (surrogate mother an American black bear). Another contender is the mountain antelope called a bongo, which is restricted to some 50 animals living in a small region in Kenya; its surrogate mother will be an eland.

Attempts have been made to clone the woolly mammoth, that became extinct 10,000 years ago, from a dead specimen found in the Siberian permafrost (surrogate mother an elephant); so far these have been unsuccessful—the DNA has become too damaged. However, there is a suggestion that a few isolated populations of woolly mammoth may have survived in remote parts of Siberia; if this turns out to be true, the species may yet be saved. Problems regarding the stability of DNA have likewise beset attempts to clone a thylacine or Tasmanian tiger from a pup preserved in alcohol since 1866.[28] Little chance, therefore, that the cloning of 65 million year-old dinosaur samples will remain anything more than science fiction. On the other hand, we may see threatened species like the cheetah and the ocelot saved by cloning. Time alone will show whether this approach really is effective for preventing the extinction of endangered animals.

An important medical development is to transplant human genes into an animal embryo through IVF in order to generate large amounts of human proteins. Patients require such proteins in order to counter the absence or loss of a particular protein, or to boost its presence. Insulin in the case of diabetes is an example of the first situation; albumin in the case of blood loss during an accident or surgery is an example of the second; thrombokinase, that helps to dissolve a blood clot, is an example of the third. To isolate these proteins from human sources has obvious limitations. Using the same protein extracted from an animal is one solution, and has worked well for insulin in the past. An alternative is to use gene technology with microbes: human genes are inserted into bacteria that then secrete the desired product. But both processes are expensive, and the yields are low. Xenotransplantation provides an alternative. So scientists have hit on the idea of introducing the human gene for the requisite protein into the germ cells of a milk-producing animal like a cow, sheep or goat.[29] By tagging the gene to one that is expressed only in mammary glands, the protein comes to be secreted in the milk. Isolation of pure human protein in large quantities is then an easy procedure.

Another technique is to engineer human genes into the germ cells of hens, so that the relevant proteins appear in the white of their eggs. From this they can be readily isolated, again in large amounts. Proteins that have potential as anti-cancer agents are currently being produced by this technique. In order to use farm animals for the preparation of human proteins, it is of course essential that they are not infected with any agent that might contaminate the protein product. Particularly important is the absence of BSE in cattle, scrapie[30] in sheep, salmonella or Newcastle disease virus in hens. But the techniques seem to work well, and the offspring of genetically modified animals continue to produce the desired proteins for generation upon generation. It is a good example of biotechnology arising out of the science of genetics and, because it is based on the use of farm animals, has been dubbed 'pharming'. The reader may wonder why one bothers to isolate the protein, sterilise it and inject it into patients. Why cannot they simply drink the milk or eat the eggs? As mentioned earlier, proteins are largely degraded in the gastrointestinal tract and for that reason administration by mouth is generally ineffective.

A potential combination of the techniques of introducing human genes into animals and transplanting animal organs into humans, is to transplant intact human cells into animals. The cells are then encouraged to grow into organs and tissues: these can then be removed from the surrogate animal host and transplanted back into humans. There is no problem about immune rejection of the organ because it comes from a human, not an animal.[31] But why are the human cells not rejected by the animal host in the first place? The trick, which has been devised by a group at the Children's Institute for Surgical Science in Philadelphia, is to inject the cells into embryos that have not yet developed an immune system. The cells that are injected are 'stem' cells similar to the embryonic stem cells mentioned above: they are undifferentiated and display fewer immune molecules on their surface. What the American scientists found by injecting human stem cells into lamb foetuses was that the adult lambs could be made to contain human cells within tissues such as skeletal muscle, heart and cartilage.

Summary

Let me return to the subject of risk, which underlies both the chapters making up Part III. In certain situations we automatically —sometimes sub-consciously—calculate risk: about to cross a busy street, for example, we look to see what traffic is approaching from either side and then take a decision to cross or not to cross. Nothing that we do in this life is risk-free. Most things that happen to us depend to a certain extent on events beyond our control and therefore contain an element of risk. To most of us, there is no such thing as an 'act of God': there are merely circumstances that are extremely unlikely. The chances of any particular situation arising can, in principle, be calculated. That, after all, is what insurance companies and bookmakers do all the time. Meteorologists may not be able to accurately *predict* a flood in Bangladesh or an earthquake in California, but they can calculate the odds. To do so, of course, it helps to have the relevant data regarding previous occurrences. In the debate about the impact of GM crops on the environment and the safety of GM foods on health, it is precisely this point that the opponents of the new technology stress: because it is novel, there is no way of calculating the odds of something going wrong. But they are only partly right.

No technological advance is so dramatic that it is impossible to calculate—at least approximately—the possibility of deleterious consequences. Scientists knew well enough the damage that the first atomic bomb was likely to inflict, and told the politicians so. That, after all, was why it was developed: to cause maximum mayhem and thereby stop a war. True, scientists did not know exactly what the long-term consequences of radioactive strontium in the body might be (it would anyway have been irrelevant to the decision to use the bomb), but they had a rough idea that radioactive fall-out would, like poisonous gas or gun-shot wounds or the terror of being killed in battle, lead to clinical problems. May I remind the doom-watchers who want all genetic modification of food and people to be halted, of the following? When Edward Jenner began vaccination against smallpox, he was accused of subverting the natural order, in the way that scientists engaged in GM research are today; yet few would now argue that vaccination against lethal diseases like smallpox, polio, typhoid or tuberculosis should be stopped. When George Stephenson introduced the first railway train to the world, doctors warned that the human body would not be able to withstand the high speeds involved (it travelled at 20 mph).

The unforeseen in gene technology—whether applied to food or to people—is largely this. When manipulating DNA, we are never sure that a gene, or an element that controls the expression of that gene, will not behave in an unexpected manner when transferred from one organism[32] to another. The possibility that unsuspected and dormant viral sequences might be transferred at the same time also exists. Am I changing my mind about the risks involved with GM foods, that I summarised at the end of the last chapter as being low? Not at all. I am merely being objective, as I promised to be at the outset. So I will readily admit that a German research group that tested the efficacy of non-infectious retroviruses as carriers for introducing modified genes into mice found that the virus had inadvertently caused some of the animals to develop leukaemia.[33] But the scientist leading these experiments pointed out that hundreds of thousands of animals treated in this way did *not* develop cancer; the odds against them doing so are in the region of 10 million to 1, although further research is clearly necessary. The possibility that genes introduced into somatic cells like lung or liver *do* find their way into the germ line, is being addressed.[34] As for the risk of falling ill from eating GM food, I repeat, this is no greater than that from eating organically grown—or any other—type of food. The risk of GM crops affecting the environment is larger, but the consequences are trivial compared to the changes man has already inflicted on the environment over the past 10,000 years. GM foods have been eaten by millions of people, and GM crops have been cultivated over many years, without any record of significant effect on health or the environment. By caving in to belligerent conservationists we may be damaging the very fabric they wish to maintain. Destruction of crops by swarms of locusts is an example. A drug called Dieldrin proved to be an effective measure against these insects, but its use was stopped because of protestations regarding its potential toxicity towards other forms of wildlife: a milder, less effective insecticide called Fenitrothion was substituted. The result? Millions of people in Africa live in fear of returning locust swarms, with devastating economic consequences. The risk involved in tampering with human genes is equally unimpressive. All medical interventions carry with it an element of risk, from taking an aspirin to undergoing a heart transplant. What we need to do in every situation is to weigh up the risk against the potential benefit.

I contend that the benefit of GM foods to a billion undernourished human beings in Africa and Asia—most of them children— outweighs any potential risks, especially those dreamt up by ill-informed protesters. I believe that the benefit of gene technology to sufferers of terminal diseases like cystic fibrosis and muscular dystrophy and cancer, of IVF to an infertile couple wishing to produce a child, of cloned brain cells to a sufferer of Parkinson's disease, of xenotransplantation to a liver patient on the verge of death, all outweigh the risks. We should thank the scientists for their quest for new technologies, not chastise them. It is not biomedical research that needs to be controlled, it is its inappropriate application. Such a dilemma was recognised already in the early seventeenth century by the English philosopher and statesman Francis Bacon: since 'knowledge is power', scientists should take an oath 'of secrecy, for the concealing of those which we think fit to keep secret; though some of those we do reveal to the state and some not'.[35] Nowadays, of course, it would not do to leave the matter in the hands of the inventors.[36] The application of science is a matter for all—scientists and laymen, politicians and voters—to decide. But please, allow logic, not cant, to determine the outcome.

Notes

1. Genes are recognised solely on the assumption that whenever the sequence of bases is able to code for a corresponding sequence of amino acids in a protein (recall the triplet code explained in Chapter 2), one is looking at a gene.
2. The words 'dominant' and 'recessive' are used in the following way. Cells generally contain two versions of any protein: that coded by the maternal gene and that coded by the paternal gene (see Chapter 2 for details). Normally these two sets of proteins are identical: the person is said to be homozygous in this regard. If one of the genes is faulty, half the proteins are normal, half are faulty (or non-existent where the bad gene makes no protein at all), a situation known as heterozygous. Provided that the faulty protein does not interfere with the functioning of the normal protein, the bad gene is termed recessive; if, however, the faulty protein prevents its normal counterpart from working, the bad gene is called dominant. Note that if both genes are faulty, the situation is homozygous once more. Disease ensues either when a person is heterozygous for a dominant gene encoding a faulty protein, or when the person is homozygous for a faulty gene (irrespective of whether it is dominant or recessive). Where an individual is heterozygous for a recessive gene, the person is usually healthy and is termed a 'carrier' of the gene, in the sense that every offspring has a 50% chance of inheriting the bad gene; when

two carriers mate, there is a 50% chance of the offspring being homozygous for the bad gene and therefore a sufferer of the disease.

3. Not all diabetics require insulin; the majority can be treated by control of the diet alone.

4. For a discussion of this topic by Francis Fukuyama, see his *Our Posthuman Future*, Profile Books, London, 2002.

5. In the form of the molecule ATP.

6. At −196 °C, just below the boiling point of nitrogen.

7. For one reason or another, Marie Antoinette did not conceive during the first 8 years of the marriage. See Antonia Fraser, *Marie Antoinette*, Weidenfeld & Nicolson, London, 2001.

8. An egg released from either of the two ovaries has to travel through one of the Fallopian tubes before it meets any sperm; once fertilised, it needs then to become implanted in the wall of the uterus.

9. Three months from conception.

10. This includes certain states of the USA.

11. Recent figures are as follows: 52 abortions per 1000 women in Peru, 45 in Chile, 44 in the Dominican Republic, 38 in Brazil, 34 in Columbia and 23 in Mexico. This compares with 26 in the USA, 17 in Australia, 15 in the UK, 14 in Japan, 10 in Finland and 6 in The Netherlands.

12. Development can be triggered by treatment with certain chemicals: sperm is not an essential component.

13. In this instance, of course, no sperm is used anyway.

14. Taeyoung Shin *et al.*, *Nature* **415**: 859; 2002.

15. Waiting for the tadpole to metamorphose into a frog was not necessary: Gurdon had made his point.

16. Although I recall attending a memorial service in a Protestant Church several years ago for a good friend who took his life after years of agonising back pain brought on initially by polio; the priest referred to 'Bill's courage' in taking his own life.

17. Another group in the USA claims to have forestalled him, but as yet confirmation of this through the scientific literature is lacking. An Italian team is said to be close on the heels of the American scientists.

18. The nervous system does not develop until well past 14 days after fertilisation.

19. See R. G. Edwards (one of the founders of IVF), 'IVF and the history of stem cells', *Nature* **413**: 349; 2001.

20. The enucleated 'host' egg does not constitute an immunological barrier.

21. Jose B. Cibelli, Robert P. Lanza and Michael D. West, *Sci. Am.* **286** (January): 42–49; 2002. But see also *Nature* **415**: 109; 2002. For a review of the relative merits of using adult stem cells as opposed to embryonic stem cells for therapeutic cloning, see Stuart H. Orkin and Sean J. Morrison, 'Stem-cell competition', *Nature* **418**: 25–27;

2002. The pros and cons of therapeutic cloning—indeed of cloning in general—have recently been addressed by experts in *Cloning* (coordinated by Anne McLaren), Council of Europe, Strasbourg, France; 2002.

22. The organism that causes African sleeping sickness. It infects cattle as well as humans.

23. The prefix 'xeno' is used to denote tissue of foreign origin. It is taken from the Greek word 'xenos' meaning 'a stranger'.

24. But see Declan Butler, 'Xenotransplant experts express caution over knock-out piglets', *Nature* **415**: 103–104; 2002.

25. Although the genes of this class of virus are made of RNA, not DNA, the body contains enzymes that are able to make a DNA copy of the RNA (see Chapter 11). The DNA could then become integrated within the DNA—in other words, the chromosomes—of the human host (there is no immune mechanism to prevent this happening). Such stretches of DNA that are essentially viral genes may then become activated at some later date and eventually form infective particles that lead to disease.

26. See Robert P. Lanza *et al.*, 'Cloning Noah's Ark', *Sci. Am.* **283** (November): 66–71; 2000.

27. See *Nature* **409**: 277; 2001.

28. The species died out 70 years ago.

29. There is no immunological barrier to manipulating genes between species in this way, since the molecules that underly the phenomenon of tissue rejection are proteins situated on the outer surface of cells, not molecules of DNA within the cell nucleus.

30. A disease somewhat similar to BSE, that is also caused by defective prions.

31. Although the donor of the cells may be unrelated to the patient requiring them, immune rejection is less severe than if they were transplanted directly from human to human.

32. Eventually even from the test tube, where it has been synthesised from scratch.

33. Zhixiong Li *et al.*, Murine leukaemia induced by retroviral gene marking, *Science* **296**: 497; 2002.

34. See *Nature* **414**: 677; 2001.

35. From Benjamin Farrington, *Francis Bacon—Philosopher of Industrial Science*, Lawrence and Wishart, 1951, p 190.

36. Although an Oath for Scientists, along the lines of the Hippocratic Oath for medical doctors, is one that is seriously being promoted by many scientists themselves.

PART IV

Speculation: a glimpse into the future

CHAPTER FOURTEEN

Extinction or survival of Homo quaerens?

*O*ne of the characteristics of searching is that you do not know what you will find. Columbus was searching for a way to reach the Indies by travelling westwards across the Atlantic: instead he discovered the Americas; 400 years on, David Livingstone was searching for the source of the Nile: what he found were the headwaters of the Congo. Newton was searching for an explanation for the movement of planets: he discovered gravity. Watson and Crick were searching for the correct structure of DNA: they discovered the way genes are expressed and duplicated. That being so, it is impossible to predict what advances lie around the corner. If you had asked anyone in 1900 to speculate on how man might be living in 2000, they might have foreseen the advent of the automobile as a more convenient form of transport than a horse and carriage or a railway train running along defined tracks, but they would not have guessed that the streets of Bombay and Bangkok, Caracas and Jakarta would become more congested with cars than those of London, Paris or New York. The advent of aircraft would not have surprised them—flying machines had been on the drawing board since Leonardo's time—but the possibility of commuting between London and New York in under 4 hours would. They might have anticipated the advent of electronic communication —the telegraph had been developed in mid-century and radio had soon followed, with Marconi sending the first transmission across the Severn Estuary from Penarth to Weston-super-Mare in 1896— but would not have thought that every schoolchild, library attendant,

QUEST

bank clerk, nurse and shop assistant would be versed in its use. They might have predicted the discovery of the north and south poles, and the ascent of Mount Everest, but they would not have imagined it feasible for men to walk on the moon.

When Max Planck put forward his quantum theory in 1900, no scientist would have predicted that its implications would lead to the everyday use of transistors, lasers or MRI scans. The nature of scientific discoveries is so haphazard, the rate of technological advance so rapid, that it is impossible to foresee the future. Serious scientists refuse to predict the course of fundamental science. When I asked a friend (a Nobel Laureate) to speculate on future discoveries in his field, he replied, 'I am an experimental scientist, not a crystal ball gazer'. Sometimes the predictions are too optimistic: the requisite technology and its financial support do not come up to scratch, and public opinion can scupper the most ingenious projects. In 1955 it was predicted that within 5 years at best and 15 years at worst, atomic-powered aeroplanes would cross the Atlantic in 30 minutes. 50 years on and it has not happened: the hazards of harnessing nuclear energy have made us wary.

The next century

You want me to try to predict what life will be like in 2100 as a result of our searches? Since I shall not be around—and neither, I suspect, will most of my readers unless they are *very* early learners who are simultaneously blessed with remarkable longevity[1]—I have nothing to lose. The doom-watchers among us, of course, think that life as we know it will virtually have ceased. Our tampering with nature and ourselves—GM crops and GM people—will lead to some catastrophic disaster. For the reasons given in the previous chapters, I do not share this view. There are people who predict cataclysmic events at every total eclipse of the sun and at the passing of a new millennium, and who mutter about the accuracy of Nostradamus' prognostications 500 years ago in forecasting President Kennedy's assassination, the end of the Cold War, Saddam Hussein's invasion of Kuwait and the death of Diana Princess of

Wales. I smile politely and change the conversation: when reason slips out of the door in the middle of a dialogue, it is best to do the same.

Of course the earth may be hit by as large an asteroid as that which collided with earth 65 million years ago.[2] The consequences of such an occurrence would indeed be calamitous, but the chances of it happening are minute.[3] Yet there are over 100,000 asteroids the size of a football field in our solar system alone.[4] We know that the probability of a small asteroid crashing into the earth with the force of 100 Hiroshima bombs on 21 September 2030 is a mere 1 in 500. Another asteroid, NT7, was also recently identified as being on a collision course with earth. Its mass is 11 billion tonnes, it is 1–2 miles in diameter, and it is orbiting the sun at 17 miles per second. If it hits earth, it will do so —on 1 February 2019—with a force of more than a million hydrogen bombs. But do not despair. Scientists are even now planning ways to deflect it from its present orbit: by attaching a huge solar-powered sail to it, by pushing it aside with a nuclear reactor, or by blasting it off course with a neutron bomb.[5]

Yet of all the species of animal and plant that might die out, surely the least likely to be affected is man: his quest for survival is too strong. Yes, man's search for extra living space, for food and for fresh water, will lead to tensions. Twenty four people are added to the world's population every 10 seconds, and by the time 8 have ticked by, a hectare of cultivatable land is lost.[6] Two-thirds of all the people who have ever lived to the age of 65 are alive today. Within 20 years, half the population of developing countries will be living in urban areas, compared with less than a third at present. Men of evil intent will try to exploit such situations[7] with ever more effective weapons of mass destruction. The technology for selectively destroying people is already to hand: the neutron bomb and lethal microbes—not to mention mass sterilisation—are examples. But it is unlikely that such an attack would go out of control sufficiently to wipe *H. sapiens* off the face of the earth. The quality of pragmatism, which is one of man's distinguishing characteristics, provides a brake against malevolent goals of global dimensions. Recall the 40 recent years of Cold War between the Soviet Union and the Western democracies, during which restraint triumphed over opportunity in the use of nuclear weaponry.

Some aspects of life in 2100 will not have changed. Controversies over new technology will persist.[8] There will still be squabbles and wars, treaties that are not kept, promises that are broken. Anarchism will be as rife as in 2000 or 1900 and acts of terror will continue to be justified on religious grounds, as they have been since the first Crusade 1000 years ago. The number of scientific break-throughs will be about the same as during the last century, but the ensuing technological advances are likely to be huge. The amount of outstanding books written, music composed or pictures painted will be no more than during the previous 100 years: those who consider that the present quality of art is already in free-fall— novels peppered with pornography, music a cacophony of sounds, prized forms of the pictorial nothing more than a can of soup or an animal pickled in formaldehyde—will be relieved. The reason for this constancy of achievement, as I have pointed out earlier, is that qualities like hatred and evil, incompetence and dishonesty, scientific flair and artistic creativity, are randomly distributed among us, and the proportion of those blessed or cursed with one or other characteristic does not change over a mere 100 years. The qualities reflect the expression of a mixture of genes that we inherit from our parents. Genes merely become reshuffled at every generation, but the total gene pool remains fairly constant. It does change slightly, but over millions, not hundreds, of years. New variants of *H. sapiens* may be emerging—no, *are* emerging—but we do not recognise them: the modifications are too subtle.

The environment changes at a faster pace, and I have emphasized that our bodily functions are determined by an interplay between genetic and environmental factors. Will alterations in the latter have affected us by 2100? Global warming is anticipated to elevate the average world temperature by as much as 60 °C over the next 100 years, compared with a 0.6 °C rise during the past century. The effect will be greatest at the poles: all Arctic ice will have melted by the turn of the next century, leaving the north pole in the middle of an ocean. The reason for such a rise in temperature is the greenhouse effect. It is caused in part by man's emission of carbon dioxide through traffic and industrial pollution, in part by methane production from an increasing number of ruminants, and in part by less carbon dioxide being absorbed by vegetation as forests are destroyed. Increases in temperature are offset or exacerbated by changes over which man has no control: variations in the global carbon cycle and in solar radiation. The first is the result of carbon dioxide from volcanic eruptions entering the atmosphere and returning as acid rain; fluctuations in the amount of carbon dioxide absorbed by plants[9] and variations in the microbial content of the oceans[10] also contribute. The second change is due to sun-spots. Man-made pollution may well be a major factor in global warming over the next century,[11] but it is by no means the only one.[12]

The consequences of global warming will be regional. The snow on the summit of mount Kilimanjaro will melt, but in northern Europe, the winters may actually be colder. Melting the ice locked in the Arctic ocean will chill the Atlantic and negate the warmth that the Gulf Stream currently brings to the British Isles and north-west Europe. The speed of the Gulf Stream has already fallen by 20% over the past 50 years. As a result London and Brussels will experience winter temperatures more typical of other regions on the same latitude: the Gulf of St Lawrence and the steppes of Siberia, both of which are frozen solid in mid-winter.[13] Conversely, the temperature of southern Europe will rise, and disease-carrying mosquitoes—transmitting viruses like dengue and West Nile Fever as well as the malarial parasite— may once more be endemic.[14] The level of the sea could rise by as much as a metre, and many coastal towns of England will need the protection of dykes that today keep the waters of the North Sea and the English Channel out of The Netherlands. These problems will be exacerbated by increased rainstorms: by the end of the century the skies over southern England will be depositing 50% more rain than at present.[15] But is global warming really so disastrous? According to that maverick duo, the late Fred Hoyle and Chandra Wickramasinghe, whom we met in Chapter 3, further global warming will be good for earth, as it will save us from the next ice age.[16] In the long term, they may be right. But so far as this century is concerned, few agree with their viewpoint.

Climatic changes will challenge the ingenuity of those who are affected, but they will have little impact on their biochemistry. The threat of malaria returning to Italy will be offset by the probable availability of a vaccine by then. Other environmental changes are more likely to leave a mark on the human population. The spread of HIV is one. In Africa, where as many as 40% of the population are infected in some countries, those resistant to developing AIDS[17] are likely to outbreed the majority who are susceptible. Such alterations in the genetic make-up of the population are happening all the time. Many people who survived the influenza pandemic of 1918 (which killed 40 million) may have done so because of a genetic advantage. Unfortunately, their descendants alive today are not necessarily protected against future epidemics because the virus undergoes continuous variation.[18] The descendants of those resistant to HIV today may therefore succumb to it tomorrow. The point I am making is that infectious microbes in the environment are responsible for genetic drift within a population: it is part of the evolutionary process. But so far as we know, susceptibility to disease is not linked to qualities like creativity or intelligence, aggression or kindness. It is for that reason that human endeavour in 2100 will not be so different from that in 2000.

Civilisations flourish, civilisations decline. Today, the term 'society' is more appropriate than 'civilisation', for man has become 'civilised' throughout the world, not necessarily by having to climb a few rungs up the ladder of achievement himself, but by passively being lifted up. Did I not say earlier that the ladder itself advances continuously upwards? That it is a moving staircase, an escalator? I am thinking particularly of sub-Saharan Africa, which has been exposed to European forms of government and technology through conquest and assimilation for several generations.[19] While slaughter and slavery decimated its population two centuries ago, famine and AIDS do so today. Yet the survivors are benefiting from Western technology in certain areas and living to an older age; it is for that reason that their production of food needs to be stepped up by new technology.

By the year 2100, the political and social map of the world will have changed. Some societies will have grown, others weakened. As the historian Oswald Spengler put it almost a century ago, 'Cultures ... bloom and age ... *but there is no ageing 'mankind'* [my italics]. Each culture has its own new possibilities of self-expression which arise, ripen, decay and never return ... [They] grow with the same aimlessness as the flowers of the field'.[20] The yardstick by which we measure success is a combination of influence and wealth: the USSR throughout most of the twentieth century had much influence with little wealth; Switzerland and Brunei had much wealth but little influence. Since the middle of the twentieth century (some historians put it even earlier), Europe has been in decline. As the English Prime Minister Lord Salisbury saw it 100 years ago, when the British Empire was still at its height: 'Whatever happens [in foreign policy] will be for the worse, and therefore it is in our interest that as little should happen as possible'. Inaction is undeniably the enemy of quest.

The diminishing influence of Europe over the past century has been matched by the ascent of the USA, whose power is still predominant at the beginning of the twenty-first century. I do not believe that a federal European Union will now reverse the trend of the past century: its stifling bureaucracy and its inflexible labour laws will render it uncompetitive in relation to other nations. In contrast, China and India, who now each contribute 20% to the world's population, should have reached their economic potential and become dominant players on the world's stage. That assumes that the south of China will not have broken away from the north — the old rivalry between the Cantonese of the south and the Mandarin speakers of the north — and that India remains a secular democracy, without Kashmir and other Muslim regions gaining independence of central government in New Delhi. The USA is likely to lose much of its influence, especially if certain States within the Union — Texas and California come to mind — were to opt for greater autonomy: political and social differences will be the reasons for secession, without a civil war this time. Within Europe, regions like Scotland and Wales, Catalonia and the Basque country, may have acquired independence of their present masters. The Middle East is unlikely to have regained the prominence it enjoyed during the first half of the past millennium (eleventh to fifteenth centuries): Islamic fundamentalism will hold it back, and the oil will have run out. Sub-Saharan Africa should witness the greatest change of any of the continents: its time for increased prosperity — currently enjoyed by a much reduced population as a result of AIDS — may finally have arrived, once the pandemic has played itself out.

Culturally as well as politically and economically, then, the emphasis will shift back—after 500 years of Western supremacy —to the East: from Europe and North America to India and China, to south-east Asia and to Japan. What is my reason for this assertion? Partly it is the 'dumbing down', the reduction to the lowest common denominator, that we are witnessing in the Western world today: in education as well as in culture. A few steps down the ladder of enlightenment. Irrespective of whether technology in the west continues to leap ahead, the education of the majority in Europe and North America—there will always be pockets of the elite—will begin to decline: it is already happening.

The International Association for the Evaluation of Educational Achievement recently studied 14 year-olds (eighth grade) in 38 countries: in science, England was ranked 9th, behind Taiwan, Singapore, Japan and (South) Korea, with the USA following in 16th place; in mathematics, England was 20th and the USA 19th, with Singapore, Korea, Taiwan, Hong Kong and Japan taking the top five places.[21] Among European countries, those of the former Eastern Bloc, like Hungary, Czech Republic and Russia itself, on average outperformed the Western democracies: their more didactic approach to teaching produces better results. It is true that the differences in achievement were not large: in science the middle-ranking countries attained a score of 88% compared with the top, while in mathematics the figure was 82%. Nevertheless, the trend is clear: the work ethic of the Far East is producing better-educated children than the more lackadaisical approach of the West. The performance of today's youngsters is an indicator of their country's performance tomorrow. When the thirst for knowledge declines, competitiveness soon wanes. An overall lowering of standards, coupled to an adherence to 'political correctness' that is actually incorrectness, ensues.

No-one nowadays is allowed to fail an examination (it is discriminatory). University graduates are barely able to write a coherent essay. In the UK a few years ago, the number of universities was doubled overnight: had the number of qualified students and teachers competent to instruct them really suddenly soared? The politicians and bureaucrats maintained that this was so, and that a large pool of able 18 year-olds and clever lecturers had long been waiting in the wings for the opportunity to engage in academic pursuits. When I was teaching at Oxford 30 years ago, a group of us young 'dons' was sent across the length and breadth of Britain to search for some of these unfulfilled scholars who were failing to gain entry to a university. We did not find them. Subsequently I located them: there were indeed students and teachers of exceptional talent, frustrated at their lot. But they were not in Manchester or Hull, Birmingham or Leicester: they were in Calcutta and Bangkok, in Accra and Baghdad, in Caracas and Mexico City. It was to enable some of them—those wishing to realise their potential in the biomedical sciences—that I subsequently founded the Oxford International Biomedical Centre. I digress.

How did the new universities of Britain fare? They flourished. The students, however, are taking courses not in philosophy, physics or psychology, but in packaging, perfumery business, pig enterprise management and popular music studies; their teachers hold professorships not in linguistics, law or literature, but in leather technology, leisure management and lighting design. If you think I am exaggerating, read Maskell and Robinson's *The New Idea of a University* for yourself.[22] We should not be surprised at this trend. The new universities were created largely out of existing polytechnics and technical colleges, and have merely remained true to their original calling: their leap in status was unaccompanied by one in intellectual curiosity. It typifies what I mean by educational dumbing down. This lowering of standards is not confined to the UK. It is happening in the USA and in other European countries as well; indeed, most cultural change since the nineteenth century is, like the prevailing wind, blown across the Atlantic from west to east. To be fair, over the past 100 years the number of children and young people receiving an education in Europe and the USA has risen enormously. My point is that growth is now being achieved at the expense of quality. So far, dumbing down has not infiltrated pockets of genuine learning like Harvard and Yale, Heidelberg and Uppsala, Oxford and Cambridge. Whether these will be able to resist the pressures of an intellectually declining society over the next 100 years one would not like to predict: the cracks are already appearing.

The reader is familiar with my views on the direction that contemporary Western art is following: a replacement of talent by *chutzpah*, of beauty by crassness, of composition by compost.[23] But cultural dumbing down embraces the whole of society. Most people —whether child or adult, married or single—do not spend their evening reading (letter-writing has all but disappeared) or listening to music: they watch television.[24] The most popular programmes are quiz shows, game shows, soap operas, gossip programmes about 'celebrities' (film stars, pop stars, fallen politicians and serial killers). The diarist has been replaced by the couch potato, the traveller in search of other cultures by the seeker of wine bars and sandy beaches. Of course, like education, far more people are able to avail themselves of entertainment and travel than a century ago, and the numbers will rise further during the next 100 years. Again, it is that very increase that is responsible for the dumbing down. Am I saying that the intellectual curiosity of the majority is less than that of a minority? Yes, I am. In any group of people, some will be intellectually more inventive, others manually more dexterous, some more athletic, others more artistic. It is the searching—for knowledge and for novel technology—of a small fraction of the population that led to the founding of primary civilisations 5000 years ago and that drove their successors upwards thereafter. Until the last century, the views of the majority had little impact on the actions of the minority, who were the innovators, the educators, the rulers: most of the people did not even have the vote.

Does an increase in living standards and a say in the governance of a country by the majority of its people then lead inevitably to its decline? Not at all. Britain was stronger at the end of the nineteenth century than it had ever been before, yet an increasing number of men were able to vote following the Reform Bills of 1832, 1867 and 1884–1885, and the standard of living had been improving since the middle of the century. Another example is that of Japan during the decades following the end of World War II. It had lost the war, but the striving of its people (coupled with Marshall Aid) more than compensated for the destruction of the country and a loss of prestige. The population was better fed, better housed and better educated than ever before, and they themselves, not the Emperor, now chose the political leaders in the Diet (recall my observations regarding hereditary rulers in Chapter 6). An educated majority does not weaken a country, it strengthens it. But a majority that has become lethargic and non-competitive heralds a nation's decline. Was this not one of the reasons for the downfall of the Easter Islanders? Did this not contribute to the demise of the Roman Empire? When searching is replaced by satisfaction, society slips a few rungs down the ladder. Aspiration is an essential ingredient for progress; arrogance is its enemy. The Nazis possessed both, but the latter proved the stronger and soon led to their downfall: China, beware. The latter point apart, I repeat that by 2100 the countries whose roots are in the Indic and Sinic civilisations—India and China, Korea and Japan, Malaysia and Thailand—will once more dominate the world: 3000 years ago the European civilisation had barely begun; today its culture is in decline. This is not an idiosyncratic viewpoint; read the French writer Jean Gimpel,[25] who foresees a similar development based not so much on 'dumbing down' as on economic decline and a consequential decrease in viable technology. The relationship between quest and human development seems undeniable.

To predict how technology will have altered the life-style of those who will be around in 2100 is impossible. Air travel should have quickened by almost another order of magnitude and tourists may be spending much of their time in space or on the moon. I say 'should' deliberately. As we saw at the beginning of this chapter, atomic-powered flight was not developed during the last century, and neither was commercial travel by rocket, despite the announcement from Bell Aviation of Buffalo in 1955 that passengers would soon be able to travel from New York to San Francisco—cruising at a maximum speed of 7500 miles per hour—in 75 minutes. The rocket's maiden flight was scheduled for 1961, but the plans were subsequently shelved. Is its realisation 140 years later too optimistic a prediction?

People in 2100 will certainly be dressed in different clothes and wearing other hairstyles. The potential for the latter is rather limited; perhaps some form of wig will return, although there will be no necessity for this by bald people, as GM hair—of any colour, that never greys—will be available. They will be eating different foods, living in different dwellings and driving different vehicles.[26] The vertical take-off car should have arrived by then; I am continuously surprised it has not been developed to date.[27]

Electronic communication will include visual displays—they are being produced even now and will be in general use over most parts of the world within a decade. Privacy? Well I suppose you can always switch everything off or shut your eyes to the monitors that stare at you from every nook and cranny of your home: displays of temperature, humidity and pollution indoors and outdoors, details of your outstanding bank loan, the price of avocados and instant three-course meals at your neighbourhood megamarket, the entertainment waiting for your patronage that evening, a run-down of the state of the greens on your favourite golf course (whether around the corner or in Tasmania), the news from cities and villages throughout the world—including the state of the liver and current sexual forays of every politician and star of screen and football field (golf and football may have been surpassed by other recreational activities, but the argument remains).

The reason for my auguries is simple. Pause and reflect on the life style of your grandparents. When they were your age, a mere half century or so ago, did their lives not differ from yours today? A little old-fashioned, perhaps? We cannot resist—even if we want to—the novel gadgets that technology throws up at us, the ever-quickening pace of life. Science and technology rarely stand still. Curiosity and change are in our genes. So shall we have learnt to subdue hurricanes and floods, volcanos and earthquakes? At present we cannot even *predict* the latter two, never mind control them. Yet earthquakes alone have cost 10 million lives throughout the world over the last century, as a result of seismic tremors that *in total* lasted less than 1 hour. The containment of floods is likely to have been achieved by building dykes the size of cathedrals along the banks of the Mississippi, the shores of Bangladesh, the rivers and coast-line of northern Europe; it is probable that by 2100 the technology for bringing rain to drought-stricken areas will have been refined and made economically viable, since it is already being developed. But the chances of controlling—let alone preventing—hurricanes, bush fires, volcanic eruptions and earthquakes are not good.

Only a decade ago, the leaders of the two greatest nations on earth—Mikhail Gorbachev of the Soviet Union and George Bush (senior) of the USA—could not meet on a destroyer in the Black

Sea *because the waves were too rough* to bring their respective craft close enough together. Each of their countries had developed the most sophisticated technology then known to man, had sent cosmonauts and astronauts into the heavens, but their rendezvous had to be cancelled. In rough weather the ferries that ply across the English Channel (La Manche) between Dover and Calais cannot put into port, and have to wait hours outside the harbour entrance for the waves to subside. If there is fog on the ground aeroplanes cannot land, and if their wing tips freeze up they cannot take off. A major snow storm brings many cities in the USA to a standstill. Man may have turned to his needs the fauna and flora on the crust of the earth, but he has been unable to control the elements above or below it. To subdue the more violent forces of nature is a challenge to which he is unlikely to have found the answers within 100 years.

On the other hand, he is planning even now to fly to Mars. In its size it more closely resembles Earth than does the Moon: gravity is one-third that on earth, not one-sixth. The journey will take 6 months; a stay of a year and a half is being planned for the first explorers of the Martian landscape. Of course they will need to take their own oxygen and food with them; water is said to be there, in the frozen state. Although by then the means of bringing along a self-sustaining little ecosystem—plants producing sufficient oxygen and nutrients—may have been devised: the ultimate source of energy will be the sun, as on earth. While some scientists are busy modifying the genes of appropriate vegetables to achieve this, others are studying the sleeping habits of black bears.[28] This is because hibernating animals have much to teach us about how to prevent muscular atrophy during long periods of inactivity and weightlessness. While on the proposed flight to Mars and back, the travellers will have lost some 40% of their muscle mass. Their bone density is likely to drop by 25%, making osteoporosis a likely outcome. In addition, the radiation absorbed en route will increase their chances of developing cancer. Yet with the advances in medical intervention that are now taking place, these problems are likely to be overcome. What do the explorers expect to find on the arid Martian surface? They[29] will be searching for footprints of any organisms that might once have lived there. Nothing as complex as an Earth-like plant or animal, but some primitive bacterium, perhaps. After all, single-celled organisms alone occupied Earth for over 2 billion years—roughly half its entire existence so far. And if the red planet does reveal forms of life, the most exciting part, of course, will be analysis of the constituent molecules: whether these prove to resemble in any way the molecules that have evolved on Earth.

Other goals will keep scientists busy throughout this century. Searching for life on a planet outside our solar system is one. The chances of discovering this by 2100 are high. The Milky Way, which is at the centre of our own galaxy, alone contains 100 billion stars; and our galaxy is only one out of some 125 billion galaxies throughout the universe. Have not the gases emitted from at least *some* of those stars coalesced to form planets in the way that vapours from our sun produced Venus and Earth, Mars and Jupiter? The answer is that they have: 75 planets have, at the time of writing, already been identified in other solar systems,[30] and the number is likely to increase to millions, if not billions, by 2100. There is therefore a good chance that some, at least, will have followed a sequence of events similar to those on Earth. The conditions for this to happen—cooling sufficiently (but not too much) and forming an insulating atmosphere so that organic molecules and some form of life can develop—are extremely stringent and unlikely; yet we know that it has happened once already. Given that it took only a billion years for life to emerge on Earth, and that many stars are more than twice as old as our sun, the assumption that such events are occurring elsewhere seems irrefutable. Indeed, they may be harbouring organisms considerably more advanced than *Homo sapiens.*

In order to test this possibility, scientists are scouring the universe for signs of extraterrestial intelligence. A radio station has been set up in the rain forest of Puerto Rico, and another one at Jodrell Bank, in Britain. Together they are scanning 20 million frequencies, listening to anything that might be coming from deep space. At the same time other instruments are searching for microwave and laser-like signals of lower wavelength.[31] So far, nothing. But within a century, who knows? And if other forms of life exist out there, will *they* have visited us by 2100? The believers in UFOs, of course, tell you that this is precisely what they have done already. The rest of us are conscious of the fact that the nearest planet so far discovered (in the constellation of Cancer) is 41 light years away. If it harbours creatures that have attained the knowledge to construct spacecraft similar to ours,[32] they would need to have set off at the time that *Homo erectus* was wandering across Eurasia: for it would take them more than 400,000 years to arrive. Our own (unmanned) Pioneer 10 spacecraft, which was launched 30 years ago, is heading for the constellation of Taurus. It passed the extremity of our solar system 19 years ago, but will take another 2 million years to reach its destination.

The next milioneum

Let us look beyond 2100, then, past another millennium, to the next milioneum.[33] The question to which you will now wish to have an answer is probably this: is our unrelenting search likely to spark off some disaster that will end man's quest for ever? Is *H. quaerens* destined for extinction? Scenarios of computers going wrong and triggering cataclysmic events, of genetically modified organisms running out of control and wiping out the human race, of robots taking over the world have been described, and not just by those using the genre of science fiction. As mentioned above, I do not share these worries. Man is the most ingenious creature on earth. He has managed to control the possible aftermath of a nuclear catastrophe through common sense, and the consequences of biological disasters—the unchecked spread of HIV, for example[34] —through scientific research, technological innovation and repeated health warnings. My conclusion, therefore, is simple: if new dangers unexpectedly arise, there is no creature better placed than man to meet them. His capacity to search for new solutions, and his mental ability to find them, will ensure his survival against all odds.

Another query is on the mind of many. Is a new species of *Homo* likely to arise over the course of time, that will eventually displace *H. quaerens*, in the way that he (perhaps) was responsible for the demise of *H. neanderthalensis*? A new species descended from ourselves, or from one of our primate relatives, *Pan troglodytes* and

Pan paniscus? Neither event is likely. In the first case, new species develop only in situations where two or more groups of their ancestor have become isolated from each other. This is what gave Charles Darwin the clue to the origin of species. He came to the conclusion that the finches on the various Galapagos Islands were different because they had lost the capacity for long flight and had therefore become separated from others of their kind. At one time a common ancestor had lived throughout the islands. Gradually a number of variant forms were thrown up on each island. Of these, one variant outgrew the others because it turned out to survive better: avoidance of predators—by having a colouration of its feathers that was a superior match for that particular environment, for example—or an enhanced ability to find food or a mate, might have been the reason. Because the conditions on each island were slightly different, the successful survivors on each varies slightly also: they became distinct species. Man has colonised the globe so throroughly that no isolated pockets are left. Moreover, he interbreeds with all others of his kind so extensively that there is little chance of a gene pool remaining separated from others for any length of time. Of course, genes are changing slowly and continuously through mutations, and it may be that a particular mutation results in an increased resistance to some new strain of lethal virus. The descendants of the resistant person who inherit the gene will then be at a selective advantage over all others. But for the reasons just given—man's mobility and his unrestricted interbreeding—such a cluster of people will not develop into a distinct species. So far as evolution out of a separate genus like *Pan* is concerned, it is an even less likely possibility. *P. troglodytes* and *P. paniscus* are threatened with extinction by man through his continual curtailment of their territory, not blessed with expansion. The chances of repeating 5 million years of human evolution in some valley of the east African rift are slim indeed. And if you think you can ape (pun intended) the process in a cage or an artificial enclosure for the same number of years, your imagination is wilder than mine.

The only place where man is likely to find an isolated breeding ground is beyond the confines of the globe: on the Moon or Mars,[35] perhaps, or on a space station in orbit. But even if it were possible to supply all the ingredients necessary—oxygen, water and food, for one—in a sustainable way for a community to be able to survive not months or years but millions of years, do you not think it likely that long before then, man's curiosity will have got the better of him and those on earth will have wanted to visit the ones in space and vice versa? Once that happens, the isolated pocket has a hole in it. And yet a self-sustaining community, like a modern Noah's Ark, might set off out of our solar system altogether, and seek life on another planet in a different corner of our galaxy, or in one beyond that. As pointed out earlier, the nearest solar system so far shown to be orbited by a planet is more than 40 light years distant. So at the present rate of space travel it would take about 400,000 years or 20,000 generations to reach it. Fine, you say: plenty of time for a new species of *Homo—H. aetheris—* to arise en route. I find myself unable to counter this, for the more futuristic a suggestion is, the more difficult to find arguments for its rejection. But then again, perhaps creatures of superior intelligence and technological know-how are already on their way here, searching for our little world. If indeed this is the case, time is on their side: they have another 7 billion years to go before our sun burns itself out and light on earth is extinguished. Long before then, however, we will already have perished. This is because prior to its end, the sun will flare up to more than 100 times its present size and heat our planet to the point that the oceans begin to boil: without water, and at such temperatures, life on earth will be as unlikely as it now is on Mercury or Venus. Human quest will have come to its end.

Notes

1. It is unlikely that the average life span will have lengthened by more than 10 years or so within the next century.
2. Whether it wiped out the dinosaurs is a matter for debate.
3. Four and a half billion years ago huge asteroids were colliding frequently with Earth. In more recent times such large impacts have taken place at least two or three times. And meteorites—smaller versions, also made of rock and metal—hail down upon us with the frequency of volcanic eruptions.

4. There are also said to be tiny particles ('strangelets'), the size of pollen grains but weighing over a ton each, that are travelling through space at 40 times the speed of sound. They are thought to be made of the subatomic particles known as quarks. Their huge momentum means that their course is barely affected by solid matter. Scientists believe that two such particles collided with the earth in 1993: one hit the Antarctic and emerged 26 seconds later from the floor of the Indian Ocean; the other hit the Pacific near the Pitcairn Islands and exited 19 seconds later from Antarctica. See the *Sunday Telegraph* of 12 May 2002. Strangelets are, however, unlikely to cause any more damage than a bullet going through a tub of butter.

5. A NASA-sponsored conference will have been held in Washington, DC, in September 2002 to discuss these issues (as reported in the *Sunday Telegraph* of 28 July 2002). See also Steve Nadis, 'Planetary protection', *Sci. Am.* **287** (October): 12; 2002.

6. Figures from the International Rice Institute, Los Baños, the Philippines. See also the article by Edward Wilson on 'The bottleneck' (an excerpt from his book, *The Future of Life*, op. cit.) in *Sci. Am.* **286** (February): 70–79; 2002.

7. Already 350 years ago Thomas Hobbes predicted that 'When all the world is overcharged with inhabitants, then the last remedy of all is war ...': op. cit. (Part II, Chapter 30, p 227).

8. Scientists will continue to tinker with genes. They may even try to recreate the common ancestor of chimpanzee and man, or an *Australopithecus* like Lucy. See *The Next Fifty Years*, a series of essays edited by John Brockman, op. cit.

9. Each year the world's vegetation (mainly forest, but also savannah and grassland) absorbs some 60 billion tonnes of carbon through photosynthesis; it releases a similar (but not identical) amount of carbon, partly through the formation of carbon dioxide at night (see Chapter 3) and partly through microbial decomposition of plant-derived matter. This figure should be compared with the amount of carbon discharged by the burning of fossil fuels by man: around 6.5 billion tonnes. See John Grace and Mark Rayment, 'Respiration in the balance', *Nature* **404**: 819–820; 2000.

10. The oceans harbour a total of some 3×10^{28} bacteria, that through their carbon and nitrogen cycles have a significant effect on climate; see John Copley, 'All at sea', *Nature* **415**: 572; 2002. So do the phytoplankton; see Paul G. Falkowski, 'The ocean's invisible forest', *Sci. Am.* **287** (August): 38–45; 2002. But whether the overall effect of the oceans on the global carbon cycle is that of a net sink or of a net source is unclear; see Paul A. del Giorgio and Carlos M. Duarte, 'Respiration in the open sea', *Nature* **420**: 379–384; 2002.

11. The Intergovernmental Panel on Climate Change (IPCC) is quite clear that 'most of the warming observed over the past 50 years is

attributable to human activities', and two of its groups are forecasting that the temperature between 2020 and 2030 will exceed by 1 °C the increase that occurred between 1990 and 2000; see Francis W. Zwiess, *Nature* **416**: 690–691; 2002. But unpredicted natural causes should not be discounted: the forest fires in Indonesia during 1997, alone, caused the global emission of carbon dioxide to double (see David Schimel and David Baker, 'The wildfire factor', *Nature* **420**: 29–30; 2002).

12. In any case, as Dr Robert E. Dickinson pointed out to the American Association for the Advancement of Science meeting in Boston on 17 February 2002, in a talk entitled 'Predicting climate change', there is so much greenhouse gas already in the atmosphere that nothing can stop the world heating up over the next century, even if the use of fossil fuels were dramatically reduced. See also Daniel Grossman, *Sci. Am.* **285** (November): 26–27; 2001.

13. But the role of the Gulf Stream in keeping northern Europe warm now appears not to be crucial. It is atmospheric currents that are the most important factor. See Richard A. Kerr, 'Mild winters mostly hot air, not Gulf Stream', *Science* **297**: 2202; 2002.

14. A mere 200 years ago, malaria was the major cause of death among people living in the salt marshes of southern England.

15. According to a study by the Climatic Research Unit at the University of East Anglia (UK), reported by Roger Dobson and Tom Robbins, 'Superstorms will raise flood threat', *Sunday Times*, 21 October 2001.

16. We should be stepping up our greenhouse gas emission, according to Fred Hoyle and Chandra Wickramasinghe, *Astrophys. Space Sci.* **275**: 367–376; 2001.

17. Because they lack a molecule on the surface of their white cells that serves as a receptor for the HIV virus. The majority of people possess the molecule and their white cells become infected when HIV enters their system.

18. Influenza, with which a billion people become infected annually is, like HIV, an RNA not a DNA virus. It therefore undergoes rapid mutation because RNA does not have as effective a 'proof-reading' mechanism as DNA.

19. The downside is a loss of traditional skills and herbal remedies.

20. Quoted by Jean Gimpel, op. cit., pp 99–100.

21. Michael O. Martin *et al.*: *TIMSS 1999 International Science Report*, International Study Center Lynch School of Education, Boston College, MA, USA (2000), pages 32 *et seq.* and Ina V. S. Mullis *et al.*: *TIMSS 1999 International Mathematics Report*, International Study Center Lynch School of Education, Boston College, MA, USA (2000), pages 32 *et seq.*

22. And if you should wish to study for a Master's degree in Airline Food, the University of Surrey at Guildford is for you. Thanks to a

generous grant from the International Flight Catering Association, a professorship in this exacting subject was recently inaugurated.

23. As with universities, the teachers of art colleges are largely to blame. Listen to former students of a typical instituton, Camberwell College of Arts in London. One complained that he could not find anyone to teach him the most basic rudiments of art. Another voiced a similar criticism: 'We did nothing about painting technique and virtually nothing about art history. It seems that if you go in doing figurative work and landscapes and come out doing figurative works and landscapes, you haven't progressed. If I'd come out doing video works of my backside, then I would have done very well' (Report from *The Times* of London, 8 July 2002).

24. See Note 39 to Chapter 3.

25. Jean Gimpel, op. cit.

26. Hydrogen gas may have replaced petrol (gasoline) as a fuel for cars. See Lawrence D. Burns *et al.*, 'Vehicle of change', *Sci. Am.* **287** (October): 40–49; 2002.

27. It was planned in the 1970s as the ULM (ultra-light motor) but never happened, largely for economic reasons.

28. Henry J. Harlow *et al.*, 'Muscle strength in overwintering bears', *Nature* **409**: 997; 2001.

29. It may well be that the human mission to Mars will be cancelled during the next few years: robots are able to carry out most of the tasks almost as well, much more cheaply, and without risk to life. See the editorial, 'Do we still need astronauts?', *Nature* **419**: 653; 2002.

30. See Tony Reichhardt, 'Planetary portraits', *Nature* **415**: 570–571; 2002; and Jack J. Lissauer, 'Extrasolar planets', *Nature* **419**: 355–358; 2002.

31. From *The Likelihood of Life on Other Planets*, a programme on UK television (Channel 4), 5 February 2001.

32. Travelling at 7×10^4 miles per hour at best.

33. There is no Latin word for a million (unlike the Chinese, the Romans considered a thousand thousand as merely 'very large' and used the phrase 'ten hundred thousand' to indicate a million). I have taken the liberty of adapting the Italian word for a million—*milione*—into milioneum in the way that a thousand—*mille*—has been turned into millenium.

34. AIDS is predicted to decline, at least in the latter part of this century.

35. See the views of Sir Martin Rees, Astronomer Royal, summarised by Adam Nathan's article, 'Destination Mars, the new Wild West', *Sunday Times*, 8 September 2002.

CHAPTER FIFTEEN

Epilogue

A straight summary of the topics covered in a book adds little to its message, and repetition is the last resort of a writer who has run out of steam. To assess, in retrospect, the soundness of a proposition, on the other hand, is not only permissable, it is surely mandatory. Let us therefore take stock.

In the Prologue I made three propositions that lie at the heart of this book. The first concerns the genetic differences between chimpanzees and humans. Our respective genomes—the totality of our DNA molecules—were shown almost two decades ago to resemble each other by more than 95%. This result can be interpreted in two ways. The first is that most of the genes of chimpanzee and man are the same, with a small number—less than 5%—being typically either 'chimp-like' or 'human'. The other interpretation is that *all* the genes are, on average, more than 95% similar and less than 5% different. I opted for the second interpretation, which leads to the conclusion that specifically 'human' genes do not exist. Scientists may search for them, but they will not find them. All they will discover are the human variants of genes present in other primates.[1] In Chapter 2 we saw that an analysis of the molecular events by which the divergence of species is brought about entirely supports that view. The argument, of course, extends throughout evolution: there are no specifically 'ape' as opposed to 'monkey' genes, and so on. All creatures that ever lived are made up of genes that can be traced back to the first multicellular member of the animal kingdom some 500 million years ago. And even that organism inherited the genes responsible for its metabolism from an archaebacterium alive 2 billion years earlier. Evolution does not produce new genes characteristic of any one species: it merely modifies existing ones and adds a few variants. We are deceived by the diversity of shape that animals assume: sea urchins and jellyfish, earthworms and ants, crocodiles and elephants. As we examine the underlying genes, we find that the wing of a bumble bee is related to the arm of a gorilla, the skin of a python to the pelt of a beaver. All structures are ultimately variations of a common theme. Of course, if we compare the genes of a chimpanzee with those of a worm like *Caenorhabditis elegans* there will be much diversity, but that is because the two organisms are separated by more than 500 million years of evolution. Consider this. There are over 10 million species of animals alive today,[2] and another 10 billion that have become extinct; we share at least 50% of our genetic make up with every one of them, but have only 30,000 genes ourselves: does this not make the existence of species-specific genes an extremely unlikely circumstance?

My second proposition was that searching is integral to all forms of life. Plants search for the sunlight that fuels their growth, and carnivorous plants search for food as well. Many microbes do the same. In that sense I have extended Alister Hardy's musing,[3] to which I referred in Chapter 1, beyond the animal kingdom to the first microbe that ever lived. It has been possible to identify some of the genes, and hence the proteins, that underly the searching process. Is there homology between the proteins involved in searching for light by plants and microbes, and the visual processes of animals, without which searching for a mate, for food and water, is impossible? The answer is that there is: I showed in Chapter 3 that several of the molecules involved in animal (and human) vision are similar to those concerned with the search and utilisation of light by plants and by photosynthetic bacteria. There is a continuum of molecular structure from the lowest to the highest forms of life: if the exploratory drive of animals is dependent on light, then it can be traced back to bacteria that first appeared on earth more than 3 billion years ago. Having written this sentence, I now find that it echoes a comment made by the philosopher Karl Popper a decade earlier: 'All living things are in search of a better world. Men, animals, plants, even unicellular organisms are constantly active. They are trying to improve their situation, or at least to avoid its deterioration'.[4]

The evolution of organisms in terms of an increasing ability for quest resolves the problems that some followers of Darwin—notably James Mark Baldwin—had at the end of the nineteenth century. To them the mind of animals did not seem to play a sufficiently important role in evolution, in the design of new creatures. In the words of the American philosopher Dan C. Dennett, they 'set out to demonstrate that animals, *by dint of their own clever activities in the world*' [Dennett's italics], 'might hasten or guide the further evolution of their species'.[5] Dennett uses a crane as an engineering analogy to describe how animals, by a 'Good Trick', might improve their organization in what he calls 'Design Space'. I have extended this idea to include all organisms —plants and microbes as well as animals—and have identified Baldwin's use of 'Mind', and Dennett's crane or Good Trick, as an organism's ability to search: the greater that skill, the more successful it becomes in evolutionary terms.[6]

The third proposition seemed at first sight paradoxical. To make the point that all organisms search, while at the same time proposing that searching is what distinguishes man from chimpanzee, appears contradictory. The discrepancy disappears by defining man's quest more precisely: it is not searching *per se*, but an increased ability to do so, that is characteristic of *Homo*. The distinction between man and chimpanzee is quantitative, not qualitative. That difference, I suggested, depends on an interplay between four attributes, a combination of which contributes to the distictitive behaviour of humans. An upright gait, which is a prerequisite for freeing the hands, had developed already in primates like *Australopithecus* and *Kenyanthropus* that preceded early species of *Homo* by several million years. Over the following 2 million years, the other qualities that typify humans gradually appeared: first, manual dexterity through a thumb that is fully rotatory, then a voice box that endows its owner with the power of speech; simultaneously with these two developments, the cortical region of the brain gradually grew in size. The acquisition of each attribute involves only a subtle variation in function and in minimal change within the underlying molecules: no more than 2 out of 715 amino acid differences between chimpanzee and man in the case of the FOXP2 protein that underlies speech and language, for example. This sits easily with my first proposition that there is no such thing as a 'human' gene.

A hundred thousand years ago, when groups of *Homo sapiens* were walking naked along the valley of the East African Rift, eating berries and hunting game—albeit with primitive weapons and tools developed already by their predecessors *H. erectus* and *H. habilis*—they did not differ so much from the *Pan troglodytes* that were living around them at that time. Since then, the genes of *H. sapiens* have hardly changed; no more than those of *P. troglodytes*. The potential of man to write and to draw, to analyse and to construct, to oppress and to humiliate, was there 100,000 years ago. We were as clever and as vindictive then as we are today. All that has occurred—especially rapidly in the last 10,000 years—is an accretion of accomplishments. As pointed out in Chapter 6, knowledge is cumulative: the achievements of one generation are passed vertically to the next, and they spread horizontally across the globe like chick-weed. Common sense, on the other hand, is as unchanging as the size of our liver or the length of the vocal cord. How well, then, does the third proposition hold up?

The more we have learnt about the behaviour of animals, and of primates in particular, the more it seems that man's ability to reason—*H. sapiens*—is not what distinguishes him from other species. Nor do I believe that consciousness is a particularly human quality. Indeed, there are those who view consciousness in humans as no more than an awareness of the environment, and in that sense are able to trace its possession back to microbes: we saw in Chapter 3 how bacteria such as *S. typhimurium* and protozoa like *Stentor*, avoid noxious stimuli by using flagella or cilia to move themselves to a new position. It is such awareness that underlies the very evolution of the animal kingdom, and I note that avoidance of danger is but the flip side of searching for food. A quarter of a century ago Richard Dawkins coined the word 'meme' as a unit of imitation to describe the cultural analogue of the gene. He derived the word from the Greek *mimeme* but shortened it to chime with 'gene', and intended it also to convey aspects of *memory* and the French *même*.[7] Just as a gene is a 'replicator' of molecular information—it is copied faithfully from generation to generation, but within evolutionary time undergoes slow variation—so a meme is a 'replicator' of ideas: of stories and songs, of habits and skills, of inventions and procedures. Somewhat like genes, these too are copied—by imitation in this instance—from generation to generation. And like genes, memes become varied with time, but at a much faster rate: in years, not millennia. Psychologists like Susan Blackmore in England believe that it is memes that set humans aside from other primates.[8] This seems to me improbable, for we know that animals from fish to mammals imitate each other all the time; Blackmore, of course, is aware of this and puts some severe restrictions on her use of the word 'imitate' in order to exclude anything instinctive, like avoiding danger. Yet, as mentioned in Chapter 4, avoiding danger is not always instinctive: moose living in Yellowstone National Park had lost the ability to recognize predators like grizzly bears and wolves after these had died out. For them to recognize such creatures as a portent of danger once more needed to be learnt, meme-like. Experiments with blackbirds show that they are capable of imitating each other for reasons other than necessity: like humans cheering at a football match, they squawk simply because other members of their group are doing it.[9] And what about the linguistic abilities of Panbanisha the pygmy chimpanzee and Koko the gorilla, described in Chapter 4? Yet language, according to Blackmore, is a typical meme. The meme concept may well illustrate some of the ways in which man uses his attributes of manual dexterity, speech and higher intellect to develop cultural patterns, but it should not be confined to *Homo sapiens*.[10] Moreover, it excludes the very quality I have considered typically human: originality of thought. Memes have no place in describing the creativity of a Leonardo or a Leibnitz, a Schubert or a Shakespeare. Invention and inspiration are surely the opposites of imitation. If memes do not underlie the human condition, what does? Is a heightened ability for quest—physical as well as intellectual— after all a more appropriate quality by which to distinguish our species from all others?

My view is that it is. Other primates stay within their habitat— man has colonised most of the globe; other primates remain on the ground—man has learnt to swim (and with a bit of help, to fly); other primates stick to their diet—man changes his at every opportunity; other primates live much the way their ancestors did—man never stops tinkering with the way he builds his shelter. Chimpanzees may be able to *use* implements like sticks to harvest termites, stones to crack nuts, or leaves to sponge themselves, but no chimpanzee in the wild has so far been observed to *make* a tool or to light a fire. Is not searching for novel ideas the most appropriate criterion by which to describe man's development of technology beyond anything imaginable in the animal world? You could argue that the cerebral features that distinguish man from chimpanzee are more accurately expressed in qualities like the ambition to succeed, the urge to create, the desire to explore, a thirst for knowledge, a craving for understanding, a yearning for challenge. But are success, creativity, discovery, knowledge and understanding not the fruits of searching? Is not a yearning to meet new challenges a form of quest? What invention has not involved trial and error, search and rejection? Have not the civilisations forged by man succeeded because of a search for novel ways of governance—autocracy, democracy, bureaucracy—and of communication—language, script, silicon chip? Which of the cultures that man has created has not been the result of a quest for utility, efficiency and art? Are scientific discoveries not the consequence of searching for a rational explanation? Is not the quality of our life the outcome of a search for improvement? Are not the current advances in genetic technology for more productive agriculture, for more effective diagnosis and therapy of disease, brought about by a quest? Chimpanzees, as well as dogs and dolphins for that matter, may well wonder about the world around them, and try to change it: but they are constrained by the relative lack of the attributes I have identified as being crucial to man's heightened proficiency for quest.

So does my description of events over the last 100,000 years— that constitutes much of this book—support the concept that man's domination of the world he inhabits is the consequence of his search? You, the reader, are the best judge of that and I await your response with anticipation, and that of my professional critics with apprehension. In order to forestall some of these, let me return to a point made in an earlier chapter. In referring to communities living a simple agricultural life away from their 'civilised' neighbours —in the Grand Valley in Papua New Guinea or along the shores of the Orinoco in Amazonia—I was careful not to attribute to them a lack of contentment: I merely noted that they had not ascended the ladder of achievement as much as others. But there are those who do not consider the escalator (Chapter 6) as leading upwards at all. To them it is a downward path: civilisation is destructive, not creative. Listen to the words of one exponent of this view, the anthropologist Robin Fox: 'Since man evolved as a hunting, omnivorous species, it follows that he will destroy animals, plants and even the other members of his species who threaten him'.[11] The pinnacle in man's history was the late Stone Age. To prevent the extinction of our species, we should strive to restore the conditions of the pre-agricultural world. We should adopt the life of the !Kung hunter-gatherers of the Kalahari in Africa, of the Yanomamo in Venezuala, of the aborigines of the Australian outback. Fox is doing no more than echoing the views of earlier writers, such as the Austrian ethologist (and Nobel Laureate for his work on the behaviour of geese) Konrad Lorenz. To Lorenz, civilisation is the same process as the domestication of animals: a regrettable and unnatural event. Although in my account of man's domination of the world I separated the two developments of agriculture and the founding of civilisations—as they are chronologically by some 5000 years—this is a minor point. If certain biologists choose to view the last 10,000 years as the Descent of Man, it is their prerogative.

My argument is different: civilisation is nothing more than a consequence of our genes. The possession of a mobile thumb, a lower-placed vocal cord and a large number of cortical neurons are the result of chance mutations in our DNA that caused *H. sapiens* to survive in neolithic times, whereas all other species of *Homo*, like Neanderthal man, died out. Why? Perhaps because they were less able to compete with *H. sapiens*' heightened ability to search. Man's monopoly of the world—that, yes, sometimes includes wanton destruction of his environment and his fellow creatures—is merely a continuation of that search. Consider it downward or upward as you will; I choose the latter simply because most people regard an increasingly sophisticated way of living as an advance, not a regression. The thrust of my argument, however, is less subjective: it is that the rate of change in our life style is greater than that of any other creature, be it a honeybee, a whale or a gorilla. And this rapidity is the result of an increased ability to exercise the innate urge for quest that resides in every living organism. Of course, I shall be accused of being a reductionist, a Darwinian who sees man's unique behaviour as merely that of a rather sophisticated animal. So be it. Did I not in an earlier book[12] deem every emotion of man, whether happiness or dispair, belief or skepticism, creativity or hatred, as eventually explainable in terms of molecular interactions? Our mind is an extemely complicated system, but complexity is not synonymous with inexplicability. Of course, the environment in which we live influences the way our molecules interact, and hence affects our behaviour as much as it does our metabolism;[13] and since our actions alter the environment —from the replacement of forests by farmland and cities to the pollution of water and air—a kind of feed-back loop between the two is set up. But that is no reason to invoke a special 'extramolecular' relationship between man and the world he inhabits in order to explain the evolution of his brain and the emergence of his culture and civilisation.

* * *

What, then, has been the message of this book? Not just to individuals, but to institutions and communities, to the nations of the world? It is simple: keep searching. A country such as Afghanistan under the Taliban, who abrogated novelty, education and art, did not survive.[14] A country like China that is bold and inventive, that experiments with novel schemes even if they sometimes fail, endures. Use the attributes with which you have been endowed—hands, voice, mind—to give full rein to your curiosity. He who seeks new trails in life prospers more than one who follows a well-trodden path. The person who retires to become a couch potato declines; the one who tackles fresh projects in old age remains astute: neurons, like muscles, last longer when exercised. Already 500 years ago Leonardo da Vinci observed that 'As iron rusts when not used, and water gets foul from standing or turns to ice when exposed to cold, so the intellect degenerates without exercise'. Cerebral searching does not mean that you have to espouse the trends of the day. If you do not like the latest shopping malls, eight-lane highways, or bustling theme parks that are growing up around your home, if you have no wish to join your colleagues in their first trip to the Moon and beyond, if you do not hanker after the sound and vision that passes for today's art, then join me in my quest: for a spot in the countryside where we may listen to the song of birds and the rustle of leaves, where we may savour the scent of nature and the aroma of woodsmoke, where we may watch a squirrel scurry away as the sun sets over the horizon, where you may plan your new project and I may write my next book.

Whatever the nature of your venture, it will surely involve an element of searching: for a successful outcome, if for nothing else. But even as you give rein to that typically human quality, I should warn you that our journey is an unbroken one:

Man is the shuttle, to whose winding quest
And passage through these looms
God ordered motion, but ordained no rest.[15]

Notes

1. And much of the 5% difference probably represents mutations in non-coding regions of DNA, as well as 'silent' mutations in genes, that have accumulated over the past 6–8 million years in chimpanzees and humans alike, and that have little functional significance.
2. The reader may wonder why I cited 10 million as the number of *all* species alive today—plants and microbes as well as animals—in an earlier chapter. The reason is that insects make up such a large majority of organisms—almost 9 million—that the rest are relatively minor in number.
3. A. C. Hardy, op. cit.
4. From Karl Popper, *In Search of a Better World: Lectures and Essays from Thirty Years*, Routledge, London and New York, 1992.
5. Daniel C. Dennett, op. cit., pp 73–80.
6. Whether evolution through natural selection explains *everything* about human (and animal) behaviour is another matter. Darwin himself left room for doubt, and Stephen Jay Gould elegantly added his own reservations in 'More things in Heaven and Earth', in Hilary and Steven Rose (eds), op. cit., pp 85–105.

7. Richard Dawkins, *The Selfish Gene*, op. cit., p 192.
8. Susan Blackmore, *Sci. Am.* **283** (October): 52–61; 2000.
9. Lee Alan Dugatkin, *Sci. Am.* **283** (October): 55; 2000.
10. See e.g. Frans de Waal, *The Ape and the Sushi Master: Cultural Reflections by a Primatologist*, Allen Lane, London, 2001, and Basic Books, New York, 2001.
11. Robin Fox, op. cit., pp 127, 218.
12. Charles Pasternak, op. cit., pp 245–276.
13. An excellent example of the reductionist approach, applied successfully to the problem of learning and memory, may be found in Eric Kandel's 2000 Nobel Lecture, 'The molecular biology of memory storage: a dialog between genes and synapses', reprinted in *Biosci. Rep.* **21**: 1–47; 2001. See also Note 27 to Chapter 2.
14. I originally wrote that sentence in the form of a prediction many months before the events during the autumn of 2001 took place.
15. Henry Vaughan, 1622–1695: 'Man', from *Silex Scintillans*.

Bibliography

The following list includes some of the articles and books I have consulted. The reader who wishes to delve deeper into certain of the topics mentioned in *Quest* may find them, as well as some textbooks I have listed, useful.

Lesley and Roy Adkins. *The Keys of Egypt: the Race to Read the Hieroglyphs.* Harper Collins, London, 2000.

Bruce Alberts, Alexander Johnson, Julian Lewis, Martin Raff, Keith Roberts and Peter Walter. *Molecular Biology of the Cell*, 4th edn. Garland Science, New York, 2002.

Karen Armstrong. *Buddha.* Weidenfeld & Nicolson/Phoenix, London, 2000.

Patrick Bateson and Paul Martin. *Design for a Life. How Behaviour Develops.* Jonathan Cape, London, 1999.

David Berlinski. *Newton's Gift. How Sir Isaac Newton Unlocked the System of the World.* Duckworth, London, 2001.

John H. and Evelyn Nagai Berthrong. *Confucianism: a Short Introduction.* Oneworld, Oxford, 2000.

Baruch S. Blumberg. *Hepatitis B: the Hunt for a Killer Virus.* Princeton University Press, Princeton, NJ, 2002.

Fernand Braudel. *Civilization and Capitalism. Fifteenth – Eighteenth Century,* vol I, 1981, and vol II, 1982 (English translation). William Collins Sons & Co, London.

British Medical Association. *The BMA Guide to Living with Risk.* Penguin, London, 1990.

John Brockman (ed.). *The Next Fifty Years.* Weidenfeld & Nicolson, London, 2002.

R. A. Buchanan. *History and Industrial Civilisation.* Macmillan, London, 1979.

Nigel Calder. *Technopolis. Social Control of the Uses of Science.* MacGibbon & Kee, London, 1969.

Luigi L. Cavalli-Sforza. *Genes, Peoples and Languages.* Allen Lane/Penguin, London, 2000.

Father Bernabe Cobo. *Inca Religion and Customs* (translated by Roland Hamilton). University of Texas Press, Austin, TX, 1990.

Peter Coles. *Einstein and the Total Eclipse.* Icon Books, Cambridge/ Totem Books, New York, 1999.

Glenn C. Conroy. *Reconstructing Human Origins: a Modern Synthesis.* W. W. Norton, New York, 1997.

Nicholas Crane. *Mercator: the Man who Mapped the Planet.* Weidenfeld & Nicolson, London, 2002.

Richard Dawkins. *The Selfish Gene.* Oxford University Press, Oxford, 1976; new edition, 1989.

Richard Dawkins. *Unweaving the Rainbow. Science, Delusion and the Appetite for Wonder.* Penguin, London, 1999.

Daniel C. Dennett. *Darwin's Dangerous Idea. Evolution and the Meanings of Life.* Allen Lane, Penguin, London, 1995.

Jared Diamond. *The Rise and Fall of the Third Chimpanzee,* Vintage edn. Random House, London, 1992.

Robin Dunbar. *Grooming, Gossip and the Evolution of Language.* Faber and Faber, London, 1996.

Paul and Anne Ehrlich. *Extinction. The Causes and Consequences of the Disappearance of Species.* Victor Gollancz, London, 1982.

John L. Esposito. *Islam.* Oxford University Press, New York, 1988.

Caesar E. Farah. *Islam. Beliefs and Observances,* 5th edn. Barron's Educational Series Inc., Hauppauge, NY, 1994.

Steven Roger Fischer. *A History of Language.* Reaktion Books, London, 1999.

Steven Roger Fischer. *A History of Writing.* Reaktion Books, London, 2001.

Robin Fox. *The Search for Society: Quest for a Biosocial Science and Morality.* Rutgers University Press, New Brunswick, NJ, 1989.

Henry Gee (ed.). Nature Insight: Astrobiology (features articles on 'The habitat and nature of early life', 'The search for extraterrestial intelligence', 'Humans in space' and other topics). *Nature* **409**: 1079–1122; 2001.

Gerd Gigerenzer. *Reckoning with Risk: Learning to Live with Uncertainty.* Allen Lane/Penguin, London, 2002.

Marija Gimbutas. *The Language of the Goddess: Unearthing the Hidden Symbols of Western Civilisation.* Thames and Hudson, London, 1989.

Jean Gimpel. *The End of the Future. The Waning of the High-Tech World* (translated from the French by Helen McPhail). Adamantine Press, London, 1995.

Jane Goodall. *The Chimpanzees of Gombe.* Bellknap Press, Harvard, MA, 1986.

Graham Hancock. *Underworld.* Michael Joseph, London, 2002.

A. C. Hardy. *The Living Stream: a Restatement of Evolution Theory and Its Relation to the Spirit of Man.* Collins, London, 1965.

Sir Thomas Heath. *Archimedes.* a volume in *Men of Science,* G. Chapman (ed.). Society for Promoting Christian Knowledge, London, 1920.

Thor Heyerdahl. *The Ra Expeditions.* George Allen & Unwin, London, 1971.

Leo Tan Wee Hin and R. Subramanian. 'Scientific societies build better nations'. *Nature* **399**: 633; 1999.

Thomas Hobbes. *Leviathan, or the Matter, Forme and Power of a Commonwealth Ecclesiastical and Civil,* Michael Oakeshott (ed.). Blackwell, Oxford, 1960; originally published 1651.

Mark Honigsbaum. *The Fever Trail.* Macmillan, London, 2001.

BIBLIOGRAPHY

David Horrobin. *The Madness of Adam and Eve: how Schizophrenia Shaped Humanity.* Bantam, London, 2001.

Nicholas Humphrey. *The Mind Made Flesh. Essays from the Frontiers of Psychology and Evolution.* Oxford University Press, Oxford, 2002.

Peter Jay. *Road to Riches, or The Wealth of Man.* Weidenfeld & Nicolson, London, 2000.

Terence Kealey. *The Economic Laws of Scientific Research.* Macmillan, London, 1996.

John Kobler. *The Reluctant Surgeon: the Life of John Hunter.* Heinemann, London, 1960.

Jaroslav Krejči. *The Human Predicament: Its Changing Image. A Study in Comparative Religion and History.* St Martin's Press/Macmillan, Basingstoke, 1993.

Richard Leakey. *The Origin of Humankind.* Weidenfeld & Nicolson, London, 1994.

Roger Lewin. *Human Evolution: an Illustrated Introduction,* 3rd edn. Blackwell Scientific, Oxford, 1993.

Roger Lewin. *Principles of Human Evolution.* Blackwell Scientific, Oxford, 1998.

Bernard Lewis. *The Multiple Identities of the Middle East.* Weidenfeld & Nicolson, London, 1998.

David Lewis-Williams. *The Mind in the Cave. Consciousness and the Origins of Art.* Thames and Hudson, London, 2002.

Bruce Lincoln. *Priests, Warriors, and Cattle. A Study in the Ecology of Religions.* University of California Press, Berkeley, CA, 1981.

C. Scott Littleton (ed.). The Sacred East Series. *Hinduism* (Mary McGee); *Buddhism* (Ornan Rotem); *Confucianism* (John Chinnery); *Daoism* (John Chinnery); and *Shinto* (C. Scott Littleton). Macmillan, London, 1996.

John Maddox. *What Remains to Be Discovered. Mapping the Secrets of the Universe, the Origins of Life, and the Future of the Human Race.* Macmillan, London, 1998.

Kenan Malik. *Man, Beast and Zombie. What Science Can and Cannot Tell Us about Human Nature.* Weidenfeld & Nicolson, London, 2000

Vincent H Malmström. *Cycles of the Su, Mysteries of the Moon. The Calendar in Mesoamerican Civilization.* University of Texas Press, Austin, TX, 1997.

Duke Maskell and Ian Robinson. *The New Idea of a University.* Haven Books, London, 2001.

Alan McHughen. *A Consumer's Guide to Genetically Modified Food. From Green Genes to Red Herrings.* Oxford University Press, Oxford, 2000.

Steven J. Mithen. *The Prehistory of the Mind: a Search for the Origins of Art, Religion and Science.* Thames and Hudson, London, 1996.

J. R. McNeill. *Something New Under the Sun: an Environmental History of the Twentieth Century World.* Allen Lane/W.W. Norton, New York, 2000.

Ernst Mayr. *What Evolution Is.* Basic Books, New York, 2001, and Weidenfeld & Nicolson, London, 2002.

John Merson. *Roads to Xanadu. East and West in the Making of the Modern World.* Weidenfeld & Nicolson, London, 1989.

Giles Milton. *Nathaniel's Nutmeg. How One Man's Courage Changed the Course of History.* Sceptre/Hodder & Stoughton, London, 1999.

Gary F. Moring. *The Complete Idiot's Guide to Understanding Einstein.* Alpha Books, Macmillan, Indianapolis, IN, 2000.

David L. Nelson and Michael M. Cox. *Lehninger Principles of Biochemistry,* 3rd edn. Worth, New York, 2000.

Daniel Nettle. *Strong Imagination: Madness, Creativity and Human Nature.* Oxford University Press, Oxford, 2001.

New Encyclopaedia Britannica, vols 1–29. Encyclopaedia Britannica Inc, New York, 1994.

Sherwin B. Nuland. *Leonardo da Vinci.* Weidenfeld & Nicolson, London, 2000.

Edwin R. Nye and Mary E. Gibson. *Ronald Ross: Malariologist and Polymath.* Macmillan, Basingstoke, and St Martin's Press, New York, 1997.

Haim Ofek. *Second Nature. Economic Origins of Human Evolution.* Cambridge University Press, Cambridge, 2001.

Stephen Oppenheimer. *Eden in the East. The Drowned Continent of South-east Asia.* Weidenfeld & Nicolson, London, 1998.

Oxford Paperback Encyclopedia. Oxford University Press, Oxford, 1998.

Charles Pasternak. *The Molecules Within Us: Our Body in Health and Disease.* Plenum, New York, 1998.

Sir Flinders Petrie. *Religious Life in Ancient Egypt.* Cooper Square Publishers, New York, 1972.

Steven Pinker. *How the Mind Works.* Penguin, Harmondsworth, 1997.

Roy Porter. *The Greatest Benefit to Mankind: a Medical History of Humanity from Antiquity to the Present.* Harper Collins, London, 1997.

V. S. Ramachandran and Sandra Blakeslee. *Phantoms in the Brain.* Fourth Estate, London, 1998.

John H. Relethford. *Genetics and the Search for Modern Human Origins.* Wiley-Liss, New York, 2001.

Hilary and Steven Rose (eds). *Alas, Poor Darwin. Arguments Against Evolutionary Psychology.* Jonathan Cape, London, 2000.

Richard Rudgley. *Lost Civilisations of the Stone Age.* Arrow Books, London 1999.

Carl Sagan and Ann Druyan. *Shadows of Forgotten Ancestors. A Search for Who We Are.* Random House, New York, 1992.

Denise Schmandt-Besserat. *Before Writing, Volume One: From Counting to Cuneiform.* University of Texas Press, Austin, TX, 1992.

Michael Sharratt. *Galileo. Decisive Innovator.* Blackwell, Oxford, 1994.

Dava Sobel. *Galileo's Daughter.* Fourth Estate, London, 2000.

Jacques Soustelle. *Los Mayas* (originally *Les Maya*). Fondo de Cultura Economica, Mexico, DF, 1992.

Irving Stone. *The Origin.* Corgi Books, London, 1980.

BIBLIOGRAPHY

Sun Tzu. *The Art of War*. Foreword by James Clavell. Hodder & Stoughton, London, 1981.

Bryan Sykes. *The Seven Daughters of Eve*. Bantam Press, London, 2001.

Keith Thomas (ed.). Founders of Faith Series: *the Buddha* (Michael Carrithers); *Confucius* (Raymond Dawson); *Jesus* (Humphrey Carpenter); and *Muhammad* (Michael Cook). Oxford University Press, Oxford, 1986.

J. Eric S. Thompson. *Maya History and Religion*. University of Oklahoma Press, Norman, OK, 1970.

Arnold J. Toynbee. *A Study of History*, vols I – VI (abridged by D. C. Somervell). Oxford University Press, New York, 1946.

Eric Trinkhaus and Pat Shipman. *The Neandertals. Changing the Image of Mankind*. Pimlico, London, 1994.

Colin Tudge. *The Day before Yesterday*. Jonathan Cape, London, 1995.

James D. Watson. *The Double Helix*. Weidenfeld & Nicolson, London, 1968.

Peter Watson. *A Terrible Beauty. A History of the People and Ideas that Shaped the Modern Mind*. Weidenfeld & Nicolson, London, 2000.

Steven Weinberg. *Facing Up. Science and Its Cultural Adversaries*. Harvard University Press, Cambridge, MA, 2001.

Richard S. Westfall. *Never at Rest. A Biography of Isaac Newton*. Cambridge University Press, Cambridge, 1980.

Michael White. *Leonardo. The First Scientist*, Little, Brown, London, 2000.

Paul Wildish. *Taoism*. Thorsons, London, 2000.

Endymion Wilkinson. *Chinese History. A Manual*. Harvard University Asia Center, Cambridge, MA, 2000.

Ian Wilmut, Keith Campbell and Colin Tudge. *The Second Creation. The Age of Biological Control by the Scientists who Cloned Dolly* Headline Book Publishing, London, 2000.

Edward O. Wilson. *Sociobiology. The New Synthesis*, Harvard University Press, Cambridge, MA, 1975.

Edward O. Wilson. *The Diversity of Life*. Harvard University Press, Cambridge, MA, 1992.

Edward O. Wilson. *The Future of Life*. Little, Brown, London, and Alfred A. Knopf, New York, 2002.

Lewis Wolpert. *The Unnatural Nature of Science*. Faber and Faber, London, 1992.

Alexander Wood. *Thomas Young, Natural Philosopher, 1773 – 1829*. Cambridge University Press, 1954.

J. Z. Young. *An Introduction to the Study of Man*. Oxford University Press, Oxford, 1971.

R. C. Zaehner. *Hinduism*. Oxford University Press, Oxford, 1962.

Semir Zeki. *Inner Vision—an Exploration of Art and the Brain*. Oxford University Press, Oxford, 1999.

Glossary

The following definitions of medical and scientific words are taken largely from the glossary in Charles Pasternak, *The Molecules Within Us: Our Body in Health and Disease* (op. cit.). For further medical terms, consult a reference work such as the *Concise Colour Medical Dictionary*, 2nd edn, Oxford University Press, Oxford, 1998; and for more biochemical information, consult J. C. Kendrew, *The Encyclopaedia of Molecular Biology*, Blackwell Science, Oxford, 1995.

Acute disease of rapid onset with severe symptoms and brief duration (contrast with **chronic**).

Adipose relating to fat, e.g. adipose tissue.

-aemia pertaining to blood.

Aetiology cause of a disease.

Agonist substance that triggers a response in a cell, such as a **hormone** or **neurotransmitter** (opposite, **antagonist**).

AIDS acquired immune deficiency syndrome; disease characterised by failure to mount an immune defence against infectious microbes, that is caused by infection with **HIV** some years earlier.

Allele one of a number of alternative forms of a **gene**.

Allergen substance, like pollen, nettles or gluten, that sets up an **immune** response in hypersensitive people, that can culminate in **anaphylactic shock**.

Alzheimer's disease neurological disorder characterised by progressive loss of short-term memory, deterioration in behaviour and intellectual performance, and slowness of thought.

Amino acids **molecules** that are the building blocks of **proteins**, which are made up of 20 different amino acids.

Anabolism building up; making more complex **molecules** by biosynthesis (opposite, **catabolism**).

Anaphylactic shock an extreme and generalised **allergic** reaction causing swelling, **oedema**, constriction of the bronchioles in the lung, heart failure, circulatory collapse and sometimes death.

Androgen steroid **hormone** (e.g. testosterone) that stimulates the development of the male sex characteristics.

Anaemia reduction in the amount of **haemoglobin** in the blood.

Angiogenesis formation of new blood vessels. Essential for development of a **tumour**.

GLOSSARY

Anoxia conditions where body tissues receive inadequate amounts of oxygen.

Antagonist inhibitor of **hormone** or **neurotransmitter** action (opposite, **agonist**).

Antibiotic a compound, usually produced by microbes, that selectively inhibits or kills other microbes (e.g. penicillin).

Antibody protein, also called **immunoglobulin**, which binds to an **antigen**.

Antigen foreign substance, such as a protozoan, bacterium or virus, which binds to an **antibody** and thereby elicits an **immune** response.

Arthritis inflammation of one or more joints; includes rheumatoid arthritis (often related to **autoimmune disease**) and osteoarthritis (often related to ageing).

Asthma narrowing of the airways in the lungs, leading to coughing, wheezing and difficulty in breathing. Often brought on by an **allergen**.

Asymptomatic not showing any signs of disease, whether disease is present or not.

Atheroma formation of fatty plaque in artery walls, which limits its blood flow and predisposes to thrombosis.

Atherosclerosis disease in which atheromatous plaques develop.

Atom part of a **molecule**; atoms have differing masses (e.g. ^{2}H, ^{12}C, ^{14}N, ^{16}O etc.).

ATP adenosine triphosphate; molecule that acts as 'energy currency' of cells; produced by the **oxidation** of foodstuffs (**glucose** and **fatty acids**) or by **photosynthesis**, and used for muscle contraction (including the pumping of the heart), pumping ions across membranes, and biosynthesis of molecules like **carbohydrates**, **proteins**, **RNA** and **DNA**.

Atrophy wasting away of a tissue or organ.

Autoimmune disease caused by attack of certain organs or tissues by the body's own **immune** system.

Benign a **tumour** or other lesion that is not **malignant**.

Blood – brain barrier prevents movement of many components of blood into brain and cerebrospinal fluid, and vice versa.

BSE bovine spongiform encephalopathy; a degenerative neuropathological disorder of cattle, associated with an abnormal **prion** protein.

Cancer a **malignant** tumour.

Capillary narrowest type of blood vessel.

Carbohydrate molecule made up of sugar units; may be single sugar like **glucose**, two sugars like lactose or sucrose, or many sugar units (a **polymer**) like glycogen or starch.

Carcinogen substance that produces **cancer**.

Cardiovascular system of heart plus blood vessels.

Catabolism breaking down of food or storage molecules (e.g. for energy; opposite, **anabolism**).

Cell cycle   sequence of events between one cell division and the next.

Cerebral cortex   the outer layer of the brain; makes up 40% of the human brain and contains 15 billion **neurons** that function in consciousness, perception, memory, thought, mental ability and intellect.

Chemotaxis   movement of microbes towards, or away from, a chemical stimulus.

Chemotherapy   treatment of disease with chemicals.

Cholesterol   molecule (a type of **steroid**) present in fatty food, as well as being made in the body.

Cholesterolaemia   too much cholesterol in the blood.

Chromosome   structure within a cell in which most of the DNA is packaged.

Chronic   disease of long duration involving slow changes, often of gradual onset (opposite, **acute**).

CJD   Creutzfeldt – Jakob disease; a degenerative neurological disorder associated with an abnormal **prion** protein; one variant of the disease appears to be caused by eating **BSE**-infected meat.

Congenital   a condition present since birth.

Cortical (cortex)   outer layer of an organ, such as the brain.

Cystic fibrosis   hereditary disease in which thick mucus obstructs the pancreas and lungs; severe respiratory infections often result.

Diabetes mellitus   disorder in which **glucose** uptake and metabolism by cells is impaired; caused by lack of, or insensitivity to, **insulin**.

Differentiation   increasing specialisation of cells during development.

DNA   deoxyribonucleic acid; molecule made up of a linear chain of **nucleotides**; certain stretches of DNA are **genes**.

Domain   structurally or functionally defined part of a **protein**.

Dominant   refers to an **allele** on a **chromosome** that determines the condition or **phenotype** (contrast with **recessive**).

Edema   US spelling of **oedema**.

-emia   US spelling of **-aemia**.

Encephalitis   inflammation of the brain.

Endemic   occurring regularly in a particular region or population.

Endocrine   **hormonal**.

Endogenous   originating within the body or a cell (opposite, **exogenous**).

Endothelial   surface lining of blood vessels and other fluid-filled cavities.

Enzyme   **protein** with catalytic function.

Epidemiology   study of epidemics, occurrence or spread of diseases within populations.

Epithelium   sheet of cells lining a surace like skin (epidermis) or alimentary tract (mucous membrane).

Erythrocyte   mature red blood cell.

Etiology   US spelling of **aetiology**.

Exogenous   originating outside the body or a cell (opposite, **endogenous**).

GLOSSARY

Fatty acid   molecule made up of a chain of carbon atoms (typically 16–24 C atoms); can be saturated (all C atoms fully hydrogenated) or unsaturated (some C atoms not fully hydrogenated).

Gastric (gastro-)   pertaining to stomach.

-gen (-genic)   'giving rise to'.

Gene   stretch of **DNA** specifying a particular **protein**.

Genome   genetic complement of an organism; also refers to total **DNA** of an organism.

Genotype   genetic constitution of an organism (contrast with **phenotype**).

Gestation   development from fertilised egg to newborn.

Glucose   molecule of formula $C_6H_{12}O_6$; most common sugar in cells and building block for **carbohydrates** such as glycogen and starch.

Haematology   study of blood and its formation.

Haem   iron-containing molecule that is attached to the **protein** globin in **haemoglobin**.

Haemoglobin   the main **protein** constituent of red blood cells, which binds oxygen and carries it from the lungs to all the organs and tissues in the body.

Hepatic   pertaining to the liver.

Hepatitis   inflammation of the liver.

Herpes   a type of virus.

Heterozygous   having inherited different **alleles** of any one **gene** from each parent (contrast with **homozygous**).

Histology   study of the structure of tissues.

HIV   human immune deficiency virus, which leads to the onset of **AIDS**.

HLA   human **leukocyte** antigen; **protein** on the surface of cells involved in recognition of foreign compounds. Persons having similar HLA types can accept each other's grafts.

Homozygous   having inherited the same **allele** of any one **gene** from each parent (contrast with **heterozygous**).

Hormone   molecule, generally a **protein**, **amino acid** derivative or **steroid**, that is secreted by one type of tissue or organ and that affects the function of another tissue or organ.

Hyper-   'raised'.

Hypercholesterolaemia   raised blood cholesterol.

Hypertension   raised blood pressure.

Hypo-   'lowered'.

Immune   response of **lymphocytes** to a foreign body like an infectious microbe, and of mast cells to an **allergen**.

Immunity   protection against infectious disease.

Immunoglobulin   protein that binds to an **antigen** or **allergen**.

Insulin   protein **hormone** secreted by the pancreas that promotes the uptake of **glucose** into tissues.

In vitro   'in glass', i.e. in a dish or test tube, outside the body.

In vivo   'in life', i.e. inside the body.

Ion an **atom** that has gained one or more negative charges (i.e. electrons), like Cl^- (chloride ion) or $SO_4{}^{2-}$ (sulphate ion), or one that has lost one or more negative charges, like H^+ (hydrogen ion), K^+ (potassium ion), Na^+ (sodium ion) or Ca^{2+} (calcium ion); when salts like NaCl (sodium chloride or common salt) are dissolved in water, they dissociate into Na^+ and Cl^- ions.

Isotope different forms of an **atom**; some heavier forms are unstable and emit radioactive radiations (e.g. ^{14}C, cf. ^{12}C).

Leukaemia **malignant** disease in which the bone marrow produces excess immature or abnormal **leukocytes**. May be **acute** or **chronic**.

Leukocyte white blood cell.

Ligand molecule that binds to another molecule, e.g. **hormone**, **neurotransmitter** or other signal binding to a receptor **protein**.

Lymphocyte class of **leukocyte** involved in **immunity**.

Macro- 'large'.

Malignant a **tumour** that spreads and invades other tissues (contrast with **benign**).

Meiosis a special type of cell division that occurs in the gonads (testes in male, ovaries in female) to produce sperm and ova (the latter subsequently mature into eggs). Four daughter cells (not two as in **mitosis**) are produced, each of which contains only a single set of chromosomes. Since the halving of chromosome pairs is random, a sperm or ovum cell contains a mixture of chromosomes: some paternal, some maternal. Further diversity is generated by the process of 'crossing over' prior to cell division, in which regions within a chromosome (i.e. particular **genes**) are exchanged between paternal and maternal chromosomes.

Metastasis spread of a **malignant** tumour from its site of origin.

Micro- 'small'.

Mitosis cell division during growth of an organism by which two identical daughter cells are produced.

Molecule smallest part of organic matter that is stable under the conditions prevailing at the earth's surface; (e.g. oxygen, water, **glucose, protein, DNA**).

Monoclonal **immunoglobulin** derived from a single **lymphocyte** (contrast **polyclonal**).

Monogenic condition, often a disorder, controlled by a single **gene** (contrast **polygenic**).

Morbidity state of being diseased.

Morphology form and structure of the body and its organs.

Mortality (rate) incidence of death in a population in a given period.

Mutagen agent (a molecule, or radiation) causing a **mutation**.

Mutation change in **DNA** which may result in altered **phenotype**; changes in germ cells are passed on to the next generation, changes in other (somatic) cells are not.

Necrosis death of some or all of the cells of an organ or tissue.

GLOSSARY

Neonatal newborn; within the first 4 weeks of life.

Neuron nerve cell.

Neurotoxic poisonous to **neurons**.

Neurotransmitter molecule involved in the transmission of nerve impulses.

Nucleotide molecule that is a building block of nucleic acids; in **RNA** nucleotides contain ribose, in **DNA** they contain deoxyribose. **ATP** is also a nucleotide.

Obesity condition where excess fat has accumulated in the body; grossly overweight.

Oedema accumulation of fluid in body tissues; formerly called dropsy.

Oncogenesis development of an abnormal growth or **tumour**, that can be **benign** or **malignant**.

Oxidise to add oxygen, or to remove hydrogen, from a molecule.

Pathogenesis origin of a disease; a pathogen is an agent (e.g. a microbe) causing disease.

Peptide molecule made up of several **amino acid** residues (typically 3 – 12), i.e. part of a **protein**.

Peripheral near the surface or extremeties.

Phenotype visible or otherwise measurable characteristic of an organism resulting from its **genotype**.

Phospholipid molecule containing two **fatty acids**, glycerol, phosphate and a residue such as choline or inositol; phospholipids are the main components of biological membranes, such as the plasma membrane that surrounds a cell.

Photosynthesis the process by which plants and certain bacteria synthesise **carbohydrates** from carbon dioxide and water, utilising the energy of light.

Polyclonal **immunoglobulin** derived from more than one **lymphocyte** (contrast with **monoclonal**).

Polygenic condition, often a disorder, controlled by several different **genes** (contrast with **monogenic**).

Polymer large molecule made up of many smaller repeating units, e.g. **proteins**, **RNA** and **DNA**, glycogen and starch, plastic.

Polymorphism genetic character that occurs in several different forms, reflecting different **alleles**.

Prenatal 'before birth'; diagnosis to detect potential disease by amniocentesis, chorionic villus sampling, or other technique.

Prion 'infectious protein'; a **protein** found normally in the body, **mutant** forms of which are associated with diseases like **BSE** in cattle and **CJD** in humans.

Protein molecule made up of a linear chain of **amino acids**.

Recessive refers to an **allele** on a **chromosome** that does not determine the condition or **phenotype** (which is determined by the allele on the other chromosome; contrast with **dominant**).

Reduce   to add hydrogen, or to remove oxygen, from a molecule.

Renal   pertaining to the kidneys.

RNA   ribonucleic acid; molecule made up of a linear chain of **nucleotides**.

Sensory   nerve impulses derived from the senses that are carried to the brain.

Sex chromosome   the X and Y chromosomes of an individual; females are XX, males XY.

Sickle cell disease   disorder in which the red cells tend to assume a sickled shape; caused by an abnormal **haemoglobin**.

Steroid   molecule like **cholesterol**, testosterone or oestrogen, that contains a characteristic ring structure.

Syndrome   group of symptoms characteristic of a particular disease.

Triglyceride   molecule made up of glycerol and three **fatty acids**; the main constituent of fatty foods and of **adipose** tissue.

Tumour   swelling, usually as a result of abnormal cell proliferation as in **cancer**; see **oncogenesis**.

-uria   pertaining to urine.

Vaccination   administration of a **vaccine** to protect against an infectious disease.

Vaccine   preparation of a microbe, or a molecule derived therefrom, that leads to **immunity** from the disease caused by the microbe.

Xenobiotic   foreign to the human body; applied to drugs and to animal tissues (e.g. for transplants).

Index

Page numbers in **bold** refer to illustrations, page numbers in *italic* refer to endnotes.

Abbott, Alison *185, 220, 303*
Abraham 262, 265
actin 20
d'Adamo, P. J. *222*
Adamson, John *221, 246*
adenine **19**, 22
adversity, challenge of 140–149
Afrikaner 132–133
agriculture 8, 9, 138, 139, 158–160, 172, 177, 179, 183, 187, 209, 228, 242, 313–332
AIDS (acquired immune deficiency syndrome) 308, 366, 367, *380*
Aiello, Lesley *78, 97, 203*
Akkadian 164, 165, 189
Alaska 70, 73, 113, 147
Aldrin, Edwin (Buzz) 130, 131, **Plate 1**
Aleut 113
Alexander the Great 118, 180
Alexandria 169, 170
alphabet 190, 191
Altamira 201
altruism 122, 123
aluminium silicate 17
America
    Central 8, 9, 140, 175–177, 199
    North 113–115
    South 8, 9, 140, 178–181, 199
Amerindian (*see also* Inca; Maya) 113–116
amino acid **19**, 20, 23, 36, 45, 54, **55**, 63, 89
ammonia 225, 226
Amundsen, Roald 129
Anasazi 181
anatomy 3, 76–81, 83, **84**, 85, **85**, 86, **86**, **87**, 88, 170, 239, 240
Anaximenes 282
Andes 140, 146, 159, 178–180
Angkor Wat 183
antibiotics 324–326

Aparicio, Samuel A. J. *303*
Aral Sea 108
Archaebacteria (archaea) 44, 46, 48, 49, 53, 54, 381
Archimedes 11, 26, 282, 283, 287
Aristarchus *300*
Aristophenes 198
Aristotle 153, 256, 257, 281, 282, 284, 285
Armstrong, Karen 275
Armstrong, Neil 130
art 171, 200–210, 228, 239–242, 364, 386
Aryan 171
Ashoka 142, 260
asteroid 34, 363, 377
astronomy 165, 170, 177, 218, 232, 255, 278, 279
astrophysics 298, 299
Atahualpa 280
Athens 151, 153
Atlantis 119, 184, 216, 218
atom 18
ATP 49, 54, 57, 65, 293
Augustine, St 125
Augustus (Octavian) 154, 155
Austen, Jane 209
Australopithecus 76–80, 85, 96, 109, 383
auxin 51, 52
Avebury 181
Averroes (Ibn Rushd) 235
Awash valley 77, 110
Aztec 125, 142, 176, 199, 223, 257, 258, 275

Babbage, Charles 226
Babu, Arvind **24**
Babylon 118, 146, 164, 165
Bach family 151, 152, 205
Bacillus thuringiensis 328, **328**, 329
Bacon, Francis 356

bacteria (*see also* microbes) 44, 48, 53 – 57,
    55, 143, 297, 298, 328, **328**, 329, *378*
Badcock, Christopher *99*
Baekeland, Leo Hendrik 226
Bagehot, Walter *162*
Baker, David *379*
Baldwin, James Mark 383
Barss, Peter *333*
Bass, Brenda L. *303*
Bede, the Venerable *274*
Beethoven, Ludwig van 201, 208
Benzon, William *220*
Berber 147, 199
Bering Strait 113, 114
Bering, Vitus *135*
Berlinski, David *301*
Berman, H. M. **21**
Betz, F. S. **328**
Big Bang 44, 299
Bilzingsleben 108
Black, Davidson 80
Blackmore, Susan 385, *390*
Blumberg, Baruch *303*
Boer 132 – 133
Bohr, Niels 187, 279
bonobo 3, *12*, *13*, **90**, **91**, 92, 93
Bosch, Carl 225
Bossidy, John Collins *136*
bovine spongiform encephalopathy *see* BSE
Boxgrove 108
Boyle, Robert 291
Bragg, Lawrence 25, 26, 151, 152
Bragg, William 25, 26, 151, 152
Brahe, Tycho 288
brain 78, 82, 85, 86, **87**, 99, 188, 189, 218,
    383, 388
Braudel, Fernand *186*
bravery 122, 123
Bray, D. **59**
Brendel, Alfred 200
Bretschneider, Joachim *185*
Briggs, Robert 345
Briggs, Winslow R. *66*
British rulers 157
Britten, Roy J. *13*
Brockman, John *378*
Bronowski, Jacob 211
Brontë sisters 209
bronze 171, 173, 223
Bronze Age 174, 223

Brown, Fred *301*
Brunet, M. *98*
Bruno, Giordano 284
BSE *40*, 298, 311, 322, 323, 352
Buddha 268, 269
Buddhism 9, 260, 268, 271, 273, *276*
Burns, Lawrence D. *380*
Burton, Charles 130
Butler, Declan *302*, *358*
Byrd, Richard 129

Cabeza de Vaca 124, 125
Cabot 128, *136*
Caesar, Julius 154, 155, 175, 177, 182
Caldas, Carlos *303*
Calder, Nigel *248*
Calvin, John 132
cancer 294 – 297, 307, 308 – 310, 322, 355,
    373
Cann R. L. *100*
Cannadine, David *162*
carbohydrate 17, 47, 48, 53, 65, 292
carbon 18, 45, *378*
    dioxide 34, 46 – 48, 53, 65, 365, *378*, *379*
Cárdenas, Maria Luz *64*
Carnac 181, 184
Carrangua 124
Caspian Sea 108
Çatal Hüyük *182*, 184
Cavalli-Sforza, Luigi L. *220*
cave art 201, 202, 227 – 229
Caxton, William *246*
Cech, Thomas R. *303*
cell 18, 23, 24, 28, 44, 45
    transplantation 343 – 347, **348**,
    351 – 353
Celts 182
Ceprano 108
Chac 257, 258, *274*
Chaco Canyon 181, 184
Chain, Ernst 280
challenge of adversity 140 – 149
Champollion, Jean-Francois 192, 193
chance *see* risk
Chargaff, Erwin 27, *40*
Chauvet 201
Chavin culture 178
chemotaxis 54 – 57, **55**, **58**
Chichen Itza 146, 177
Chichester, Francis 130

Chicurel, Marina 67
chimpanzee (*see also Pan paniscus; Pan troglodytes*) 3 – 6, 12, 36 – 39, 74, 79, 81, 83, 86, 89, **90, 91**
  brain **87**
  cortical neurons **87**, 89, 188
  DNA **6**, *389*
  genes 5, 6, **6**, 36, 37, 381
  hand **85**
  larynx **86**, 88
Chimu culture 178, 259
China 8, 9, 139, 140, 142, 143, 146, 154, 172 – 174, 205 – 207, 367, 368, 388
Chinese (*see also* Sinic)
  accounting 188
  astronomy 278, 279
  beliefs (*see also* Buddhism; Confucianism; Daoism) 254, 255, 273
  bureaucracy 154, 156
  civilisation 149, 172 – 174, 216
  dynasties 172 – 174
  script 194 – 196, **194**, 215
  technology 231 – 233
chlorophyll 49, 66
cholesterol 17
Christian Scientist 133
Christianity 9, 204, 211, 261 – 269, 273
chromosome 24, **24**, 25, 27, 31, 36, 40, 41, 96, *101*, 110
chromosome number
  chimpanzee 36
  coyote 31
  dog 31
  donkey 31
  fox 36
  horse 31
  human 36
  wolf 31
Cibelli, Jose B. **348**, *357*
circadian rhythm 52, 53
civilisation 8, 140 – 149, *160*, 163 – 222, 366, 386, 388
  Egyptian **141**, 166 – 170
  Inca **141**, 178 – 180
  Indic **141**, 171, 172, 371
  Mayan **141**, 177
  Minoan **141**, 174, 175
  Sinic **141**, 172 – 174, 371
  Sumerian **141**, 164 – 166
CJD 40, 296, 298, 310, 311

Clark, Kenneth 211, 239, 247
Clavell, James 237
climate change 145, 159, 183, 364, 365, *378*, 379
cloning 343 – 349, **348**, 351, 357, 358
Clovis 113, 114, *135*
Cobo, Bernabe 258, 259, 275
Cohen, Fred E. *303*
Coles, Peter **290**
Collard, Mark 97
Collins, Michael 130
Columbus, Christopher 11, 119 – 123, *136*, **Plate 1**, 361
computer 226, 227
Conduitt, John 287
Confucianism 268 – 271, 273, 276
Confucius 209, 232, 255, 270
conquest 117, 118, 125, 164 – 166, 169, 170, 171, 174, 180, 235
conquistador 125, 180
continental drift 109
Cook, James *136*
Cooper, George *64*
Copernicus, Nicolaus 280, 284, 285, 288
Copley, John *378*
Coptic 191
Cornish-Bowden, Athel *64*
Cortés, Hernando 125, 176
Crane, Nicholas *136*
Crete 8, 9, 140 – 142, 174, 175
Creutzfeldt-Jakob disease *see* CJD
Crick, Francis 26, 27, 291, 361
Cromwell, Oliver 156
crops
  genetically-modified 313 – 332
  yields 182, 314, 315
Crowder, Thomas R. **190, 194, 229**
cryptochrome 51, 53
crystallography 26
culture (*see also* civilisation) 144, 207, 366 – 368, 386, 388
cuneiform 189, 230
Curie family 151, 152
Cuzco 178 – 180, *181*
cystic fibrosis 337, 338, 342
cytosine 22
Csikszentmihalyi, Mihaly *68*

Dalrymple, William 275
Dante Alighieri 198

Daoism (Taoism) 268–271, 273, *276*
Darwin, Charles 32, 33, 51, 81, *98*, *99*, 109,
    151, *161*, 265, 269, 280, 281, 286, 291,
    301, 376, 383, 388
dating techniques 74–76, 163
Dawkins, Richard 10, *13*, 384, *390*
Descartes, René 286, 287
Democritus *300*
Dennett, Daniel C. *41*, 383, *389*
deoxyribose **19**
Deutsch, David *304*
Diamond, Jared 3, 36, *43*, 115, *135*, *186*, 197,
    220, *245*
Dias, Bartolomeu 125, 126, *136*, 233
Dickens, Charles 207, 208
Dickinson, Robert E. *379*
Dictyostelium discoides 57, **58**, **59**
diet 78, 79
Dingle, Hugh *97*
dinosaur 34, 35, 351
DNA (*see also* chromosome; gene) 2, **6**, 7, 17,
    18, 20, 22–29, 36, 37, *39*–*43*, 168,
    296–298, *303*, 316, 335, 337, 345, 387,
    389
  mitochondrial 95, 96, *100*, 116, 344
Dobson, Roger *379*
Doolittle, Russell F. *64*
double helix 26, 27
Dover, Gabriel *13*
Druyan, Ann *12*
Duarte, Carlos M. *378*
Dugatkin, Lee Alan *390*
'dumbing down' 368–370
Dunbar, Robin 5, 187–189, *219*
Dictyostelium discoides 57, **58**, 59

Easter Island 115, 224, 371
Eddington, Arthur 289
Eddy, Mary Baker 133
Edwards, Robert 341, *357*
egg 27–29, 340–342, 344, 345, 347,
    351–353, *357*
Egypt 8, 9, 140, 142, 143, 278
Egyptian civilisation **141**, 166–170, 182,
    215–217
  beliefs 252, 253, 259, 273
  script 191–193, **Plate 4**
Einstein, Albert **Plate 8**, 237, 238, 273,
    280, 281, 288–291, **290**, *301*, *302*
electronics *226*, *227*, 361, 362

Eliot, George 209
embryo 27, 29, 341, 342, 344, 347, **348**,
    349, 351, 352
Empedocles 282
Enard, Wolfgang *99*
environment 143, 145, 150, 318   324, 355,
    362, 364, 384, 388
Eratosthenes *136*, 170,
Erickson, Clark L. *186*
Erik the Red 120
Erikson, Leif 120
Escherichia coli 54, 57, 316
Eskimo 113
Euclid 170, 282
Eudoxus 282
Euphrates 143, 145
Everest 129, 130, 362
evolution 32–34, 44, 45, *63*, *64*, 374–377,
    383, 384
  of man 4, 10, 73–97
exploration 8, 11, 105–108, 117–131,
    277–300, 373–375

Faraday, Michael *304*
Farah, Caesar E. *275*
Farrington, Benjamin *358*
fat 17, 78, 203, 292, 337
Fehr, Ernst *136*
Ferdinand II and Isabella I 119, 121, 132,
    134
fertilisation 27
Fiennes, Ranulph 130
finger 4, 76, 85, **85**, 86
Fischer, Steven Roger *246*
flavin 51, 60, *66*
floods 164, 184, 185, 251, 258, 372
Florey, Howard 280
food 3, 54, 62, 78, 79, 179, 209, 232
  safety 315–318, 324–328
  production 313–315, 377
foraminifera 35
Forbes, Allen **190**, **194**, **229**,
Ford, Henry 226
fossil 74–83
Fourier, Jean Baptiste 192
Fox, Robin 387, *390*
FOXP2 gene 88, 89
FOXP2 protein 89, *99*, 383
Franklin, Benjamin 280, *304*
Franklin, Rosalind 26, 27

INDEX

Fraser, Antonia 357
French rulers 157
Freud, Sigmund 274
Fuchs, R. L. **328**
Fuhlrott, Johann Karl 81, 82
Fukuyama, Francis 357

Gachter, Simon 136
Gadagkar, Raghavendra 43
Gagarin, Yuri 130
Galapagos 32, 109, 376
Galileo Galilei **Plate 6**, 264, 273, 280,
283–285, 288
Gama, Vasco da 125, 126, 233
Gandhi, Indira 314
Gandhi, Mahatma 261
Gee, Henry 64
gene (*see also* under specific proteins like
haemoglobin or insulin) 5–7, **6**, 9, 10,
24, 25–27, 31, 35–37, 41–43, 92, 203,
316, 322, 323, 356
disorders 336–339, 342, 343
flow 30, 109, 110, 366
modification 307, 309, 313–332, **328**,
354–356, 362
therapy 336–339, 355, 356, 362
transplants 315, 316, 321, 323, 328, **328**,
336–339, 340, 352, 353, **355**
variants, generation of 28–30, 364, 366,
382
genome 12, 27, 36, 335, 336
genus 35–37
Georgia 107
Gibbs, W. Wayt 42
Gibson, Mary E. 302
Gigerenzer, Gerd 332
Gimbutas, Marija 186, 220, 229, 245
Gimpel, Jean 379, 380
Giorgio, Paul A. del 378
Giza 146, 167–169, **Plate 2**, 278
glass 169, 234
Gleeson, Janet 248
Glendinning, Victoria 221
Glenn, John 130
glucose 17, **19**, 338,
glutamate **19**, 23, 40
GM *see* gene modification; gene therapy
Goodall, Jane 12, 276
gorilla 74, **84**, 93
Gould, Stephen Jay 239, 274, 389

Grace, John 378
Gratzer, Walter 41, 302, 304
Great Rift valley 8, 75, 77, 79, 81, 83, 384
Great Zimbabwe 181, 183, 184, 186
Greece 118, 140, 279
Greek
alphabet 191, 197
beliefs 255–257
culture 153, 154, 170, 181, 182, 197, 198
science 282, 283
philosophy 9, 153, 154, 256, 257
greenhouse effect 34, 320, 364
Grossman, Daniel 186, 379
guanine 22
Gurdon, John 345
Gutenberg, Johannes 232
gypsies 131–132

Haber, Fritz 225
haemoglobin 6, 20, **21**, 26, 29, 30, 40, 41,
150, 337
Halley, Edmund 286, 287
Halobacterium salinarium 48, 49, 54
Hammond, B. G. **328**
Han dynasty 174, 196
Hancock, Graham 183, 186
hand 76, 83, 85, **85**, 86, 89, 383
Hangzhou 206, **Plate 5**
Harappa 171
Hardy, Alister, 10, 11, 13, 382, 389
Harlow, Henry J. 380
Harvey, William 280, 291, 293
Hawking, Stephen 304
Heath, Thomas 301
health (*see also* medicine)
risks 315–318, 324–328, 355
Helicobacter pylori 295
heliotropism 50, 52
helium 17
Henson, Matthew 129
Herculanaeum 175
heredity 23–28, 149–158, 203, 204
Heyerdahl, Thor 115, 217, 218
Hillary, Edmund 130
Himmler, Heinrich 12
Hinduism 9, 142, 193, 253, 254, 260, 261,
268, 271
Hipparchus 170
Hippocrates of Chios 282
Hitler, Adolf 11, 149

Hittite 164
HIV 76, *302*, 308, 350, 351, 366, *379*
Hobbes, Thomas *186*, *378*
Holt, Robert A. *302*
Homer 198, 255
Homo 10, 36, 75, 77–82, 85, 94, 95,
    105–111, 139, 227, 375, 383, 387
Homo aetheris 377
Homo ergaster 95
Homo erectus 79, 94, *99*, 105, 107, 108, 227,
    375, 384
Homo habilis 79, 94, *99*, 106, 384
Homo heidelbergensis 95
Homo neanderthalensis 81–83, 85, 96, 110,
    111, 187, 375
Homo quaerens 10, 375
Homo sapiens 2, 7, 30, 39, 47, 76, 83, 86, 88,
    92–97, *99*, 110–117, 139, 187, 227,
    363, 364, 374, 384, 386
Hooke, Robert 286, 287
Hooker, Joseph 33
Horrobin, David 202, 203, *220*
Hoyle, Fred 45, *64*, 365, *379*
Huala, Eva 66
Hudson, Henry 127, 128
Hughes, Robert *135*
Huguenots 134
human
    attributes 4, 5, 38, 39, 73–97, 383
    brain **87**
    cortical neurons **87**, 188
    DNA **6**, *389*
    evolution 73–97
    genes 5, 6, **6**, 36, 37, 381, 384
    hand **85**
    larynx **86**
    migration 106–117, 131–134
    potential 149–152, 209
    genetic similarities 30, 96, 110, 111,
        115–117
    skeleton **84**,
human immune deficiency virus *see* HIV
Humphrey, Nicholas 201, *220*, *276*, *301*
Hunt, John 130
Hunter, John 340
Huxley, Thomas 33
hybridisation 36, *42*, 75
hydrogen 17, 18, 45, 225, 380
    bond 23, *39*, *65*,
Hyksos 169

ice age 107, 113, *135*, 145, 159, 184, 251
Inca 125, 142, 146, 178–180, 199
    civilisation **141**, 180, 181, 188
    beliefs 258, 259
India 8, 140, 142, 212, 213, 367, 368
Indic civilisation **141**, 145, 371
    beliefs (*see also* Hinduism) 253, 254
    languages 193
Indus 171
infectious disease 139, 212, 213, 231, 233,
    234, 238, 292–295, 352, *358*, 366
inheritance 27–29, 339, *356*, 364
    of human potential 149–152
    of leadership 152–158
insulin 6, 20, **21**, 27, 328, 336–338, 352
Inuit 113, 147
in vitro fertilisation *see* IVF
involuntary responses 2, 62, 63
Irish 134
iron 223, 224, 231, 233
Iron Age 183, 224
Irving, Washington 214, *222*
Islamic
    religion 9, 234, 261, 265–268, 367
    culture and technology 170, 233–235
Israel 133, 134
IVF 339–343, 351, 352

Jagiellon dynasty 157
Jainism 271
Java Man 108
Jay, Peter 242, 243, *248*
Jayaraman, K. S. *221*, *333*,
Jenner, Edward 292, 293, *302*, 354
Jesus 262, 266–268, *275*
Jews 133, 134, 261, 262, 267, 268, 271
Jomon culture 183, 184
Joyce, Gerald F. *63*
Judaism 9, 261, 262

Kandel, Eric *390*
Kant, Immanuel *98*
Kassite 164
Kauffmann, S. A. *248*
Kealey, Terence 277, *300*
Kenyanthropus platyops 78, 383
Kendrew, John 26
Kepler, Johannes 288
Kerr, Richard A. *379*
Kershaw, Peter *135*

Khoikoin 132
Kilwa island 183
King, Thomas 345
Klasies river 110
Knossos 174, 175, 197, 198, *222*
Koch, Robert 280, 292, 293
Koran (Qur'an) 234, 266, 267
Koshland, D. E. **55**
Kramer, S. N. *274*
Krejci, Jaroslav *274*
Kubey, Robert *68*

Lake Victoria 183
Lamarck, Jean-Baptiste 32, 265
Langridge, William H. R. *334*
language 8, 38, **90, 91**, 92, 93, 108, 112, 116, 165, 171, 187–200, 218, 281, 383, 386
L'Anse-aux-Meadows 120
Lantian 108
Lanza, Robert P. **348**, *357, 358*
Lao Tzu 270, 271
larynx 4, 83, 86, **86**, 88, 383
Lascaux 201
leadership 107, 108, 152–158
Leakey family 77, 79, *98, 99*
Leibnitz, Gottfried 280, 286, *301*, 385
Lepenski Vir 183, 184
Lewin, Roger **86**, *98*
Lewis-Williams, David *220, 274, 276*
Li, Zhixiong *358*
life
    dependency on light 46, 47
    molecular basis 17–28
    origins 44, 45, 374
    quality 211–215
light 46–54, 62, 65, 66, 69, 192, **Plate 7**, 208, 239, 241, 257, 286, 288, 289, **290**, 382
Lincoln, Bruce *274*
Lindahl, Tomas, *97*
Linear A. **190**, 196, 215
Linear B. **190**, 197, 215
Linnaeus, Carl 92
Lissauer, Jack J. *380*
literacy 212
literature 197–199, 207–211
Littleton, C. Scott *276*
Livi-Bacci, Massimo *248*
Livingstone, David 361

Lorenz, Konrad 387
Louis XVI *162*, 340
Lowell 128, *136*
Lucy 77
Luther, Martin 263, 264
Lyell, Charles 33
Lysenko, Trofim Denisovich 32, 284, 285

Machu Picchu 179, 180
Mack, Steve *41*
Maddox, John *64*, *304*
Magellan, Ferdinand 126
magnetotaxis 56
Maimonides 235, 267
malaria 29, 30, 292, 293, 296, *302*, 365, *379*
Malik, Kenan 3
Malmström, Vincent H. *135*
Malta 184
man *see* human, *Homo*, etc.
Manson, Patrick 292
Mao Zhedong 148, 149, 215, 270
Mapungubwe 183, 184
Marco Polo 233
Marconi, Guglielmo 361
Martin, Michael O. *379*
Maskell, Duke 369
Maspero, H. *274*
mathematics 165, 170, 195, 215, 216, 218, 234, 282, 283, 286
Maudsley, Henry 203
Maya 140, 142, 146, 177, 199, 215, 216, 257, 258
Mayan civilisation **141**, 180, 181, *185*
    beliefs 257, 258
McHughen, Alan 332, *334*
McTaggart, Lynne *276*
mechanics (*see also* physics) 283, 284, 286–288
Medawar, Peter 5, *12*
medicine 9, 165, 230–231, 234, 291–296, 336–353, 355, 356
meiosis 31
meme 3, 384, 385
memory 72, 73, 384, 385
Menzies, Gavin, *136*
Mendel, Gregor 25, 28
Merbach, M. A. *68*
Mercator, Gerardus 126, 127
Merson, John *247, 300*
Meselson, Matthew *247*

Mesopotamia (*see also* Sumeria) 8, 142, 143, 164–166, 170, 171
meteorite 44, 45
microbes (*see also* bacteria) 18, 44, 45, 297, 298
migration 70–73
  birds 70, 71
  butterfly 71
  Homo, early 106–111
  H. sapiens 111–117
  humans, current 131–134, 159
  locust 70
  plankton 71, 72
  plants 72
  reindeer 70
  whale 70
  wildebeest 70
Milligan, Max *186*
Ming dynasty 174, 233
Minoan civilisation **141**, 142, 147, 174, 175, 181, 182, 196–198, 215, 216,
Mithen, Steven J. *12*, *245*
mitochondrial DNA 95, 96, *100*, 116, *135*, 344
Modjokerto 108
Mohammed *see* Muhammad
Mohenjo Daro 171, 181
Moivre, Abraham de 287
molecular biology 296–298
molecules 2, 7, 17–28, 45, 292, 294
Monet, Claude 11, 208, *221*
money 243–244
Montague, Lady Mary Wortley 231
Monte Verde 114
Montezuma 125
Moring, Gary F. *302*
Mormon 133, *136*
Morris, Desmond 3
Morrison, Philip *219*, *300*
Morrison, Sean J. *357*
Moxon, Richard *333*
Mozart 151, 208, 280
Muhammad *247*, 265–268
Mullis, Ina V. S. *379*
multiregional origin 110–111
Munro, H. H. 93, 94, *100*
Murray, John 33
muscle 20, 83, 373, 388
Muslim (*see also* Islamic, Muhammad) 190, 263, 265–268

mutation 29, 31, *40*, 86, 117, 376
Mycobacterium lepri 18
myoglobin 26
myosin 20

Nadis, Steve *378*
Nakagaki, Toshiyuki *67*
Narmada 108
Nathan, Adam *380*
Neander valley 81, 82
Neanderthal Man *see Homo neanderthalensis*
Nemecek, Sasha *135*
neocortex 188, 189
neolithic *see* Stone Age
Nepenthes albomarginata 62
nerve *see* neuron
Nettle, David 203, 204, *220*
neuron 4, 188, 189, 218, 300, 383, 387, 388
neurotransmitter 294
Newcomen, Thomas 224
Newton, Isaac **Plate 7**, 273, 279, 280, 285–288, *301*, 361
Nile 143, 145–147, 166, 168
Nitra 183
nitrogen 17, 45, 56, 225
North Pole *97*, *98*, 126, 129, 362
Nowak, Martin *219*
nucleic acid (*see also* DNA; RNA) 292
nucleotide **19**, 23, 45, *63*
Nuland, Sherwin B. *41*, *247*, *300*
numbers (*see also* script) 169, 189, 195, 215, 216, *220*
Nye, Edwin R. *302*

Octavian *see* Augustus
Ofek, Haim *98*, 109, *135*
Olduvai Gorge 11
Olmec 175, 176, 224, 257, 258
oncology 294–296
Oppenheimer, Stephen 183, *186*, *274*
organic
  food 318, 319, 324
  molecules (*see also* molecules; DNA; protein; etc.) 17, 44, 45, 47
  remains 74
organs 18, 28, 338–353
  transplantation 338, 349–351
Orkin, Stuart H. *357*
Orrorin tugenensis 73

Ottoman empire 156, 234, 244
oxygen 17, 18, 20, 45, 377

Palenque 146, 177
Pan paniscus 3, 30, 39, 74, 109, 376
Pan troglodytes 3, 30, 39, 74, 109, 375, 376, 384
Panbanisha **90, 91**, 92, 93, 385
paper 170, 177, 232, 234
papyrus *see* paper
Paracas culture 178
Parmenides *301*
particle physics 298–300
PAS domain 60, 61, *68*, 89
Pasternak, Boris *221*
Pasternak, Charles *302, 390*
Pasternak, Leonid **Plate 8**, *221*
Pasteur, Louis 292, 293
Patagonia 111, 114, 115
Patterson, Francine 93
Pauling, Linus 26
Peacocke, Arthur *276*
Peary, Robert 129
Peking Man 80, 81
Pennisi, Elisabeth *43*
Perkin, William Henry 225
Persia 118, 164, 169, 190
Peru 140
Perutz, Max 26
Petersen, Arne Friemuth 273, *276*
Petric, Flinders *274*
Phoenecian 170, 191
phosphate **19**, 22, 61, *99*
photosynthesis 47–50, 54, *65*
phototaxis 54
phototropin 51, 52
phototropism 50–52, **50**
Physarum polycephalum 59
physics (*see also* astrophysics; mechanics; particle physics) 288, 298–300
physiology 83, 239, 240, 291
phytochrome 51, 52
Picardie, Justine *276*
Picasso, Pable 208
Pilgrim Fathers 128
Pinker, Steven 99, 160, *162*
Pizarro, Francisco 125, 180
plague 233
Planck, Max 362
plankton 71, 72

plants 44–53, **50**, 60–63
Plasmodium falciparum 30, *302*
plastics 226
Plato 153, 184, 216, 256
Polynesian 113, 115, 116, 148
Ponce de Leon, Juan 123
Popes 156, 157
Popper, Karl, 187, 188, *219*, 262–264, *301*, 382, *389*
population 158, 242, 313, 363
Porodin 183
pottery 163, 179, 183, 228
precision grip 4, 85, 218
Presbyterian 132, 134
Pretorius, Marthinus 132
primary civilisations 140–149, **141**
printing 232
prion *40*, 298, 300, *358*
protein (*see also* specific proteins like haemoglobin and insulin) 2, 7, 17, 18, 20, **21**, 23, 24, 28, 29, 36, 37, *39*, 40, 78, 296 298, 352, 353
Protestant 134, 157, 263–265, 273, *357*
protoctista 57–59, **58**
Prusiner, Stanley B. *303*
psychiatry 294
psychology 294
Ptolemy 119, *136*, 279
pyramid 164–169, 176, 177, 178, **Plate 2**, **Plate 3**, 217, 218, 224, 232, 273, 278
Pythagoras *136*, 165, 282

Qin dynasty 174, *185*, 196, 254
Qing dynasty 174, *185*
quality of life 181, 211–215
quest (*see also* search)
  ability to 4, 12, 78–92, **84**, **85**, **86**, **87**, 209, 383, 385, 386
  derivation 1
Quetzalcoatl 176, 258
Qur'an *see* Koran

radiocarbon dating 74
Rayment, Mark *378*
Rees, Martin *380*
Reichhardt, Tony *380*
Relethford, J. H. *135*
religion 9, 125, 171, 232, 249–271, 281, 343
  American, central 257, 258

religion (*continued*)
  American, south 258, 259
  Chinese 254, 255, 273
  contemporary faiths 259–273
  Egyptian 252–253, 273
  Greek 255–257
  neolithic beliefs 228, 229, 249–251
  Sumerian 251–252, 273
Reppert, Steven M. *67*
respiration 47, 48, *65*
retinol 48–50, 60
rhodopsin 48–50
Ridley, Mark 11
risk 309–313, 318–324, 331, 332, 353–356
RNA 17, 296–298, *303*, 330, *379*
Robbins, Tom *379*
Robinson, Ian 369
Roman
  culture 154, 155, 182
  empire 148, 156, 179, 371
  leaders 154, 155
  republic 154
Rose, Hilary and Steven *13, 160, 274, 389*
Rosen, Charles *220*
Rosetta Stone 191, 192, **Plate 4**
Ross, Ronald 292, 293
Rous, Peyton 293, 294, 307
Rousseau, Jean-Jacques *12*
Rubik, B. A. **55**
Rudenski, Aram *300*
Rudgley, Richard *135, 160, 220, 245*
rulers 152–158, 215
Ruse, Michael *276*
Rutherford, Ernest 237

Sachs, Jeffrey *248*
Saddam Hussein 238
Sagan, Carl *12*
Sahul 112
Salisbury, Lord 367
Salmonella typhimurium **55**, 316, 384
Sand, George 209
Sangiran 108
San Salvador 120
Savage-Rumbaugh, Sue 38, 93
Schaffhausen, Hermann 82
Schimel, David *379*
schizophrenia 202–204
Schmandt-Besserat, Denise 229, 230
scholarship 200–210

Schubert, Franz 385
Schweitzer, Albert 125
science 9, 239–240, 277–300, 368, 386
Scott, Robert 129
script (*see also* numbers) 163, 170, 181
  Egyptian 169, **190, Plate 4**
  Indic 171
  Mayan 177
  Minoan 169, **190**
  other **190**, 228–230, **229**
  Sinic 172, 173, 194–196, **194**
  Sumerian 169, 171, 188, 189, **190**, 230
Seagrave, Sterling *136*
search (*see also* quest)
  by animals 1, 6, 7, 70–72, 382, 386
  by man 1, 6–8, 117–131, 211, 298–300, 361, 375, 382, 386
  by microbes 1, 6, 7, 53–59, **55, 58**, 71, 72, 382
  by plants 1, 6, 7, 50–52, **50**, 62, 72, 382
Seed, Richard 346
Seminole 123
Sephton, Mark A. *64*
Shakespeare, William 198, 199, 280, 385
Shang dynasty 172, 173, 231
  language 193, 194
  script 193–196, **194**, *220*
Sharratt, Barney **Plate 6**
Shermer, Michael *41*
Shin, Taeyoung *357*
Shinto 269, *276*
Shipman, Pat 99
Shock, Everett L. *64*
sickle cell 29, 30, *40*
silicon chip 226, 227
Simson, Sarah *98*
Sinanthropus pekinensis see Peking Man
Sinic (*see also* Chinese)
  civilisation **141**, 145, 146, 371
  skeleton 76–81, **84, 85, 86**
Smil, Vaclav *245*
Smith, Harry *66*
Smith, Joseph 133
Snow, John 212, 213
Socrates 153, 256
Solomon, Susan *136*
South Pole 129, 362
space
  exploration 298, 299, 374, 375
  flight 130, 131, 373–375, 377

species 35, 92, 109, 363, 382, *389*
    definition 30, 31, *41*, 92
    generation 30–35, 375–377
    preservation 351, 352
    speech 4, 83, **86**, 88, 89, 92–94, 383
Spence, Kate 278, *300*
Spengler, Oswald 366
sperm 2, 28, 340, 341
Spirulina 318
Stalin, Josef 32, 149
staphylococci 143, 329
Stentor **58**, 59, **59**, 384
Stephenson, George and Robert 225, 354
Steptoe, Patrick 341
Stone Age 158–160, 227–231
Stonehenge 181, 184, 224
streptococci 143, 329, *333*
Sturm, Richard A. *100*
sugar (*see also* carbohydrate; glucose) 20
Sumeria (*see also* Mesopotamia) 8, 145
Sumerian civilisation 140, **141**, 142, 145,
    164–166, 215
    beliefs 251, 252, 273
    script 188, 230
Sun Tzu 235–238, *247*
Sunda Land 112
Swartkrans 107
Sykes, Bryan 116, *135*
symbols **190**, 191, 194, **194**, 197, 215,
    228–230, **229**
Szabo, Peter *63*

Tagliatela, Jared 91
Takahashi, Joseph S. *67*
Taliban 212, 388
Tang dynasty 196, 231, *233*
Taoism *see* Daoism
Taylor, Barry L. *67*, *68*
technology 8, 9, 149, 180, 223–244, 281,
    298, 299, 364, 371–375, 386
    Egyptian 166–170, 228
    for dating samples 74–76
    gene 313–332, **328**, 336–353, **348**, 362
    Inca 179, 180
    Indic 171, 228
    Mayan 177
    Minoan 174
    modern 224
    Sinic 172, 173, 228, 231–233
    Stone Age 227–230

sub-Saharan 183
Sumerian 164–166, 228
telescope 284, 289, 298, 299
Templeton, Alan R. *135*
Tennyson, Alfred 144, 145
Tenochtitlan 176
Tenzing, Norgay 130
Teotihuacan 146, 176, 257
Ternifine 107
Thales of Miletus 282
Theresa, Mother 12, 125
Thompson, J. Eric S. *185*, *186*
thumb 4, 85, **85**, 86, 218, 383, 387
thymine 22
Tigris 143, 145, 164, 166,
Timbuktu 183
tissues 18
tools
    chimpanzee 386
    human 79–81, 106, 109, 227, 386
Tolstoy, Lev 210
Toltec 176, 257, 258
Toynbee, Arnold 140, 117, 180
transplantation
    cells 343–347, **348**, 351–353
    genes 315, 316, 321, 323, 328, **328**,
        336–339, 349, 352, 353, 355
    organs 338, 349–351
Trinil 108
Trinkhaus, Eric *99*
triplet code 23
Trollope, Anthony 209
Tudge, Colin *160*
Turing, Alan 226
Turkana 77, 79
Tyndale, William 263

Ubeidia 197
upright gait 4, 76–78, **84**, 85, 89
Ur 164, 262
Uruk 164, 229

vaccination, vaccines 231, 292, *302*, 310,
    316, 327, 331, 366
valine 23, *40*
Valladas, H. *220*
Vaughan, Henry *390*
Venice 156
Venter, Craig 335, 336
Ventris, Michael 197

Venus' flytrap 62
Verma, Ram S. **24**
Vermeer, Jan 280
Vespucci, Amerigo *136*
Vidal, John *334*
Vinci, Leonardo da 8, *41*, 210, 238–242,
  241, *283*, *300*, 361, 385, 388
virus 18, 297, 298, 307, 308, 331, 350, 352,
  358
vision 7, 46–48, 69, 382
vocal cord 4, 83, **86**, 86, 89, 218, 228, 383,
  387
Voltaire 280

Waal, Frans B. M. de *12*, *390*
Walden, George *221*
Waldseemuller, Martin *136*
Wallace, Alfred Russel *32*, *41*, *89*, *99*, 286
Walters, Alan 244
Wambugu, Florence *333*
war 231, 235–238, 255, 364
water 17, 18, **19**, 46, *65*, 224, 254, 373, 377
Watson, James 26, 27, 291, 361
Watt, James 224
Wayne, Robert K *42*
wealth 214, 242–244, 254, 299, 367
Weaver, David R. *67*
Weinberg, Steven *304*
West, Michael D. **348**, *357*
Westfall, Richard *301*
Whistler, James McNeill 245
White, Michael 247
Whiten, A. *12*
Whittle, Frank 226
Wickramasinghe, Chandra 45, *64*, 365, *379*
Wilberforce, Samuel 33
Wilberforce, William 33
Wildish, Paul *276*

Wilkins, Maurice 26, 27
Williams, S. L. *100*
Williams, Tennessee 1
Wilson, Edward 129, *136*
Wilson, Edward O. *13*, *42*, 107, *134*, *378*
Wind, J. *219*
Wolpert, Lewis *247*, *274*, *300*, *301*
Wolpoff, Milford 110, *135*
Wren, Christopher 287
Wright, Karen *67*
Wright, Orville and Wilbur 226
Wycliffe, John 263
Wyndham, John 47

Xenotransplantation 349–353, 356
Xia dynasty 172, 173
X-ray 26

Y chromosome **24**, 96, *101*, 111, 116, *135*
Yangzi 172
Yellow River 143, 172, 193
Yersinia pestis 233
Young, Brigham 133
Young, J. Z. **85**, **87**
Young, Michael *67*
Young, Thomas 192, 193
Yucatan 140, 143, 146, 177, *185*, 199, 257

Zapotec 176, 177, **Plate 3**
Zeki, Semir *221*, *300*
Zen Buddhism 269
Zhang Heng *247*
Zheng He 122, *136*, 233
Zhou dynasty 173, 255
  script 195
Zhoukoudian (Chou-K'ou-tien) 106, 108
Zhulin, Igor B. *68*
Zwiess, Francis W. *379*